16th International Youth Tournament
11th – 23rd April, 1963

INFORMATION

THE FOOTBALL ASSOCIATION
22 Lancaster Gate, London, W.2

CRYSTAL PALACE

FOOTBALL LEAGUE DIVISION ONE

...ERPOOL

...th AUGUST, 1969

...OTBALL ASSOCIATION CHALLENGE
CUP COMPETITION

FINAL

LIVERPOOL

F.A. CUP HONOURS
WINNERS
1965
Runners-up
1914, 1950, 1971

NEWCASTLE UNITED

F.A. CUP HONOURS
WINNERS
1910, 1924, 1932,
1951, 1952, 1955
Runners-up
1905, 1906, 1908,
1911

...TURDAY, 4th MAY 1974
Kick-off 3 p.m.

INTERNATIONAL YOUTH TOURNAMENT

FINAL TIE

THE EMPIRE STADIUM, W...

TUESDAY, 23rd A...

...ENGLADBACH

ANFIELD IRON
The Autobiography

www.**rbooks**.co.uk

ANFIELD IRON
THE AUTOBIOGRAPHY

Tommy Smith

BANTAM PRESS

LONDON · TORONTO · SYDNEY · AUCKLAND · JOHANNESBURG

TRANSWORLD PUBLISHERS
61–63 Uxbridge Road, London W5 5SA
A Random House Group Company
www.rbooks.co.uk

First published in Great Britain
in 2008 by Bantam Press
an imprint of Transworld Publishers

A CIP catalogue record for this book
is available from the British Library.

ISBNs 9780593059586 (cased)
9780593061190 (tpb)

Addresses for Random House Group Ltd companies outside the UK
can be found at: www.randomhouse.co.uk
The Random House Group Ltd Reg. No. 954009

The Random House Group Limited supports The Forest Stewardship
Council (FSC), the leading international forest–certification organization.
All our titles that are printed on Greenpeace–approved FSC–certified
paper carry the FSC logo.
Our paper procurement policy can be found at
www.rbooks.co.uk/environment

Mixed Sources
Product group from well-managed
forests and other controlled sources
www.fsc.org Cert no. TT-COC-2139
© 1996 Forest Stewardship Council
FSC

Typeset in 11/15pt Plantin by
Falcon Oast Graphic Art Ltd.

Printed in the UK by
Clays Ltd, Bungay, Suffolk

2 4 6 8 10 9 7 5 3 1

This book is dedicated to Sue – the love of my life –
to our children, Darren and Janette, and all our family.

Acknowledgements

I would like to thank the following who, by way of expertise, recollection or friendship, helped significantly in the creation of this book: Julian Alexander and all at Lucas Alexander Whitley; Ken and Jean Bolam, Ian Callaghan, Jimmy Case, Dean Statham and Phill Dann; Tommy Docherty, Joey Jones; Tony Jo; John Keith; Liverpool FC; all at the *Liverpool Echo*; Kenny Rogers; Arthur Montford; Dave and Christine Scott; all at Transworld publishers, in particular Emma Musgrave, Giles Elliott and Doug Young; and John Turnock.

I would like to say a big thank you to Les Scott, who worked with me on this book. Les collaborated on the autobiographies of, amongst others, Sir Stanley Matthews, Jimmy Greaves, George Best, Tommy Docherty and Fred Trueman, and has written extensively for the press. Les is widely regarded as being one of the finest football writers in the country and when I decided to commit my story to book form, I had no hesitation in asking him to lend a helping hand. Thanks for everything, Les, you made sure I never had to 'walk alone'.

For Jane, Lauren, Ruby, Toni and Charley.

Tommy Smith, 2008

Contents

1

THE QUALITY OF MERSEY

I'M BORN AND BRED IN LIVERPOOL, A CITY THAT TAKES THE ROUGH with the smooth. Life here has always been a mixture of the two, and its people are just the same. I am who I am. I know who I am and where I am, a knowledge I share with the Inland Revenue, the VAT people and *Readers' Digest*. I'm no saint. Ian St John is the only saint as far as I'm concerned. But I have integrity and have always known the difference between right and wrong. Right is good, wrong is not good. It's that simple.

I've lived on Merseyside all my life. Even when I played for Swansea, I still lived here. I know Liverpool like the back of my hand. I know what the city is and what it has done to me. I know about belonging, which people are mine. My people are down-to-earth, honest and upfront. They are hard-working, compassionate, considerate, respectful of others and their property, yet have a hard edge. Anyone who threatens me, or my lot, well, I'm in their face straight away. That's how it is in this city; that's how it was when I played for Liverpool. Those who wanted to mix it, we were in their faces, giving much more than we got. Not pretty, but sometimes the beautiful game is not about being pretty, it's about winning personal battles in order to help win a game. 'Don't take any shit from anybody,' Bill Shankly once told me. I never forgot his words, so I've never taken shit from anybody, not then, not now.

Of course there is another side to me, that of the family man, the loving husband, father and grandfather, the good friend. Those who really know me see me for what I really am. Those whose only knowledge of me comes from having seen me play have their own ideas as to what sort of person I am – the other person. It's all relative, depending on which team you played for or supported. I haven't played competitive football for some twenty-five years, but that 'other person' still exists, in the memory of others.

I was at Liverpool for nigh on eighteen years during which time, the European Cup Winners' Cup excepted, I won every honour club football has to offer – and more than once. I was proud to captain Liverpool for a number of seasons and played under both Bill Shankly and Bob Paisley, widely regarded as two of the greatest managers British football has ever produced. I also had the honour of playing for my country under Sir Alf Ramsey at youth, under-23 and full international level, so make that three of the greatest managers in British football.

I have never before written my autobiography. There was a book published in the seventies which carried my name and which, up to a point, told my story. It was supposedly my autobiography, though in truth I had hardly any involvement in it whatsoever. It was written by a football journalist; I didn't even meet the publishers. That I have decided to write my autobiography now is simply down to the fact that I feel the time is right. I feel I have now lived 'enough life' to make my story interesting. Older and wiser as I am, my opinions on football past and present, and my personal experience of some of football's greatest and most memorable games and its most colourful characters, will hopefully make for an entertaining read. Only you, the reader, can decide how successful I've been in that aim.

Public opinion of me is that I was a hard man. Well, that's true, but I would like to think there is much more to me than my reputation for crunching tackles. In recalling my career in football and what has happened in my life since, I hope to convey to readers the Tommy Smith known to my family, close friends and team-mates.

I was born on 5 April 1945, when Britain was still at war. Legend has it that within a month of giving birth to me my mother rang the War Office, told them about me, and the following day Hitler surrendered.

I believe I was born with football in my blood – which was red, of course, not blue. There are no half-measures in Liverpool, either in pubs or football. My grandfather and father were both loyal Liverpool supporters, so there was no argument about which team I was to support. Only my devotion to Liverpool Football Club would prove to be somewhat deeper than that of loyal support. Simply in making reference to my birth, I quash yet another legend, one perpetrated by Bill Shankly himself, who on more than one occasion when referring to me said, 'Tommy wasn't born, he was quarried.'

I was born into a house at the bottom of Arkles Lane, which was within earshot of both Liverpool's Anfield stadium and Everton's equally historic Goodison Park. My parents were Martin and Margaret, and I was their only child. Initially my dad worked as a lorry driver, delivering fruit and vegetables, but later gained employment as a foreman at the docks. When I was still a baby we moved into a flat that overlooked a coal yard, in Buckingham Street in the Everton district of Liverpool. Within a matter of months we gained a 'transfer' from Everton to 9 Lambeth Road, which was again within earshot of both the mighty grounds. My earliest memory of football is of hearing the roar of the crowd whenever a goal was scored. The sound was like muffled thunder. Come twenty to five on a Saturday, when the game finished, if I heard another roar it was a sure sign that either Liverpool or Everton, whichever team was playing at home that day, had won.

I enjoyed my childhood. Ours was a happy home, and although household chores in the 1950s were labour intensive, I suppose I received more attention from my parents than other boys I knew, particularly those who came from large Catholic families, because I was an only child.

The fifties is often shunted into the margins of social history for being an age of frugality, a dull, drab and somewhat repressive decade that sits glumly in the shadow of its younger sibling, the attention-grabbing swinging sixties. My impression of the fifties is different. Looking back, those years seem to me to be one of the most significant decades in our history. The Beatles, the Rolling Stones, the Mini car and the radical fashion designer Mary Quant may be synonymous with the sixties but they were all products of the fifties; likewise Bill Shankly as a manager. The fifties may have begun with rationing still in place and the nation hanging on to a sense of itself as a world power, but it quickly evolved into a time of emerging opportunities, particularly for the first working-class generation to benefit from the new education programme and the National Health Service. I was one of the young people afforded new opportunities, and I grabbed them with both hands.

My first school was St John's Roman Catholic School (no, not named after Ian St John, though he'd like to think so!) where I did well in my studies, particularly in maths. I was football mad, and played at every given opportunity. The school had a play area situated on the roof of one of the buildings which took the shape of the letter 'H'; it was divided into two sections by corridors. Ball games were not allowed on the roof play area, so we boys played a version of football with a piece of wood some three inches long by an inch wide. Two games would take place simultaneously, separated by one of the corridors. The roof was layered with sheets of weatherproof felt; the daily wear and tear this material was subjected to turned the surface of the felt to powder. This powdery substance lent itself to sliding tackles, which, I believe, was where my ability to tackle and win a ball first began.

My memories of early childhood are, in the main, happy ones. When not playing football, reading or doing the household chores that were expected of me, like any other lad I liked to watch television. In the late fifties there were only two TV channels, BBC and ITV. One of my earliest TV memories is of watching *Quatermass and the Pit*, a BBC science fiction drama I loved but which scared me half to death. The series featured the character Professor Quatermass (played by Andre Morell), a highly moral British scientist who was forever being confronted with sinister alien forces in his capacity as the pioneer of Britain's space exploration programme. The series was immensely popular; it seemed the whole country tuned in to watch it. It really was scary stuff. I remember an episode in which an alien craft landed in a churchyard. A man who saw the craft ran away, tripped and fell. The path he lay on began to undulate and an eerie scratching noise could be heard from within the craft. The fact that we were never shown the alien fuelled my imagination and, I suppose, added to the element of drama and fear. The following day at school there would be only one topic of conversation: 'Did you see *Quatermass*?' Even our teachers watched and raved about it. I was an impressionable young boy, and that eerie image of the undulating ground in the churchyard remains with me to this day.

My other favourite programmes were *Robin Hood* and *The Phil Silvers Show*. *Robin Hood* starred Richard Greene as Robin and was a classic adventure series. The programme always began with an arrow being shot from a bow. The extraordinary aspect to the programme's opening titles was that a camera followed the trajectory of this arrow and plainly visible in the background was a set of telephone wires. I used to think, 'I've spotted this, why haven't the makers of the programme?' The title music to *Robin Hood* was very popular and was often requested on the Saturday-morning radio programme *Children's Favourites*, which I often listened to. The title music was written and sung by Dick James, who went on to become a highly successful music publisher and once managed Elton John. What always intrigued me about the *Robin Hood* song was the part of the lyric which referred to Robin and his men travelling the English countryside to help the people of the king and ended with the line 'and they still found plenty of time to sing'. There were heroes, and there were heroes. The subjects of other TV children's dramas, Sir Lancelot, Francis Drake and William Tell, also had great adventures in which they performed good and heroic deeds, but to my mind Robin and his men had the edge over them all. Having helped the poor, preserved Richard's status as king, freed those who were wrongly imprisoned and fought the evil Sheriff of Nottingham, Robin and the lads still found plenty of time to sing. Not for the odd minute, note you; they had 'plenty of time'. Talk about panache.

The Phil Silvers Show was not a series aimed at children but was a favourite of mine as a boy. Phil Silvers played Sgt Bilko, the larcenous leader of a motor pool in the US army whose life was dedicated to money-making schemes. Bilko never did make it rich because his Achilles heel was that he had a heart of gold, which I suppose was why his character was so appealing. Bilko's platoon was a minor miracle of casting. Every one of them had striking facial features, none more so than the obese, slobbery, dim-witted but loveable gargoyle Private Doberman. Though Bilko's schemes invariably failed, he always managed to persuade his men that his latest scam was going to be a winner. The plots, multi-layered and quick-moving, and the lines he spoke had me in stitches. It has been years since I watched the show but I can still remember some of those golden lines. When about to tell his men of a 'sure-fire' scheme: 'This is it, boys. Have your hips fitted for Jaguars.' When he found himself in hot water, one of Bilko's ploys was to curry favour with the officers' wives, which he did by means of blatant flattery. 'Mrs Hall, what you do for an angora sweater! Why, if you lived in France, they'd build a park and name it after you.' I loved

Sgt Bilko because his character brought to mind some of the Liverpool 'get-rich-quick scallys' I'd heard my dad and Uncle John talk of.

Every summer Mum and Dad took me to Rhyl for a fortnight's holiday in a caravan. I always looked forward to this, and in the weeks preceding it I would be excited beyond belief. There was only one occasion when I was really disappointed with my dad, and that involved the money Mum saved for one of these holidays in Rhyl. Dad liked a gamble. It wasn't an obsession, but every now and then he'd enjoy a flutter. Not far from where we lived was a field where, occasionally, the menfolk would gather to play 'toss' for money. A week prior to us going on holiday Mum went to check the tin in which she kept our holiday savings only to find it short. It transpired that Dad had dipped into the money and subsequently lost it playing 'toss' on the back field. Mum was furious. We no longer had enough to pay for all three of us to go on holiday, so Mum told Dad he'd have to stay at home.

In the caravan next to ours were my Aunty Rosie and her family. Throughout the holiday, Mum was forever saying to my Aunty Rosie, 'I wonder how Matty is getting on?' Mum was still mad with Dad, but like me, she knew the holiday was not the same without him. The time he gambled away some of their savings and couldn't join us on holiday was one of the few occasions I felt genuine sadness as a boy.

The thing about growing up in what would be referred to as a 'normal' family is you never consider yourselves to be normal, in the way you see other families as normal. For all we were considered a normal family, I saw Mum, Dad and myself as having quirks that would be a great source of embarrassment to me should they ever be revealed. What I didn't realize as a boy is that every family has its own quirks and idiosyncratic ways that mark them out. 'All happy families resemble one another, but each unhappy family is unhappy in its own way,' wrote Tolstoy in *Anna Karenina*, and every normal family is, in its own way, not normal.

This realization dawned on me when Mum and I returned from Rhyl to find Dad and my Uncle John eating tea. Tea consisting of kippers which Dad had generously smeared with strawberry jam. He and Uncle John ate this curious juxtaposition of food with some relish, ignoring the protestations of Mum, who appeared somewhat disgusted by it all. I was simply amused, though I did think it odd. I was of the mind that no other family in our neighbourhood would ever sit down to such a bizarre meal, and I prayed that knowledge of the kippers and jam would never pass beyond our front door.

Mum was a very good cook, and I loved the meals she made for us. Particular favourites of mine were salted fish and a meat and vegetable stew known as scouse, the speciality dish of Merseyfolk. On Sundays we enjoyed a roast dinner, beef and lamb alternating. These were the standard, affordable options for Sunday roast in the 1950s. Chicken wasn't widely available and was expensive; as such it was only eaten to celebrate very special occasions, such as Christmas Day or a Liverpool away win.

Dad worked in the vegetable and fruit wholesale business at the docks, so whatever was in season we had a-plenty. People didn't need the government or nutritionists to tell them they needed 'five-a-day'. We ate vegetables because we knew they were good for us, and we knew this because our mothers told us. Each vegetable was blessed with its own beneficial qualities – something Mum unfailingly reminded me of with every serving: 'Parsnips, bursting with vitamin B, gives you energy'; 'Butter beans, full of protein, Tommy'; 'Carrots, full of vitamin C, good for your skin and eyes. You ever seen a rabbit wearing glasses?'

Out of sheer necessity, Mum, in keeping with most women of the time, used imagination and ingenuity to make the Sunday roast last until Tuesday, sometimes to Wednesday, depending on how perilous a state the family budget was in that week. On Monday she might use some of the roast to make bubble and squeak, a dish that relied heavily upon cabbage ('full of iron'), which Dad always ensured we had plenty of. We might also have beef or lamb sandwiches for Monday supper. On Tuesday Mum would often make scouse with the remnants, carefully scraping the bone to ensure no morsel went to waste, and cooking the meat with onions ('good for your blood'), carrots and whatever other vegetables were to hand.

I rarely had a school dinner. Mum preferred me to take a packed lunch, which I ate in the school dining hall alongside the other 'packed lunchers', separate tables marking us out from those who ate school dinners. The 'packed lunchers' took sandwiches. A regular favourite of mine was roast pork ribs, which to my school pals must have seemed as unorthodox a packed lunch as Dad's kippers and jam tea had appeared to me.

Marked out as I was from those who ate school dinners, I felt marked out again among my fellow 'packed lunchers'. A sense of somehow being different pervaded my childhood. As I said, little did I know at the time that all families had their little indulgences which they kept to themselves. That was brought home to me in later years when talking to Gordon Banks, who told me that when eating Sunday lunch his father would heap strawberry jam on to his Yorkshire pudding. Banksy's father and my dad were around the same age, so I can only assume this unorthodox use of jam was a generational thing, going back to their childhood when jam was considered a treat.

From the age of around seven I was expected to help out around the home, putting my toys away, keeping my bedroom tidy and so on. As I got a little older I was expected to do chores as well. At the age of twelve I would come home from school, peel potatoes and other vegetables and put them on a low gas on the cooker in preparation for Mum coming home from work. We had a backyard as opposed to a garden and I was forever in the yard kicking a ball against its whitewashed walls. The ball made scruffy marks on the walls, especially in wet weather. As I had made these marks, it was my job to whitewash the walls, which I did some four times a year.

I did numerous other chores too: cleaning shoes, washing up, sweeping the carpet and helping with the weekly wash. I never considered myself badly done to. Mum and Dad both worked, household work was very labour intensive, and I was only too happy to help out. The only time I did take umbrage was when I stayed for a few days with my nan and grandfather in Norris Green, when Mum went into hospital for an operation to remove bunions. I never warmed to my grandfather who came across to me as a nasty man, even to Nan. One day he made me clean all the windows in the house, inside and outside. I did it, but reluctantly, as I felt he was simply taking advantage of me and my situation.

As I said, my dad was a big Liverpool supporter, but often he couldn't afford to go to games, let alone take me. However, nothing would keep me from seeing my heroes. When Liverpool were playing at home, I would walk down to Anfield, arriving some twenty minutes before the end of the game for what was called 'three-quarter time', when the exit gates would be opened in readiness for the mass exodus at the final whistle. As soon as I saw the first exit gate open at the Kop, I was through the gap and on to the terraces.

Statistics show that the majority of goals scored today occur in the final period of the second half when players are tiring. It was no different back in the 1950s. Given that I only saw twenty minutes of home games I managed to see quite a number of goals. I can clearly remember Liverpool playing Manchester City in an FA Cup tie. Right at the death, Billy Liddell blasted the ball and it flew into the net. Pandemonium broke out on the terraces and on the pitch when the referee disallowed the goal: he had blown his whistle for full-time just as Billy connected with the ball. The following Monday morning at school every lad was talking about Billy's disallowed goal. The majority had not been there to see it and had only read about it in the newspapers or heard about it from their dads. I, however, had seen it, and for free. In fact I'd had a right royal view, on the Kop looking down on both Billy and the referee as the controversial incident unfolded before my very eyes. If there could ever be such a thing as a ten-year-old dining out on a story, it happened to me that day.

For all that I was football mad, I did well at school. I took an interest in all subjects and loved to read. At St John's I did well in my studies, so well that at the age of eleven I won a scholarship to Cardinal Godfrey College. Cardinal Godfrey I can best describe as a secondary technical school of some note and reputation where, among other subjects, I was taught algebra and French. Such opportunities were not available to working-class kids prior to the war. My scholarship was representative of the new opportunities afforded to young people from poorer backgrounds in the 1950s.

Many of the teachers at Cardinal Godfrey College were Christian Brothers, but quite a number of them didn't behave in a loving Christian manner – far from it. Even minor indiscretions, such as forgetting your metalwork apron, were punished with a caning. I remember one lad who, having left his apron at home, knew he would be in for 'six of the best'. Unbeknown to us, his fellow pupils and the teacher in question, in readiness for his punishment he pushed a sheet of tin down the seat of his trousers. As the Christian Brother gave him four swift strokes of the cane across the backside, we lads began to pack away our books because we thought the bell had gone.

I excelled in maths. I remember one occasion when a teacher was writing out a series of problems and equations on a black-board. I worked out the answers and wrote them down as he went along. When I presented my book to him he couldn't believe I had worked out the answers so quickly, nor could he understand how I had arrived at the correct answers as I had used a different system to his. Rather than praising me, he became angry, accusing me of having somehow acquired the solutions from his teaching notes. The sense of injustice sat heavy with me for weeks. I was not a disruptive pupil but I felt I wanted to get back at the teacher for his attitude towards me. Rather than being insolent, however, I worked even harder in maths, my success serving to confound him even further.

I felt I was popular at school. I gained kudos among my fellow pupils not just because they saw me as a decent footballer, but also because I could look after myself and adhered to fair play. One day I was sitting at my desk when a boy who was a noted bully came into our classroom. He spat at another lad, only for the spittle to splatter across my blazer. I told him to wipe it off and received a two-word reply for my trouble. Incensed, I jumped up, ran towards him and butted him. We fell to the floor wrestling with each other until a teacher, Tom Burke, intervened. Tom was one of the teachers at the school I really warmed to. He was a football fanatic, he supervised school teams, and in class he was a superb teacher. He pulled us apart and asked what the fight was all about. The bully said I had butted him, and when asked by Tom if this was true I told him it was. Tom asked why I had done such a thing, and I explained about the spitting and the bully's response to my request that he clean my blazer. Tom was at pains to explain to me that that was not the way to respond, but he knew what sort of lad I was through football so I received only a mild rebuke. When he turned to the bully, his demeanour changed. 'Bullies are cowards,' he said. 'You're a bully, so what does that also make you?' He then went on to severely reprimand this lad for his general behaviour and the way he treated other pupils, ending with the words, 'And if I hear of you bullying or spitting at another boy again, I'll butt you!'

From that moment on, no lad at the school ever caused me trouble again. I wasn't a troublemaker, and I wasn't a source of grief to my fellow pupils, but from that day I went through school assured and confident in my own ability to look after myself and, if need be, others. It was an ability and confidence I took into my career as a footballer with Liverpool.

My mum and dad were very supportive of my football and always ensured I had good boots. I was fortunate that at both schools I attended I had teachers who were enthusiastic about football and offered me good advice. I played football at every opportunity. As there were very few cars in our neighbourhood in the 1950s, we played in the street. On several occasions, however, a wayward shot broke a window, so in the end parents put the kibosh on us kicking a ball around in the street and we boys took to playing on an old bomb site off Lambeth Road. There was no grass and the uneven ground was pitted with stones and glass. We put down our jumpers for goalposts and would quite happily play football for hours at a time. The lad who owned the ball was the most popular boy in the neighbourhood, and never short of friends.

I am sure those games instilled in me and my pals a sense of responsibility and a notion that one had to adhere to rules in life if you were not to spoil things for other people. We had no referee to apply the rules of the game. When a goal was scored we restarted the game with a kick-off from what passed as a centre spot. When a foul was committed, a free-kick was taken and no one took umbrage. We seemed to accept that if anyone did not play by the rules of football, the game would be spoiled for everyone. Those games played without supervision taught us that you can't go about doing just what you want because there are others to think of. Of course it was not a conscious thought at the time, but those kickabouts on the bomb site taught us the rules of society and prepared us for life.

Today you rarely see a group of boys having a kickabout, which perhaps is a contributing factor to the crime and unsocial behaviour we so often hear about. Some kids simply haven't learned the principle that both the game and society have rules and it displays consideration for others if you stick by them. Youngsters today, for all their comparative sophistication and knowledge of computers, mobile phones, iPods and what have you, are still basically the same as lads in my day, no better and no worse. I am convinced that many of them would benefit from taking up a sport, even from a kickabout with mates in a park. Football reflects society, and if you know the value of sticking to the game's rules, you're more likely to be unselfish in the wider world.

From the bomb site we graduated to a shale surface we called the Rec which was situated at the rear of my first school, St John's RC. In truth, the surface of the Rec was little better than the bomb site. It too was uneven and pitted with stones, and it also had pot-holes. If you could control the ball when it was played to you across that surface, you were on your way to becoming a serious footballer. Many was the time we boys finished a game and walked home with blood streaming down our legs from having executed a sliding tackle on the treacherous surface. In summer we also played cricket on the Rec with a cricket ball so old that the leather had long since perished, reducing it to a ball of hard cork. No one possessed cricket pads, and wearing short trousers when facing bowling was an adventure in itself. Due to the very uneven surface the hard cork ball bounced up at speed and at all manner of angles, which concentrated the batsman's mind wonderfully. Eyes were trained on the ball at all times. We all became adept with the bat, for no other reason than a deep-seated desire to protect our bare legs from a severe bruising, or worse.

The only even surface we found to play football on was a main road that linked Commercial Road with Dock Road. During the week and on Saturdays this was a very busy road with lorries and horses and carts transporting goods from the docks to various warehouses. On a Sunday, however, the road was quiet and deserted, which made it ideal for playing football. The only thing we boys had to worry about on a Sunday was the presence of the police. As soon as we saw a policeman walking towards us, we would scarper. On one occasion, however, we were so engrossed in our game that we didn't see a policeman approaching until he was there among us. My mates ran off, but I had put down my jumper as one of the goalposts. It was while I was trying to retrieve the jumper that he collared me.

The policeman asked me my name.

'Tommy Smith,' I told him. A reply which brought me a clip round the ear.

'Don't try and be funny with me,' he said.

He asked where I lived. I told him my address on Lambeth Road and, still holding me by the collar, he frogmarched me back to our home. When we got there he knocked on the door, which was eventually opened by my dad.

'What's going on?' asked Dad.

'Is this lad yours?' asked the policeman.

Dad confirmed the fact, and my name.

'He's been playing football on a main road. It's not on. It's dangerous. I've given him a clip round the ear.'

'And I'll give him another one,' said Dad, and he duly did. 'Now get in this house. How many times have I told you never to go near that main road?' He pulled me through the door and pushed me up the hall.

On seeing this, the policeman appeared satisfied. 'I was going to issue him with a caution, but I'm happy with the action you have taken, so we'll leave it at that.' And with that he went on his way.

When dad came back inside, I said, 'You have never told me not to go near that main road.'

'I know, but I've saved you from a caution from the police,' he said. 'And don't ever do anything that brings the police to this house again.'

I never did.

Dad was a wily man. He knew how to appease that policeman and he saved me from going into his book. There was a stigma about a police caution in those days. There was shame attached to it, and I was grateful to my dad for what he did. Later, when a clutch of clubs wanted to sign me, one of them was Manchester City. But there was never a possibility of my joining them because Dad's words remained with me: 'Keep away from that Maine Road.'

I got into a few scrapes as a boy, but nothing serious. I enjoyed my childhood and early teens. I ate toast made from chunks of white bread smeared with full-fat butter, and ate the fat on bacon, roast ribs and fried chips. I drank Vimto and Tizer fizzy pop, but I was never an ounce overweight because I was always out playing football, cricket or generally running around. I had fights and occasionally came home with cuts and bruises, but I got over it. I was fortunate enough to do well at school and pass exams. The fact that some kids failed exams wasn't considered to be the fault of teachers or a failing school; people simply accepted that some kids were brighter than others. A Big Mac was what my dad wore in the winter. Coke was something that fired the church boiler. Grass was something to be mown, and a joint was what you had for Sunday dinner. A chip was something you ate out of news-paper. Hardware was a hammer and nails, and software a Fair Isle sweater. Going all the way meant staying on the bus to the terminus, and the only swingers were trapeze artistes. The only thing that came ready to serve was tennis balls, and the only auto-matic sprinkler system for pitches was the club cat. I didn't have an iPod, a picture-text mobile, a computer, Nintendo or a DVD player. I had friends. When we moved to a new house, I went into the street and made new friends. I went to the Rec to play football and cricket. I caught buses or walked around Liverpool to play for my school team or Liverpool Boys. No one accosted me and no one interfered with me. Like every other lad, I was out there in the big wide world without a parent by my side and yet, though it's unthinkable today, I survived.

That is not to say that my childhood was without tragedy. I was devastated when Dad died. Double pneumonia took him, and to this day I can recall the moment I heard the tragic news. At first it was thought he had a heavy cold, or so we were told by the doctor. When his condition deteriorated he was confined to bed at home, but even then, as a fourteen-year-old boy, I was never aware of the serious nature of his condition. One day in December 1959, after training with Liverpool Schoolboys at Penny Lane, I caught a bus a part of the way home to Everton Valley, and when I got off I was surprised to see my cousin Rosie waiting for me. I knew something was amiss because her eyes were welled with tears.

'I've got some bad news, Tommy,' she informed me. 'Your dad has died.'

Her 'news' hit me like a bolt from the blue. I was immediately overcome with shock and emotion. I couldn't take it in because I couldn't think straight. For a few moments I could do nothing but stand and stare at her. Her face was full of sadness and pity. She took my arm and together we walked down – of all streets – Smith Street until we reached Lambeth Road.

From the few words that were spoken I gathered that Rosie had been sent to meet me by my mum, but not with the intention of breaking the tragic news to me. Rosie, however, was so upset she had not been able to control herself. A part of me was angry that I had not been told how grave dad's illness was, but I suppose Mum had kept that from me to protect me, and also because she lived in hope that he might recover. Sadly, he never did.

Following my father's death, all my beliefs about religion and the Church were crushed, and in crass circumstances. After Dad's funeral, relatives and friends gathered back at our house. The local priest, Father Songhurst, was also present, supposedly to offer comfort and condolence. Everyone displayed due respect and reverence except Father Songhurst, who helped himself to copious amounts of alcohol and ended up in a drunken state, his speech slurred. When he left our home I watched through the window as he made his way along our street. He was unsteady on his feet, swaying from side to side, and must have bumped into the bay window of every house. That experience did it for me, and from that moment I ceased to be a regular church-goer. I still occasionally attend church today, but only for weddings and funerals, and I do so only out of respect for those for whom the service is being held. For nearly fifty years now I have adhered to my own interpretation of religion, which I carry in my heart and my head. Quite simply, it is this: I believe that to be religious is to be aware of the difference between right and wrong. As reasoned and rational people we know what is right and what is wrong; you don't necessarily need the Church to tell you that. I suppose what I am saying is that religion is a matter of personal conscience.

My mother must have been devastated by my father's death too, but such was her strength she never disclosed her feelings to me. Mum came across as being ever stronger, and she assumed the role of my dad. Mum had to be strong as money became too tight to mention. Over time I became increasingly aware that the special meals and treats I had once taken for granted were becoming scarce, eventually becoming strangers to our dining table. Cheaper cuts of meat were bought from the butcher's. Soup made from whatever was to be found in the kitchen appeared weekly, then twice a week. I never made Mum aware of the fact that I had noticed. I knew she was struggling to keep us both. It soon reached the stage where Mum couldn't afford our house in Lambeth Road, so we moved to my nan's house in Norris Green.

I was football mad and harboured a dream that one day I would be good enough to play for Liverpool. I vowed that should my dream ever be realized I would help Mum, repay her for all she had done for me, particularly in the time following the death of my father.

Mum didn't know much about football, but she encouraged me in my love of the game as she believed Dad would have done. When I was awarded the scholarship to Cardinal Godfrey College I was disappointed to find it was primarily a rugby school. It did have a football team, however, and with Mum's backing I soon established myself in the school team.

The school is situated only about a mile from Anfield, the home of my heroes. The biggest thrill of my life to that point was that I had actually played at Anfield. That honour had come in the 1955–56 season. I was ten years old and playing for my school against Arnott Street School. At the end of every season Anfield staged the final of the city schools' cup competition. The games were played over the full-size pitch, but because we were so small, I can remember they had to lower the crossbar for the game otherwise there would have been a cricket score. In the event, we lost 2–1.

Such were my performances for Cardinal Godfrey that at the age of thirteen I was playing for the school under-15 team. This was considered some achievement as the physical difference between a thirteen-year-old and lads coming up to the age of fifteen was quite marked. It was around that time that it was first pointed out to me that I had a talent for football the other boys didn't possess. Curiously, rather than coming from a teacher, this observation came from a fellow pupil whose name, sadly, I can't now recall.

I was playing for Cardinal Godfrey one Saturday morning. At one point I received the ball, looked up, shouted for a team-mate to run behind the opposing defence, and as he did so, with the outside of my boot I played a curving pass for him to run on to. My team-mate ran on to score. In the changing room after the game this lad came up to me.

'That pass you played to me, did you mean it?' he asked.

'Of course I did,' I replied, somewhat taken aback at the nature of his question.

'I think you have something,' he said.

'What do you mean?'

'I mean, have it in you to be a footballer. I've never seen anyone do what you do on a football field.'

I was so surprised to hear him say this that I didn't know how to reply. I just said, 'I hope so, thanks.' On the way home I wondered if my pal could be right, and hoped he was. It was the first time anyone had suggested I might be good enough to make a career out of football. As I said, I can't remember this lad's name, let alone what he ended up doing for a living, but I like to think he went on to be a good scout for some club.

It was at this stage of my development that I achieved a hat-trick of appearances at Anfield that was to change my life. One Monday I played for Cardinal Godfrey under-15s in a local schools cup final against St Teresa's. I played centre-forward at the time and scored twice in a 5–1 victory. One player who stood out for the opposition that day was Chris Lawler; he and I would become team-mates at Anfield and play alongside each other in some of Liverpool's most legendary games. A few days later I appeared at Anfield again, this time against the senior division of my old school, St John's, who included in their ranks David McManaman, the father of Steve. We won 4–2 and I scored again. On the Saturday morning it was cup final number three, a second showdown with St Teresa's. We won 2–1 and I managed to score another goal. It was an incredible seven days for me as a thirteen-year-old boy, not just to win three cup finals but to have played three times at my beloved Anfield. I had attended Liverpool home games on many occasions, but to play on the same pitch as my heroes and to be inside the hallowed dressing rooms filled me with excitement and awe. My achievements for my school team had earned me selection for the Liverpool city schoolboys' team in which, during the following season, I established myself as centre-forward.

My performances in those three schoolboy cup finals, and my subsequent performances for Liverpool Boys, did not go unnoticed by Liverpool Football Club. I was playing as centre-forward or inside-left for Liverpool Boys and had formed a prolific striking partnership with Tommy Wright, the pair of us scoring over forty goals in some thirteen matches. At the time Tommy and I were aware a number of clubs were running the rule over us, but neither of us got carried away. Scouts were always present at games involving Liverpool Boys. In the event we both enjoyed lengthy careers in football (Tommy with Everton) and played for England – as defenders!

Since early childhood it had been my ambition to be a

professional footballer with Liverpool; should that dream not be realized, I wanted to be an architect. As I had done particularly well in physics, maths and design at school I felt this would help me in that field, but all along I prayed my ability as a footballer would one day be noticed by a Liverpool scout. Eventually that day came.

When I was coming up to my fifteenth birthday I received a letter from Liverpool inviting me to meet their new manager with a view to awarding me a place on their groundstaff, which in those days amounted to being a youth player. I was ecstatic to receive this letter, but there was a problem. Following my fifteenth birthday I still had a year to do at Cardinal Godfrey College as under my scholarship I was expected to continue at school until I finished my exams at sixteen. What's more, due to Mum's financial situation, Liverpool Council had consented to pay her £1 a week toward my upkeep – a nominal amount by today's standards but a Godsend to Mum at the time.

Mum took me to see the Liverpool manager, Bill Shankly. This was in February 1960, and it was the first time I had met the man who was still to create his revolution at Anfield. Even so I was in awe of him as I knew of his history as a great player with Preston North End and Scotland, and what he had achieved when cutting his managerial teeth at Carlisle United, Grimsby Town, Workington and Huddersfield Town. Shankly had only been at the club for a few months and was still finding his feet, but to me he came across as being very positive and ambitious. Bill listened to my mother as she outlined my ambitions, which amounted to nothing more than wanting to be a professional footballer with Liverpool. On hearing this, his eyes sparkled.

'Tell you what I propose, Mrs Smith,' he said. 'Let's give Tommy the chance of realizing his dream, his ambition. What say you agree to him joining our groundstaff? We'll pay him seven pounds a week.'

Mum and I both looked at Shanks as if we had won the treble

chance on the football pools. Seven pounds a week was a very good wage for an adult, let alone a fifteen-year-old. Mum then explained to Shanks that the council paid her a pound a week upfront for my maintenance, and should I leave school early she would have to pay that money back.

'I'm no mathematician,' he said, 'but I know a pound a week, over a year, comes to fifty-two pounds. What say you, this club pays the fifty-two pounds to buy your Tommy out of school?'

So it was that Liverpool paid £52 to Mum, who in turn passed the money on to the council so that I could leave school and join their groundstaff.

Before leaving his office, Mum surprised me, and somewhat embarrassed me. She didn't know much about football but, from whatever source, she had learned Liverpool had never won the FA Cup. A fact she mentioned to Bill Shankly. 'But this club will win the FA Cup one day,' Mum added, 'and when it does, Tommy will be in that team.'

'I shall look forward to that day, Mrs Smith,' replied Shanks, seemingly relishing the thought.

Once outside the ground I said to Mum, 'Why did you have to say that stuff about the FA Cup? It was embarrassing, made me feel a big head.'

'I wanted to impress him. Show you had ambition and that you believe in him and what he's hoping to achieve at this club.'

In May 1965, Liverpool did win the FA Cup, beating Leeds United in a memorable final. I was a member of that Liverpool team. In the Wembley dressing room after the game as we celebrated our success, Bill Shankly came up and put an arm around me. 'See, your mother was right, son,' he said. 'Always listen to your mother. She knows.' Over five years had passed since Mum first took me to see Bill Shankly and said those words, but amid the euphoria and celebrations of that Wembley dressing room, he remembered them. What a man.

2

THE GIRDER OF GIRTH

MY PRIORITIES WHEN JOINING LIVERPOOL WERE TWOFOLD: TO EARN myself a professional contract, and then to make it into the first team as soon as possible. Bill Shankly's priority was to guide Liverpool to promotion to the First Division, as soon as possible, and, as he is often quoted as saying, 'to build Liverpool into a bastion of invincibility'.

He had a monumental task on his hands. All the club had going for it was potential. For all that Anfield was almost a holy place to me, in truth it was a ramshackle ground badly in need of renovation. In terms of size the training ground at Melwood was more than adequate, but, like Anfield itself, tired and shabby. As for the team, arguably it was more in need of renovation than Anfield itself.

Shanks joined from Huddersfield Town on 30 November 1959 and had been at Anfield for only four months prior to my signing for the club. He'd had an inauspicious start, losing his first two games in charge, but following victory over Charlton Athletic in his third match he had begun to make his presence felt. He set about creating a policy that included the setting-up of an organized and, hopefully, productive youth system which he saw as an essential part of his plan for turning Liverpool into a highly successful club. When not devoting himself to team matters he was improving facilities at the club, which at the time were woeful. His attention to detail was phenomenal. One of the first tasks Shanks applied himself to was to upgrade the utilities that serviced Anfield. The club was strapped for cash, but he persuaded the board to spend £3,000 on a pipeline to bring water in from Oakfield Road so that all the toilets around the ground could be flushed.

I was only fifteen years old but so keen to learn that I was taking everything in. I wasn't the only one. Even at such a tender age it was apparent to me that Shankly was assessing everything and everyone at the club, including the directors. The existing backroom staff of Bob Paisley, Reuben Bennett and Joe Fagan were all known to Shanks. When Shanks had been manager of Grimsby Town he had tried to sign Fagan on three occasions from Manchester City, which I suppose says volumes for what Bill thought of Joe's character and application. Shanks was obviously happy with his backroom staff as all three kept their jobs. On the playing side he gave all the pros a fair chance to prove they could do a job for him before reassessing the situation and having a clear-out. Some players immediately benefited from his presence. Shanks's predecessor, Phil Taylor, had placed full-back Gerry Byrne on the transfer list, but Shanks soon took Gerry off the list and gave him a new contract. It was to prove a decision that not only benefited Gerry but the club, as he developed into one of the finest full-backs in the country.

On 1 May 1960 I reported to Anfield for my first day as a member of the club's groundstaff. From the off I was as keen as mustard to impress Bill Shankly, but when I arrived at the ground just before nine a.m. the only other people present were nine fellow groundstaff boys. We gathered in what was known as the 'pigeon loft' at the back of the main stand, so-called because in the pre-war years reporters had dispatched their running and final match reports back to their newspapers by pigeon. Shanks later told us how, when he was playing Scottish junior football, a furious sports editor of the *Glasgow Evening News* once took to task a rookie reporter covering his first game for not sending him the result of an important junior game in the Highlands. According to Shanks, the greenhorn reporter informed his editor, 'I told the pigeon "Won two-nil" and sent it on its way. It's not my fault the bird forgot everything I said.' As boys, we hung on to Shanks's every word, but without exception we all believed he was having a joke with us that day. True to character, he insisted he wasn't. The thing about Shanks was, when questioned about a tale such as this, he would be so convincing in his insistence that the story was true that you began to believe it.

I thought my only boss would be Shanks himself, but I soon discovered I was answerable not only to his backroom staff but to other staff as well: head groundsman Arthur Riley and his assistant Jack Webb; maintenance manager Kenny Myres and his assistant Sammy Roach; the head groundsman at the Melwood training ground, Eli Wass; even the club's full-time painter and decorator, 'Harry the Paint'. If from this you deduce that my early days at Anfield were not just about applying myself to football, you're spot on. It was made apparent to every member of the groundstaff that we were expected to perform a variety of duties that were not strictly football-related. Should any youngster take umbrage at this, it would reach the ears of Shanks and the miscreant would be out on his ear. So, wanting to impress, I did what I was told, be the instructions from Shanks, Bob Paisley or Harry the Paint.

Having gained experience of the Anfield pitch as a schoolboy, I was keen to set foot on what I saw as the hallowed turf as soon as possible. I didn't have long to wait. As we groundstaff lads were sitting in the 'pigeon loft', head groundsman Arthur Riley approached with several old tracksuits over one arm. Having introduced himself, Arthur told us to don the tracksuits; he then marched us on to the pitch. Instead of a ball we were handed garden forks and spades, and under his supervision we were set to work preparing the pitch.

In the afternoon a lorry appeared through the exit gap between the Kop and the main stand. The driver manoeuvred the vehicle so that the cab faced the Kop, and then commenced to deposit what must have been about fifty tons of topsoil on to the pitch near the corner flag. Arthur organized us into a line along the goal-line and gave each of us a garden sieve. For the next fortnight we painstakingly made our way to the other end of the pitch, sieving the existing soil as we went and extracting every small stone and piece of debris, which we placed into wheelbarrows. That done, and having binned the debris and stones, it was back to the Kop where we loaded the topsoil on to the wheelbarrows. Yet again we painstakingly made our way from the Kop to the Anfield Road end, spreading the top soil, raking it across the pitch and bedding it in with our shoes. Arthur followed, meticulously spreading grass seed, careful to ensure that no square inch of the pitch received more than another.

It took us almost three weeks to prepare the pitch, during which time I never so much as saw a football, let alone practised with one. When it was done, Arthur shocked us rigid when he disappeared into the main stand and returned brandishing a shotgun. He obviously saw the concerned looks on our faces so he eased our anxieties by saying, 'It's like the Tranmere forward line: it only fires blanks.' We took it in turns to 'guard' the pitch. Whenever pigeons settled, we fired the gun in the air, which prompted the birds to scatter and soar up into the rafters of the stands. With no match reports to carry back to editors, it was only a matter of time, however, before the pigeons returned and the gun would have to be fired again. The process was repeated seemingly ad infinitum.

With the pitch finally prepared for a new season, I was assigned to Harry the Paint. During my career at Liverpool many were the times when the supporters 'painted the town red'; that summer I quite literally painted Anfield red. Under the watchful eye of Harry, I painted the dressing rooms, the toilets and, most difficult of all, the stands themselves. If there were health and safety regulations in force in the summer of 1960, Liverpool Football Club hadn't heard about them. Harry and assistant maintenance man Sammy Roach erected scaffolding in the stands and tied us groundstaff lads to the steelwork with ropes to ensure we didn't plummet to the floor. As well as it being precarious work, it was also tedious. Every surface, niche and angle of the girders and rafters of the stands had to be painted.

Just when I was beginning to think I might have been given more opportunity to play football if I had become an apprentice painter and decorator, Bill Shankly appeared one morning with news that was music to my ears. It was a Thursday morning in June. I remember the Everly Brothers were number one with 'Cathy's Clown'. There was also a song by Jimmy Jones in the top ten entitled 'Handyman' which contained the line 'I'm just a handyman around here', the irony of which was not lost on me.

'Boys,' said Shanks, 'I hear you've all done good work. You've all made a good start at the club, which pleases me, so there'll be no work today. Today, you'll be playing your first game for this club.'

He proceeded to inform us that we should get changed and assemble in the car park outside the main stand. This was the moment I'd been waiting for, the chance to show Bill Shankly and his staff what I could do in the name of Liverpool Football Club. As I joined my fellow groundstaff colleagues to get changed, we speculated about who the opposition might be. As we had been asked to assemble in the car park, we thought we were going to play a team on their home ground, travelling to our destination by coach. Someone suggested it might be the Everton youth team; another lad believed it would be Tranmere Rovers; even Manchester United was touted. This notion of playing the youth team of another club was given further credence when the ten of us were joined in the car park by Shanks and his entire backroom staff: Bob Paisley, Reuben Bennett and Joe Fagan.

We hung around for a few minutes, then suddenly I heard the sound of what I took to be the engine of a coach approaching from around the corner. Deep intake of breath. 'This is it,' I told myself. 'Off for my first game. Show them what you can do, Tommy.' My excitement was immediately quelled when rather than a team coach turning the corner into the Anfield car park, I saw a Liverpool Council dustbin lorry. To a man – or, rather, boy – all of us groundstaff lads descended from tenterhooks, only for our excitement to be immediately rekindled by the approaching sound of another groaning engine. 'This'll be our coach,' said one of the lads. I felt deep disappointment when another council dustbin lorry turned the corner, and that was superseded by incredulity when a third bin lorry turned into the car park. Fourteen bin men tumbled out of these vehicles. Bill Shankly stepped forward, handed them each a yellow bib and said, 'Right, boys, are you ready for a good hiding? I've got a top team out against you today.'

We played against the council dustmen on the car park, the fact that it was fourteen-a-side not seeming to bother anybody. In addition to playing, Shanks acted as referee in what was the most bizarre game of football I played in eighteen years at Anfield. There was no time limit, and the game, played in a highly com-petitive manner, carried on for over two hours, only ending when Shanks was of the mind that we had such a lead we could not be pegged back. It was a little quirk of Shanks's that he took on to the training ground at Melwood: five-a-side games involving his team could last for hours until his side got their noses in front. After the game Shanks was full of praise for us groundstaff lads. 'I wanted us to beat them bin lads at all costs, and ye came through with fly-ing colours,' he told us. 'Well done, boys.'

To Shanks, every game of football, be it a five-a-side match at Melwood, a game against Liverpool Council bin men on the

Anfield car park, or an FA Cup Final at Wembley, had to be taken seriously and won. It was all part of his philosophy of instilling into every player at the club what he called the 'winning mentality'. Shanks paid meticulous attention to detail and preparation. He believed that if players did not take a practice game seriously, it would 'take the edge off their game' and weaken their 'mentality for winning'. I can only imagine what he would have thought of the tenure as manager of England of Sven Goran Eriksson, who, it seemed to me was of the mind that results and performances in so-called 'friendly' internationals were of no great importance. Such an attitude was anathema to Shanks, for whom the term 'friendly match' simply did not exist. Given the woeful, insipid performances of England under Eriksson, I am sure many will agree with me in thinking that Shanks had the right idea. As he once told us, 'If ye fail to prepare, then prepare to fail.'

Shanks created and actively encouraged a competitive spirit within the club. Players could be arguing and squaring up to one another on the training ground during a five-a-side game. Such an incident never made the tabloid newspapers in those days, and never served to make Shanks believe discipline among the players was crumbling. On the contrary, he liked to see competitiveness boiling over. On such occasions he would turn to Bob Paisley or Joe Fagan and say, 'If they're fighting each other over a "goal" in a five-a-side, imagine what they'll be like when it's for real.' This was all part of the 'Shankly psychology'. He had countless little rituals that might have appeared insignificant to an outsider, but to Shanks and his backroom staff they were the vital ingredients in the formula that would turn Liverpool into a major force not only in British but in world club football.

As the 1960–61 season approached more of my time at Anfield was taken up by training, but this was interspersed with the other duties I was expected to perform as a member of the groundstaff. This meant cleaning the boots of the senior pros, keeping the ground tidy, and more maintenance work.

Bob Paisley was a jack-of-all-trades and a master of every one of them, the original Bob the Builder. He was Bill Shankly's assistant and right-hand man, but his lofty status didn't stop him mucking in. Bob had begun his football career as an amateur in his native County Durham with Bishop Auckland, with whom he won an FA Amateur Cup winner's medal before joining Liverpool. It was while playing for Bishop Auckland that he completed his apprenticeship as a builder and bricklayer, skills he would utilize when he and Shanks began their Anfield renaissance.

One day in the summer of 1960 I had just finished sweeping the paddock terrace when Bob approached.

'Smithy, come with me,' he said. 'I have a little job for you.'

He walked me to the Kop and we made our way down to one of the turnstile booths where a voluminous girder was cramping the style of the turnstile operator.

'Saw off the end of that girder,' said Bob, casually handing me a hacksaw as if he had asked me to cut a piece of plywood.

My jaw must have dropped because he then said, 'What's up?'

'Well, it's, er, a big girder and I've only got this hacksaw and—'

'Just do it, Smithy.'

I did do it, but it took me a fortnight to saw through what had become known around Anfield as 'the great girder of girth'. When the end piece finally clanged to the ground I heaved a great sigh of relief. My arm was aching so much I thought it might join the end of the girder in dropping off. It was not without some delight and satisfaction that I went to see Bob and told him, 'Job done.' Having seen for himself the evidence, Bob then set to work mixing cement and bricking up, the bricks having been ferried by yours truly. It had been one hell of an undertaking, and all to make life a little more comfortable for the turnstile operator.

In my early days at the club, Bob did any amount of maintenance and development work at the club. There was a band box roughly where the home bench is today. The box had accommodated the members of whichever local brass band provided music before and during the half-time interval of every home match. In 1960, however, the playing of pop records over what was called the Tannoy system had superseded brass bands as far as pre-match and half-time entertainment for supporters was concerned. Though the occasional local band still appeared at Anfield throughout the sixties, the band box, which afforded a unique close-up view of play, was no longer considered necessary. As Shanks said, that the local Co-op brass band had a better view of play than the manager and his staff was crazy; it showed the priorities of this club had been all wrong. Bob demolished the old band box, and with his mortar board and trowel built 'home' and 'away' dug-outs. Bob was rightly proud of the finished job. It seemed to mean as much to him in terms of achievement as any major trophy success – and he had plenty of those.

Bill Shankly's influence at Anfield was all-encompassing, that of Bob Paisley no less so. Football has much to do with balance, and in Shanks and Paisley the club reaped the benefits of a management team that enjoyed all the precision of a spring-balance. Shanks was brash and full of himself in the most positive way imaginable, Bob was exactly the opposite. But opposites attract, they say, and this was very much the case with Shanks and Paisley. Their respective approaches to players and games were different, yet, curiously, they sang from the same hymn sheet.

Shanks was not a practical man in the sense that Bob was, yet he too would muck in to do work around Anfield that a contemporary manager would consider unthinkable. One night the Liverpool chairman, T. V. Williams, called in to Anfield at around half nine to collect some paperwork. The offices were dark and deserted, but just as he was about to leave, Williams noticed a light shining from the steps of one of the exits in the Kop. Illuminated by the light, Williams saw a box of tools on the terracing. Curious to know who was on the premises at such an hour, he walked over to the Kop and proceeded down the steps at the back of the stand. The light was coming from one of the toilet blocks where he found

31

Shanks and Paisley in overalls, painting the walls and ceiling.

Bill Shankly, ably assisted by Bob Paisley, was hell-bent on making Liverpool a force to be reckoned with. They had great respect for the club's supporters and did not want the people who paid their wages, and those of the players, to have to put up with a shabby ground and poor, in some cases degrading, facilities. Should the club not be able to afford the cost of outside help, such was his and Bob's devotion to the club and its cause that they were willing to paint toilet blocks themselves and maintain the plumbing of the loos and sinks so that they were functioning normally come matchday. The dedication and commitment we players felt for the club were largely engendered by Shanks and Paisley. Leadership is action, not position. As a player, how could you not give your all in the knowledge that the management were doing that and more? I never took umbrage when asked to do maintenance work. To me it was all part and parcel of my football education at Anfield. What's more, I knew Shanks and his staff were monitoring how we young lads applied ourselves to the tasks we were given. It gave them a good indication of character.

At Christmas, Bill Shankly held a party for the senior pros, groundstaff and his backroom staff. Everyone was expected to do a 'turn', either solo or as part of a group. Someone had the idea of singing 'Ten Green Bottles' complete with dramatic actions, so we groundstaff lads set about rehearsing. We needn't have bothered. We were jeered off stage after only two green bottles had descended. At the end of the night, Shanks took to his feet and gave a speech which was to have a profound effect on me. He loved Hollywood gangster movies, particularly those featuring James Cagney, which appeared to have a cathartic effect on him. Having seen one, for days afterwards he would adopt Cagneyesque speech and mannerisms. Sure enough, he delivered his Christmas party speech in the same style. It was bizarre, humorous, poignant and profound. 'OK, you boys, you listen to me, and listen good,' he said, hitching up his shoulders. 'This club is going places, see? Big places. And I want you to remember this. Foist is foist and second is no good.' It wasn't so much a prediction as a statement of fact. On the way home that night I repeated the phrase over and over to myself – 'Foist is foist and second is no good'. It became my mantra at Liverpool, and that of many other players too. When I got home my mum asked me if I'd had a good time at the party. I felt like saying, 'Look, Ma, I'm on top of the world!'

I did feel on top of the world. I had achieved my childhood dream of signing for Liverpool. But in truth, I knew I had a long way to go to fulfil my ambitions.

In 1960–61, Liverpool fielded five teams. The first team were in the Second Division, while the reserves played in the Central League along with the reserve teams of such clubs as Everton, the two Manchester and Sheffield clubs, Wolves, Burnley, Leeds United, Aston Villa, West Brom, Bolton and Newcastle United. Prior to Shanks's culling of the staff he had inherited, the main-stays of the first team were goalkeeper Bert Slater and centre-half Dick White (the only 'ever presents' in 1960–61); Gerry Byrne, who had just taken over at left-back from Ronnie Moran; Johnny Molineux; wing-half Tommy Leishman; inside-forwards Jimmy Melia, former England winger Alan A'Court, Johnny Morrisey (more of whom later), Kevin Lewis and a young blond-haired Roger Hunt. Leading the line in attack was Dave Hickson, who achieved the notable and rare distinction of being idolized by both Liverpool and Everton supporters; he had been signed from Goodison Park, much to the chagrin of Evertonians. Few of these players would survive the Shankly cull as he revolutionized the club with a view to achieving swift promotion from the Second Division.

The A team, which I first played for, were members of the Lancashire League Division One which boasted the youth teams of, among others, Everton, Manchester United and City, Preston, Blackpool, Bolton and Burnley as well as the reserve teams of

Rochdale and Southport. Liverpool B team, which comprised groundstaff and amateur players, played in the West Cheshire League. Finally there was the C team which, although it did include members of the groundstaff, largely consisted of amateurs, non-contract players, trialists and promising schoolboys. The C team played in the Lancashire League Division Three, against Everton C and the reserve or youth sides of local non-League clubs.

It was common for members of the groundstaff to begin their Anfield careers playing for either the B or C team. The management must have thought I had something going for me, however, because I bypassed these sides and went straight into the A team as a centre-forward. I can recall very little of the games I played in that first season, but one match has stuck in the memory, and for good reason. In January 1961 we played Everton A. For Liverpool, a game against Everton at any level is considered a 'must win' game. Local as well as club pride is at stake, and prior to a game against Everton, even in the Lancashire League, it was drummed into us that whatever we did we must not come off the pitch having lost the game. On that day we beat Everton A 5–1, and I was fortunate enough to score a hat-trick, our other goals coming from Phil Green and Frank Twist.

Since joining Liverpool in May of the previous year it had been indicated to me that my development was good. Training had improved me physically and my performances in the A team had continued to get better. I had a number of goals to my name, but scoring a hat-trick in a 'must win' game against Everton really brought me to the attention of Bill Shankly and his backroom staff. For all that I was in my salad days at Anfield, I was well aware that Shanks was assessing every player connected with the club, be he in the first team or a trialist in the C team, with a view to over-hauling the playing staff. I think everyone knew he was planning a big clear-out and I was determined to stay at the club. Not only that, I wanted to prove to him and his backroom staff that I was good enough eventually to be given an opportunity in the first team.

Of the team that beat Everton A, as far as I can remember Phil Ferns, Bob Davies, Frank Twist, Phil Green and myself were the only ones awarded pro terms. Goalkeeper Bernard McLaren was not a member of the groundstaff, but had been offered a twelve-month contract following a trial period at the club. In the event I was the only one of this group who went on to make a real impression in the first team, though Phil Ferns did play a number of matches. The youth system Shanks and Bob Paisley wanted for the club was still in the planning stage. In time, however, it would prove highly productive. In 1977–78, of the thirty pros on the books, eighteen were homegrown, including Ian Callaghan, Phil Thompson, Brian Kettle, Jimmy Case, Sammy Lee, David Fairclough, Howard Gayle and Alan Harper. In 1960–61, despite Liverpool running three junior sides, few players graduated through the ranks to the first team. John Manning played for the A team against Everton that day, but left Liverpool soon after, though he did go on to enjoy a lengthy and successful career with Tranmere Rovers. Of the players who plied their trade in the B and C teams at the time, only Bobby Graham and Gordon Wallace went on to become first-team players.

I was in the game long enough not to be surprised by what fate can have in store for a footballer. For instance, at the time Liverpool had a reserve-team player, Sammy Reid, who fell foul of Shankly's cull of the playing staff. Sammy returned to his native Scotland where he plied his trade mainly among the part-time professional clubs. However, he went on to make an indelible mark on the history of Scottish football. In 1967, while playing for Berwick Rangers, Sammy scored the goal that knocked Glasgow Rangers out of the Scottish Cup in what many newspapers described as the 'greatest Scottish giant-killing act of the century'. Football can be a fickle mistress. There are any number of players who produced consistently good performances for their clubs during the course of lengthy careers who are now all but forgotten. Conversely, it can take a second to score a goal, and a player who scores one that secures a historic victory, such as Sammy's for Berwick, can go on to enjoy legendary status and a certain immortality in the game. *C'est la vie, c'est le football.*

One of the new rules introduced by Shanks was that all players had to change for training at Anfield, then travel by coach to the Melwood training ground. Following morning training, players made the return trip to Anfield where they would shower or enjoy a bath. This system was adopted by successive Liverpool managers, Bob Paisley, Joe Fagan and Kenny Dalglish, only for it to be abandoned when Graeme Souness took over the reins. As with every idea introduced by Shanks, there was good reason why we changed at Anfield and travelled to Melwood. The foundation of the training was basic skills, control, passing, vision, awareness, exhaustion and recovery. When training was completed, players were perspiring heavily. Shanks didn't want us to go straight into a bath or shower; we would then sweat all day because our pores hadn't closed. After training, and a quick cup of tea, he and his backroom staff had us players walking around the training ground before taking the coach back to Anfield. He believed that by the time we reached Anfield our pores would have closed and only then would we be ready for a bath or shower. Today, most clubs send players out after training or a match for what is called 'warming down'; in 1960–61, Liverpool was the only club doing this. It's yet another example of Bill Shankly's attention to detail. I remember a player from another club thinking this was silly. Believe me, nothing Liverpool ever did in the way of preparation for matches was silly. Bizarre, perhaps, but silly? Never.

Bizarre was the appropriate word for the way we groundstaff lads travelled to Lancashire League matches at Melwood – in a Rolls Royce. The 'Roller' was older than any player on the staff, so old the joke was it was insured against Viking raids. It was like a hearse and it was used to transport kit and balls to and from

Anfield for junior matches. We were issued with our bus fare, but instead we would all pile into the Rolls Royce. Eleven lads in that car was a tight squeeze, but somehow we managed it. The driver was a good old guy called Fred, so small he was just about able to see over the top of the steering wheel. Knees bent and on chests, some faces pressed against the windows, we'd set off for Melwood, passing the church hall where the Beatles were reputed to have played their first gig, the one years later everybody said they went to but didn't. Every journey in that old Rolls Royce was an adventure in itself, not least the one made when a pea-souper descended upon Liverpool.

That day you could hardly see your hand in front of your face. There was little chance of the game being played but we had to turn up for the referee's inspection. 'Show willing,' as someone said. About a mile from Anfield, old Fred took a right turn into what looked like Pinehurst Avenue. Pandemonium reigned inside the car when we realized he was going the wrong way down a dual carriageway. There was laughter, but of the nervous sort. Footballs were grabbed and held in front of heads and bodies – the first makeshift airbags. I fought with Phil Green for the right of protection afforded by the kit bag. Fingers were crossed, and I dare say those in the front seat had reason to cross their legs too. Thankfully, Fred managed to negotiate his way back on to the right side of the road and everyone made as if they had only been pretending to be scared.

'If we had hit anything, this car's built like a tank,' said Fred.

What sort of tank? someone asked.

'Fish tank,' Fred replied, and we all made for the balls and kit bag again.

In the second half of the 1960–61 season I made five appearances for Liverpool reserves. I was still a few months off my sixteenth birthday so I suppose the fact that I had been chosen at such a tender age indicated that the management believed I had potential. Playing for the reserves filled me with awe and excitement as it gave me the opportunity to play alongside my boy-hood idol, Billy Liddell.

Billy was *the* legend of Liverpool Football Club. He had been at Anfield for twenty-two years and was in the twilight of his career; he made only one first-team appearance in 1960–61, bringing his tally to 537 games. He could play any position in the forward line. He had achieved fame as a winger but he was a taker as well as a maker of goals, scoring 229 for Liverpool. He was a member of the Liverpool team that won the Championship in 1947; Bob Paisley was also a member of that side. During the fifties, when Liverpool were struggling, the performances of Billy alone often secured points, so much so that the fans took to calling the club 'Liddlepool'. Billy was rated as one of the greatest British players of all time. Strong, fast and fearless, his consistently good performances earned him twenty-eight caps for Scotland plus eight unofficial appearances during the Second World War. The curious thing about Billy was that throughout his career at Anfield he remained a part-time professional. By day he worked in the city as an accountant. He had a great sense of humour, too. I once asked him, because I genuinely didn't know, what the difference was between an accountant and an auditor. He replied, 'Auditors are people who left accountancy because they found it too exciting.'

It was just days after my sixteenth birthday when I first played alongside Billy in a reserve match against Aston Villa at Anfield. In his pomp Billy had had pace, power and one of the most explosive shots in football, but those days were, sadly, over. On the day, I played inside-left, partnering Billy on the flank. The game was only a minute or so old when I received the ball and played a pass down the left wing for Billy to run on to, just like he used to when I watched him wide-eyed from the Kop. Billy never moved. Minutes later I repeated the scenario, side-footing the ball into space behind two Villa defenders. Again Billy did not move.

'Son, play the ball to ma feet,' he said, turning on me. 'Got that? To ma feet, son!'

Old footballers, unlike soldiers, do not simply fade away; the end is much more brutal than that. The game has little affection for ageing players. Bejewelled careers are often ended with an almost callous abruptness. But retirement and decline are facts of football life, to be accepted without question. A player never loses skill or football nous, it's his legs that go. If someone was to throw me a football now, I could still display the skills I had when I was twenty-seven; what I can't do now is the running. That was the case with Billy Liddell. He was in the dying embers of his career, his pace had deserted him and he needed his team-mates to play to his remaining strengths. Years later, I would find myself in exactly the same situation.

I took Billy's directive on board, began to play the ball into his feet, and he commenced to make the ball do the work, hitting short and long balls with Swiss-watch precision and accuracy.

I learned another valuable lesson during this game against Villa reserves, one that was to stand me in good stead for the rest of my time in football. At right-back for Villa that day was Stan Lynn. Stan was a gnarled, seasoned pro for whom the beautiful game had become tinged with cynicism. He knew how to get through a game, how to survive, and how to gain the upper hand psychologically. During the first half I accelerated past Stan with the ball, much to his annoyance. When the ball subsequently went out of play, I had to run past him again in order to take up a defensive position.

'You little shit,' he snarled. 'If you go past me again, I'll break your back. I have kids like you for 'king breakfast.'

I was stunned. No player had ever spoken to me like that on a football pitch. For the first (and last) time I felt frightened on a football pitch. The next time I received the ball, I found myself thinking about Stan rather than what I was going to do with it.

The match ended 1–1, our goal coming from Willie Carlin who went on to create a little bit of football history, winning promotions with four different clubs: Liverpool, Wolves, Carlisle United and Notts County.

After the game I gave the matter of Stan and his threat some considered thought. I began to realize the power of psychology on a football pitch. You have to be 100 per cent physically fit to play football, but that day I learned you also have to be 100 per cent fit mentally. Stan and his threat had thrown me; I didn't play my normal game because I felt intimidated. They say all the best ideas are adopted and adapted. Indeed, after that match I decided to use Stan's mind games to my own advantage. In the following games I found myself turning to opponents and issuing a warning. 'Do that again and I'll break your leg.' I had no intention of doing so, but to my delight I found that snarling such a threat was often enough to put an opponent off his game, if not to nullify him altogether. The legend of the 'Anfield Iron' was in the making.

There is a postscript to this story and it concerns a spot of gardening at Bill Shankly's house. Shanks and his wife Nessie lived in West Derby in a house from which it was possible to see Everton's training ground. They loved their garden, but Shanks hated gardening with a passion. So he got us groundstaff lads to do it. One day I was doing some weeding and general tidying when Shanks came out for a chat. I can't remember how we got on to the topic – perhaps I mentioned the Stan Lynn incident – but during the course of our conversation Shanks said something I was never to forget. 'Don't take any shit from anybody, no matter who it is,' he told me. From that day on I never did. On the subject of psychological games, he went on to tell me, 'If you can win a game before you go out on the pitch, then win it.'

Given that 1960–61 was my first season at the club and I'd only just turned sixteen, I was pleased with the progress I had made. Liverpool finished third in Division Two, with Ipswich Town promoted as champions and Sheffield United as runners-up. On the face of it, it had been a decent season for the club, but Bill Shankly was not satisfied. No sooner had the last ball been kicked than he started his 'clear-out'. In addition to getting rid of twenty-four players, he set about recruiting.

In the early summer of 1961 he signed centre-half Ron Yeats from Dundee United for £30,000. Ron would come to be known as the 'colossus' – little wonder, given that he is six feet three inches tall and built like a vending machine. Ron had just completed his National Service and had been playing for Dundee United on a part-time basis when Shanks signed him. The day Ron arrived at the club Shanks took him into the boardroom and invited the press along to meet him. Purposefully, he kept the press boys waiting outside for a few minutes. Shanks was in awe of Ron's height and physique and wanted the press lads to feel the same way. Having built up the tension, he then ushered them in with the words, 'Come, lads, come and take a walk around our new centre-half!'

In 1961 it was still common for many players to obtain alternative employment during the close-season. Having arranged board and lodging for Ron, Shanks had to fix him up with some sort of income as the club nigh on shut down for six weeks during the summer. This in mind, Shanks asked Liverpool chairman T. V. Williams if he could have a word with some of his business associates with a view to getting Ron a summer job. A few days later Mr Williams called in to Shanks's office and informed him that a business friend of his might be able to fix up Ron with a temporary post in his car dealership.

'Thank you, Mr Chairman,' said Shanks, 'but there's no need. I had a word with a pal of mine. I've managed to fix the Yeats boy up with a job.'

Mr Williams enquired as to what sort of work Ron would be doing.

'Lifeguard on Southport beach,' replied Shanks.

Mr Williams gave Shanks an incredulous look. 'But Yeats can't swim,' he said.

'No,' said Bill, adding with great satisfaction, 'but he can wade out for two miles!'

The signing of Ron Yeats was followed by that of Ian St John, who joined us from Motherwell for the then considerable fee of £35,000. Shanks later told me the story of how, when he had gone to see the board to ask permission to sign Ian and told them how much it was going to cost, one director said, 'I'm against this. We can't afford to sign him.' To which another director, Mr Sawyer, replied, 'We can't afford not to. It's part of Bill's job to find players who can take this club forward, and it is part of our job to find the money for them.' Mr Sawyer told Shanks to go ahead and sign St John and the board would somehow come up with the money, which they did. Shanks never forgot the support he was given by Mr Sawyer. In truth, he had little time for directors and share-holders, but of Mr Sawyer, who always backed his judgement of players, Shanks would later say, 'That man was really and truly the beginning of Liverpool. The director who not only believed but understood what I was trying to do.'

Liverpool still had one game outstanding, the Liverpool Senior Cup Final against Everton. Ian St John had only been at the club a matter of days, but Shanks played him in this game. It may only have been a local cup final but a crowd of over 51,000 was there to see it, including yours truly. Ian was up against Brian Labone, who would go on to play for England in the 1970 World Cup. Brian was only young at the time but a class act even then; still, Ian ran riot, scoring a hat-trick in a 5–1 victory. No one had bigger smiles on their faces that day than Shanks and Mr Sawyer.

Shanks believed in building a team in the traditional way – that is, one with a strong spine: a good goalkeeper, centre-half, middle-man and centre-forward. He now had his centre-half and centre-forward, and in goalkeeper Bert Slater and inside-forward Jimmy Melia he had, if not great, then dependable occupants of the other positions.

I may have been mad about football since early childhood, but I did have other interests. I had always liked to read, and in my early days with Liverpool I had a great love of thriller and detective novels. Perhaps it was an extension of my childhood excitement at the exploits of Quatermass and Robin Hood. Whatever it was, I certainly took a book with me whenever we went on coaches or stayed in team hotels. I read the first of Ian Fleming's James Bond novels before the first Bond movie, *Dr No*, hit the screens, which really began the Bond phenomenon. Other thriller writers I enjoyed reading were Raymond Chandler, Dashiell Hammett and Francis Durbridge.

At the age of sixteen another interest entered my life: girls, or, to be precise, one girl in particular. I was so devoted to football I'd had little time for dating, but in my first year at Liverpool I did go out with a couple of girls. The second of them came across as very nice but our relationship ended the night of our first and only date when I walked her home. She lived next to Goodison Park and appeared to be an Evertonian. That did it for me; for some reason I couldn't bring myself to call on her again.

A few weeks later I ran into a pal of mine, Mike Kelly. I hadn't seen Mike for a while and during the course of our conversation he asked if I was seeing anyone. When I told him no, he asked if I would be up for going on a blind date with a girl he knew. It turned out the girl Mike was keen on always seemed to be with her best friend. Mike went on to tell me that this 'friend' was a lovely girl but a bit shy, and he suggested the four of us went dancing at the Locarno ballroom. Faint heart and all that, I said yes.

My date was a girl called Susanne. Mike wasn't wrong: she was a lovely girl, if a tad shy. In truth, Mike hadn't done her justice. The moment I saw her I was struck by how beautiful she was. She was of slim build, with short blonde hair, and though she appeared nervous I was soon aware of her wonderful personality and very taken with her engaging smile. I fell for Susanne straight away, even when she told me she had no interest in football whatsoever. Sue and I started seeing each other on a regular basis. We were very happy, but she did have one reservation.

'How old are you?' she asked one evening as we walked back to her home.

'Sixteen,' I replied.

'God! You know I'm eighteen?' There was a look of concern on her face.

'So what?' I replied.

'You never told me you were only sixteen!'

'The age gap needn't be an issue,' I told her. 'We enjoy being with each other. If your friends are true friends, they'll be happy for you that you've found someone you are happy with. And that's the main thing, whether you're happy when we're together.'

She seemed content with that, with everything, and so was I.

When we reported back for training prior to the 1961–62 season, we groundstaff lads had to undertake another monumental task. Shanks was not happy with the penalty area at the Kop end. Rain wasn't draining away properly and as a result the penalty area often resembled a quagmire. The solution, we were told, was simple: dig up the penalty area to a depth of over six feet, lay new pipes and drains, replace the soil, add some topsoil and then seed it. That was some job. It took eight of us nigh on two weeks just to dig it all out. We went to such a depth we had to be helped out of the hole by Arthur the groundsman and his staff. Eventually the job was done to the satisfaction of Arthur and Shanks. What's more, it transpired that we had done a good job. That penalty area never held water again.

In keeping with many clubs, Liverpool started their pre-season programme of matches with a game between the first team and the reserves. At Liverpool it was billed as Reds v. Whites; other clubs had variations on this theme: Possibles v. Probables, Blues v. Stripes and so on. These matches were preceded by a game of some forty minutes between two teams comprising the rest of the playing staff and trialists. The crowd would grow in number as the afternoon progressed until there were some 24,000 present for the game between the Reds and the Whites. Such matches are an anachronism these days but once proved popular with supporters starved of any sort of football for three months in the summer.

That July I received a boost to my confidence when I looked at the team sheet and saw my name down as one of the reserves for the Whites. Past experience of having watched this sort of game told me that those named as reserves were invariably given a run-out at some point in the second half, if not for the duration.

During half-time, Shanks entered our dressing room and said, 'Get ready, Smithy, you're going on as centre-forward for the Whites.' I needed no second telling. However, my enthusiasm and excitement were suddenly tempered when I realized this meant I was going up against the colossus, Ron Yeats. Ron could intimidate opponents by his sheer size, let alone his ability. Whenever an opponent was proving difficult Ron would adhere to the purist football dictum by advising team-mates to 'send him down the 'king line and I'll kick him over the 'king stand'. In short, not a man to mess with.

My team were trailing 2–0 to two Roger Hunt goals when we won a corner. Johnny Morrisey drove it across the penalty area, I ran from deep, met the ball with the meat of my head, and a split second later the net took on the shape of a humongous gumboil. Perhaps it was the joy of scoring at Anfield in front of all those spectators; perhaps it was youthful exuberance fuelled by coursing adrenalin; or maybe a combination of the two. How else can I explain what I did next? Having seen the ball balloon the net, I turned, and there was Ron Yeats standing next to me.

'Pick that out, you big lumbering twat!' I heard myself saying.

I spent most of the rest of the game trying not to beat the American and Russian space programmes by becoming the first human being to orbit the earth. Ron was not a happy man, particularly after the game, when Shanks asked him, 'Big man, how did a sixteen-year-old beat you in the air?'

Incidentally, my eyes must have deceived me that day. I

estimated there were around 24,000 present at Anfield, but from the number of people who have since told me they were first to spot my potential as a boy when I beat Ron Yeats in the air to score for the Whites against the Reds, the attendance must have been nigh on a quarter of a million.

The season proved a successful one for the club. Roger Hunt created a club record by scoring forty-one League goals, while Ian St John chimed in with eighteen and Jimmy Melia and Kevin Lewis also hit double figures. Liverpool were runaway champions of Division Two. Bill Shankly had achieved the first part of his plan for the club, by returning it to Division One.

The outstanding performance of the first team that season was great for the club, but not such good news for me. I spent the entire campaign playing in the reserves. One incident I do recall was my first ever goal for the reserves. It occurred at Oakwell against Barnsley reserves; Phil Ferns took a corner and I rose to head home. It didn't do us much good though: we lost 2–1. I reasoned that at sixteen going on seventeen I was still making good progress, but in truth I had been champing at the bit, hopeful of making my first-team debut.

Mindful of the words of advice given by Shanks himself, not to take shit from anybody, I went to see him with the intention of asking when I would get my big chance.

'Come in, come in, Smithy, son,' said Shanks, smiling broadly. 'Have a cup of tea and a Yo-Yo. They're the toffee ones.'

'No thanks, boss,' I said. 'I've just come to ask when I might be getting my chance in the first team. I think I'm good enough.'

'Your chance will come, Tommy, son, just keep working hard,' he told me, only to add, 'Tell you what, it's been a while since you've been to our house. Come round some time soon and I'll take you out into the garden. I'd love my roses to see you!'

Shanks had an amazing way of disarming players who were not content with their lot. He spoke in such a way that you left his office thinking you were the best thing since sliced bread and damn lucky to be at the best football club in the world. Some years later Liverpool had a player called Bobby Graham who, in the days when only one substitute was named, was unhappy with being regularly named on the bench and felt he deserved a place in the first team. One day after training, Bobby took Shanks to task about this. 'Jesus Christ, Bobby, son,' said Shanks, 'when you started out in this game you would have more than settled for being the twelfth best player in the world!'

I really did think I was good enough to break into the first team, but Shanks and Bob Paisley did not share my opinion, not then. During the summer of 1962, however, I received a fillip when the club offered me professional terms. I was now no longer a member of the groundstaff, and as a first-year professional I earned the princely sum of £18 a week. This development encouraged me greatly. If Shanks thought me good enough to be a full-time pro, I reasoned, he also thought I was future first-team material. When I received the news I couldn't wait to get home and tell Mum, who of course was delighted for me.

I began the 1962–63 season as I had finished the previous season, however, as a regular reserve-team player. I continued to work hard and developed not only my personal game but physically as well. I filled a number of positions in the reserves: centre-forward, inside-left, right-half and even right-back. It was all part of my 'Anfield education'.

Liverpool more than consolidated their return to the top flight, finishing in eighth position. Any satisfaction at this was tempered by the fact that near neighbours Everton won the Championship, in so doing finishing seventeen points ahead of us – and this in the days when only two points were awarded for a victory. But the fact that Liverpool had not struggled in the First Division strengthened Bill Shankly's hand at the club. Slowly but surely he wrested control away from the directors and share-holders. In the course of 1962–63 there were two watershed moments in this respect.

The first involved Tommy Leishman who, following the arrival of Willie Stevenson from Glasgow Rangers, had lost his place at left-half. Tom played eleven matches in 1962–63, filling in for defenders who were injured. Tom didn't feature in the future plans of Shanks, but this didn't stop Shanks standing by him when Tom was subjected to some heckling by a shareholder in the directors' box during a game. Unfortunately for the shareholder in question, Shanks heard his less than complimentary comments. He was fuming, and immediately after the game he headed for the board-room. Shanks was well aware that Tom had struggled in the match, but he wasn't going to allow anyone directly connected with the club to pillory one of his players so publicly.

In the boardroom Shanks found himself talking to a club official and he pointedly cursed and swore when mentioning the conduct of the Liverpool shareholder that afternoon. The shareholder in question was keeping out of Shanks's way, but he sent one of his gofers across to ask if Shanks would curb his language. The terrified gofer gingerly tapped the Liverpool manager on the shoulder. Shanks immediately spun around. His eyes blazed as the gofer pointed to the shareholder and passed on his ill-judged request.

'You're right,' Shanks roared. 'You do well to point that clown out. The idiot who has the temerity to publicly ridicule one of my players!'

The room fell silent as Shanks continued his verbal fusillade.

'Are you trying to make an idiot of me in front of all these people?' asked the shareholder angrily when Shanks had finally finished his piece.

'The good Lord beat me to it!' Shanks replied, and on that note he strode out of the room.

The following Monday morning this story was all over the changing room. I laughed when I heard it, thinking to myself, 'Yes, the boss doesn't take shit from anybody.'

A few weeks later there was another incident which served not only to strengthen Shanks's power and presence at Liverpool, but to lay down the foundations for the club culture he was attempting to create. Johnny Morrisey was not your archetypal winger. He was tough, hard-tackling and hotly competitive. Due, in the main, to the form of young Ian Callaghan, Johnny had not made an appearance in the first team during 1962–63. About halfway through the season the Liverpool board, seemingly thinking him surplus to requirements, sold Johnny to arch rivals Everton, and they did so without fully consulting Shanks. Shanks was livid. He went to see the directors, threatened to resign and told them in no uncertain terms that they were never to do such a thing again. He went on to remind the board that he was the manager and therefore it was he who decided which players stayed and which players left the club. Shanks was so forceful in his view that the board had no choice but to be compliant for fear of losing him.

The matter, however, did not end there. Eager that there should be no repeat of such an incident, Shanks drew up a list of club rules and regulations and had them printed into a little book – a red book, of course, a bit like *The Thoughts of Chairman Mao*. Every member of staff was issued with a copy, including directors and shareholders. In essence it was Shanks's code of practice for the club. In addition to saying what was expected of players in terms of conduct, attitude, dress, general appearance, training and match preparation, the little red book detailed the club's chain of command. The manager would convey instructions to players during matches via the team captain; it was also permissible for the captain to receive instructions from the manager's assistants, Bob Paisley, Joe Fagan and Reuben Bennett. Should the captain receive instructions or advice about play from directors or shareholders, he was to ignore it. The captain was responsible for matters on the field, and as such he was allowed to give his own instructions as he thought fit. Given that Ron Yeats was now captain, on reading this I assumed it was a green light for 'send him down here etc.'. The book also committed to print the responsibilities of each member of the staff, including Shanks himself. One aspect of his remit as manager was the signing or releasing of players. Should the signing or transfer of a player involve a fee, he would conduct the business in consultation with the board of directors.

Everyone now knew what was expected of them. There were no grey areas, no confusion and, importantly from Shanks's point of view, no further usurping of his authority. The foundations had been laid for the culture of the club that would rise to become one of the most successful in the world.

My performances for the reserves in 1962–63 brought me to the attention of England Youth, who in April were due to compete in the Junior World Cup – or, to give it its official title, the 16th International Youth Tournament. Initially I was invited to trials at the Cliff, the then training ground of Manchester United. I was thrilled when about a week later I received a letter from the FA informing me of my inclusion in the squad.

I had attended the trials as a right-half, and that is the position in which I played in England Youth's warm-up matches. The first of these was a game against Coventry City first team which we lost 2–1. We then played Sheffield United reserves at Bramall Lane, winning 3–2, before a final game at Wimbledon's Plough Lane against the open-age England amateur team. We lost that one 4–0, but these games were all part of the toughening-up process. Our coach, Wilf McGuinness of Manchester United, wanted us fit, mentally and physically, as well as familiar with one another's style of play.

Things began to take shape when England Youth travelled to Switzerland and on 21 March beat the home side 7–1 in Bienne. We had a very strong squad of players which included Len Badger and Bernard Shaw (both Sheffield United), Phil Beal (Tottenham), Lew Chatterley (Aston Villa), George Jones (Bury), David Pleat (Nottingham Forest), Johnny Sissons and John

Charles (West Ham United), David Sadler (Manchester United), Jon Sammels (Arsenal), Mick Leach (QPR), Graham French (Shrewsbury Town), Denis Thwaites (Birmingham City) and our skipper, a fey little lad noted for his genteel tackling – Ron Harris (Chelsea). All those players went on to enjoy highly successful careers in the game. Curiously, the one position in which players did not go on to carve out successful careers was that of goal-keeper. John Cowen (Chelsea) was the regular number one. He did make the Chelsea first team but he never quite managed the level of success in the game enjoyed by other members of the team. Likewise John's deputy, Don Roper (Bradford City), and outside-left Ray Whittaker (Arsenal).

As had been the case for the forthcoming 1966 World Cup, England had been invited to stage the Youth World Cup, as opposed to conducting a campaign of application, which is the case nowadays. As hosts, England Youth qualified for the finals automatically, which meant we missed out on the preliminary group stages which would have afforded us a further opportunity for familiarization as a team. England were drawn in Group C along with Holland, Russia and Romania. Scotland found them-selves in Group A with West Germany, Greece and Switzerland. The other home nation to qualify was Northern Ireland, who were in Group D along with Belgium, Sweden and Czechoslovakia. Group B comprised Italy, France, Hungary and Bulgaria.

I think it came as a surprise to most when England, Scotland and Northern Ireland topped their respective groups. It was a marvellous achievement by the home nations, particularly Scotland, who got off to a bad start losing 2–1 to West Germany. The Germans had a strong squad (was it ever thus?) which included Franz Beckenbauer and four other players who eventually went on to play for the full national side.

We began our group by beating Holland 5–0 at Wimbledon's Plough Lane. Romania were then defeated at Highbury (3–0), and we clinched top spot with a 2–0 win against Russia at White Hart

Lane. The semi-finals saw us pitched against the 'auld enemy', Scotland. The game took place at the White City Stadium, which was not a regular football ground but curiously was chosen as a venue for the 1966 World Cup over the likes of Highbury and White Hart Lane. A White City crowd of 21,978 saw the Scots prove stern opposition but we managed to score the only goal of the game.

Our opponents in the final were Northern Ireland who, after drawing their semi-final 3–3 against Bulgaria, went through on the drawing of lots. The match took place at Wembley before a crowd of 59,567 and the England team that lined up before them read as follows: John Cowen; Len Badger, Bernard Shaw; me, Lew Chatterley, Ron Harris; Graham French, Jon Sammels, George Jones, John Sissons and Ray Whittaker. I remember the early exchanges being rather even, but once John Napier put through his own goal, despite the Irish playing some really good football we never looked back. We went on to win 4–0, a winning margin that could have been more but for a superb performance from the Northern Ireland goalkeeper, Pat Jennings.

The newspapers were all in agreement: it had been one of the finest games seen at Wembley for a long time. I felt very proud to have helped England Youth win the Youth World Cup. It was widely hailed as a superb achievement, and to have been part of it not only thrilled me but proved a massive boost to my confidence. I knew on returning to Anfield that Bill Shankly and Bob Paisley were going to congratulate me and hopefully one day soon recognize my worth by giving me my chance in the first team.

1962–63 was the season of the 'Big Freeze'. Snow fell in some parts of northern England and Scotland prior to Christmas; the rest of the UK saw snow on Boxing Day and were to keep on seeing it for over two months. I remember this period particularly well. On 29 December fourteen inches of snow fell in parts of London, and they got off lightly! In early January twenty-three inches of snow fell on Liverpool within twenty-four hours. The North-East and Scotland were brought to their knees by blizzards that resulted in snowdrifts measured at over eighteen feet in parts of County Durham. On 23 January the night temperature in Hereford was recorded at −20.6°C, the lowest ever in England. The River Thames froze and the ice was measured at three inches at Windsor, which was nothing compared to the nine inches recorded on parts of the Tyne and the pack ice seen on the Mersey. Television showed pictures of the sea frozen up to a hundred feet offshore at Southport. The snow lay deep for sixty-seven days yet I can never recall a school closing. The trains ran, too. Most were late, but they ran, thanks to the work of snowploughs and the sterling work of gangs of labourers who cleared snow from the tracks with shovels. I remember Liverpool Corporation buses with chains affixed to their tyres to enable them to ascend the hills in the city. People went to work every day, it just took a bit longer.

The Big Freeze played havoc with fixtures. Only three third-round FA Cup ties out of thirty-two went ahead as scheduled; fourteen of these ties were postponed ten or more times. Having drawn their third-round tie on 3 January, Blackburn Rovers and Middlesbrough had to wait until 11 March before replaying. On one Saturday in January only four games took place in England, and only five on 2 February. The following Saturday, England managed seven matches but the entire Scottish League programme was wiped out. Having beaten Blackburn Rovers on 22 December, Liverpool managed to play only another two League matches between then and March. The reserves managed just three Central League matches from mid-December to March.

With nigh on five hundred matches postponed, the Football League had no alternative but to extend the season until the end of May; in the event, the final League game took place at Workington on 1 June. Clubs had to cram matches into April and May. Liverpool played seven League fixtures and an FA Cup semi-final against Leicester City within three weeks in April. With matches coming thick and fast, players had no time to recover from injuries, one such player being Liverpool right-half Gordon Milne. It was expected that Jimmy Melia would deputize for Gordon. Only for yours truly, the winds of providence were blowing a gale that week.

Jimmy Melia was a stylish inside-forward, good enough to be chosen by Alf Ramsey for England. For me, however, Jimmy never adhered to the Shankly dictum of giving everything irrespective of the type of game. In early May a practice game took place between the first team and the reserves at Melwood. I had the job of marking Jimmy, who tended to coast in such games. I played Jimmy off the park, which apparently impressed Shanks, though to be fair, Jimmy was carrying an injury.

Bill Shankly was something of a dichotomy in that he was a traditionalist who readily embraced new ideas. He was always on the lookout for technological advances in the treatment of injuries, and had purchased a machine from Germany that was supposedly a miracle cure for muscular problems. Shanks was very proud of this machine and made no secret of the fact that it had cost £2,000 – a considerable sum of money at the time. The first beneficiary of this 'wonder' machine was Jimmy Melia, and Shanks invited a number of the players to see it in action. Strapping was wrapped around the area of injury which would then vibrate, massage and, as a consequence, apply heat to the sore point. The intensity of the vibration, and thus the amount of heat, was controlled by a dial which had a scale of one to ten.

We gathered in the physio's room and watched intently, and with not a little expectation, as Shanks strapped Jimmy's leg, telling him he would soon be fit to play in the forthcoming match against Birmingham City. Shanks then turned the dial on the new machine to number two.

'How's that, Jimmy, son?' asked Shanks.

'Can't feel a thing, boss,' replied Jimmy.

'It's just warming up, give it time.'

Two minutes passed.

'Feel anything?' asked Shanks.

'Nothing,' replied Jimmy.

Shanks turned the dial to number five.

'How's that?'

Another couple of minutes passed.

'No difference,' Jimmy informed him.

Not a little irritated, Shanks proceeded to crank the dial to number eight. Still nothing to report from Jimmy. Shanks was becoming very frustrated now. He whipped the dial to the maximum of ten.

We waited.

'Can't feel a thing, boss,' said Jimmy.

'Bloody German rubbish!' shouted Shanks, flinging both arms in the air in frustration and annoyance. 'They can have it back, and I want my money back!'

At this point Bob Paisley entered the room. He surveyed the scene, calmly walked over to a socket on the wall and flicked the switch. Jimmy's strapped leg immediately shot into the air and his whole body juddered manically as if he was having an epileptic fit.

'Turn it off, turn it off!' he screamed.

Bob turned off the machine and we players went across to scrape Jimmy off the ceiling.

Embarrassed and disgusted by the fiasco, Shanks made for the door.

'What does all this mean?' Jimmy whimpered.

'It means Smithy's playing against Birmingham,' said Shanks.

On 8 May 1963, a matter of weeks after my eighteenth birthday, I made my Liverpool debut against Birmingham City. It is a night that is indelibly printed in my mind. I felt that everything I had worked so hard for had finally come to fruition. To this day I can still recite the Liverpool team: Tommy Lawrence, Chris Lawler, Gerry Byrne, me, Ron Yeats, Willie Stevenson, Ian Callaghan,

Roger Hunt, Ian St John, Gordon Wallace, Alan A'Court. Birmingham were a decent First Division team and included in their ranks goalkeeper Colin Withers, Terry Hennessey, Trevor Smith, Mike Hellawell, Jimmy Bloomfield and Ken Leek, all renowned players. Oh, and at right-back they had Stan Lynn, the seasoned pro who had frightened the life out of me two years earlier, in so doing teaching me an invaluable lesson.

My mum had remarried, and she was there in the stand with my new stepfather, Richie Morton, who had been a decent footballer in his own right, having played for Liverpool Schoolboys in the 1920s. As I took to the pitch I turned, saw Mum and gave her a wave. I did so in appreciation of all she had done for me. As we kicked in my mind went back to the day when she took me to Anfield to meet Shanks. I knew how proud she would be to see me playing in the first team.

A little older now, and a lot wiser, Stan Lynn's scare tactics had no effect on me. We blitzed Birmingham that night, winning 5–1, Roger Hunt scoring two of our goals. I was gloriously happy, and not a little relieved, to get through the game without making a telling mistake. The Liverpool supporters were great to me. Knowing it was my debut they applauded almost every time I touched the ball, which gave me great encouragement. It was the beginning of a wonderfully warm relationship with the club's supporters that I am happy to say continues to this day. After the game, Shanks and Bob Paisley were full of praise for me, saying that I had contributed in a positive way to the game and had played well. As a Liverpool lad and a Liverpool supporter, it made me feel something I'd never felt in my life before; a mixture of pride, excitement, joy, satisfaction and, no exaggeration, ecstasy consumed my being. I experienced the first natural high of my life.

When I came out of the ground, Mum and Richie were there to meet me. Mum said, 'Come on, let's go home and have a cup of tea, and you can tell us all about it.' But I declined her kind offer and told them I would see them later.

I went for a walk around the terraced streets of Anfield. I just wanted to stay close to the ground, relive and savour every moment of what had been the most fantastic night of my life. I can't imagine today's players doing that, even if they wanted to. I was the happiest lad in Liverpool – no, make that the world. When I started to walk there were still a few supporters hanging about, but soon I had the streets to myself. There is something desolate about the environs of a football ground in the aftermath of a game. Streets that a few hours ago had been alive with humanity and expectation were returned to stillness and silence. The sudden contrast seemed to envelop each and every street with a certain sadness, but it was a sadness that failed to penetrate the ecstasy I felt. The detritus of a football match – chip papers, fag packets, cigarette ends and pages from newspapers – blew aimlessly around the streets like urban tumbleweed. Thin rain began to fall, illuminated by the streetlamps. The pavements shone long and dingy yellow, and here and there puddles in the gutters were rainbowed with oil. I could hear televisions babbling from within the terraced houses. Through gaps in curtains I caught glimpses of safe, slippered, waterproof hearths, which served to instil in me the feeling that, for all that the streets were cold, wet and deserted, all was well and comfortable this night.

I kept on walking the silent streets, always keeping the ground within sight, as if I couldn't bear to part from it. I ran the game through my mind, committing to memory my every touch of the ball; playing a through-ball to Roger Hunt; contesting a high ball with Ken Leek; tackling Mike Hellawell. I replayed every goal, my part in the build-up and celebration, the reaction of the crowd. I had always been confident of making it into the first team, yet a small part of me, buried deep within, wondered if I was deluding myself, living a dream that could never be realized. Now that small part of me had been extinguished. I told myself that no matter what the future had in store for me I had played for Liverpool; the record books would testify to that and no one could take that away from me. I felt a certain satisfaction with this, yet I was also wholly unsatisfied. One game was not enough for me. I wanted to be playing every week, to devote myself to representing the club. I told myself that if I played regularly for Liverpool until I was thirty-five and suddenly died, that would be fine. I was eighteen, and that night life had no meaning for me beyond a career in football with Liverpool.

I walked the streets for some two hours before making my way home. I went to bed straight away, but couldn't sleep. Yet again I ran the game through my mind, reliving every moment, savouring the highly charged atmosphere of the night. Eventually I drifted into the arms of Morpheus and dreams of future games and success with Liverpool.

3

AMBITION LIKE A TORRENT

HAVING MADE MY FIRST-TEAM DEBUT I FELT THERE WAS A FUTURE for me at Liverpool. Following my debut against Birmingham City, Chris Lawler and I laughed about our days on the ground-staff and dreamed of a glorious future together in the first team. But though I had been told I had done well against Birmingham City, I immediately reverted back to the reserves for the remaining three matches of the season. I was very disappointed, and I told Shanks as much. Typically, he turned my situation on its head. 'It's good that you're very disappointed, Tommy, son. If you didn't feel disappointed it would tell me your attitude is all wrong. Your time will come. Nothing is slower than time to the man who expects. Keep working hard, be patient.'

During the close-season Shanks strengthened the first team with the signing of winger Peter Thompson from Preston North End for £35,000. Tommy Lawrence assumed the role of first-choice goalkeeper at the expense of Jim Furnell, and as the 1963–64 season progressed some of the stalwarts of the days in the Second Division – Tommy Leishman, Kevin Lewis and Alan A'Court – found themselves being eased out. Once again Bill Shankly and

Bob Paisley demonstrated that they had a great eye for emerging talent. As in the case of Ron Yeats, Ian St John and Willie Stevenson, who had been signed for a bargain £6,000 from Glasgow Rangers reserves, Peter Thompson was an instant success at Anfield. With his neatly cut hair and 'West One' style clothes that were all the rage with mods, Peter appeared the epitome of 1960s male fashion. With Peter on one wing and Ian Callaghan on the other, the pair wreaked havoc among opposing defences. The Everton legend Dixie Dean was even moved to say he would have loved to play at centre-forward with Peter and Ian on either wing. They were, he said, the best pairing he had ever seen.

I knew Peter had style the moment he turned up at Anfield to sign for the club. He was wearing a 'mod' pastel striped jacket, Ben Sherman tab-collared shirt and white hipster trousers, and he drove a blue MG sports car. His signing generated so much interest that over a thousand supporters were at the ground to see him. Shanks was keen as mustard to land his man. Peter was also keen to sign, but he made a faux pas during the talks by asking for a signing-on fee. A business friend of Peter's had advised him to do this, but when he brought the subject up, Shanks went berserk. 'I'm giving you the chance to play for the greatest club in the world, and you ask for illegal money! You have the temerity to ask us to pay you to sign for this great club? *You* should be paying *us*! This tells me there's a flaw in your character. Now get out!' Peter was so shocked and flabbergasted that he immediately grabbed a pen that was lying on Shanks's desk and hastily signed the contract that had been placed before him. As Peter later told me, it was the best thing he ever did.

He enjoyed a great first season with the club. His mercurial performances on the wing resulted in him being an ever-present in the first team, and he soon learned he had to immerse himself in the culture of the club and to adhere to the idiosyncratic ways of Bill Shankly. One morning at Melwood we were walking off the training pitch when Shanks approached Peter and said he wanted a word. It transpired that Shanks was not happy with the colour of Peter's sports car.

'I'm very disappointed in you, Thommo,' he said. 'You're still driving a blue car. You play for Liverpool, not Everton. Any type of car, any colour but blue. Get rid of it.'

He did.

Having consolidated in Division One the previous season, in 1963–64 Liverpool finally shed the mediocrity that had dogged the club since the early fifties by surging to the League Championship. I remained ever hopeful of being called up to the first team, particularly as only one of the opening four League matches was won. However, as the season progressed results improved, and then became sensational. Wolves, Stoke City, Sheffield United and Ipswich Town were all hit for six and Arsenal for five in the space of a few heady months. Having hit such a rich vein of form I knew Shanks would be loath to change the side. It left me wondering if I would ever be given a run. Nothing hurts when you are winning, and this was very much the case as far as the first-team players were concerned. If any of them did take a knock, if it wasn't serious he didn't let on for fear of losing his place. With opportunities for first-team places at a premium, I again spent the entire season in the Central League side.

I remember the reserves starting the season with a 2–0 win at home to Manchester City. A few weeks later I was on the scoresheet when we beat Blackburn Rovers 4–0, our other goals coming from Alan A'Court and Phil Tinney, who scored twice. The season ended on somewhat of a high note when we beat Tranmere Rovers 2–1 to win the Liverpool Senior Cup. I scored from the penalty spot and Phil Ferns netted the decisive goal before an Anfield crowd of 9,000. I may only have been a regular in the reserves, but the fact that I had maintained my place in that team made me feel very much a Liverpool player during what was a historic period for the club and the city as both underwent a metamorphosis.

The season proved to be one of the most sensational and memorable not only in the history of Liverpool Football Club, but also for the city itself, and I consider myself damn lucky to have been there when it all happened. The race for the First Division title had for the most part been contested by Liverpool, Manchester United, Everton, Spurs and Chelsea. For a while it was nip and tuck, but following a 3–1 defeat at Everton in early February, Liverpool lost only one of their next twelve League games which proved enough to secure the title. We finished as champions on fifty-seven points, four ahead of runners-up Manchester United and five ahead of near neighbours Everton, who had to settle for third. Only Spurs (ninety-seven) scored more goals than Liverpool (ninety-two), but whereas Spurs conceded eighty-one goals, Liverpool conceded only forty-five, which in the days of open, attacking football nigh on passed for a 'watertight' defence.

The title was clinched on 18 April in sensational fashion with a 5–0 demolition of Arsenal, and we still had three matches to play. The only fly in the ointment that day concerned the attitude of Everton, who had won the Championship the previous season. Liverpool had asked Everton if they could send the League Championship trophy to Anfield so that the players could be presented with it should they beat Arsenal. Everton refused, saying they had to 'do things by the book' – that is, return the trophy to the Football League for later presentation to Liverpool should we win the title. Undaunted, someone in the club office had a papier-mâché copy of the trophy made. Following victory over Arsenal, Ron Yeats was presented with this and the lads carried it on a victorious lap of honour around Anfield. Photographs of this appeared in all the newspapers, and the football annuals of that year. I'm sure countless people around the country were at a loss to understand why Ron was carrying a papier-mâché trophy; perhaps only now they will learn why. The papier-mâché trophy came to symbolize the attitude that ran throughout the club: we would not be beaten, and if there was a problem we would somehow get round it, even if the solution was a little Heath Robinson. The papier-mâché trophy was looked upon fondly by everyone, so much so that two years later, when Liverpool won the title again, it made another public appearance, this time alongside the real Championship trophy.

The Arsenal game was a watershed for Liverpool in more ways than one. It helped launch the club into the nation's conscious-ness. Though obviously we were not aware of it at the time, winning the League Championship in 1964 marked the beginning of an age of football imperialism for the club that was to last for some thirty years. Anfield was packed for every home match, and the fact that Everton had contested the title race throughout the season added to the fervour and excitement. Not only were the clubs at the forefront of English football, the city of Liverpool had achieved a hitherto unknown fame throughout the world, not least because it was the home of the Beatles.

London will always be the nation's centre for commerce, government and popular culture. Whenever a new movement in music or fashion evolves, however, invariably it emerges in a provincial city before gravitating to the capital. The so-called swinging sixties had much to do with popular music, colourful fashion, comedy, hip poets and the youth revolution, much of which had emerged in Liverpool. In 1963–64, Liverpool was the place to be. The country, and a good part of the world, were gripped by Beatlemania. The Rolling Stones may have rocked harder, and Bob Dylan may have been smarter, but neither could claim the cultural impact of the Beatles. The 'Fab Four' were in tune with the times. They were also in tune with their home city, which in no small way contributed to Liverpool becoming the hub of British popular culture at the time. To me, the Beatles are the ultimate pop group, one of the few bands to transcend the limit-ations of their art to produce music that, though it had its roots in Liverpool, became universal.

They were at the forefront of what was called the 'Mersey Beat', a musical movement which had grown out of the city's clubs and pubs and included artistes such as the Searchers, Gerry and the Pacemakers, Cilla Black, the Merseybeats, the Scaffold and Billy J. Kramer and the Dakotas. All these artistes had at one time or another in their fledgling careers played at the Cavern Club. Seemingly overnight, a small music club in a nondescript street in the city centre became the most famous in the world.

I saw any number of bands at the Cavern in the early 1960s, but this club was just one of some two hundred or so in the city providing a possible venue for the estimated three hundred local bands doing the rounds at the time. Those bands and singers I have mentioned went on to achieve success and fame, but bands that were little known nationally, such as Faron's Flamingos, the Remo Four, the Undertakers, Rory Storm, and Nicky Crouch and the Mojos, were just as popular with Liverpool teenagers. In addition to the Cavern I went to numerous other clubs – not particularly to drink, rather to see the groups – such as the Blue Angel, the Iron Door and the Jacaranda. The latter was owned by Allan Williams, one of the city's great characters who in May 1960 gave the Silver Beetles, as they were then called, their first pro gig.

The club I frequented the most, however, was the Royal Tiger, which was situated just off the entrance to the Mersey tunnel. The club was owned by Chris Lawler's father-in-law and was very popular with Liverpool and Everton players, who happily mixed socially. The club had an upstairs-downstairs arrangement: live acts played downstairs whereas upstairs was for sitting and chatting. I remember once seeing Cilla Black perform; she sang a popular number entitled Let's Jump The Broomstick'. We were all so naive, no one more so than Cilla, that the sexual innuendo was lost on us. The Liverpool and Everton players liked the Royal Tiger because its door policy ensured that no drunks were admitted. The non-footballers who attended the club were never a source of trouble, which made for a very convivial, hassle-free atmosphere. In all the years I frequented the Royal Tiger I only witnessed one 'incident', and that involved our skipper, Ron Yeats.

Following a Merseyside derby, Liverpool and Everton players would still mix together at the Royal Tiger, irrespective of what had happened on the pitch. We would rarely mention the game. One night, however, a guy, seemingly an Everton supporter, started to goad the wife of Ron Yeats. Players from both teams politely asked this guy to leave Ron's wife alone, but he was having none of that. He continued to have a go at her about the game, Ron's worth as a footballer, and so on. Again he was politely asked to desist, but he continued his verbal tirade. He became more and more uncouth until finally he made a very insulting remark. Ron immediately took to his feet and with a fist attempted to locate the back of the guy's head via his face. It was as if an unseen force had gripped the back of the guy's jacket and yanked him backwards. With a startling momentum he shot through the air and across a table before coming to rest on the floor, his face pressed against the wall. The hubbub of the club ceased for all of two seconds as people took in the scene; then everyone simply returned to their respective conversations. The amazing thing was the guy lay there on the floor for a good half hour and attracted as much attention as an empty fag packet. A lad ferrying a tray of drinks to his friends didn't take the blindest bit of notice; he casually stepped over the prostrate body as he might a cricket boundary rope. Eventually the guy did regain consciousness and staggered out of the club, no doubt wondering what the hell had hit him.

As I said, in the sixties I saw many bands at the Cavern, but my connection with this famous club in Matthew Street runs a little deeper. When my footballing days were over I had numerous business interests in the city, and one partnership was with a local lad whose background was delivering solicitors' writs and working as a club doorman but who had saved a bit of money and gone into property development. In 1980 we bought the lease of the Cavern

Club and redeveloped it. It was seedy and very rundown, but we restored it to its former glory and built a pub above the club and named it Abbey Road. The Cavern was back in business as a venue for bands, the majority of them local. But while the pub thrived, the Cavern was anything but a money spinner. A few years later I sold the lease, and I now have no connection with either the club or the pub. However, the fact that I did once 'own' a famous piece of Liverpool's cultural history, albeit in days far removed from when the Beatles played there, is still a source of pride to me.

I got to know most of the Liverpool bands of the 1960s, but unfortunately not the Beatles. The nearest I ever came was when attending social functions at which they were also present. I always longed to go up and chat with one of them, but there was always a crowd around them and I felt my presence would only add to what appeared to me to be their obvious angst.

One band I did get to know well was the Scaffold, which comprised the poet Roger McGough, John Gorman and Mike McGear, who is the brother of Paul McCartney. Mike was a big Liverpool supporter and later in the sixties he invited me and a number of other players to sing along with the band in the chorus of a recording of the song 'Lily The Pink', which reached number one in the charts in November 1968. I had another connection with the Scaffold, albeit a tenuous one. In the mid-sixties they released a song entitled 'Thank You Very Much' which was also a hit for the band. It was a novelty song really, one which included the line 'Thank you very much for the Aintree iron'. At the time Liverpool supporters had dubbed me 'The Anfield Iron', something which the band picked up on: they changed the lyric to 'Thank you very much for the Anfield Iron'.

In addition to producing pop stars, in 1963–64 Liverpool also produced a great many comedians. So plentiful were they at this time that the city achieved national fame for what was termed 'Scouse humour'. Freddie Starr, Stan Boardman and Ken Dodd became very popular with their respective versions of Scouse humour, but the most famous comic to emerge during this period was a close pal of mine, Jimmy Tarbuck, whom I'd first met one night in the Royal Tiger when out with Susanne. Jimmy's brand of Scouse humour and mop Beatles hairstyle captivated the nation. He shot to fame when he landed the job of hosting one of television's most popular programmes, the variety show *Sunday Night at the London Palladium*. The transition proved seamless: Jimmy simply told the jokes he had been telling when doing the rounds of Liverpool pubs and clubs. If not exactly the city's working-class culture, it was Liverpool's perceived working-class sub-culture. Stock phrases such as 'tatty head' and 'wack' formed an integral part of Jimmy's stage act and were adopted at least temporarily by the nation.

Even poetry became mainstream. *The Mersey Sound*, an anthology featuring the work of poets Roger McGough, Brian Patten and Adrian Henri, became a best-seller in 1967 and encouraged thousands of working-class teenagers to read poetry; prior to its publication they probably thought poems were for middle-class arty-farties. The poems of McGough, Patten and Henri were accessible because many dealt with the nuts and bolts of everyday life in a humorous but poignant way. We were all wrapped up in the Liverpool scene and, quite literally, supported one another. The poets came to watch the football, and the footballers read their poetry. The success of these poets owed much to the fact that we young people thought of their work as simply being part of the pop movement.

The popular TV police drama *Z Cars* was based in the city. The programme's theme music, the traditional tune 'Johnny Todd', was synonymous with Everton: it was played through the loud-speakers when the team took to the pitch at Goodison Park. The reason Everton adopted the tune was simply that the TV version was subtitled 'The Boys In Blue'.

Anything and everything to do with Liverpool was popular in 1964. Even TV programmes based in other cities were seemingly not complete without someone from Liverpool in the cast, the most notable example being Johnny Speight's *Til Death Us Do Part*. It was set in London's East End but relied heavily for its humour on the prickly relationship between its main character, the West Ham-supporting, working-class Tory bigot Alf Garnett (Warren Mitchell), and his Scouse, socialist, Liverpool-supporting layabout son-in-law Mike, played by Anthony Booth. At the time it was hip and fashionable just to be from Liverpool. Liverpool was where it was happening.

Underpinning this great movement in popular music, comedy, drama, poetry and fashion were the city's two successful football clubs, in particular new champions Liverpool and our enigmatic manager Bill Shankly. The club's renaissance under Shankly co-incided with this explosion of popular culture on Merseyside. It was a hell of a coincidence, but it put the club in the vanguard of English football and even made our supporters famous. The fans who congregated on the Kop had taken to singing 'You'll Never Walk Alone', the song which is now the anthem of the club. Rather than paying homage to Richard Rodgers and Oscar Hammerstein, who penned the song for *Carousel*, I'm sure the majority of our supporters associated the song with Gerry and the Pacemakers whose version topped the charts in October 1963. As for why Liverpool supporters adopted the song, I shall tell you.

Gerry Marsden, lead singer with Gerry and the Pacemakers, was and still is a Liverpool fanatic. He was often a guest of the players at home games and became friends with Bill Shankly. Gerry is a smashing lad. Shanks took to him straight away and always made a point of having a chat with him whenever he visited Anfield. In the summer of 1963 we embarked upon a short pre-season tour of the Continent. Prior to our leaving, Gerry visited Anfield and pre-sented Bill with a taped recording of what he informed us was to be Gerry and the Pacemakers' next record, 'You'll Never Walk Alone'. We travelled by coach, and the driver played taped music, which prompted Shanks to get up and ask if he would play Gerry's tape. The driver obliged, and when the song had finished, Shanks was in awe of what he had just heard. He took to his feet and made his way to the back of the coach where the players were seated.

'Did ye hear that, lads? That song of Gerry's, "You'll Never Walk Alone"?'

We told him we had.

'What a song! It's like that psalm, "Yea, though I walk through the valley of death". From now on, "You'll Never Walk Alone" will be *our* song.'

Football writers from the local papers were travelling with our party and, thirsty for a story of any kind between games, filed copy back to their editors to the effect that we had adopted Gerry Marsden's forthcoming single as the club song. The rest is history.

The song is an uplifting, optimistic, never-say-die number which seemed to embody the attitude that ran through the club at the time – which I suppose is why it appealed so much to Shanks. As for its enduring popularity with our supporters, it was a song which became a massive hit, one recorded by a local band who were themselves Liverpool fans, added to which the words of 'You'll Never Walk Alone' are highly memorable. It is not an up-tempo song so it lends itself to community singing and is in a key most people find comfortable. Little wonder, then, that having been endorsed by Bill Shankly and the players it was so readily adopted by the Kop.

As for the fame Liverpool supporters enjoyed, in particular those songsters on the Kop, this again had much to do with TV and, of all programmes, *Panorama*. Wanting to capture the social and cultural phenomena of Liverpool in 1964 when Beatlemania was at its height, *Panorama* devoted a whole programme to the city. It told of the impact of the Beatles and many of the other groups that were part of the 'Mersey Beat'; it also featured the city's comedians, writers and poets as well as the two football clubs which had re-emerged as the hub of the community. BBC cameras were present at that final home game of the season against Arsenal which, if Liverpool won, would result in the club winning the First Division Championship for the first time since 1947. Liverpool, as we know, were on fire that day, but in the main the cameras were trained on the tumultuous Kop as supporters swayed en masse singing the Beatles' 'She Loves You' and the song they had read in the local papers that Bill Shankly had adopted as the club anthem, 'You'll Never Walk Alone'.

When the programme was broadcast the following week it proved a watershed moment for English football. The *Panorama* reporter John Morgan was seen standing in front of the Kop as supporters of all ages sang their hearts out; it really did come across as some sort of cultural phenomenon. The appearance of the Liverpool supporters on such a 'highbrow' current affairs programme afforded the Kop national exposure to an audience that went far beyond the confines of football. Supporters of whatever hue, and those who had only a passing interest in the game, were in awe of what they had seen. Supporters of other clubs immediately took to copying the Kop, crowding together and indulging in community singing, though the atmosphere and dynamics of that moment at Anfield proved impossible to replicate.

A few years ago I saw a video of that *Panorama* programme. All these years on, and the sight of the Kop in full cry in 1964 is still a moving experience. John Morgan's commentary is hopelessly over-the-top and patronizing, though; perhaps it even came across like that at the time. Football in 1964 was still widely regarded as a sport played by and largely watched by working-class men. I suspect for Morgan and the programme's presenter, that pillar of the establishment Richard Dimbleby, what they saw that day at Anfield was as alien to them as some tribal ritual in Papua New Guinea. Which is probably why Morgan spoke of the Kop's rhythmic swaying as being 'as rich and mystifying as any ritual on a South Sea island' and their singing 'tribal and full of inventive ferocity to signal to supporters of other clubs they should not impinge upon their sacred territory'. Morgan's wrap-up words, however, appeared to owe much to his having watched Jimmy Tarbuck at the London Palladium. 'See how these truly fanatical Liverpool supporters are in touch with Wacker, the spirit of Scouse.'

The airtime given to the massed singing of those two songs that had become synonymous with Liverpool, and the collective euphoria that had descended on Anfield that day, ensured that the Kop and its supporters joined the bands, comedians and poets in achieving national fame. Anyone and everything from Liverpool at the time was, to coin a popular term of the day, 'fab'. A matter of months after Liverpool won the Championship, one of the city's MPs, Harold Wilson, won the General Election and became Prime Minister. In May 1965, the American beat poet Allan Ginsberg visited the city and described it as 'the centre of the consciousness of the human universe'. Believe me, I was there, and that is just how it seemed.

I knew I was 'knocking on the door' for a place in the first team when Bill Shankly included me in the squad for the 1964 summer tour of North America. Shanks didn't usually join the team for summer tours as he preferred to stay at home and enjoy his creature comforts. He wasn't with us when we flew out to the USA and neither were Roger Hunt, Gordon Milne and Peter Thompson, who were on tour with England; but to the surprise of just about everybody Shanks joined us in New York prior to the visit to Chicago and I'm convinced he did so because of Chicago's past connection with Al Capone. As I said, he loved gangster movies.

The president of the fledgling American Soccer League was Kurt Lamb, who also acted as our guide on the tour. One day I was sitting with some of the lads in the hotel lounge when Kurt approached us looking very perplexed. 'Your boss, is he for real?' he asked. 'He wants to see Al Capone's car in Chicago, visit the New York bar of famous boxer Jack Dempsey, then Boot

Hill. Boot Hill? The guy watches too many cowboy movies.'

That was Shanks. His knowledge of America was largely gleaned from movies, which gave him a curious take on what society in the USA was like. I think he saw life there as being a cross between *Angels With Dirty Faces* and *High Noon*. He also struggled to come to terms with the time difference, resolutely refusing to alter his watch. On his first night with us he went to bed at five p.m. because his watch showed ten p.m. At three a.m. a member of the hotel staff found him in the dining room, dressed, shaved and waiting for Bob Paisley, Joe Fagan and Reuben Bennett to join him for breakfast. He was genuinely taken aback when the member of staff told him it was three in the morning and suggested he went back to bed.

We were in Chicago to play the Monterey club from Mexico. The game took place at the famous Soldier Field ground, which normally staged American grid-iron football and athletics. Soccer, as it was always called over there, was very much a minority sport in America at the time, and the reason for tours by clubs such as Liverpool was to help promote the sport in the major cities, particularly among Americans of European descent whose support was seen as imperative if football was to take off in the States.

I was delighted to be selected to play at inside-left against Monterey, and saw my inclusion in the side as a golden opportunity to show Shanks that I could do a job in the first team. Within minutes of the game starting I played the ball out to Alan A'Court on the left wing. Alan took off and I made progress down the left channel. I glanced across to the wing hopeful of receiving the ball, only Alan wasn't there: he'd disappeared into a sandpit normally used for the long jump which for this game, had been covered with squares of turf. After much fuss, Alan was extricated, the turf was reinstated and the game continued, but mainly down the right wing.

After trailing to Monterey we pulled back to win the game 2–1. In the dressing room after the game, Shanks was full of praise for my performance. 'This lad dug us out of a hole today,' he said, referring to yours truly, only for Ronnie Moran to immediately pipe up, 'He had to dig out Alan A'Court as well . . . literally.'

Soccer may have been in the embryonic stages of its development in the country but they had a number of innovative ideas, several of which British football later adopted. One such idea was the Man of the Match award. At the time we didn't bother with such a thing, but the Americans saw it as a small but important aspect to give added credibility to games. I was voted Man of the Match against Monterey. Such an award for a friendly game is no big deal, but it heartened me. Following the praise Shanks had given me, the fact that independent people had considered me the best player in the game served as a boost to my confidence. I knew I could play in the first team and do a good job.

Following a game in New York we were invited to a party held by one of our hosts. All the players and management went along, and as we didn't have a game for a week we all enjoyed a few beers. All except for Phil Chisnall and Phil Ferns, that is, who enjoyed a lot of beers. The pair drank so many, in fact, that for the remainder of the tour we nicknamed them 'Budweiser' and 'Schaffer'. To this day Phil Chisnall, who had joined the club for £30,000, enjoys an almost unique status at Anfield – he is one of only two players Liverpool have ever signed from Manchester United (the other, Tom McNulty, was signed in 1949)! Also present that night was the American singer and guitarist Del Shannon, who in addition to being very successful in the USA had had a number of big hits in the UK. Later in the evening some of the lads, full of brio thanks to the beer, asked Del to get up and give us a song. At first he made as if he didn't want to, but when the whole room urged him on, he took to his feet.

We all settled down as Del produced a guitar from somewhere and then launched into 'Runaway'. Eyes blinked as we struggled to come to terms with what we were hearing: he sang out of key and was often flat. People shifted uncomfortably with embarrassment, and I found myself staring down at the carpet. When Del finished the number he flung his arms out wide and smiled broadly as if expecting tumultuous applause. There was applause, but only of the polite sort, and not much of that. Undaunted by this and seemingly unaware of the mood of the room, with a loud whoop he launched into 'Swiss Maid'. If anything his singing of this was even worse. After what seemed like an eternity he reached the last verse. Pockets of conversation had broken out all around the room. Aware now that he had bombed, he flung down the guitar and returned to the company of a man I took to be his agent. It was then that Phil Chisnall and Phil Ferns took to their feet. 'You want to hear a song, we'll give you a song – and in key!' shouted Chis. The pair launched into 'Old Shanty Town' and, much to my surprise, rendered a cracking version of the song. When Chis and Fernsy finished there was wild applause and cheering. It was all too much for Del, who stormed out of the room in an obvious strop.

A minute later someone came up to Ron Yeats and said, 'That Del Shannon, he's leaving and he's wearing your coat.' Ron needed no second telling. He ran out of the room, literally collared Del and dragged the coat off his back. Del offered no resistance – who would to Ron? – and having had the coat removed he removed himself from the building, sharpish.

Then Ronnie Moran went up to Big Ron.

'Ron, been looking for you,' he said. 'I've just seen another guy walking out with your coat on.'

'What'd he look like?' asked Ron, ready to make another bolt for the staircase.

'Bloody ridiculous, it was like a tent on him,' said Ronnie.

We all burst into laughter.

From New York we flew to St Louis to play a local team. On the coach journey from the airport to the hotel, our chairman, T. V. Williams, approached Bob Paisley complaining of constipation and asked if he had anything to relieve the problem. Bob carried all manner of medical products in a holdall, and he gave

T. V. two packets of laxative chews to alleviate his discomfort.

It was early evening by the time we had checked in to our hotel so we went for a walk around the hotel grounds to stretch our legs. During the course of this walk, T. V. asked Bob if he had any more of the chews. Bob was taken aback.

'What have you done with the two packets I gave you?' he asked.

'I've eaten them,' replied T. V.

'They're not sweets,' said Bob, somewhat concerned. 'You'd better get back to the hotel, and quick.'

Our walk was immediately abandoned and we headed back to the hotel. T. V. Williams began walking at what can best be described as a leisurely stroll. After a few hundred yards his stroll turned into a sprightly walk, which in turn developed into route-march pace. With the hotel entrance in sight, the route march turned into a jog, then a run. He was sprinting by the time he got through the hotel door, but for all his efforts he never made it back to his room. He had to stand in the foyer in agony waiting for the lift to descend. When it finally arrived on the ground floor and its doors opened, so did T. V.'s bowels. Panic gripped his face as he lost control – of everything. Racked with embarrassment and obviously uncomfortable, he took hold of Bob's arm and pleaded to be taken to his room. Bob and Reuben Bennett accompanied him there and helped him change. It had been one hell of a bodily evacuation which ruined not only his underpants and the trousers of his suit, but also his shoes. Hotel staff were summoned, but on seeing the state of T. V.'s soiled apparel they flatly refused to have it cleaned and it was consigned to the furnace for burning.

Unbelievably, T. V. had travelled to America with only one suit, no spare trousers, and just the one pair of shoes. That night we were due to attend a welcoming dinner held by our host club, St Louis Stars. T. V. now had another dilemma, as attempts to find a men's clothing shop that was still open proved futile. Eventually, Bob Paisley came up with the answer. T. V. Williams was a gaunt man, six feet three inches tall. There was only one player in our party of similar height, our skipper, Ron Yeats. Bob set off for Ron's room to borrow some trousers and shoes.

I'll never forget that night as long as I live. With the players seated at their tables, the evening began with our directors and management making their entrance, announced by the Master of Ceremonies. One by one they entered the room and took their seats. When T. V. Williams came in we players were agog. I had never seen, and have never seen since, a seventy-eight-year-old man wearing a blue pin-stripe suit jacket and herringbone hipster trousers with white leather belt and Cuban heel boots.

Despite the sartorial inelegance of our chairman, our tour of the USA went well. I featured in all five games and was pleased with my performances. I was keen to get back to Liverpool, however, and for a very good reason.

I had been seeing Susanne for nigh on four years, we were very much in love (we still are), and we had decided to get married. Given that I had just visited the USA for the first time in my life, there was a certain poignancy to the date we had chosen for our wedding: 4 July – American Independence Day. I had just had my nineteenth birthday, but I knew Susanne was the right girl for me. I'd gone to see Shanks and Bob to give them my news, and both were delighted for us. I was only on the fringe of the first team and I didn't have a great deal of money, certainly not enough to put a deposit down on a home of our own, so I asked Shanks if the club could help us out. They did. Susanne and I were given a club house in Maghull for which we paid the club rent, a decent little semi which Sue soon turned into a beautiful home. Our next-door neighbour was Phil Chisnall – 'Budweiser' of the slightly over-enthusiastic drinking pair on our American tour.

For a variety of reasons, then – my encouraging tour of the States, a feeling that I was good enough to play in the first-choice side, and my new status as a married man – now I was really pressing my claim, keen for the opportunity to establish myself at the club. I began the 1964–65 season with the reserves, as usual. I was disappointed with this but determined to give my all in every game, knowing that anything less would indicate to Shanks that I wasn't ready for the first team.

The reserves kicked off the season with a game at Derby County. Goals from George Scott and Alan A'Court gave us a 2–0 victory; more importantly, from my point of view, I felt I had a good game. When on duty with the reserves, immediately the game is over the first thing everyone wants to know is how the first team got on. We heard they had beaten Arsenal 3–2. I was delighted they had won, but human nature being what it is I felt every good result would act as a barrier to my chances of being picked for the first team.

That game against Arsenal created a little bit of television history, as it was the first one ever to be featured on the BBC's new football programme *Match of the Day*. The BBC and ITV had done a deal with the Football League to broadcast highlights of matches: ITV were to show highlights of games on a Sunday on a regional basis, the BBC highlights of one match only on a Saturday evening. *Match of the Day* was the brainchild of the controller of BBC2, David Attenborough, and began life on that channel, which at the time not all of the UK could receive. It was a godsend to football fans; England games, the FA Cup and European finals apart, there had been no football on television. For all that *MOTD* comprised but a single game, the novelty of seeing a League match on TV, even in the form of edited highlights, proved immensely popular, and as audiences grew the programme switched to BBC1.

That *Match of the Day* began life on BBC2 was testimony to the fact that TV bosses, and major industries such as banks and building societies, didn't see football as one of the major cultural phenomena of the twentieth century. Football was still regarded as the bastion sport of the working class. Clubs existed on gate money and donations from directors and their supporters' clubs. The bedrock support was working people who had little in the way of disposable income. The game was immensely popular but not cash rich, so it was not the attraction to big business it later became – a fact borne out by the match programmes I have from 1964–65. The Liverpool programme comprises twelve pages and can easily be folded and put in your pocket – a far cry from the 'magazine' style programmes of today. The companies that advertised on its pages knew their market: Higson's, Bent's and Threlfall's beers; Park Drive and Senior Service cigarettes; Whitney's car dealership (for Ford); British Railways (excursions to the next away match); and the Liverpool Supporters' Club, which met in a room at the wonderfully named Cabbage Hall cinema. Other adverts are for tobacconists and newsagents-cum-sweet shops, and there's one for what is quaintly described as a 'gents' outfitter and supplier of work wear apparel'. Like football at the time, these adverts were parochial, placed by local businesses that provided the city's working people not only with products and services, but its social glue – much the same as the club itself. The multinational companies shunned football; they had yet to realize how they could benefit from the game. Only in the late seventies, when television's insatiable appetite for the game fuelled further interest, did the big companies see the potential. Big businesses paid big money to advertise in match programmes, and small businesses could no longer compete, not only in terms of advertising in match programmes but, as it transpired, on the high street too.

Ian St John picked up an injury against Arsenal and I was hopeful of receiving a call-up for the game at Leeds United the following Wednesday. On Sunday, however, I learned I was to play for the reserves on Monday night at home to Manchester City. My inclusion for this game indicated to me that I wasn't to be considered for the Leeds match. Manchester City reserves were beaten 4–1, and I managed to get on the scoresheet courtesy of a penalty, but what pleased me most was that I produced what I believed was another good performance. Still, the following morning the team sheet showed Phil Chisnall in place of the injured St

John, just as I had suspected. Leeds had been promoted the previous season but offered ample evidence that they were not to be overawed by their new-found status by beating Liverpool 4–2.

On the Friday morning after training Shanks took me to one side and gave me the news I had been longing to hear: he was promoting me to the first team for the game against Blackburn Rovers on 29 August. I was excited beyond belief and couldn't wait to give Susanne and Mum my wonderful news.

I was the proudest lad in the ground when I ran out at Ewood Park behind skipper Ron Yeats. I was determined I wouldn't let myself or Shanks down. Mindful of the fact that this was a rare opportunity for me, I gave it my all. After about a quarter of an hour I played the ball through to Roger Hunt who made progress before cutting the ball back across goal to where Phil Ferns was following up to give us the lead. Seven minutes later the Blackburn defence was all at sea trying to defend a cross from Ian Callaghan; the ball broke to me and I tucked it away as sweet as a nut. When that ball hit the back of the net, I jumped so high I thought I might clear the roof of the stand. My first goal for Liverpool in my second match; it was as if my dreams were coming true. The goal was a tremendous boost to my confidence, and following the restart I seemed to have an extra edge to my game as we tore into Blackburn.

One of the attractions of football is its unpredictability. Blackburn had lost their opening two games, and at half-time we had them on the rack. The second half, however, was played out to a totally different script. Blackburn had a number of top-quality players such as Ronnie Clayton, Brian Douglas, Keith Newton and John Byrom. Five minutes after the restart, it was the latter who pulled a goal back. Mick Harrison then converted a penalty. All our assertiveness appeared to desert us as Blackburn played with increasing purpose. Ten minutes from the end their pressure paid dividends when Andy McEvoy scored what proved to be the winning goal.

Having squandered a two-goal lead I expected Shanks to tear into us, but he didn't. He hardly said a word. I learned this was how he was in the wake of defeat. He knew emotions were high immediately after a game and would never take the team or an individual player to task for fear of something being said in the heat of the moment that would later be regretted. He saved his words until Monday morning at Melwood, as he always did on the rare occasion of a Liverpool defeat.

On the journey back to Liverpool on the team coach I was racked with contrasting emotions. I was happy with my performance and delighted with my goal, but to have lost, particularly after being two goals to the good, dampened my spirits. It had been nigh on sixteen months since my debut; this bitterly disappointing game now made me anxious about my first-team prospects. We had conceded nine goals in three matches and won only one of them. I felt Shanks would ring the changes.

I needn't have worried. I kept my place in the team for the return game against Leeds the following Wednesday night. When Leeds took the lead in the first half it seemed as if we were about to continue our poor start to the season. In the second period, however, we dominated the game. With twenty minutes remaining Peter Thompson cut in from the left and rifled a low shot past Gary Sprake. Ten minutes later Ian Callaghan intercepted a pass from Billy Bremner, accelerated down the right and crossed low. I had made up good ground, and the ball sat up just right for me. I got my head over it and drove it low past Sprake. Anfield erupted, and I felt pretty darn good too. It was the stuff of my dreams. Two goals in two matches. I felt I had arrived in the first team and all I could think of was keeping my place.

As reigning champions, though, we were not firing on all cylinders. Following the euphoria of victory over Leeds, we drew 2–2 with Blackpool at Anfield. One of the unwritten laws of football is that every club has its bogey side. Players and managers change over the years but a club will have opponents who invariably get a result against them season after season. In the case of Liverpool this has been Leicester City. Following the draw against Blackpool we travelled to Filbert Street and Leicester did for Liverpool again, winning 2–0.

When the team sheet went up for our next game at Sheffield Wednesday, Bobby Graham was at number ten, and so was I – in the reserves. I was very disappointed, but again I vowed to myself I would work harder than ever to regain my place. Having experienced a relatively prolonged taste of first-team football, I wanted more. For all that I had scored two goals, I reasoned inside-left was not my best position – I felt much more comfortable playing in defence – and should I produce some very good performances at wing-half where I played most of the time for the reserves I would be given another opportunity with the first team. I took no satisfaction from the fact that Liverpool lost to Sheffield Wednesday, a bad result that was followed by worse when we were beaten 4–0 at Anfield by Everton. Two wins from eight matches was the worst run the club had had under Shankly. Then, after the Everton debacle when my hopes of a recall were high, the first team suddenly clicked. Aston Villa were dispatched 5–1 and a 3–1 victory over Sheffield United followed, back-to-back wins that were the beginning of a good sequence of results. To compound my anxiety, on 7 November Liverpool signed Geoff Strong from Arsenal, and a few days later he made his debut against Fulham at inside-left.

As champions, that autumn the club embarked upon its first ever sojourn in European competition. I was disappointed not to be involved in the first round of the European Cup but Liverpool managed to squeeze through without me, defeating Reykjavik of Iceland 11–1 on aggregate. This set up a second-round tie against Anderlecht which everybody knew would prove a totally different kettle of kedgeree.

In 1964 Belgian football was in the ascendancy in Europe.

Dutch clubs had only just stepped up from part-time to full-time status, and French football was far from the force it is today, but Belgium had produced a crop of top-class players, most of whom played for Anderlecht. Two months earlier Belgium had drawn 2–2 with England at Wembley, a game in which the Belgians had dominated for long periods. Two of our players, Gordon Milne and Peter Thompson, played for England in that game and had returned to Anfield full of admiration for the way Belgium had played. Gordon and Peter were not the only ones to recognize their worth: Shanks had watched the game too, and as the Anderlecht tie drew nearer, for once he appeared genuinely nervous about the opposition. Shanks had been so impressed by the technique and all-round play of the Belgians he was even talking about us playing a defensive game in the first leg at Anfield. This set me thinking: perhaps I might have a chance of playing. When he announced the team I was thrilled to hear my name.

Having been given the number ten shirt, I thought I would be playing as a striker, but Shanks had a plan to combat and confuse Anderlecht, and it involved me. He told me that rather than playing upfront I was to play as an extra defender. The Anderlecht team contained seven players who had been in the team that had given England such a torrid time of it at Wembley: Heylens, Cornelis, Plaskie, Puis, Jurion, Vebiest and Paul Van Himst. Van Himst, far and away Anderlecht's best player, played behind the target man and had been pinpointed by Bob Paisley as a potential threat. Bob was worried that for all his strengths, Ron Yeats was all left peg. 'I want you to be Ron's right leg,' Shanks told me. 'Against these Belgians, I want you to win the ball and find a red shirt, preferably Callaghan or Thompson, and I don't want to see you over the halfway line.' I couldn't believe it. We had home advantage in the first leg and Shanks was preaching caution.

That game against Anderlecht was one of the milestones. When we entered the dressing room and saw the strips hanging on the pegs we were surprised to see the style had changed. It was the first time Liverpool wore the all-red strip. Gone were the white trim on the red shirts, the white shorts and the red and white stockings. Liverpool were now the 'Reds' in every sense of the word. After the game Shanks would tell us, 'When you boys took to the pitch tonight, you were like a fire burning.'

As soon as the game got underway I was surprised when the Anderlecht number four began to mark me man for man and continued to do so for the first twenty minutes. Anderlecht players were used to man-marking the player who directly opposed them: their centre-half marked our centre-forward, Ian St John; their right-back picked up Peter Thompson; and so on. Their number four, finding himself with no one to mark, simply drifted forward and stuck with me. Until, that is, the penny dropped with the Anderlecht bench and he received instructions to do otherwise.

Liverpool adopted a 4–4–2 formation on the night, nearly two years before Alf Ramsey adopted the same system in the World Cup. To be truthful, 4–4–2 was nothing new, even in 1964. Blackpool had played a version of it when winning the FA Cup in 1953, and numerous other clubs had tried it over the years with varying degrees of success. On the night it worked a treat for us: we dominated the game and won 3–0 with goals from Roger Hunt, Ian St John and Ron Yeats. After the game Bob Paisley went up to Big Ron and said he wanted to check his nose. When Ron asked why, Bob said, 'You scored tonight. You must have had a nosebleed when you crossed the halfway line being so far upfield.' Shanks was full of it, telling us that we had played one of the best teams in Europe off the park, which was true. Liverpool had now signalled their entry into Europe (to be honest, any team in the Football League would have beaten Reykjavik). As I said, it was a milestone night. In an all-red strip we proved we could not only compete with but beat a team considered one of the best in Europe. From a personal point of view it was the night Shanks went on record as saying, 'The game marked out Tommy Smith as a fine player. The boy has arrived.'

Such a compliment from the boss didn't go to my head. Just as well, because I found myself as the stand-by reserve for our next game, at home to Tottenham Hotspur. The match after that was at Burnley, and again I was named in the twelve to travel. Everyone was expected to muck in at the club – prima donnas were strictly personae non gratae at Anfield – and it was accepted that the travelling reserve would help carry the skip containing the strips on away trips. When we arrived at Turf Moor I made my way to the rear of our coach and took hold of one end of the skip.

'What are you doing, Smithy?' asked Bob Paisley, who had hold of the other end.

'Helping you with the skip,' I replied.

'Get yourself in the dressing room,' he said. 'You're playing.'

It was the first I knew, but I needed no second telling.

We stormed to a 5–1 win, and I never looked back from that point on. Having yearned for so long for a decent run in the first team, my performances at last earned me a regular place. I felt as Columbus must have felt when he realized he hadn't sailed over the edge of the world.

In the return leg against Anderlecht I was determined to give Paul Van Himst another difficult night, and the consensus was that I did just that. Ten minutes into the game I launched into a tackle that let him know I was there on the pitch. I won the ball cleanly but my momentum carried me under and through the Belgian, who shot into the air.

'Nutter!' screamed Van Himst, pointing to his head with a jabbing finger. 'You, nutter and dangerous bastard!'

'Yes,' I said in a calm voice, 'and don't you forget it.'

Van Himst continued to swear and shout at me, but I simply ignored him and didn't say another word. I smiled to myself – I knew I had him.

Anderlecht found no way through our defence, and a minute from time Roger Hunt swept in the only goal of the game to make it 4–0 on aggregate. There were still any number of top-quality teams left in the competition, but characteristically Shanks was convinced that, even though it was our very first season in Europe, we could go all the way and win the European Cup. 'Fear no one; let them fear us,' he told us. 'The greatest thing about this club is not where we stand, but where we are going.'

Our good form continued on a freezing cold December day when we exacted revenge on Blackburn Rovers, beating them 3–2 at Anfield. Roger Hunt added to his season's goal plunder by scoring twice and I chipped in with our other goal. We had now gone nine matches without defeat, and on Christmas Day night we set off for the north-east full of confidence for our Boxing Day fixture against Sunderland, who had been promoted along with Leeds United, but unlike Leeds had struggled to make an impact in Division One. In fact they were scrubbing about near the foot of the table and would have been among the relegation places but for an unbeaten home record. They had been picking up a little form, though: they had beaten Everton 4–0 at Roker Park which was followed by their first away victory of the season at Leicester, then a 3–0 home win over Chelsea. I knew we would be in for a tough game.

A crowd of 50,000 was at Roker Park on what was another bitterly cold day. As we filed from our dressing room towards the tunnel, a voice boomed out of the loudspeaker system: 'Ladies and gentlemen, boys and girls, please give a warm Wearside welcome to our visitors today, reigning First Division champions, Liverpool!' We took to the field to warm applause. To me, this incident serves as further proof of how the game has changed over the years. If opponents received such an introduction these days, particularly Liverpool, Manchester United or Chelsea, they would be roundly booed if not subjected to vitriol from some supporters. It was different back then. Fans were no less fervent in their support of their club than the fans of today, but first and foremost they were supporters of football and they respected visiting teams, particularly those that had won trophies.

We dominated the first half. Gordon Milne gave us the lead, and just before the interval I slipped the ball through a square Sunderland back four for Willie Stevenson to make it 2–0. We knew Sunderland would come out in the second half and have a go, and so it proved. Nicky Sharkey pulled a goal back for the home side, only for Willie to restore our two-goal lead. Five minutes from the end a goal from George Mulhall gave Sunderland renewed hope, but we comfortably held out for what was a deserved 3–2 victory.

In his match report in the *Daily Mirror*, Frank Wilson wrote, 'In Tommy Smith Liverpool have a player who belies his tender years. Tough tackling, uncompromising yet with an abundance of skill, Smith, not yet twenty, looks the finished article. Should he continue to produce performances like this, an illustrious career at Anfield lies before him.' Mum committed that one to the scrapbook. Good or bad, I never took what the press said to heart, but I did take heart from Wilson's words. At times a team has to carry a young player as young footballers are notoriously fickle, on fire one game, anonymous the next. Senior pros and the manager will make allowances for inexperienced players, but I felt I was contributing to the team in a consistently positive way. My self-belief was being vindicated by Shanks and Bob Paisley through the very fact that they were now picking me regularly. Seemingly, now, I had also received the endorsement of the press. My performances against Anderlecht, Burnley and Sunderland helped cement in me the notion that I was now a member of the first team rather than a fringe player. I felt very much a part of the set-up, though I never saw myself as 'the finished article'. Far from it: I knew I had a lot of hard work and learning to do, and I knew anything less than total commitment would see me back in the reserves.

We finished the season in seventh position, seventeen points adrift of Manchester United (two points were still awarded for a win), who clinched the Championship on goal average from Leeds United. Having won the title the previous season I knew seventh place would not satisfy Shanks whose aim was still to make Liverpool the dominant force in English football. Winning the League Championship is hard, but retaining the title is harder still. We were still on a learning curve, but Shanks and Bob Paisley never rested in their efforts to improve us as individuals and as a team. Our undoing was our away form. Five victories from twenty-one games on our travels had to be improved upon. We would subsequently spend a lot of time at Melwood working on keeping possession of the ball with a view to controlling games. 'Football is a simple game,' Shanks told us one day. 'If we have the ball then the opposition can't score.'

Liverpool were coming of age, a fact borne out by that first assault on the European Cup. Having disposed of Reykjavik and Anderlecht we faced our toughest European assignment thus far against Cologne in the quarter-final. The first leg took place on 10 February before a capacity crowd of 60,800. Cologne included in their line-up Weber, Overath and Loher, who would play for West Germany in the 1966 World Cup Finals; Schumacher, Regh, Pott, Sturm and Mueller were also internationals. We knew we were in for a very difficult game against the West German champions but, as ever, Shanks was confident we would achieve a favourable result.

When playing on the Continent, Shanks and Bob Paisley were always keen for us to see a little of the city we visited. Usually this took the form of a 'leg stretcher' – Bob's term for a walk – often undertaken the day we arrived at our destination, either in the afternoon or evening, depending on the time of year. It was the first time any of us had been to Cologne and the two things that struck me about the city were its cathedral and the 4711 cologne factory across the river Rhine. The cathedral walls still bore the scars of the Second World War when hand-to-hand fighting raged across the city. Shell and bullet marks were clearly visible. I should imagine they are still there today, pertinent and poignant reminders that war is no respecter of anyone or anything.

Shanks and Bob educated us, and not only in terms of football. Whichever foreign city we visited, they would glean a few facts from the tourist brochures and relate them to the players as we went about our walk. Shanks informed us that construction of the cathedral had started in the thirteenth century but the work wasn't completed until the late nineteenth century, prompting Ian St John to say, 'They must have had Bob and Smithy working on it.'

Seeing the 4711 factory from a vantage point across the Rhine brought back memories of my childhood. When I was a small boy, 4711 seemed to be the only fragrance used by Mum and my aunties. On those occasions when I endured the illnesses all boys seemingly had to endure – chicken pox, measles, mumps and whooping cough – I would be confined to bed and Mum would call for the doctor. People were in awe of the doctor. For a start, he was one of the few people we knew who had a car. A house visit from the doctor would send Mum into a flurry of activity. My bed sheets would be straightened and smoothed, the pillows fluffed. Having been told not to disrupt the bedding I would sit upright, static, afraid to move while awaiting his arrival. Mum would put a few drops of 4711 on a handkerchief, dab my face, then place the handkerchief in the top pocket of my pyjama jacket. This ritual was conducted by all mothers with ailing sons and daughters. Just as the Queen must think every town and city in Britain smells of new paint, Liverpool doctors in the early 1950s must have laboured under the misapprehension that the natural body smell of every kid was that of eau de cologne.

As we suspected, Cologne proved tougher opposition than Reykjavik and Anderlecht. We were happy to return to Merseyside with a goalless draw, confident of beating Cologne at Anfield, but the tie was wiped out due to a blizzard, which meant Cologne had to make another trip to Merseyside. It didn't daunt them: the rearranged match also ended goalless.

There were no penalty shoot-outs in those days, so both teams played a deciding tie on neutral territory, which turned out to be

Rotterdam. It was often the case that such ties attracted a meagre attendance, but not this one: a capacity crowd of 55,000 was at the Spangen Stadium to see what proved to be a dramatic night of football. We broke the stalemate by racing into a two-goal lead courtesy of St John and Hunt. Cologne, however, were made of stern stuff. They wouldn't lie down, continued to launch attacks, and pulled a goal back before equalizing late in the game. At the end of extra time we still could not be separated, so the tie had to be decided by the toss of a disc.

It was a wholly unsatisfactory end to what had been an epic battle. If the disc came down on the red side, we would go through to the semi-finals; should it fall on the white side, Cologne would progress. With the two captains as witnesses, the referee flipped the disc in the air. Unbelievably, it came down and stuck on its side in the mud. The tension was unbearable. When the referee flipped the disc for a second time I couldn't see which side it landed on, but Ron Yeats's leap for joy told me all I wanted to know.

I felt for the Cologne players. They had battled hard throughout and played a sporting game, and it was a cruel way to exit the European Cup. Our success, such as it was, was not without irony. In the three matches and extra time of this decider, when flipping the disc to decide who would call for which way play would commence, Ron Yeats had lost the toss every time. When it first became apparent that Ron had called correctly and it was Liverpool who would go through, I glanced across to the bench. Rather than being carried away by the euphoria we all felt and running over to join in our celebrations, Shanks calmly walked over to the Cologne coach and his backroom staff to offer his commiserations and sympathy.

In our first season of European competition we were through to the semi-finals of the European Cup. Our opponents were Inter Milan, seasoned veterans of Europe. We didn't fear Inter; on the contrary we were confident of beating them as we feared no one.

But curious and deeply suspicious circumstances were to turn our European dream into a nightmare.

I finished the 1964–65 season with twenty-five League games under my belt and four goals. I had settled into the position of right-half, successfully fulfilling the role asked of me as 'Ron Yeats's right leg'. Just to have played regularly in the first team filled me with a sense of great achievement; the icing on the cake that season was our success in the FA Cup.

Our run began with a trip to West Bromwich Albion where in front of a packed Hawthorns goals from St John and Hunt gave us a 2–1 victory. It proved a tie not without incident, most notably when, with minutes of the game remaining, someone in the crowd blew a whistle. At the time West Brom were laying siege to our goal. Thinking that the referee had blown for time, Ron Yeats picked up the ball with the intention of handing it over to the match official. His face fell like an undercooked cake when the referee did blow his whistle and pointed to the penalty spot. Policemen went into the crowd in search of the miscreant, but as far as we were concerned the damage was done. Justice is not always seen to be done in football, but it was that day. Albion's Clive Clark stepped up, put the penalty wide, and we heaved a collective sigh of relief.

What was on paper an easy tie at home to Stockport County of Division Four in round four proved to be anything but. The day of the fourth round coincided with the state funeral of Sir Winston Churchill. There was a minute's silence before the game, and in keeping with every other ground the club flew the Liverpool flag at half mast. In the sixties a minute of silence was deemed a suitable period of time for the nation to pay their respects to one of the greatest Britons who had ever lived. These days paying our respects to those who have passed on often involves two minutes, sometimes three, of collective silence. It's as if the extended time is somehow even more respectful, indicative of a genuine, somewhat deeper sense of mourning, which I don't believe it is.

It was a bitterly cold day when we played Stockport. The Anfield pitch was frozen solid, treacherous underfoot. I doubt such a pitch would be passed as playable these days, but then it was not a cause for concern. Pitches were generally in poor condition in mid-winter and the rock-hard state of ours in late January was simply deemed 'par for the course'. We never adapted to the hard slippery surface. Stockport were bottom of Division Four and seemed to regard the tie at Anfield as an opportunity to gain some pride from what was proving to be a terrible season for them. They almost won it, too. Not only do you need a good team to win a cup competition, you need luck, and we had some that day. With the score at 1–1 and the game deep into added time, Gerry Byrne saved our bacon when he cleared off the line.

In the 1960s, an FA Cup replay took place either the following Tuesday or Wednesday night. Attendances for FA Cup matches in the 1960s were in excess of what they are today, invariably larger than League games. Curiously, as opposed to now, the police in those days had no problem supervising replays at short notice, likewise the clubs and the FA in terms of arranging them. Shanks was convinced we had been handicapped by the icy pitch at Anfield and in the few days before the replay he too acted swiftly to ensure there would be no repetition. Having checked the weather forecast and learned that it would be another freezing cold night, Shanks bought the entire team what he told us were 'magic' boots. Rather than having conventional studs, these boots had a special moulded rubber sole comprising grooves that went off at right angles to one another. Prior to the game we went out on to the Edgeley Park pitch to try them out. The pitch was heavily sanded and hard underneath, but I found that the boots enabled me to twist and turn quickly without losing my footing; they also had adhesion when I took to my toes to sprint. The consensus among the lads was that the boots would work their 'magic'. There was no repetition of the scare Stockport had given us at Anfield. Roger

Hunt scored twice on the night, and such was our dominance we could have won by six.

In round five we were drawn at Second Division Bolton. The cup really worked up a head of steam come the fifth round. Players and supporters, sensing that Wembley was only three games away, began to feel the effects of the age-old malady, cup fever. Players considered an appearance in an FA Cup Final at Wembley as the pinnacle of a career in the game. I was some months short of my twentieth birthday, I had just begun to establish myself in the first team and I had all my career ahead of me, yet I too began to get the collywobbles at the thought of playing in the fifth round of the FA Cup.

Players, supporters and officials had nothing but the highest regard for the FA Cup. It's the oldest club cup competition in the world with a history and tradition to match. The cup was all about glory and it was unthinkable a manager would field anything less than his strongest possible team for a tie. I find it sad that the involvement of a handful of clubs in what is now called the European Champions League (the big clubs always said they wanted a European Super League, and gradually we are being made to sleep-walk towards it) and the attitude and influence of some foreign coaches in English football have combined to lessen the standing of the FA Cup. What I find equally irksome is that having demonstrated a certain contempt for the FA Cup and the history and traditions of the game in this country by fielding weakened teams, their example has been sheepishly followed by other managers. The money-driven Champions League, and annual qualification for that competition, is the priority of the big four in English football; for the rest, survival in the Premiership is the number one priority. Which is why most Premiership clubs now pay little more than lip service to the FA Cup by fielding below-full-strength teams. Reflected glory has always had a part to play in football, which is why we have managers of clubs in what is now termed the Championship and League One also fielding weakened teams in the cup. Invariably these managers justify this by saying, 'The League is our bread and butter.' When I hear managers say such a thing I think to myself, 'Do me a favour. Stop trying to be a big-time Charlie. Think of how a good cup run will energize your players, supporters, the town's people – and boost club coffers.'

No one viewed our tie at Bolton as being anything less than of vital importance to the club. That everyone took the FA Cup very seriously was reflected in the attendance that day: a capacity crowd of 57,500 crammed into Burnden Park to see a pulsating match full of blood and thunder, in keeping with the traditions of the cup. Chances were few and far between for both teams, but when Ian Callaghan was presented with an opportunity he took it, rising to get on the end of a cross from Peter Thompson to head past Bolton keeper Eddie Hopkinson. As soon as I saw the ball hit the back of the net I sensed that should we not do anything silly we would be home and dry. It was the type of game that appeared to have only one goal in it, and so it proved. Incidentally, Cally played 640 matches for Liverpool and scored forty-nine goals, but this was the only one he scored with his head.

As I said, every club appears to have a bogey team, and down the years Liverpool's has invariably been Leicester City. So it was not without apprehension that we travelled to Filbert Street for our next match. In 1962–63 Liverpool had been involved in an epic FA Cup semi-final against Leicester City at Hillsborough. Referring to this semi-final in his autobiography *Banksy*, Gordon Banks said, 'There was only one team in it, and they lost 1–0.' Liverpool had laid siege to the Leicester goal that day but a combination of brilliant goalkeeping from Banksy and resolute defending denied us. The statistics for the game tell their own story: Liverpool had thirty-eight attempts on goal (three of which hit the bar), Leicester three. One of that trio of attempts was by Mike Stringfellow, and it proved the decisive one.

At the end of that game Gordon Banks was walking off the pitch when his Leicester team-mate Frank McLintock said, 'Banksy, you and the crossbar played a blinder today.' Banksy and Frank were some six yards apart, and walking between them was a tearful Ian St John. The moment was captured by a photographer from a Sunday tabloid newspaper, but it was the subsequent action of the newspaper that was to cause a furore among Liverpool supporters and result in Banksy receiving a lot of grief. The photograph was cropped, omitting Frank McLintock. When the picture appeared in the newspaper the next day it showed Banksy appearing to laugh at St John under the headline 'Banks Mocks Tearful Saint'. Knowing this to be a contrived story, one that would be sure to incense Liverpool folk, Ian St John was on the phone to Banksy that very day. Saint told Banksy he knew he had been 'set up'; he knew it was a cheap piece of contrived journalism from the news-paper concerned. That was all well and good, but Saint couldn't telephone every Liverpool supporter to explain what had happened. A few weeks later, when Leicester visited Anfield, Banksy was sub-jected to a torrent of abuse, particularly from the Kop. Saint felt he had to set the record straight and stand up for Banksy's integrity, so he gave an interview to the press to explain the situation. Having been incensed by what they perceived to be cruel insensitivity on the part of Banksy, Liverpool fans now turned their wrath towards the newspaper that had misled them. For the record, the next time Leicester City played at Anfield, Banksy was given a rousing reception. His performances against Liverpool apart, the Kop respected his prowess as the world's greatest goal-keeper so much that they continued to give him warm applause whenever he took his position in goal.

In March 1965 Banksy produced another inspired performance against us at Filbert Street. At one point a shot from Ian Callaghan took a wicked deflection off the back of Leicester defender Richie Norman. Having flung himself to his right to save Cally's effort, Banksy suddenly twisted and changed direction in mid-air to palm away the deflection to his left.

Many people are of the mind that if a goalkeeper makes a string of good saves he is a quality goalkeeper. Well, he's got something going for him for sure, but to my mind what makes a great goalkeeper is how few saves he is called on to make. This was very much the case with Banksy, and Ray Clemence too. At this stage of his career Banksy organized his defence so well and his positioning and angling was so spot on that opposing forwards found themselves with very few opportunities to fire a shot at goal. When you are presented with no gaps in front of goal, invariably you look to pass the ball to a team-mate in the hope that he might create an opening. In our sixth-round tie at Filbert Street, Banksy presented us with precious few opportunities. By the same token we also defended well, and the final score was 1–1.

The replay at Anfield was little different. We took the game to Leicester but for the best part could not break them down. Fifteen minutes from the end I played the ball to Gordon Milne who in turn found Cally. He immediately made ground down the right before cutting the ball back across goal, and there was Roger Hunt to blast us into the semi-finals. Anfield was a cacophony of noise as 53,000 fans, suddenly relieved of tension, gave vent to their emotions. We were but one hurdle from Wembley.

The draw for the semi-final pitched us against Chelsea at Villa Park, with Leeds United meeting Manchester United at Hillsborough. At this stage of the season we were embroiled in a hectic schedule of fixtures. Our semi-final against Chelsea came just three days after the nail-biting third European Cup quarter-final meeting with Cologne in Rotterdam. We flew direct to Birmingham from Holland, arrived at our hotel late on the Thursday afternoon, and after an evening meal took to our beds. On the Friday morning after breakfast, Shanks called a team meeting in which he didn't say much at all. After the meeting Bob took us out for some limbering up. We then had lunch and took to our rooms. I read a book for a while before getting some much-needed sleep.

The following day when we arrived at Villa Park, Shanks didn't give a team talk. Instead he produced a printer's proof of what was Chelsea's '1965 FA Cup Final Brochure'. 'Boys, they think you are not worth turning up for,' said Shanks. 'They must do, because they've only gone and produced a Cup Final brochure. Chelsea think they're already at Wembley. Go out and show them, boys.' Shanks didn't say another word. He and Bob Paisley left the room, leaving us to read the proof of the Chelsea brochure, complete but for a blank page where the details of our semi-final game were to appear.

Shanks knew exactly how we would react. We were incensed that Chelsea had had the arrogance to compile a Cup Final brochure prior to our semi-final. If the Cologne game had been lingering in the minds of some players, it wasn't now. We didn't need an added incentive to beat Chelsea. Having read this brochure, I felt there was no way we were going to lose the game. Shanks liked to get our blood boiling. Following that meeting, it was so hot it was in danger of vaporizing.

The setting of Villa Park was wholly appropriate for an FA Cup semi-final. On every visit to Villa Park, the grandiose Victorian redbrick frontage with its grand stairway and pedimented towers served to remind me of the history and traditions of English football. Founded in 1874, Villa is one of the oldest clubs in the country. At the time, their total of seven FA Cup wins was a record. The club and the ground appeared to me to be synonymous with the big-match atmosphere of the FA Cup. As numerous clubs before us had experienced, the stadium stood as the gateway to Wembley and glory. No one viewed it as an FA Cup cul-de-sac in which beaten semi-finalists are buried and forever forgotten, because players don't think that way. Players are always optimistic, full of hope, dreamers even. You go to Villa Park for an FA Cup semi-final never thinking you will lose. You don't contemplate that. It's negative thinking, too painful. Some players believed it was better to get knocked out in the third round rather than suffer the bitter disappointment of defeat in the semi-finals. Defeat in the semi-finals was seen as being worse than losing in the final itself, because at least defeated finalists got to play at Wembley, which was revered as it was only used for the FA Cup Final and international matches. The fact that football only used Wembley for special occasions planted in players the belief that an appearance there meant they had achieved something special in their careers. To play at Wembley meant you were no longer a journeyman.

When the teams took to the pitch, Villa Park was a seething, swaying mass of humanity. Over 67,000 spectators packed the stands and terraces. I looked up towards the Holte End and saw a tumbling mass of people. There had been a downpour some twenty minutes before kick-off, and the fans on the terraces were so tightly packed that the combination of the body heat they generated and the soaking they had been subjected to produced voluminous clouds of steam that rose off their backs and drifted up towards a battleship-grey sky. As the game was about to get underway, the roar of a hurricane-ravaged ocean appeared to sweep down from the Alp-like terraces. The noise was so loud it smothered the shrill blast of the referee's whistle, as an avalanche of snow would the sound of a doorbell.

Tommy Docherty had assembled a youthful Chelsea team, rich in talent and full of exuberance. Young as they were, Chelsea had balance. Peter Bonetti had emerged as a rival to Gordon Banks as England's number one goalkeeper. Ron Harris was a tough-tackling, no-nonsense defender who liked to get forward to demonstrate that he had much more than a sledgehammer tackle in his repertoire. Eddie McCreadie sang from the same hymn sheet as Harris, while Marvin Hinton as a defender was as versatile, and always composed. Hinton was not a robust player; his strength was immaculate timing in the tackle. He played some 450 games and I bet you could count the fouls he committed on the fingers of one hand. Added to that, Barry Bridges, John Hollins, Bobby Tambling and Terry Venables were all top-quality players who were takers as well as makers of goals.

Bob Paisley had earmarked Terry Venables as the hub of the Chelsea team around whom every move seemed to revolve. Bob had watched Chelsea and was of the mind that as a result they could be predictable. An opening might present itself, but rather than take that option Venables would call for the ball, and such was his influence on his team-mates, he'd get it. We didn't man-mark players, we played a zonal system, so prior to the game Bob said, 'Be mindful of your responsibilities. If Venables wanders into your zone, you pick him up tight.' Shanks added his bit too. Firstly, close down quickly on Hollins and co.; that way we would starve Venables of service. Shanks's second point concerned Peter Thompson. Peter was a super winger. He had so much ability he could take on a full-back, beat him, turn, beat him again, turn into his opponent yet again and beat him a third time. 'That,' as Shanks told Peter, 'is your problem, Thommo, son. You're in danger of disappearing up your own backside.' Shanks reminded Peter that while he was doing this Roger Hunt, Saint and Cally were constantly having to reposition to keep themselves on side before receiving the ball, which was true. 'Football is a simple game, Thommo.' It must have been about the ten thousandth time I'd heard Shanks say this, and it would be far from the last. 'Strikers need the ball early, the earlier the better, so deliver it at the first opportunity.' Peter needed to be more direct, Shanks went on. He had the speed and ability to go past defenders, so why not cut inside and have a go at goal?

Energized by the thought of being one game away from Wembley and further fired up by the arrogance of Chelsea having already produced a Cup Final brochure, we tore into them from the start. We dominated the first half, but come half-time we had nothing on the scoresheet to show for our efforts. Little was said during the interval other than that we had to be patient. Both Shanks and Bob felt the break would come.

Shanks may have said little, but Willie Stevenson had plenty to say – to Peter Thompson. The pair were always on at each other.

Willie was a great passer of the ball but not the best at 'getting stuck in'. Willie was forever on at Thommo, saying he had to drop back to help him win the ball. Willie would say that he would sprint forward in support of Peter only for him never to release the ball. Peter would come back along the lines of 'I can't give you the ball because you can't keep up with me.' And so they went on, like a pair of old fishwives.

'If you're not going to pass to me, then bloody well cut inside and have a pop instead of holding the ball and disappearing up your own backside,' said Willie as the pair left the changing room.

'The boss told you that,' I piped up.

'Don't you bloody start, I have enough with him,' said Peter, pointing to Willie.

In the 63rd minute Thommo received the ball on the left and instead of taking on Eddie McCreadie he veered inside, sped past Marvin Hinton and took the ball to within a yard of the angle of the six-yard box before firing low past Peter Bonetti. Villa Park, or at least the sizeable red contingent within it, instantly became one giant agitated mass of jumping bodies. A fearsome, vociferous noise swept down from the terraces and assailed my ears. I looked at the Chelsea players; the expressions on their faces told me they didn't think they were going to make it. The goal brought more urgency to Chelsea's play but we comfortably dealt with everything they threw at us. Minutes from the end, Thommo decided to be direct again. McCreadie couldn't time his tackle and instead of playing the ball he played one of Thommo's. The referee had no hesitation in awarding the penalty. If Willie Stevenson had any nerves, he didn't show them. He calmly stepped up, drove the ball high to Peter Bonetti's left, and I knew we were Wembley bound.

Disappointed as he was, Chelsea manager Tommy Docherty was gracious in defeat, as he always was. The Doc came into our dressing room, told us we deserved our win and wished us good luck for Wembley. Shanks and the Doc were good friends, and as we celebrated making Wembley with pints of milk, the pair disappeared in search of something a little stronger to remind them of their homeland.

Shanks's psychology had worked again. We'd had little time to recover from our game against Cologne and the travel involved before playing Chelsea in what was another crucial game. But if any of us were feeling the effects of tiredness, Shanks knew that showing us Chelsea's Cup Final brochure would restart the adrenalin. Once we had read it we couldn't wait to get at Chelsea and give those smug upstarts a lesson.

There is, however, a postscript to this story. Over the years I too became good friends with Tommy Docherty. When I sat down to write this part of my book, I rang the Doc to ask why, all those years ago, Chelsea had thought fit to produce such a brochure before they had even played Liverpool.

'What Cup Final brochure?' asked Tommy.

It transpired that no one connected with Chelsea in 1965 could recall a Cup Final brochure even having been discussed, never mind produced.

'I would never have sanctioned such a thing,' the Doc went on. 'It would have been suicide to bring out such a thing before the semi-final. It would have made Liverpool even more determined to beat us.'

I told the Doc we had all seen the printer's proof.

'Tommy, if that copy is still around today, get hold of it and look at it closely,' said the Doc. 'Somewhere within its pages you'll probably find the words "Printed in Liverpool".'

Shanks was a good psychologist. Only now, forty-two years on, am I beginning to realize how good.

4

EE-AYE-ADDIO . . .

FOR NIGH ON FOUR YEARS I HAD BEEN ITCHING TO GET MY CHANCE in the first team. It may have been spring, but as the 1964–65 season reached its business stage I felt I had walked into a tornado of first-team activity. Games came with a regularity T. V. Williams's bowels would have yearned for. In five and a half weeks starting from 1 April, Liverpool played ten League matches, a two-legged European Cup semi-final and an FA Cup Final. And the ten League matches were completed in a hectic spell between 1 and 26 April.

It is amazing now to think that during this period of thirteen games, Shanks called upon the services of just twelve players. The Liverpool team ran off the tongue like a well-known nursery rhyme: Lawrence, Lawler, Byrne, Milne, Yeats, Stevenson, Callaghan, Hunt, St John, Smith and Thompson. In all probability there would not have been any changes, but Gordon Milne sustained an injury that saw him replaced by Geoff Strong, who had been signed for £40,000 from Arsenal.

Gordon was the son of Jimmy Milne, who gave sterling service to Preston as a player, trainer and manager. Shanks saw Gordon as a fetcher and carrier of messages in midfield. In essence, Gordon's job was to take the ball off the opposition and play it forward to Cally, Roger Hunt, Thommo or Saint, which he did with a minimum of fuss but to maximum effect. When Gordon sustained the injury that would result in him missing the FA Cup Final, we were very lucky to have such a quality replacement in Geoff Strong.

At Arsenal, Geoff Strong played as a front man, usually at inside-right. Shanks is on record as saying that when he and Bob Paisley bought Geoff they 'didn't buy him as an attacker or anything specific at all, more as a footballer, like they used to in the old days'. Geoff was a Swiss Army knife of a footballer. He could play upfront, in the centre or on either flank of midfield, as right-back or, as he was often used, as a sweeper. Shanks always maintained that if he had signed Geoff five years earlier he would have turned him into a truly great player. As it was, he was a very good player, cool as a mountain stream, a player who possessed a very astute football brain.

I remember when Geoff first arrived at Liverpool he was really put to work by Shanks and Bob. We had training boards at Melwood which were used to improve a player's touch, technique, fitness and stamina. When you put the ball in the back of the net it doesn't come back out; likewise when you play a pass to a teammate, chances are he'll take the ball on. Not so when you play a ball against the boards, of which there were four formed into a square. Shanks liked to work players in the boards because when you played the ball against one of them, naturally the ball came straight back. Shanks would tell us to do the rounds of the boards, playing the ball against one board with, for example, your left foot, taking the return in your stride, shielding it and dribbling a little before playing the ball off the second board, and so on. You just kept doing the rounds. It was basic stuff, but Shanks considered it very important practice because opponents can come in on your blind side and win the ball if you can't control and shield it. Taking a short pass in your stride when the ball is hit straight at you is not an easy thing to do, and Shanks saw it as a key skill that every Liverpool player had to master.

When Geoff first arrived from Arsenal he found our training difficult. It wasn't that we trained harder than Arsenal, just that it was different because we trained to play football. We would have two or three minutes of intense work, torture really, with a thirty-second breather, and would repeat this process over and over. Geoff wasn't used to this; neither was he used to working the boards. The first few weeks of training at the club came as a shock to him. The area inside the boards was twenty-five yards long by forty-five yards wide. Shanks would position a player at either end to feed footballs, and away you went. It was control, dribble, shoot, sprint, control the second ball fed to you, dribble, shoot, sprint, only to then receive another ball. You would do this for three minutes, then rest and take deep breaths for thirty seconds. Then the whole process would start again. You had to do this for twenty to twenty-five minutes. When Geoff first attempted it, he lasted for only five minutes before being physically sick. Shanks was understanding but unrelenting. Over the weeks, every training day, Shanks worked Geoff in the boards until he could do twenty-five minutes in there like the rest of us. The day Geoff achieved this, Shanks was beaming. 'Now you're ready to play for Liverpool,' he said.

That Geoff applied himself fully to the board work and all the other tasks asked of him with no murmur of complaint pleased Shanks and Bob. His improved fitness, stamina and ball control apart, the way Geoff had worked in the boards told them a lot about his character. It was in keeping with the qualities Shanks wanted to see in us all: honest, hard-working, resilient, motivated, dedicated to the cause. The level of fitness, stamina and work rate Geoff achieved was all the more remarkable for the fact that he was at the time a regular smoker. Neither Shanks nor Bob had a problem with this as it didn't seem to affect Geoff's performances. Generally speaking, at the time the majority of players in the game did not smoke, but those who did were not chastised for it or seen as pariahs, as they would be today. Cigarette smoking was still acceptable in society and I think just about every team in the land had at least a couple of players who indulged. Immediately upon entering the dressing room after a game, the first thing Geoff did was light up. In all my years in football, he was the only player I ever saw smoke in the shower. He would hold a cigarette between his thumb and forefinger and position them in towards his palm, using the other three fingers close together to keep off the spray. He had it down to an art. The fag never came into contact with water. Occasionally he rolled his own. There is a photograph of the team in the dressing room immediately after the 1965 FA Cup Final. We can all be seen drinking pints of milk, except for Geoff, who has a roll-up on the go.

In the days when playing for your country was seen as an indication that the player concerned was the best in his chosen position in the whole land, Geoff Strong was the only player of this Liverpool team not to win an international cap. I find that a shame, as Geoff was a tremendous player, worthy of a call-up by England. As Shanks told him on more than one occasion, 'Your compensation for being snubbed by your country is that you play for the greatest club in the world.'

Following those ten League games in twenty-six days in April, we had a four-day respite before meeting Leeds United in the FA Cup Final at Wembley on 1 May. In recent years the FA Cup Final has lost much of its exclusivity, pomp and circumstance, partly because the venue had to move to the Millennium Stadium while Wembley was being redeveloped, and partly due to television's saturation coverage of the game. The Millennium Stadium is a superb sporting venue, but it lacks the history, tradition and ivy-covered venerability of even a redeveloped Wembley. It's not the bricks and mortar, design or aesthetics, but the venue itself that engages the spirit. Wembley, corporate-fuelled as it may be now, still induces in people a profound sense of history, tradition, football legend and folklore. From the very first FA Cup Final at the stadium in 1923, Wembley inspired a reverence all of its own. Over the decades it took on the aura of ritual and ceremony that allowed great moments of Cup Finals and internationals to remain sharply defined. Can you readily recall FA Cup Finals at the Millennium stadium? Switching the FA Cup Final to Cardiff was a necessity, but in so doing much of the magic and sense of occasion suffered as a result.

Throughout the 1950s and 1960s the only live matches to be broadcast on TV were England games, the European Cup Final and the FA Cup Final. The fact that the latter was the only live TV game to feature English clubs served to increase the sense of exclusivity felt by players and supporters for the FA Cup Final. The nation would sit down to watch it as it was history in the making. Reputations were made and legends created at Wembley during the course of an FA Cup Final. As TV executives might now say, the Cup Final was a water-cooler moment for the entire nation. Now, with live football on our screens every day of the week, sometimes three times a day, and every match hyped to the limit, the FA Cup Final is in danger of being seen as 'just another game'. I find this gradual erosion of the significance of the FA Cup, in particular the final, sad. Money, more than ever, propels the game these days at the expense of its tradition and spirit.

Of course money played a part in football in the sixties, particularly where the FA Cup was concerned. The big difference was, in the past players had to rely on bonuses to get anything approaching a good wage. In 1965 I was on £30 a week, less tax. The other 'junior' player, Chris Lawler, was on the same money, while the rest of the team were on £35. On top of basic pay we would receive a pound for every thousand spectators above 28,000 who attended home games. When we played away, irrespective of the attendance we received the same crowd bonus paid for the previous Saturday's home game. If we featured among the top six in the First Division, the crowd bonus was doubled. In addition to this we received £2 for a win and £1 for a draw. Everyone was happy with the bonus system. There was a genuine incentive to give of our all. Like my team-mates, I didn't want to be earning just over £20 a week net, I wanted to be taking home around £55. To achieve that we had to be in a winning top-six side playing the sort of entertaining football that drew 40,000-plus to Anfield. I must emphasize, however, that first and foremost we played for the shirt and a genuine love of the game. Pardon the pun, but the money, important as it was, was a bonus to me. At no point during my career was I ever aware of a player not giving of his all in a game, certainly where Liverpool was concerned. We played for the shirt, but there is no doubt in my mind that the club's bonus system gave an added edge to our performances.

I do wonder what incentive there is for players nowadays. Today's top footballers earn such large salaries that there appears to be no room for incentive. Premiership players not selected for the first team don't turn out for their club's reserve team, they sit in the stand, and in some cases still earn £50,000 a week. Fifty grand a week for not having to put your ability as a footballer on the line week after week is ludicrous to me. In February 2007, Liverpool's Craig Bellamy was fined two weeks' wages – £80,000 – following an incident that occurred during a club break in Portugal. I wonder how much of an imposition that fine was on Bellamy? Given the highest wage I earned while a Liverpool player, it would have taken me nigh on three and a half years to earn Bellamy's wages for a fortnight.

Prior to the 1965 Cup Final, the Liverpool board said they would pay every player a bonus of £1,000 if we won the FA Cup. This was great news. Chris Lawler and I sat down with pencil and paper to work out how much money might be coming our way. Sue was creating a home for us, we had discussed what we needed, and I saw some of the FA Cup bonus as a way of paying for the various things she had in mind, and also for a car, which at the time we didn't have. We had been led to believe that the Cup Final would be treated like a home match in terms of a crowd bonus. Should we win the cup, as we were determined to do, I worked out that I would receive a £30 basic wage, the £1,000 bonus for having won the cup and, based on the traditional Wembley attendance of 100,000, a £72 crowd bonus. So victory at Wembley would bring us £1,102.

The Liverpool board, however, had different ideas. We were told that the usual crowd bonus would not be forthcoming as we were playing on a neutral ground. The players were not happy about this, but to a man we didn't want to make a scene as we didn't want to come over as being one of those teams who tarnished the achievement of having reached Wembley by squabbling over money. We felt we had to let our feelings be known, but rather than demand to see the board en masse it was decided it would be more dignified and diplomatic if one player met with the directors to discuss the matter on behalf of the entire squad. As skipper, Ron Yeats was the natural choice.

Ron put forward our case, citing the fact that our contracts allowed for us to be paid a crowd bonus when playing at the ground of another club, the amount being the same as the previous bonus paid based on the attendance of the last home match. Once again the board reiterated that Wembley was a neutral venue. It was then that Ron played what he thought was his trump card: we had been paid a crowd bonus following our defeat of Chelsea in the semi-final, which had been played at a neutral venue. So the board played their trump card – and talk about being pedantic. Ron was told that the wording in our contracts was specific. A crowd bonus would be paid to players when 'playing at the home ground of another club'. The venue of the semi-final, Villa Park, was the home of Aston Villa. This being so, the board had consented to pay the crowd bonus, in keeping with the exact wording of our contracts. Wembley Stadium, Ron was reminded, was not the 'home ground of another club' and therefore the board were not contractually bound to pay us a crowd bonus.

I was not alone in thinking the board's argument as thin as a greasy spoon café soup, but we had no choice but to accept it. The only alternative was a row, which could result in bad publicity and, worse, upset the spirit in the dressing room. The chagrin we felt was added to when we learned that Birmingham City players had each been paid a £1,000 bonus for having avoided relegation to Division Two. In addition to this, the crowd bonus due from our last home game against Wolves was only £2 because the Kemlyn Road stand was closed due to redevelopment which reduced the capacity at Anfield to just over 30,000.

'Look at it this way,' Ron told the players matter-of-factly. 'If we lose against Leeds at Wembley, we'll collect our basic plus a two pound crowd bonus from our last game against Wolves. We've battled through seven matches to reach the final. Now I don't know about you, but I haven't flogged my guts out to get to Wembley only to walk away with thirty-seven quid, less tax – less where Tommy and Chris are concerned. So, if we want a decent pay day from the cup, I suggest we go out and win it.'

The matter was put on the back burner until after the Cup Final, when it was agreed we would put our grievances to Shanks in the hope that he would talk to the board. The reason for this was that it was an unwritten rule that we wouldn't 'talk money' in the dressing room. We had talked about it in relation to Wembley, but we all agreed to let it lie after that.

Both Liverpool and Leeds United received an allocation of 15,000 tickets for the final, which meant that 70,000 tickets went to – well, God knows who. For years the allocation of Cup Final tickets to the respective finalists had been a contentious issue in football. Liverpool and Leeds were among the best-supported teams in the country. The allocation was not only meagre, it was scandalous. That said, it was a slight improvement on previous years, when only 12,000 tickets per club were made available.

The FA Cup Final was supposedly about 'the people', that is the players and the supporters of the finalists. This was only ever partly true. The Cup Final was the showpiece of the English football season but it was also the FA's annual beano, an occasion for the FA to 'reward' administrators in county FAs for their work, support and loyalty, which in the main were voluntary. The final was also an opportunity for the blazer brigade in the FA to hobnob it with politicians, celebrities, staff from foreign embassies, directors of major companies and a plethora of establishment figures, all of whom received complimentary tickets.

The FA was always concerned about the black market for Cup Final tickets and was forever at pains to stress that anyone who sold them for profit would be punished. In truth it was a black market the FA themselves had created. Many of the complimentary tickets issued by the FA were given to people who had no interest in football and didn't want to attend the final. Subsequently, many of them found their way into the hands of touts and profiteers. Each Liverpool player received twenty-five tickets, which in hindsight was generous: for other finals in which I later appeared, the allocation was twelve tickets per player. I gave my tickets to my immediate family, relatives and close friends. There were a few grumbles from certain uncles and cousins who missed out, but to be honest, there always are in these situations. You never please everybody. For the vast majority of supporters, even if over the years their club appeared in two or three Cup Finals, with such a miserly allocation of tickets attendance at an FA Cup Final represented a once-in-a-lifetime experience.

Liverpool supporters went in search of Cup Final tickets any way they could, and I suspect the same was true of Leeds fans. All manner of stories hit the local press. One featured the Liverpool fan who managed to obtain his ticket from a relation who worked in the British Embassy in Lima; another told the story of the supporter whose mother was given a Cup Final ticket by the well-meaning wife of a prominent politician whose house she used to clean. Proof positive of the unfairness of the FA's haphazard ticket allocation policy. Somehow or other, many of our supporters did manage to get hold of tickets: on the day in question an estimated 40,000 Liverpool supporters were present at Wembley.

We left Lime Street station and travelled to London by train. On arriving at Euston we boarded the coach that was to take us to our hotel in Weybridge and during the journey listened to *Desert Island Discs* on the radio. The programme was presented by its creator Roy Plomley, and his 'castaway' that day was none other than Shanks. Shanks loved music, but in the main his tastes were very conservative. On visits to his home I had noticed LPs by Jim Reeves, Kenneth McKellar, Harry Secombe and Pat Boone, the latter a collection of favourite hymns. The eight records Shanks chose as a desert island castaway reflected the music he enjoyed listening to at home. The part of *Desert Island Discs* that most intrigues the listener is probably the subject's choice of a 'luxury', and a book to accompany the Bible and the complete works of Shakespeare. Shanks chose as his luxury item Liverpool Football Club, 'so I could continue my work of creating a great football club'. The book he chose, in keeping with his Scottish roots, was a compilation of stories by John Buchan. Amazingly, he then came up with a connection between Buchan and our appearance at Wembley. 'Buchan, great Scotsman, great writer of adventure stories, which I would never get tired of reading,' Shanks told Roy Plomley. 'He wrote *The 39 Steps*, of course, and did you know, Roy, that there are thirty-nine steps leading up to the royal box at Wembley? There are, and as part of our adventure at Wembley I'll be looking forward to my boys ascending the thirty-nine steps to receive the FA Cup.' How Shanks knew there were thirty-nine steps leading up from the pitch to the royal box I don't know, but it turned out he was right.

A number of reserve players together with directors and club staff arrived on the Friday night to stay at another hotel. We also learned that the club had invited members of Liverpool's 1950 Cup Final team to join us the following day. Liverpool was very much a family club – once a red always a red. It seemed as if it was going to be very much a 'family' occasion.

On the Friday night we went to the London Palladium. Top of the bill was Liverpool's Ken Dodd in 'Doddy's Here'. In my opinion, no comedian is as funny as Doddy and I was delighted when he told the audience that Liverpool's Cup Final team was in the theatre and called for the house lights to be put on. We all stood up and received warm applause, after which Doddy launched into a series of gags about our Cup Final opponents.

'Leeds, their manager, Don Revie, he's had them doing special training for the Cup Final. He placed eleven dustbins on the pitch and told his players to weave in and out of them as part of their training. I think you are going to be all right, boys. The dustbins won 2–1!

'Liverpool will win the Cup and qualify for Europe. I'll give you lads some advice on how to score in Europe. Down by the canals in Amsterdam is best.

'To commemorate reaching Wembley for the first time, the Leeds players have made a record. It's their version of "It Might As Well Rain Until September". Meteorologists say it's the worst since records began.

'That Jim Storrie, who plays for Leeds, he's been appointed coach to Britain's Davis Cup tennis team – and rightly so. If anyone knows how *not* to put the ball into the net it's him.'

And so Doddy went on, until our stomachs ached and the pain was so much we had to force ourselves to stop laughing.

After the show our coach returned us to our hotel. We were in such good spirits we all began to sing 'You'll Never Walk Alone' as we made our way down Piccadilly. As we sang, Shanks jumped to his feet and asked our driver to open the door so passers-by could hear. 'The Leeds players will all be in bed,' he said. 'I want all London to know how happy my boys are to be at Wembley, how confident they are of winning.'

I roomed with Chris Lawler and we both had trouble getting to sleep that night. Chris was the first friend I made when joining Liverpool as a fifteen-year-old in the summer of 1960. He was a year older than me, but I had come across Chris on several occasions when playing for my school football team, Cardinal Godfrey College, against his school, St Teresa's. On my first day at Liverpool I gravitated towards Chris simply because he was the only person I knew, albeit not that well. Chris and I became good friends, and room-mates when we both graduated to the first team. The curious thing about my friendship with Chris was that in all the years we played alongside each other and roomed together, I don't think we had a meaningful conversation. Chris is the quietest person I have ever encountered in my life. He was a terrific full-back, he would join in the laughter with the rest of the lads, but he hardly ever spoke. When we were rooming together I would try to engage him in conversation, perhaps about a book I was reading, or a pop record I'd heard, but the most I could get from him was a monosyllabic reply. It wasn't that he was glum or rude; he was, as I said, a man of very few words.

A football team comprises all manner of personalities and, oddly, whichever team you play for at whatever level, each will have certain 'types'. The bubbly, outgoing sort with the infectious personality (Kevin Keegan); the hard man (me); the studious intellectual (Steve Heighway); the joker (Joey Jones); the butt of jokes (Ian Ross); the incessant talker (Terry McDermott); and the player who hardly says a word (Chris Lawler). No one at Anfield commented on Chris's reluctance to engage in conversation. He was simply accepted for who he was.

I did get to know a lot about his character, though, as did the rest of the Liverpool team. His deeds on the pitch and the way he reacted to certain situations during games spoke volumes about what sort of man he was. When the chips were down, he never gave up. When the going got tough, he never shirked a challenge or hid; on the contrary, without fail he was always brave. Should I, for example, be caught out of position, he would come across and cover for me. Chris never panicked and was always cool under pressure, so much so that he became Liverpool's regular and, arguably, most celebrated penalty-taker. He was, in short, a great team player.

I say that Chris never hid, but I remember one occasion when he'd probably have preferred to. The players always looked forward to training on a Thursday at Melwood because invariably we would spend the morning playing five-a-side. Not that these matches were animated recreation; on the contrary, they were as keenly contested as an FA Cup Final. The element of competition had much to do with the fact that Shanks and his backroom staff would each have a team. There was no time limit on these games, other than the fact that Shanks would always bring a game to an end when his side were in front. Should Shanks's team be trailing, that game could continue for over an hour until his team took the lead. Then and only then would he call time.

Bill Shankly was an enigma, and a man of contradictions. He willingly embraced new ideas, but was also a traditionalist. He was, at times, chillingly cold, at other times a man of genuine warmth and love. He was a hard man, but also compassionate. He seemed worldly, yet all he appeared to know about was football – and boy how he knew the game! He wanted his players to keep cool heads, but encouraged us to be fired up when the occasion demanded it. He believed the players had to care about and show passion for the game, even a five-a-side game, if we were to be successful as a team and as individuals. 'Some think football is a game played with the feet, but they are wrong. Ye play the game with this,' Shanks would say, pointing to his head, 'and this!' he would add, pointing to his heart. He actively encouraged arguments between players as he believed it stirred our passion for the game. In those Thursday-morning five-a-side matches, for instance, Shanks insisted that cricket stumps were used for goalposts because he knew their use would result in much arguing – and demonstrations of passion – when two teams contested whether a shot hit at a height above the top of a stump would have passed between the posts or not.

One Thursday I was playing in a team that included the Liverpool captain, Ron Yeats, whose neck could dent an axe. We were playing Shanks's team. Watching was Chris Lawler, who was sidelined because of an injury. I can't recall the exact score; suffice it to say the two teams were level when Shanks fired a shot at our goal. Immediately the ball passed over one of the stumps acting as a post, Shanks blew for time. Ron, however, took issue with Shanks and said the game had to continue as the ball had passed wide of the goal. Shanks was having none of this; he insisted the ball had passed between the two stumps and claimed the goal. The debate continued, became a little heated, and eventually even more heated. At one point the pair eye-balled each other, or at least eye-balled each other as best they could given that Shanks was nine inches shorter than Ron.

'Ye argue wi' me, son? I'm telling you that was a *goal* – and a beauty at that!' said Shanks in characteristically forceful manner.

'And I'm tellin' ye, boss, it was *not* a goal,' said Ron, holding his ground.

'Right!' said Shanks, turning towards Chris, who was still standing on the sidelines. 'Let's get an unbiased opinion.'

He strode across to where Chris was standing.

'Ye see what happened there, son?'

'Yes, boss,' replied Chris nervously.

'That great shot of mine, goal or no goal?'

Chris began to tremble like autumn leaves on a tree.

'Well? Did the ball pass over or under?' demanded Shanks.

Chris hesitated for a moment before replying in a trembling voice, 'Over. No goal.'

Shanks was so shocked he took a step back and his jaw dropped. 'Jesus Christ, son. You've been at this club eight years and have never said a word. And now, when you finally do speak, it's a bloody lie!'

It wasn't nerves that kept me awake the night before the 1965 FA Cup Final, but anticipation and excitement, and I suppose the same was true for Chris. I kept thinking, 'What a way to end my first full season in the first team.' I couldn't believe my good fortune. I was going to play for Liverpool in a Cup Final, just as my mum had predicted when we first met Shanks. I had up to this point always thought great things happened to other people, never me. That night it really hit home how fortunate I was. I had a wonderful wife who I was madly in love with, a love that was fully reciprocated. I had a fantastic mum, and I played for the club I had always dreamed of representing. I thought about the time Mum and I had to move to Nan's in Norris Green because she could no longer afford the upkeep of the family home; how Mum was so grateful for the £1 a week she received from the council. As I eventually drifted towards sleep I made a vow to myself that I would never do anything to spoil the life I had now been blessed with.

On Saturday morning we assembled for breakfast at eight, though some of the players were so keen to get going they had been up since six. Most of the lads had cereal, fruit juice, and toast with honey, but I stuck to my normal routine. On the day of a game I never ate breakfast. I would have a cup of coffee, perhaps two, but no solids. After breakfast I joined Bob Paisley and the rest of the lads for a walk down the high street to buy news-papers. We had a light lunch at noon, when again I only had a cup of coffee. At the risk of offering too much detail, after coffee at lunchtime I then always went to the loo. When arriving at a ground I would again go to the loo, so that when it came to my taking to the field for a game I knew there was no food in my system. That was my pre-match routine throughout my career, and on the occasion of the Cup Final it was no different. I felt I had to rid my system of food so that I was cleansed and carrying no excess weight. It was part physical, part psychological. Abstinence from food just made me feel better, more relaxed and up for battle, though I doubt such a regime would go down well with sports nutritionists today.

Both Shanks and Bob Paisley had played in Cup Finals – in Bob's case the 1939 Amateur Cup Final. They told us to take it all in, to savour every moment of the day and commit it to memory as we might never have another chance. As Shanks told us, 'Memory is the art of attention.' The trouble is, on Cup Final day you've got the game and your opponents on your mind. I found myself concentrating so hard on the challenge ahead that I had to make a real conscious effort to commit events to memory, though I was determined to do just that.

We left our Weybridge hotel for Wembley around 12.30 p.m. The FA had arranged for a police motorcycle escort to pick us up en route but, for whatever reason, it never turned up. Our driver parked the coach up for a time, but when it became apparent no escort would be arriving Shanks told him to head for Wembley. A couple of miles from the stadium the road was so stiff with traffic we ground to a halt. Just when it looked as if we might be late, one of the lads spotted a police motorcyclist, and Bob was sent to ask if he would act as our escort. With the police motorcyclist doing his best to clear the way, we painstakingly made our way to Wembley.

We had the radio on, and at one point the presenter referred to the traffic chaos in the vicinity of Wembley. 'All roads leading to the stadium are heavily congested,' he announced. 'One of the vehicles caught up in the traffic jam is the coach containing Liverpool's 1950 Cup Final team.'

'Hear that? This must be the worst traffic jam ever!' quipped Ian St John, at which we all broke into laughter and the tension eased.

Our coach eventually arrived just after two o'clock. Shanks

alighted and immediately headed for a group of Liverpool supporters standing by the gates that afford entry to the tunnel and dressing rooms. He had a few words with these lads and it transpired that two of them had travelled down hoping to buy tickets from touts. Shanks was having none of that. He pulled from his jacket pocket a pair of tickets. 'Pay me next season,' he said to the two now wide-eyed fans.

As was the custom, having settled into our dressing room we then went out to inspect the pitch. TV commentators always refer to this as the players 'soaking up the atmosphere'. In truth, until about ten minutes before kick-off there was little atmosphere within Wembley to savour, but we literally did soak it up as the rain was coming down like stair rods. It is not easy to reach Wembley and it is not easy to play there. Many players found its powerful atmosphere too much for them; others found the pitch's soft Cumberland turf tiring and unsuitable to their game. With the rain we knew the soft pitch – it was like playing on moss – would soon sap energy and provide problems for the goalkeepers as the ball would come off the surface like a bar of soap.

'It'll take stud,' said Chris Lawler, digging his fingers into the lush turf. 'One about four inches long.'

We'd had a short team meeting at the hotel, and Shanks's pre-match talk simply recounted the salient points of that meeting. He reminded us that the Wembley pitch was normally a holding turf, but with the rain the ball would be scooting around. He told us to play it simple; nobody should do any extra running with the ball. 'That way,' he said, 'you save your strength, and you'll need to on this pitch.' That was all he needed to say. We all knew our respective jobs and what was expected of us. But as we made our way out of the dressing room, he offered some final words. 'Whatever you do, don't be the victim of circumstances, let circumstances be dictated by us. Boss the game. Win the Cup for Liverpool.'

As the teams lined up in the tunnel awaiting the signal from the referee to take to the field, Shanks turned to the Leeds captain, Bobby Collins.

'How you feeling, Bobby, son?'

'Awful,' replied Bobby.

A broad grin broke out across Shanks's face.

In the silence of the cavernous tunnel amid an atmosphere laden with nervous tension, the shrill blast of the official's whistle was like a banshee screaming overhead. Having been issued with the signal, the crocodile of red and white shirts in front of me slowly began to move. We were off.

I had played at Wembley before, for England Youth, but had never experienced an atmosphere such as that which greeted the two teams as we emerged from the gloaming of that tunnel. On seeing Shanks and Don Revie at the head of their respective teams, Wembley erupted. The vast terraces suddenly produced evidence of their partisanship as they bloomed vivid red or virgin white. A rumbustious roar swept around Wembley's bowl only to be suddenly smothered by the sonorous collective chant of 'Liv-er-pool', in which each syllable was stretched to breaking point. Not to be outdone on their first visit to Wembley, the Leeds fans roared their riposte of 'You-night-ted', aware that the simple monosyllable 'Leeds' would not carry the same gravitas.

Mercifully the rain had stopped, but there appeared to be more in the low grey clouds that hung over the stadium. The juicy emerald turf felt very soft underfoot as we made our way to the halfway line for the presentations. The 100,000 people present seemed to me to be miles away. Wembley looked massive, much bigger than my memory of it when playing for England. I knew thousands of pairs of eyes were on me, millions watching on TV, but in that vast arena, rather than feeling any sense of importance, I felt small, insignificant and vulnerable. Further rain was forecast, which would only make conditions more difficult – the sort of conditions in which players are forced into making mistakes. I prayed

Left: Me aged three, dreaming even then, hands on knees as if posing for a team photograph.

Above: My dad (*right*) with army buddy. During the Second World War, Dad served with the Gurkhas in the Far East.

Right: Mum and Dad larking about. They were loving parents and my childhood was a happy one.

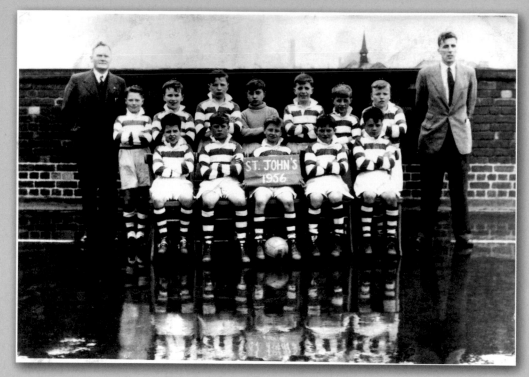

Above: St John's Primary School team – that's me third from left in the back row. The teachers are Mr Thomas (*left*) and Mr Hargreaves, both of whom gave me great encouragement in my studies and at football.

Below: Cardinal Godfrey School pose with the Liverpool Catholic Schools' Shield. I am second from left in the back row. A few weeks later, I received a letter from Bill Shankly inviting me to join the Liverpool groundstaff.

Right: On holiday in London, 1958. Mum and I with my cousin in pram pose outside Buckingham Palace. I never thought that one day I would be invited to the Palace.

Above: Aged fifteen, on holiday at the caravan site in Rhyl, doing my best to boost Brycreem's profits.

Left: The house in Lambeth Road where I grew up. This is 1973 and, as you can see, 'nets' were still fashionable in windows.

Left: Sue and me on our wedding day, 4 July 1965. I took some stick for getting married on Independence Day.

Above: Sue and I enjoy a night out with Chris Lawler and his wife, Geraldine. Chris was the first pal I made when I joined Liverpool, and we remain good friends to this day.

Left: Me, Mum and my step-father, Richie Morton, who was a good footballer, having played for Liverpool Schoolboys in the 1920s.

Left: With Sue and our daughter Janette outside our home in Maghull. Just after this was taken Janette fell and I had to rush her to hospital where she had stitches in a wound to her mouth. Parenthood, eh?

Above: I was on tour with the Jack Charlton XI in Hawaii when I received confirmation of my MBE. (*L to r*) Ian Callaghan, Tony Dunne, John Hurst, anon, Jack, me, George Wood, Bobby Charlton, Chris Lawler, Alex Stepney, Peter Lorimer, anon. (*Kneeling*) Alan Suddick, anon and Ralph Coates.

Right: A very proud day, with the family at Buckingham Palace following the investiture ceremony for my MBE. After the presentation by Her Majesty, you have to walk backwards so as not to turn your back on the Queen. I didn't know where to look.

Opposite page: Following my retirement as a player I went into property development. Here I am 'mucking in' just as everyone had to do at Anfield.

Top: With the family and a lamp. I designed our house, including the wooden cabinets needed to hold trophies, football mementoes and, being an avid reader, books.

Above: With (*l to r*) Ian St John (quizmaster), Andy King, Lou Macari and Mick Channon on a Granada TV quiz programme that combined football and general knowledge. As I keep reminding them – I won by a mile!

Right: In the gym getting in some training for playing against Leeds United.

Left: Kevin Keegan presents... the Liverpool Echo Shankly Memorial Award...

BILL SHANKLY
He made the people happy

that I wouldn't make a mistake that would prove telling.

Playing in an FA Cup Final is like being in a school photograph. Should you appear on it as a gormless-looking youth, even if you go on in life to develop the looks of Johnny Depp and be as successful as Richard Branson, your school mates will forever remember you as that gormless youth. Likewise, how you appear in an FA Cup Final is how you will be remembered as a player, not only by your own supporters but by the nation. A player may have performed heroics on the way to Wembley, his goals or performances may have been instrumental to his team having reached the final, but all that will be forgotten should he drop a clanger on the big day. A poor performance or one telling mistake on the day will dog a player not only for the remainder of his career but for the rest of his life. Ask Gordon Smith (Brighton, 1983) or John Aldridge (Liverpool, 1988). I am sure they would testify to the truth of that. Conversely, should a player be inspired on Cup Final day, what up to that point may have been a journeyman career can suddenly become one of legend and football immortality, as in the case of Ian Porterfield (Sunderland, 1973), Bobby Stokes (Southampton, 1976) and Roger Osborne (Ipswich, 1978). A Wembley Cup Final not only acts as a microcosm of a career, it will often determine reputation and standing in the game. That is the intangible magic and power of the FA Cup Final, something I feel some current managers and players would do well to remember.

The twenty-two men who faced one another at three o'clock that day were Tommy Lawrence, Chris Lawler, Gerry Byrne, Geoff Strong, Ron Yeats, Willie Stevenson, Ian Callaghan, Roger Hunt, Ian St John, me and Peter Thompson for Liverpool; Gary Sprake, Paul Reaney, Willie Bell, Billy Bremner, Jack Charlton, Norman Hunter, Johnny Giles, Jim Storrie, Alan Peacock, Bobby Collins and Albert Johanneson for Leeds. It seemed barely credible that the noise within Wembley could get louder, but it did when the referee, Mr Clements, got the game underway. A full-throated guttural roar swept down from the stands as if 100,000 people were giving vent to their suppressed nerves and aggression. The roar immediately detonated the game. From a standing start players instinctively leapt into a cauldron of frenzied activity. The ball moved about like a pinball and players thudded into tackles as both teams strove to take that first vital beach-head.

I got an early touch on the ball, played a simple pass to Willie Stevenson and felt good. In any game, but particularly a Cup Final, it is important for a player not to make a hash of his first touch and then to use the ball to good effect. The fact that I had controlled the ball with one touch and made a decent pass boosted my confidence. Conditions were very tricky underfoot, and I found myself having to concentrate simply on running, something I and all the other players would normally do instinctively.

Just how difficult the conditions were became apparent as early as the third minute. Gerry Byrne went into a challenge with Bobby Collins, who went over the top on Gerry, a heinous crime as far as pros were concerned. In an attempt to avoid him, Gerry fell awkwardly. Gerry was one of the game's tough guys. It was not like him to go down, so as soon as I saw him lying motionless on the turf I immediately thought his injury was a bad one. Bob Paisley leapt from the bench to attend to him. At first I thought he had injured his ankle, and so did he. He was pointing at it, his face grimacing with pain. Bob checked the ankle and seemed satisfied that no serious harm had been done, but just to be on the safe side he gave it a blast with the ice spray. He then helped Gerry to his feet, and that must have been when the true nature of the injury became apparent to Bob. Gerry complained of a shooting pain across his right shoulder. Bob inspected the shoulder, produced the spray, went into a huddled conversation with Gerry, patted his cheek and said he would be OK. But as Bob left the pitch,

I noticed a look of concern on Gerry's face. He carried on, though, displaying no evidence of being uncomfortable.

The first half produced a fierce, taut battle with few chances, and come half-time the game was goalless. It was during the interval that we learned the extent of Gerry's injury. As soon as he entered the dressing room, Bob told him to sit down and attempted to remove his shirt. Gerry grimaced and protested that it was too painful. The club doctor was summoned. He and Bob gingerly took the shirt off Gerry's back. It transpired that Gerry's right collar bone was split, and the shattered pieces were grinding together. I could only imagine the pain he was feeling. The club doctor attempted to freeze the injured shoulder but to no avail.

Shanks asked Gerry if he could carry on playing. Gerry never hesitated in saying 'Yes.' In the days before substitutes were allowed, an injured player would usually be asked to play on the wing where he would not be involved too much in the heat of battle. Even if the injury was truly debilitating, the theory was that even a hobbling player made some contribution as he had to be marked by an opponent. So I thought Shanks would ask Gerry to go out on the wing, drop Willie Stevenson to full-back and ask Thommo to play deeper in Willie's role on the left of midfield. Shanks, however, had another idea. He praised Gerry for the fortitude and bravery he had shown in the first half. 'Most important of all, you didn't let on how bad the injury is,' Shanks said. 'The extent of your injury must be kept a secret from Leeds. If they get a sniff that something is really wrong, they'll play on it.' He told Gerry to continue at left-back and asked the rest of us to help out by clamping down on the service Albert Johanneson had been receiving from Bell and Giles. 'Starve Johanneson of the ball, that's what we have to do,' Shanks told us.

Heaven knows what sort of pain Gerry endured throughout the second period, but endure it he did. We did our best to lighten his load, carrying out Shanks's orders to cut down the service to Johanneson. Amid a frenetic final fraught with physical challenges, this strategy brought a moment of levity.

Johanneson was creating a little piece of football history as the first black player to play in a Wembley Cup Final. A South African by birth, Albert was a smashing lad and a very good winger. He wasn't the best at riding and taking a tackle, but with the ball at his feet he was lightning quick; this and his close control were usually enough to take him past the best of full-backs. So Albert was a danger with the ball at his feet, but starved of service his effectiveness could be nullified. Aware that Albert was not getting into the game in the second-half, at one point the Leeds manager, Don Revie, leapt to his feet in frustration.

'Get it out there to Albert!' he screamed to Bell, Collins and Giles. 'Get it wide to the white shirt!'

I was on that side of the pitch and heard this, but I doubt the Leeds players could hear Don above the noise and pandemonium. Our bench did. Bob Paisley had a really dry sense of humour. He shouted over to Revie, 'You're wasting your time, Don. The whites are snookered behind the reds!'

Both benches rippled with laughter. Shanks was rolling about, this was exactly the sort of oneupmanship that tickled him pink. Even the normally stoic Revie had the semblance of a smile on his face. That was one of the moments I committed to memory, and I'm glad I did. This was an FA Cup Final, and a bitterly contested one at that, yet amid the torturous tension there they were, having a giggle. Somehow I can't imagine Arsène Wenger and Sir Alex Ferguson doing that during a Cup Final.

After ninety minutes of what in truth had been unremarkable football, the game remained goalless. Incessant rain throughout the second half hadn't helped. The ball was coming off the surface like a rocket, which tested the control and technique of even the most accomplished players. Wembley's sodden springy turf resulted in a lot of heavy legs, mine included. It was a game for stout hearts, and no one displayed this more than Gerry Byrne. He was in tremendous pain but, mindful of Shanks's words, he never showed it. In fact, rather than muddling through the game, Gerry was making a real impact. Not content to sit back he went forward at every given opportunity, and when on the defensive he never shirked a tackle. His presence of mind and mental strength were remarkable. He certainly appeared undaunted at the prospect of having to play an extra thirty minutes.

Three minutes into extra time came the moment I had dreamed of. Gerry Byrne, of all people, burst down our left-hand side, glanced across, saw Roger Hunt making ground and delivered a perfect cross. Rather than hammering the ball with his forehead, Roger glanced it towards goal. Gary Sprake, who had not thought it prudent to move, stood crestfallen, and the red contingent inside Wembley erupted.

Rather than rocking them, the goal seemed to galvanize Leeds. Their play took on an extra urgency and they began to pour forward in numbers. Norman Hunter lobbed the ball to a point just inside our penalty box where Jack Charlton nodded it back into the path of the onrushing Bremner. Billy could really connect with a ball, and without breaking stride he hit a volley that was still rising when it ballooned the roof of Tommy Lawrence's net.

Light travels faster than sound. When a goal is scored at Wembley there is the briefest hiatus before the thunderous noise from the stands reaches the ears of the players on the pitch. When I saw Bremner's shot hit our net this split second seemed surreal. I thought it hadn't actually happened because there was no noise. No sooner had this thought come into my head, however, than the tumultuous roar of the Leeds fans assailed my ears and pressed home reality. I had gone from ecstasy to agony in a matter of minutes and the contrast was hard to come to terms with.

We had it all to do again, and to a man we set about doing just that. The goals injected life into what had been a far from classic final. It was as if having breached each other's defences both teams were suddenly aware further goals were indeed possible. The game now swung from end to end as we all went in search of a winner.

There were nine minutes of the second period of extra time remaining when I made progress down the middle, evaded a challenge from Bremner and played the ball out to Ian Callaghan. Cally danced past Willie Bell and, from out on the right, crossed the ball to a point between Sprake's near post and the six-yard box. Ian St John had escaped from Jack Charlton and was steaming towards the near post. Saint almost arrived too early to meet the cross, and for a split second it seemed as if the ball would travel behind him; but then he took to the air, jack-knifed his body, bent his neck and made contact with the ball with his head. With Sprake in no-man's-land, the ball flew through the gap between the near post and Paul Reaney standing on the line in the middle of the goal. Once again an ear-splitting roar avalanched down from the stands and resonated around the stadium. I danced with joy – and I don't mean one of the Beverley sisters.

Having already conceded a lead to Leeds we were adamant there would be no repeat performance. Revie's team were doughty fighters, though. In the minutes that remained Leeds gave it their all, but Ron Yeats in the heart of defence kept a tight rein on everyone around him, team-mates as well as opponents.

I shall never forget the happiness that coursed through my body as I ascended what were indeed thirty-nine steps to receive my winner's medal from Her Majesty the Queen. Ron led us up to the royal box, followed by Tommy Lawrence, Thommo, Willie Stevenson and me. Her Majesty said, 'Well done.' I said, 'Thank you, ma'am,' and shook her gloved hand. When presented with my medal I said 'Thank you, ma'am' again, and looked up just in time to see Ron hoisting the cup aloft to the delight of our supporters. The refrains of 'We've won the cup, we've won the cup, ee-aye-addio, we've won the cup' reverberated around the stadium and seemed to go on for ever. Wembley had heard nothing like it, and I had felt nothing like it. True unadulterated ecstasy.

Following the customary lap of honour, I sat in the dressing room staring at my little gold medal contained within its blue velvet box. It had taken Liverpool seventy-three years and 207 ties to win the FA Cup. It had been a real team effort, but Gerry Byrne's courage and heroics ensured he would take his place among the legends of FA Cup Finals.

We celebrated our success by drinking pints of milk. Photographers appeared in the dressing room asking for a celebratory shot with the cup, and we were only too happy to oblige. One of them later sent me a print, which I still have. The photograph shows Ron Yeats holding the cup while Willie Stevenson, Roger Hunt, Thommo and myself fill it with milk. In the background is Gerry Byrne, his shoulder now strapped but sporting the broadest of smiles. Next to me is Geoff Strong with a roll-up in his hand. Geoff is with us but seemingly in body only: he has a glazed expression on his face and appears to be miles away. His detachment was, I am sure, simply down to the fact that he was exhausted after having covered every blade of grass on Wembley, rather than the effects of his tobacco. Honest!

That night a few Double Diamonds were supped at the club's post-Wembley banquet at the Grosvenor in Park Lane, but not to excess; three days later we were due to meet Inter Milan in the first leg of the European Cup semi-final. Joining us on the night were the members of Liverpool's 1950 Cup Final team (they eventually made it) and a number of other ex-players the club had been in contact with.

I shall never forget the train journey back to Liverpool. A little after noon on Sunday we arrived at Euston to be met by a crowd of well-wishers and photographers. Having boarded our train, the press boys asked if they could have a shot of Ron Yeats leaning out of the window of the carriage door, FA Cup in hand, and he complied. In the days when teams travelled by train this was the traditional post-Cup Final photograph, one that would appear in just about every newspaper and football annual. It is a small part of football culture that is now lost for ever.

As our train travelled further north, people began to appear at the line-side to wave and offer their congratulations to us. The nearer we got to Liverpool, the more people there were. I remember a family standing by a fence in a field holding a makeshift sign that read 'Well Done Reds'; and a farmer, or perhaps a farm worker, standing on the seat of his tractor triumphantly waving a Liverpool scarf. From Runcorn onwards, houses that backed on to the railway were bedecked with Liverpool scarves, flags, hastily made posters and red bunting. Framed in the windows of their houses excited families waved to us, and without fail we all waved back. When we arrived at Lime Street station I couldn't believe how many people were there to welcome us. Yet again the refrain of 'Ee-aye-addio, we've won the cup' rang out loud and long. I felt a strange mixture of pride and humility. Seeing all these people reinforced in me how important football was in their lives.

It saddens and annoys me when I hear people in the modern game calling for FA Cup replays to be scrapped, and for the competition to be seeded. I think to myself, 'Who the hell are they to besmirch what is the oldest and greatest club cup competition in the world?' The FA Cup retains a degree of importance to those clubs whose turnover runs into millions of course, but often that has much to do with their failure in what they perceive to be more important competitions. To me the FA Cup is not simply about the final or winning it. I have always seen it as being of vital importance to those clubs who can hardly afford to give their visitors a half-time cup of tea. To the big clubs the cup can mean further prosperity; to the likes of Rochdale or Barnet it may represent survival. I remember when Liverpool beat Stockport County on our way to Wembley. The disappointment felt by those connected with Stockport was tempered by the fact that our two ties had generated much-needed money for the club. As one County director told us, 'It's taken the pressure off. The money we've made from these two games will ensure we're OK for the next year, maybe two.' Every club belongs to the family of football. Our game is not simply about the Premiership, or the needs and requirements of four or five clubs in that League, it is all-embracing. Certain current managers who ought to know better should be aware of that.

The magic of the FA Cup has much to do with its content and conditions. When I say content, I mean the participating teams, from Arsenal and Aylesbury to Manchester United and Marine. That such clubs have a chance to meet one another suggests to me that the FA Cup is the most democratic competition in the world, – another reason to preserve it in its current state. What has changed is the importance accorded to a meeting of peers. Nowadays, if Chelsea are not drawn against Arsenal, or Liverpool against Manchester United, the round in question is thought to be flat and bereft of interest. Peer drawn against peer has always guaranteed interest, of course, but when I was a player the true romance of the cup came in the form of Crewe being drawn against, say, Spurs, or Stockport having to travel to Anfield. Fans savoured the prospect of a real upset, and the competition thrived on this. Hope is the lifeblood of football – that on the day itself the underdogs will confound the natural order of things. Against this great tide of media indifference, it must be acknowledged that the BBC do cover all of the early round ties – even if they involve non-league clubs. However, I'm not sure that the impact of this is really discernible in other media.

As the gap between rich and poor in football widens – it now resembles an irreversibly cavernous gulf – the prospect of giant-killing recedes. Astronomic wages, Premiership myopia and institutional arrogance now reign rather than objectivity and common sense. A Premiership manager with little sense of history and tradition, of football as a family, but who possesses an eminently

127

quotable turn of phrase may call for replays to be scrapped as to his mind they are an unwarranted intrusion in an already congested season, but supporters of Stoke City, Stockport or Stalybridge have every right to laugh with the rest. Giant-killing is often a case of answering insult with injury. When a big club meets a small club in the FA Cup, as Manchester United found when meeting Exeter City in 2006, the stars are playing against themselves as well as the journeymen who are racing about all over the pitch with nothing to lose and nobody to belittle them if they do. The journeyman player of the small club with no fears and responsibilities can turn the game into a lottery: anything can happen, and occasionally the unthinkable does. That is just a part of the magic of the FA Cup.

Tradition is a more tangible thing. In the cup the present can draw on the past as surely as a landlord draws off a pint from a barrel. It is something which creeps into the bricks and mortar of a club, something which sustains and inspires when the moment is right. Yeovil Town, Hereford United, Chesterfield, Wrexham and Exeter City have, over the years, been testimony to this. Clubs such as this come alive when they compete in the FA Cup. It's as if they hear bugles and smell gunpowder. The hills and streets echo with the clamour of battle and they fear no one and nothing. When such clubs meet their so-called superiors, there is no humility. This may well be a romantic view, but there is romance in the FA Cup. That, to me, is what it is all about, and for me the romance endures. The deeds of smaller clubs in the competition enrich and illuminate our dark winter days. A select band of big clubs dominates English football, they are expected to win things and they form an orderly queue as they await their turn; but every now and then in the cup an underdog will cross the game's precisely defined social boundaries. A mouse is heard to roar, and the nation listens. Giant-killing also takes place in the World Cup, the League Cup and every competition devised by football administrators except, curiously, the one competition that is now the Holy Grail for our top clubs, the European Champions League. But shocks in the FA Cup somehow shock us most of all. For me, a competition that can produce such a reaction must always be respected and, above all, preserved.

As a footnote to our success in the FA Cup in 1965, the players did receive their winning bonus, but not the crowd bonus. Sue used some of the money to improve our home, and I treated myself to my first ever car. I bought a Morris 1100, second-hand but in good condition. Such a modest acquisition is a far cry from the Ferraris and Mercedes driven by today's young Premiership players, but I was as happy as Larry with my purchase. No longer would I be referred to in the Anfield dressing room as 'Tommy Smith, the well-known pedestrian'. For Sue and me the idea of taking the car on holiday, or for a drive on a Sunday, delighted us. We were gloriously happy. Life was good.

In between our appearance at Wembley and the game against Inter, Chris Lawler married his fiancée Geraldine. There was to be no honeymoon for Chris and Geraldine though, not yet. What's more, with the Inter game looming, Chris had to spend his wedding night sleeping with me – not in the literal sense I hasten to add. In preparation for the Inter game the team stayed at the Norbeck Hydro in Blackpool. Chris didn't complain about being separated from his wife. Then again, even if he had taken umbrage his protestations would have comprised little more than a couple of words.

Over the years there have been any number of fantastic nights at Anfield, but I doubt there was ever one with such a highly charged atmosphere as the night Liverpool met Inter Milan. Still delirious at having won the FA Cup, Liverpool fans were in fine voice. Anfield was heaving and there didn't seem to be a fag paper's width between the supporters who massed on the Kop and Anfield Road end. Kick-off was 7.30 p.m., but such was the desire to see this game the gates were closed just before six p.m. with a full house of over 54,000 inside. When our team coach arrived at Anfield it appeared a reserve team game was about to take place as there was no one about. As we made our way into the ground Ron Yeats asked a steward, 'Where is everybody?'

'They're in the ground already. They started arriving just after one o'clock. We've had to close the gates.'

Prior to the kick-off, Shanks told the two injured players, Gerry Byrne and Gordon Milne, to go out and walk around the perimeter track with the FA Cup. The sight of Gerry and Gordon with the cup nigh on raised the roof. The noise was deafening. I wondered what sort of effect the crowd and frenzied atmosphere were having on the Inter players. It brought to mind what Wellington said to his generals about his British troops prior to Waterloo, along the lines of: I don't know about the French, but they frighten the hell out of me. I knew the Inter players could hear the noise of the crowd in their dressing room and I hoped the atmosphere our supporters had created would, if not exactly frighten the hell out of them, then have an unsettling effect on their nerves.

Shanks made one enforced change to the team that had won the FA Cup: Ronnie Moran, playing his penultimate game for the club, replaced Gerry Byrne at left-back. As Shanks quipped to Gerry, 'I would have played you tonight, Gerry, son, but someone gave the story of your broken shoulder to the press, so the cat's out of the bag.'

The Inter team carried an awesome reputation. It was star-studded, boasting players of true world class in the Spanish pair Luis Suarez and Joaquin Peiro, the Italian internationals Giacinto Facchetti, 'Bruno' Burgnich, Sandro Mazzola and Mario Corso, and Brazil's flying winger Jair. They were managed and coached by arguably the most celebrated coach in Europe, Helenio Herrera, the Argentine who had implemented a highly effective *catenaccio* system of play. Herrera's version featured a four-, sometimes, five-man defence marshalled by a sweeper, relying on swift breakaways to get a goal. Once Inter took the lead in a game, that was it, they shut up shop, content to absorb and smother every attack that came their way. The system was difficult to play against and dire to watch, but it had brought Inter unprecedented success. They were Serie A champions in 1963, runners-up the following year, were poised to take the title yet again, had reached the final of the Italian Cup, and were the holders of the European Cup and the World Club Championship having recently beaten Independiente. Their pedigree was not in question.

A ferocious noise rocked Anfield when Ian St John got the game underway. The Kop was an undulating swathe of vociferous humanity, the atmosphere inside the ground incendiary. The Inter players must have wondered what the hell had hit them. Roared on by our fans, we took the game to the European champions from the start. Only four minutes had elapsed when Ian Callaghan seized on a pass from Geoff Strong, sped down our right flank and crossed for Roger Hunt to hit a sumptuous volley past Sarti – a technique Roger had worked on and perfected when 'working the boards'. The response of our fans nigh on popped my eardrums.

Many a side would have folded after such an early set-back in such a volatile atmosphere, but Inter, confident of their own ability to ride out storms, refused to be intimidated. They began to probe and prod before offering evidence of their class. A series of one-touch passes were exchanged before Sandro Mazzola was put in the clear to puncture the hysteria on the terraces.

The comparative lull was only fleeting. Just after the half-hour mark Ian Callaghan won a free-kick a yard or so outside the Inter penalty box, took the kick himself and planted the ball in the back of the net. Such was the response of the crowd to his effort, if he had stood for Parliament that night he would have been elected. And five minutes before half-time, Chris Lawler embarked upon one of the attacking sorties he was famous for. He progressed deeper and deeper into the Inter half of the field before rifling a shot from twenty yards that all but ripped the net from its stanchions. Our euphoria, however, was short-lived. The Austrian referee, Karl Krainer, disallowed Chris's effort, ruling Geoff Strong to be offside. Geoff vigorously protested his innocence, but Mr Krainer was having none of it. TV pictures later proved Geoff to be right: he was onside when Chris shot at goal.

We went in search of further goals in the second half but had to wait until the 75th minute before our efforts were rewarded. Ian St John made it 3–1, and minutes later had a header which took the paint off Sarti's left-hand post. Had that gone in it would, I am sure, have spelled 'Goodnight Vienna' for Inter; as it was, our 3–1 victory was sufficient to send us to Milan confident of becoming the first British club to appear in a European Cup Final.

Shanks later went on record as saying that our game against Inter was the greatest night he ever experienced at Anfield, which is saying something. The electric atmosphere apart, I think Shanks singled out the match because it was the first time Liverpool had pitted its wits against the true elite of world football and had not been found wanting. Three days after appearing in the FA Cup Final our performance against Inter raised the bar. We ran the Italian side into the ground and, to be honest, outclassed what was a top-class team. Shanks was delighted. I think he saw this victory as a watershed for the club, a vindication of everything he had done since arriving at what was then a middling Second Division club with a ramshackle set-up and ground. 'Inter have been beaten before,' he told us, 'but tonight, boys, they were defeated. We outplayed one of the best teams in the world. We have arrived.'

In preparation for the return leg we opted to stay at a hotel overlooking Lake Como rather than one in Milan itself. Shanks and Bob were of the mind that we would get more peace and quiet out near the lake, but it didn't quite work out that way. The locals were less than accommodating. On the first night of our stay we couldn't get to sleep because, of all things, the ringing of bells in a nearby church. I don't think anybody wanted to take issue with the church, but the fact that the bells began ringing around ten at night and continued until after midnight made Shanks believe this was more than simply a case of enthusiastic campanologists. The following morning Shanks and Bob walked down to the church and asked to see the monsignor. During their meeting they respectfully asked if he could stop the bells ringing that night so we could get a good sleep. Apparently the monsignor appeared sympathetic but said he couldn't comply with such a request; there would be bell ringing again that night and we would just have to put up with it.

One of the reasons for choosing this particular hotel was that nearby was a football pitch. It wasn't anything special, like a park pitch really, but adequate for light training and practice. Arrangements had been made for us to use the pitch, but on arriving at the designated time we found the grass being cut by a groundsman. We hung about until that job was done, only for the groundsman then to insist on doing some 'vital work' to the pitch itself. Shanks was having none of this. He told us to take to the pitch and, via our interpreter, told the groundsman his 'vital work' would have to wait. It appeared that moves were afoot to disrupt our preparation, but what frustration and annoyance we felt was nothing compared to what was to come.

The San Siro was full to its capacity of 90,000. The atmosphere at Anfield for the first leg had been electric but sporting; the San Siro emanated a different mix. The atmosphere on the night was vicious and poisonous. When Tommy Lawrence took to his goal for the pre-match kick-in, smoke bombs and flares rained down from the stand behind him. Fortunately the distance between Tommy's penalty area and the stands was such that none of these missiles landed anywhere near him, but the smoke they emitted enveloped him in a fug, and it was all we could do to keep Geoff Strong away from it.

Egged on by the hostile crowd, Inter set about trying to retrieve the tie. I had a feeling it was going to be one of those games where controversy was but a single step away, and I wasn't wrong. At the time it was usually the case that match officials handled both legs of a European tie, but for some reason the referee from the first leg, Mr Krainer from Austria, had been replaced by Ortiz de Mendibil from Spain. Krainer had disallowed what we felt was a legitimate goal by Chris Lawler at Anfield, but apart from that the consensus was that he'd had a good game.

Some fifteen minutes had passed when Mr Mendibil awarded Inter an indirect free-kick just outside our penalty area. Mario Corso was standing over the ball and we marked up, naturally expecting him to lay the ball off, or flight it into the box for a team-mate. Instead he curled the ball past Tommy and into the net. The San Siro immediately erupted but I was unperturbed as the ball hadn't touched anyone on its way into the net. It was with utter disbelief that I then saw the referee point towards the centre circle to signal a goal. I joined the rest of the lads in contesting the decision, but Mr Mendibil waved away our protests. To say our bench was animated is putting it mildly. Shanks and Bob rarely, if ever, disputed a decision. Experience had taught them the folly of trying to persuade a match official that he had made an error, but both took to their feet to let their views be known.

At the time there existed an appreciable difference between how rules were interpreted on the Continent and in Britain. Continental football was far less tolerant of physical challenges, which were considered part and parcel of the British game, in particular any contact with the opposing goalkeeper. Conversely, shirt pulling, jabbing fingers into ribs and diving to obtain free-kicks, anathema to our game, met with a benign reaction in countries such as Italy and Spain. So it came as some surprise when Peiro was allowed to level the aggregate score after kicking the ball away as Tommy Lawrence was about to clear it upfield. The incident was very similar to a later one involving Gordon Banks and George Best during a Northern Ireland–England international at Windsor Park. On that occasion, in 1971, Banksy threw the ball in the air and was about to kick it upfield when George flicked it away with a boot and subsequently put it in the net. George never made contact with Banksy at any time, but the goal was disallowed for 'ungentlemanly conduct'. Not only did Peiro kick the ball away from Tommy, he barged into him prior to doing so, but the goal was allowed to stand, which is more than Mr Mendibil would have been doing if I'd had my way.

Our fate was sealed when Inter secured a second successive appearance in the final with what I have to say was a superb goal. Corso and Suarez exchanged a series of passes before the latter found Facchetti on the overlap. He rifled the ball past Tommy Lawrence.

Minutes from time, Cally, Roger Hunt and I combined to set up Ian St John, who swept the ball past Sarti. I jumped in the air like a witch doctor, but my joy was short-lived. Mr Mendibil disallowed Saint's effort. To this day no one knows why, most of all Sarti himself. I saw the look of agony on his face when Saint put the ball in the net; he didn't think there was anything wrong with the goal. But it didn't stand. I was fuming when the match restarted, as were all the lads. Not long after that the game was over, as was our dream.

What happened next I am not proud of. All I can say in my defence is that I saw the red mist. I was walking towards the steps that lead down into the bowels of the San Siro when a bottle came hurtling through the air and smashed at my feet. I looked down, then up, and saw the referee in front of me. Out of pure instinct I kicked him hard on the back of the leg. Strange thing is, he never looked round and his steps never faltered. He just kept on walking and descended the steps without saying a word. That didn't just tell me something, it told me a lot.

I felt we had been dealt a great injustice. Referees have good games and bad games, just as players do. Arguably a referee will make fewer mistakes during the course of a game than a player. Generally speaking, they give what they see, something I was always conscious of when playing. To a man we felt we should have had that place in the European Cup Final. I was sickened as I sat in what was a very depressed dressing room. I turned to Chris and said, 'I would rather we were totally outplayed and lose five-nil, than lose like that.' He agreed.

As we left the San Siro, the football journalist Sam Leitch, who worked for the BBC and the *Mirror*, asked Geoff Strong for an interview for television.

'What did you think of the referee?' asked Sam at one point. Geoff's response was so extreme that Sam's jaw dropped. 'We can't broadcast that. Temper it please, Geoff,' he said, indicating to the camera and sound men that they should keep rolling.

'Yeah, OK,' said Geoff.

'Your impression of the performance of the referee tonight, Geoff?' reiterated Sam. Geoff's second reply was no more publishable than his first. We all felt that two of Inter's goals should never have been allowed, simple as that, and we were not the only ones to question what had gone on. Newspapers placed the referee's handling of the game under a microscope and UEFA conducted a full inquiry, but Mr Mendibil was exonerated and no action taken.

I had completed my first season as a regular in the first team. That alone would have been a source of great satisfaction and pride to me. The fact that I had won an FA Cup winner's medal and appeared in a European Cup semi-final I saw as a wonderful achievement, far more than I had dared hope for. I looked upon it as a sign that my career was really taking off at the highest level. I had always believed I possessed sufficient talent to play top-class football, and now I felt I had gone some way to proving that. But the final fortnight of what had been a long season induced in me marked and contrasting emotions. From the ecstasy I felt at winning the FA Cup and beating Inter at Anfield, my emotions had plummeted to bitter disappointment and anger at the manner of our defeat in the San Siro. They say you never stop learning in football. I was learning not just how to play the game but how to cope with the gut-wrenching emotional roller-coaster football invariably becomes.

5

CREATION OF A FORCE

FOLLOWING OUR SUCCESS IN THE FA CUP I JOINED THE ENGLAND under-23s for a short tour on the Continent. In April I had played against Czechoslovakia at Elland Road. The game ended goalless, and on my return to Anfield Bob Paisley asked for my comments. I remember telling him, 'England are very well organized at the back and don't give much away, but I don't think they have many goals in them.' Truer words have rarely been spoken. We played three matches while on tour which resulted in a 1–0 defeat against West Germany and goalless draws against both Czechoslovakia in Liberec and Austria in Vienna. I was the only Liverpool player in the squad but I knew most of the players and became particularly friendly with the Chelsea quartet of Peter Bonetti, John Hollins, Bert Murray and Bobby Tambling, against whom I had played on several occasions. The squad also included Gordon West (Everton), Alan Ball (Blackpool), Nobby Stiles (Manchester United), Martin Chivers (Southampton), Vic Mobley (Sheffield Wednesday), Mick Jones and Len Badger (Sheffield United), George Armstrong (Arsenal), Bobby Thomson (Wolves) and Paul Reaney (Leeds), all of whom went on to enjoy lengthy careers at the highest level in English football.

It had been a long, hard season but I threw myself into that tour. I am a patriot, and I love my country. Representing England at under-23 level was a source of immense pride to me; I also saw my selection as recognition of the standard I had achieved in my career to date. But I was under no illusions. I knew that in order to cement my place at Liverpool and stay at the top in football I would have to work even harder at my game. As Bob Paisley often said to the players, 'Rest on your laurels in this game and very soon you won't be in the game.'

On my return from the tour, Sue and I enjoyed a holiday before I reported back to Anfield to prepare for the new season. In the event it was not only a new football season I was preparing for. Sue had given me the most fantastic news of my life: she was expecting our first child. I was excited at the prospect and threw myself into prospective fatherhood. The local health authority ran a programme called 'Preparing Men for Parenthood' which consisted of someone taking us to a fourth-floor room and telling us to throw our money out of the window. Joking apart, I enjoyed the course, and when Sue gave birth to our son, Darren, I felt my life was complete. Friends had forever been telling me that life changes with the arrival of a baby. I appreciated this, but it wasn't until Darren arrived that I realized the full truth of those words.

As all new parents discover, everything is turned upside down when a baby comes into your life. I don't think we ever experienced such tiredness as we did in those first six weeks after Darren was born. Sue, of course, took the brunt of it and proved to be a brilliant mother. She had Darren into a routine right from the start, which ensured, more or less, that he slept for the majority of the night – a godsend to me as I had to have a decent night's sleep because of football. There were occasions, however, when it was 'my turn'. This resulted in me doing things which prior to Darren's birth I would never have imagined myself doing: listening to the World Service at one in the morning while giving him a feed; discussing the quality of sleep suits; taking an interest in curtains for the room we had set aside as his bedroom. But life was good. Sue and I felt we were no longer simply man and wife, we were now a family.

While I was away with England under-23s the FA met and sanctioned a Football League proposal to allow substitutes in League games. From the start of 1965–66 managers would be allowed to name one substitute who could replace an injured player at any stage of a game. Geoff Strong, who else, has the dubious honour of being the first substitute ever used by Liverpool, replacing Chris Lawler, who had picked up a minor injury. The season was only a matter of weeks old when managers began to introduce substitutes for other reasons – a tactical change, or to replace a player who was performing below par. If a game was won managers also took to introducing the substitute in the final minutes to reward him for being a good pro and a low-maintenance player – that is, training hard throughout the week and not taking issue with the fact that he wasn't in the starting eleven. The 'reward' was that the substitute then received appearance money, even if he was only on the pitch for a minute. The rule stating that the substitute could only come on for an injured player was therefore soon ignored by managers, match officials and administrators alike. In just about every instance it resulted in the substituted player adopting a limp when he left the pitch in an effort to imply that his manager was complying with the law – and also, I suspect, to salvage some personal pride from the fact that he was being taken off. As you would expect, the FA and Football League turned a blind eye to the manipulating of the new rule but clamped down on minor indiscretions. What's more, their wrath was directed at the smaller clubs rather than the big clubs which might kick up a fuss at being disciplined. Gillingham was the first club to be disciplined for offending against the new substitute rule. They received a fine and a warning for not informing the referee that they had changed their nominated substitute prior to their game at Oldham. And some Gills fans think their club has never made football history.

Liverpool's first competitive match of the season was the Charity Shield against new champions Manchester United at Old Trafford. The emphasis that is now placed on qualification for the Champions League has also had a corrosive effect on this annual 'all for a good cause' private party that unimaginative football writers and broadcasters refer to as 'the traditional curtain raiser to the season'. Liverpool meeting Manchester United in the Charity Shield would be par for the course these days, the only credible alternative contenders being Arsenal and Chelsea. In 1965 the meeting of Liverpool and Manchester United in the Charity Shield was a rarity. As champions in 1964 Liverpool met West Ham United; Burnley, Wolves, Nottingham Forest, Bolton, Everton, Ipswich Town and Spurs had all contested the trophy in previous years. The involvement of such clubs in the Shield indicated that English football was a democracy in which it was still possible for a provincial club – one with the suffix of 'Town', for example – to win a major trophy.

The Charity Shield was usually staged at the home ground of the champions primarily as a reward to the club and its supporters – something the home club invariably recognized by reducing admission prices. In the 1970s the Shield was first staged at Wembley, and admission prices rose accordingly. In recent years the Shield took up residence at the Millennium Stadium before reverting back to the new Wembley. I don't have an issue with this, but why have the marketing johnnies thought it fit to change the name of the trophy to the Community Shield? We are told this was done because match receipts, rather than going to charities alone, also now go to community projects. Has it nothing to do with the fact that the Shield is now less charitably inclined, it being the case that only around a third of the match receipts go to 'good causes'? Officials may argue that this is still significantly better than in the past when the Shield might have been played out to a crowd of

30,000 paying reduced admission, and the trophy did not benefit from TV and marketing promotion which has afforded it greater commercial revenue. It is an argument that holds some water, but one that to my mind does little to lessen the nagging suspicion that the Community Shield might be just another money-making venture for the FA, Wembley and the big clubs.

We drew 2–2 with United. It was not considered vital that there should be a result in such a fixture, so there was no penalty shoot-out. Both clubs kept the Shield for six months. It seemed a charitable thing to do.

A week later we kicked off the season against Leicester City at Filbert Street. Gordon Banks didn't play as he'd broken his wrist in a pre-season friendly, which may have had something to do with the fact that we came away with a 3–1 victory against our 'bogey' side. Curiously for the start of a season, we didn't have a game in mid-week, so it was the following Saturday when we entertained a mid-table Sheffield United at Anfield. It turned out to be a less than auspicious occasion. We lost 1–0, a result that produced another classic piece of Shanks humour. Immediately after the game the secretary of the home club had to telephone the Football League to inform them of the result, goalscorers and attendance. Shanks saw our secretary Peter Robinson in a corridor and asked if he had telephoned yet. Robinson confirmed he had. 'Well, ring them again,' Shanks told him, 'because they won't believe it.'

We salvaged some pride the following Wednesday night with a 0–0 draw in the return fixture at Bramall Lane. I always found it strange to play at Bramall Lane as it was a three-sided ground, the John Street side opposite the main stand accommodating the cricket pitch and pavilion used by both Sheffield and Yorkshire cricket clubs. That Bramall Lane was open and exposed on one side never affected my performance, but it did affect the atmosphere generated by the supporters which seemed, in part, to drift away.

One win, a draw and a defeat was not the best of starts, but we then produced something like the performances we were capable of. A 3–2 win at Blackpool was followed by a 5–1 victory at Upton Park against a West Ham side that included Moore, Hurst, Peters et al. Far and away the highlight of what proved to be a good September in which we lost only one of seven League matches (2–1 at Spurs – that man Greaves again) was the 5–0 hammering of Everton at Anfield. It was Liverpool's highest margin of victory over their Merseyside rivals since the club had returned to the First Division under Shanks, and the result delighted him. Playing for Everton that day was Johnny Morrisey, the player the Liverpool board had sold without consulting Shanks. Johnny was not your archetypal winger, he was a real hard nut who probably hurt more full-backs than hurt him. In my opinion he was something of a bully, and I don't think I was alone in thinking that. Prior to the game, Shanks had taken me to one side. 'We're playing Everton today, Smithy, son,' Shanks said, as if I needed reminding. 'Could get nasty. If you get sent off today, just make sure Morrisey ends up in hospital.' It appeared that Shanks wasn't keen on Johnny either.

As things turned out I didn't get sent off, and Johnny didn't end up in hospital. It wasn't that sort of game. We were up for it, Everton weren't, and we played them off the park, a fact emphasized by a photograph that appeared in many of the Sunday newspapers. It captured the moment of our fourth goal, scored by Roger Hunt. The Liverpool players are full of gritty determination and action, while in the background Everton's Alex Young can be seen standing with his hands on his hips. Evertonians had dubbed Alex 'The Golden Vision' because of his superlative performances. He remains a Goodison Park legend, but when Evertonians saw this shot of him with his hands on his hips as we tore about their penalty area, he took some stick I can tell you.

I managed to get on the scoresheet, opening our account by heading home from a corner. For the record, the other goalscorers on this momentous day were Hunt (two), Willie Stevenson and

Saint, who netted the fifth and final goal. When that goal was scored, one of our supporters created a moment of derby legend and folklore. He ran on to the pitch, presented the Everton goalkeeper, Gordon West, with a handbag and quickly disappeared back into the crowd leaving everybody roaring with laughter, Everton fans included. Gordon was in fact a very good goalkeeper and couldn't have done much about any of the goals that day. I've known many players with a better sense of humour than him, but he needed one in the weeks that followed. Apparently everywhere he went in the city Liverpool fans would come up to him and ask, 'Where's your handbag, Gordon?' The incident was received with humour by the police as well. To the best of my knowledge the supporter in question wasn't apprehended and charged with any offence. It was seen as it was intended, as a light-hearted bit of tomfoolery, with no harm done. I'm not sure that officials today would regard it in the same way. Thank goodness for progress, eh?

Many of the Merseyside groups of the day supported Liverpool. The lead singer of one group, however, Johnny Kidd (Freddy Heath) of Johnny Kidd and the Pirates, who originally came from London, had a liking for Everton. On stage Johnny dressed in costume as a pirate complete with eye patch. Following that crushing defeat of Everton someone in the dressing room mentioned that Johnny Kidd had been at the game. 'Aye, and we gave Everton such a hammering, in the second half he was wearing his patch over his good eye,' replied Ian St John, quick as a flash.

A pleasant diversion from trophy chasing occurred when some Liverpool players were asked to participate in an episode of the BBC sitcom *Til Death Us Do Part*. I mentioned earlier how the two main characters in this comedy, Alf Garnett (Warren Mitchell) and his son-in-law Mick (Tony Booth), were fans, respectively, of West Ham and Liverpool. Johnny Speight wrote an episode which involved Alf and Mick travelling to Anfield for a West Ham game. They boarded the same train at Euston that carried the West Ham team, which offered an opportunity for cameo appearances by Bobby Moore and Geoff Hurst. Alf and Mick were seen attending our game against West Ham in January. That day Peter Thompson had a 'blinder', scoring both goals in a 2–0 win and generally wreaking havoc among the West Ham defence, Bobby and all. I was involved in the build-up to both goals, and lo and behold, when the episode was shown, there I was on *Til Death Us Do Part*. Cut away to Alf screaming, 'Get that Smith, bloody Scouser!' My involvement in the programme was tenuous to say the least, but it's with pride that I lay claim to the fact that I featured in an episode of one of the great British sitcoms of all time.

We made an early exit from the FA Cup in round three when Chelsea beat us 2–1 at Anfield to exact revenge for the semi-final defeat we had inflicted upon them the previous season. As holders, the fact that we had gone out of the competition at the first time of asking was disappointing but tempered by the knowledge that we were contesting the Championship and once again making real progress in Europe, this time in the Cup Winners' Cup.

We could not have wished for a tougher, or more attractive, start to our European Cup Winners' Cup campaign: in the first round we were drawn against Juventus. We lost 1–0 in the first leg in Turin to a goal from Leoncini, but, unlike the game against Inter, we had no cause for complaint. Our preparations and the match itself passed without incident, Juve shoe-horned a goal out of what was a very tight game, and we flew home fancying our chances. In the return leg, goals from Chris Lawler and Geoff Strong gave us a 2–0 half-time lead from which Juventus never recovered. We subsequently accounted for Standard Liège from Belgium and Honved (Hungary) before the semi-final draw produced the tie the British press had been hoping for – Celtic v. Liverpool.

Jock Stein was in the process of creating his great Celtic team. They were on course to win the Scottish League title, which in turn paved the way for their becoming the first British side to win the European Cup. When people talk about big clubs, invariably they are referring to the size of the club itself, financial wherewithal and trophies won. To me, Celtic is one of the really big clubs in world football because every game they play generates a truly big-match atmosphere. Unlike, for example, at Juventus or Ajax. A capacity Parkhead generates a unique atmosphere. It's as if Celtic's history and tradition seep from every brick, acting as a stimulus to supporters whose love and fanaticism for their club are extra-ordinary. The tie was a meeting of two clubs experiencing a renaissance, pitting Shanks against Stein, two good friends. Even at this stage of their managerial careers it was seen as a clash between two of the sages of the game – correctly, as it turned out, two managers on the brink of football venerability.

Parkhead was in full cry. When Stevie Lennox gave Celtic the lead the raucous din of 84,000 spectators could probably have been heard in Edinburgh. Celtic went in search of further goals that would put the tie out of our reach, but never came near to doing that. Having quelled Celtic's thirst for a second we gradu-ally began to assert ourselves, which rendered the home supporters uncharacteristically muted on occasion. Minutes from time, Geoff Strong played in Roger Hunt and only the outstretched leg of keeper Ronnie Simpson denied us what I felt would have been a deserved equalizer. We were satisfied rather than happy to come away from Parkhead with a single-goal defeat. I was confident we could take Celtic at Anfield but felt it would be far from an easy task.

I really enjoyed the experience of playing at Parkhead. Ap-pearing before a massive partisan crowd can be daunting for some players. They become so anxious that they make a tentative start, hoping they will play themselves into the game, or rather that team-mates will help them do it. The crowd and atmosphere begin to get to them and the longer the game goes on the more it becomes an uphill struggle. Rather than being intimidated by a large baying crowd I found I enjoyed the big occasion – in fact the bigger the better. Rather than feeling apprehension before the start of such a game, I couldn't wait to get out and be involved. So focused would my concentration be during a match like this that I wouldn't be aware of the crowd most of the time. But even in total concentration there are times when the noise of a passionate home crowd breaks in; you'd have to be made of stone for it not to. Even the highly charged atmosphere of a Parkhead packed to the rafters failed to unnerve me, however; on the contrary, I felt it gave my game an extra edge.

The Celtic supporters who travelled in their thousands to Anfield did so with a reputation for not being the most tolerant in defeat. Nowadays Scottish football fans enjoy a very good name for sportsmanship and engendering the notion that football is a family game. It is ironic that at a time when hooliganism was rare in football, certain elements of the Celtic and Rangers faithful had a reputation for creating havoc when fuelled with drink. Nerves were on edge on the night, not only those of players and supporters, but the police too. This may have had something to do with the first incident of the night. What was at first thought to be smoke from a fire on the terraces turned out to be nothing more than a large cloud of steam rising off the backs of the rain-soaked Celtic fans in the capacity 54,000-plus crowd. At least that was the interpretation reached by the police. Given the sheer volume of beer and spirits Celtic fans had taken on to the packed terraces, the presence of so much steam may not have been entirely the result of collective body heat causing rainwater to condense.

The first half was evenly contested and tight; we knew we had to be patient. With half-time approaching we were awarded a free-kick some twenty yards from goal. As the Celtic defence organized itself I noticed a gap and fancied my chances. Having picked my spot, to the delight of the majority in the crowd I had enough composure to drive the ball low and hard past Ronnie Simpson. In the 67th minute, Geoff Strong, limping due to a cartilage injury, headed home a cross from Cally to send our supporters wild with excitement and Liverpool a step nearer a first

European final. Celtic, however, were far from done. Minutes from time Joe McBride had the ball in our net, only for both the referee and linesman to rule offside. It was then that it began to rain bottles.

There was no doubt in my mind that the goal was offside. The Celtic players' questioning of the decision was half-hearted, and the following day's newspapers were in agreement: the referee had been right to disallow the goal. A good many Celtic fans, however, were incensed by the decision and they gave vent to their ire by throwing beer bottles on to the pitch. And I am not talking half a dozen – they came down in their hundreds. Unfortunately those hurling them from the back of the Anfield Road end couldn't reach the pitch and many Celtic supporters at the front of the stand suffered head injuries. For a few minutes chaos ensued. The police swarmed on to the terrace as we players stood agog, wondering what the hell was going to happen next. After five or so minutes order was restored and players from both teams helped our groundstaff remove the bottles to the perimeter track. It was as we were doing this that Ron Yeats turned to me and said, 'Hey, Tommy, tomorrow morning you and me'll come and collect all these bottles and take them down the offy. There's threepence on each of them. There's so many we'll get more than our bonus.'

I don't know exactly how long there was to go when the bottles started to cascade on to the pitch, but I suspect it was longer than the one minute subsequently played by the referee. I have no proof, but I was of the mind that he curtailed the game for fear of more trouble erupting. Celtic players accepted the final whistle without any qualms, and needless to say, so did we. We were through to the final of the European Cup Winners' Cup, Liverpool's first appearance in a European final – which co-incidentally meant a return to Glasgow.

Over the years I became good pals with a number of the Celtic players and have appeared at occasional dinners and charity functions with Billy McNeill, the Celtic skipper that night.

Without fail, whenever Billy and I meet, he always says the same thing: 'Hey, Tommy, you do know it was onside.'

My reply never varies: 'Offside, Billy. Every newspaper and book agrees.'

'Had a great view of it,' he'll say.

'From fifty yards away?'

'Forty. Don't exaggerate.'

Borussia Dortmund had accounted for holders West Ham United in the other semi-final, winning 2–1 at Upton Park and 3–1 in Dortmund. Their line-up included goalkeeper Hans Tilkowski, Sigi Held, Lothar Emerich and Hans Libuda, all of whom would figure prominently for West Germany in the 1966 World Cup Finals. No exaggeration, we dominated the game, but time and again Tilkowski denied us; on the occasions when he was exposed, Kurrat and Paul came to his rescue. Dortmund weathered the storm and against the run of play took the lead when Emerich, scorer of four against West Ham, played a glorious through-ball to Held, who lived up to his name by holding on to the ball as he rode a challenge before coolly slipping it past Tommy Lawrence.

Rather than it being a balmy night as you sometimes get in early May, the weather in Glasgow was wet and windy. The famous 'Hampden Swirl' – the stadium's cavernous bowl causes the wind to circle the pitch in gusts – prevented either side from producing classic football. Undaunted, we kept plugging away, and our pressure bore fruit when a scramble in the Dortmund box ended with Roger Hunt prodding home an equalizer to send the final into extra time.

To be truthful, though we had Dortmund on the rack for long periods, we were not playing to standard. At times we lacked our usual edge and appeared disjointed. Even so, I still thought we were going to do it as we had restricted Dortmund to swift break-aways. But it was from one such attack that they delivered the killer blow. Emerich and Held combined well before the latter found Libuda wide on the right. Whether Libuda meant it as a cross or a shot I don't know, but he lobbed the ball towards our far post and it sailed over Tommy's head. Ron Yeats had a lot of ground to cover and made it up, but in attempting to head clear he could do no more than help the ball into the net. My heart momentarily sank.

In the minutes that remained we gave it everything we had but, as they had on all but one occasion, Dortmund kept us at bay. When the final whistle blew I glanced across at Ron. His face sported a deeply agonized look; he gave a deep sigh, then his upper body seemed to collapse and he bent forward so much I thought his head would touch his knees. Ron's body language said it all. For a second time in as many seasons we had experienced the unpalatable taste of bitter disappointment and frustration with a major European trophy within our sights.

Following defeat to Dortmund we had one League match left to play, away to Nottingham Forest, and there was cause for celebration on the night as we had already wrapped up the League Championship. Following our faltering start we had chipped away at points before hitting a rich vein of form that saw us embark upon an unbeaten run of eighteen matches that lasted from late October until late February when, surprisingly, we went down 2–0 at Fulham, who were battling to avoid relegation. Thereafter we lost only one of our remaining ten matches, against Burnley, with whom we were contesting the title along with Leeds United, Manchester United and Chelsea. Our form saw us pull away from our rivals to clinch the Championship six points ahead of Leeds, who denied Burnley the runners-up spot on goal average. I was elated to have played my part in helping Liverpool win the Championship. I was tasting success in my career, I liked it, and I wanted more. As Ian St John said the night after the Forest game, 'Success in football isn't everything, but it's a long way ahead of what comes next.'

Unthinkable as it would be today, Liverpool used only fourteen players throughout the entire season. Gordon Milne and Geoff

Strong often vied for the number four shirt, though Geoff's versatility also saw him deputize in the odd game for Chris Lawler and Willie Stevenson. Alf Arrowsmith played three matches, on two occasions replacing Roger Hunt when he was on England duty, and Bobby Graham made one appearance. Apart from that it was the team that ran off the tongue like a familiar nursery rhyme. To be honest, but for the occasional injury and Roger Hunt's selection for England, I doubt whether Shanks would have made any changes to the team in the course of a season that comprised fifty-three competitive matches. I was also proud to have played for England under-23s and for Young England against the full England team at Stamford Bridge in what had become an annual meeting on the eve of the FA Cup Final.

Nothing, however, could match the euphoria I felt at helping Liverpool win their second Championship in three seasons. My progress and development had coincided with those of the club itself. You must never stand still in football, and my career, the team and the club were forever developing as Shanks and Bob worked to realize their ambitions for Liverpool. Shanks's attention to detail continued to be phenomenal. Certain aspects of the game which might have been overlooked at other clubs were considered to be of vital importance by Shanks and Bob. For example, we would spend time working on throw-ins, and once it had been established what should be done we were expected to stick to it. When taking a throw-in we were told never to throw the ball above knee height to a team-mate; that way he could control the ball or lay it off with one touch. If the player taking the throw-in wanted the ball returned, then and only then was it OK to throw the ball at head height. In order to play a team-mate into space from a throw-in we had a simple ruse. The Liverpool player wanting the ball from a throw-in would run up to the team-mate about to take the throw and shout, 'Leave it! I'll take it.' Thinking this player was about to take the throw, the opposition would leave him be, only for the player to carry on running down the line and receive the ball from the designated taker of the throw.

In winning the Championship we conceded thirty-four goals, which was the lowest total in the entire Football League. At a time when the emphasis was on scoring goals and not conceding them, thirty-four goals was considered a meagre tally against. It was also a time before detailed match statistics were compiled, but Frank Butler of the *News of the World* wrote a piece commenting on how few goals we conceded from free-kicks from which the opposition would invariably be caught offside. One of the reasons for this was that Shanks and Bob had Ron Yeats give us a call. We would mark up the opposition on the edge of our penalty area while Ron's eyes were trained on the member of the opposition about to take the free-kick. A split second before he made contact with the ball, Ron would call 'Out!' or some other one-word code. Immediately we heard this we would all run forward, leaving our opponents in off-side positions just as the ball was kicked. We might not catch everyone offside as opponents would run with us, but invariably one would be caught out, and one was enough. It was a simple tactic, but it worked many times in our favour.

Shanks and Bob never complicated matters. Their ideas were simple but highly effective. Over a period of time the more of these ideas we incorporated into our play, such as the taking of throw-ins and defence of free-kicks, the more we appeared to outsiders to have adopted a distinctive way of playing, which led to football writers suggesting there was 'a Liverpool way'. In some respects they were right, but really there was no conscious effort on the part of Shanks and Bob to create a system of play unique to us, it was just attention to detail and applying ourselves to basics.

As you will need no reminding, that summer England won the World Cup. Like everyone else, I was overjoyed. I was pleased for Alf Ramsey: through my involvement with the under-23s I had got to know and respect him. I was also delighted for my Liverpool team-mate Roger Hunt, who I felt had played well throughout the competition, and for Ian Callaghan who, lest we forget, featured in the group stage.

As a result of England's success, the FA Cup Final that year between Everton and Sheffield Wednesday is often overlooked. Which is a shame as it was one of the best finals staged at Wembley, and I was lucky enough to be there to see it. Liverpool and Everton players may have been adversaries on the field, but we were good friends off it. With some of the other lads I went down to Wembley to offer the Everton lads some encouragement. At one point they appeared in need of it too, irrespective of the source. Trailing 2–0, things looked bleak for Everton, but they stormed back to beat Sheffield Wednesday 3–2. Derek Temple's winning goal followed a mistake by Wednesday's Gerry Young who took his eye off the ball when taking a simple pass, which resulted in the ball slipping under his boot. Temple was on to it like a flash and the cup, as well as the Championship, was Mersey bound.

Young's error emphasizes my earlier point about the Cup Final acting as a microcosm of a career. Gerry Young gave years of sterling service to Sheffield Wednesday, but for many, all he is remembered for now is that one mistake he made at Wembley. On the other side of the coin, Everton's hero that day was Mike Trebilcock, a somewhat mediocre player who had sensationally been included in the team at the expense of Everton's England centre-forward Fred Pickering. Trebilcock justified his inclusion by scoring the first two Everton goals. Largely as a result he continued to ride high in the affection and estimation of Everton fans, even though the rest of his career more accurately reflected his usual form: little over two years after being Everton's Wembley hero, Mike found himself playing for Torquay United reserves in the Western League.

Everton's success in the FA Cup led to the very first Merseyside-contested Charity Shield. Usually the fixture was staged at the home of the League champions, but such was the desire of people to see the game that it was switched to Goodison Park, whose capacity was some ten thousand more than Anfield. If our supporters and, more recently, those of Everton had found FA Cup Final tickets hard to come by, those for the Charity Shield were even scarcer. Despite a capacity of nigh on 65,000 and no 'neutrals' to carpetbag tickets, thousands of fans were still disappointed. It seemed that everyone in the city wanted to see the local derby featuring the League champions against the FA Cup holders. Indeed, that summer the whole country was football mad.

England's success in the World Cup buoyed not only English football but the nation. In the 1950s, referring to the general lifestyle of the population, Harold Macmillan told us that we'd never had it so good; that may have been true then, but in 1966 it appeared life was even better. Industry was booming, particularly the motor industries based in Merseyside, the West Midlands and East London, whose manufacturing output struggled to meet demand. The Mini is synonymous with the sixties, but family saloons such as the Ford Cortina and Morris 1000, while they didn't have the iconic status of the Mini, proved more popular with working people who now had the financial wherewithal to buy a car. Traditional industries such as coal mining, steel, shipbuilding and fishing, though not of the strength they had been in the past, were by and large still thriving. New industries, which had prompted Harold Wilson to talk of 'Britain's white hot technological revolution', were beginning to make an impact. Britain was the hub of popular culture, particularly where music and fashion were concerned. The Beatles, about to enter their 'All You Need Is Love' phase, still reigned supreme. Britain seemed to be blossoming and prospering, and England's World Cup success added to a feeling that the country was on the up. As George Harrison replied when asked by a music journalist why he continued to live in England where he paid 90 per cent tax, 'Because England's where it's at.'

As far as football was concerned, Merseyside had come to

epitomize the success English football was now experiencing. The two major domestic trophies had taken up residence in the boardrooms at Anfield and Goodison, and the World Cup went on show too. Before the Charity Shield, the skippers, Ron Yeats and Brian Labone, led a unique lap of honour. They carried the League Championship trophy and FA Cup, won by their respective clubs, while Roger Hunt and Ray Wilson, England team-mates that summer, proudly displayed the World Cup. The 65,000 crowd at Goodison Park that day not only basked in the goldleaf sunshine, they also basked in the glory of the teams they supported. The game itself was played in a great spirit. It was competitive and entertaining, and from our point of view it produced the right result, a goal from Roger Hunt ensuring that our season got off to a good start.

Sitting in the stands that day was a fifteen-year-old trialist from Glasgow whom Shanks was very keen to sign. The lad stayed a fortnight at Anfield, played a game for our B team against Southport, and impressed everyone, but homesickness got the better of him. Much to the disappointment of Shanks and Bob, he decided to go back to his native Glasgow where he returned to junior football before eventually signing for Celtic. It would be another eleven years before Kenny Dalglish returned to Anfield.

Two days after our success in the Charity Shield, Everton signed Alan Ball from Blackpool for £110,000. The transfer was a record deal between British clubs, and as Alan was one of England's World Cup heroes the story made headlines in all the newspapers. Shanks was never happy when a good news story from Goodison dominated the back pages, nor was he enamoured with Alan's reported comments about being delighted to have joined such an ambitious club as Everton. Having read the reports of the deal, Shanks felt Alan needed to get matters into perspective, so he took it upon himself to ring him.

'Congratulations, Alan, son,' said Shanks. 'You're going to be playing your football next to the greatest club in the world.'

This was no throw-away line from Shanks. He firmly believed it to be true.

Shanks also believed that his Liverpool team were good enough to win the Championship again. In the first weeks of the 1966–67 season several top First Division clubs went the way of Everton, spending heavily to strengthen their teams. Spurs signed Welsh international Mike England for £95,000 from Blackburn Rovers; Arsenal paid £50,000 to Chelsea for George Graham and Tommy Baldwin, and £55,000 for the Huddersfield full-back Bob McNab; Sheffield Wednesday secured the services of John Ritchie from Stoke City for £75,000; and Chelsea used part of the fee received from Arsenal for Graham and Baldwin to pay Aston Villa £100,000 for Tony Hateley – a world-record fee for a non-international player. Another centre-forward renowned for his prowess in the air, Wyn Davies, joined Newcastle from Bolton for £85,000. At the time these were all substantial transfers. Interestingly, three of the top teams, Manchester United, Leeds and Liverpool, seemed happy with their squads and didn't add to them.

That is not to say that Shanks was totally inactive as far as transfers were concerned. There was one position he was keen to improve upon. Tommy Lawrence was a good goalkeeper, but when news broke that Leicester City was willing to sell Gordon Banks, Shanks was keen to buy. Banksy had emerged as one of the best goalkeepers in the game and would eventually be widely considered number one in the world. He was one of England's World Cup heroes too, and seemingly Leicester were looking to cash in on their prize asset; they felt they had a ready replacement in teenager Peter Shilton.

Shanks met with the Leicester directors and Banksy and a fee of £60,000 was agreed, which at the time was a world record for a goalkeeper. Banksy was more than keen to come to Anfield, so it seemed a done deal. When Shanks returned to the club, however, matters changed. Banksy was surprised and disappointed to receive a call from Shanks to say that the Liverpool board had refused to pay the money. Big fees for goalkeepers were unheard of at the time, basically because although many directors understood what a top centre-forward could bring to a team, they didn't appreciate the worth of a top-class goalkeeper. Shanks tried to persuade the Liverpool board that Banksy's contribution would be worth every penny of the £60,000 as he could 'save' Liverpool some twenty goals a season, but to no avail. The deal fell through, and Liverpool missed out on one of the greatest goalkeepers of all time.

It seems that directors of other clubs did not appreciate the true worth of a goalkeeper either. Following Shanks's failure to persuade our board to part with £60,000, Banksy then had talks with both Manchester United and West Ham but a deal never materialized – and it wasn't because of Banksy's wage demands. To the consternation of most people, but particularly Banksy himself, he stayed at Leicester until March 1967, when Stoke City manager Tony Waddington paid the club the asking fee.

It is incredible to think that England's number one had trouble getting fixed up with a new club; no less incredible is the fact that Shanks failed to land his man. I say this because by this time Shanks really had a position of authority within the club. The board recognized what he had achieved in turning the club around, so to this day I can't understand how he didn't persuade them to part with the money for Banksy. After his retirement, Shanks gave an interview to John Keith of the *Daily Express* in which he said, 'We had a great team in the sixties. If I had been allowed to sign Gordon Banks when he was available, or if Ray Clemence had matured as a goalkeeper at that time, then we'd have won the European Cup and all the cups under the sun.'

As I said, Tommy Lawrence was a good goalkeeper, but not quite as good as Banks or Clemence. I believe Shanks was probably right in thinking that had Liverpool had a world-class keeper in the late sixties we would have won numerous trophies. Though we were always to be there or thereabouts in domestic football and a force to be reckoned with in Europe, further trophies eluded us until 1973. But it would be wrong of me to put Liverpool's dearth of success in those years simply down to the lack of a world-class goalkeeper. Other factors were to have a telling effect.

It has often been said that England's success in the 1966 World Cup signalled a glorious new dawn for English football. In truth, it was a sunset. England's success in 1966 was really the culmination of the revolution that had taken place in the English game following the watershed defeats against Hungary in 1953. Gradually, over thirteen years, English football had removed its head from the sand and caught up with developments in world football, particularly where coaching was concerned. Come 1966, England proved they were no longer the pupils but once again the masters. Tottenham Hotspur had offered a broad hint of what was to come in 1963 when they trounced Atlético Bilbao 5–1 in the 1963 European Cup Winners' Cup Final, becoming the first British team to win a major European trophy. Liverpool too had played a part, reaching the European Cup semi-final and the final of the Cup Winners' Cup. English football was waking up, once again becoming a force to be reckoned with.

But the age of innocence, of cavalier, attacking football, was over. It wasn't the fault of Alf Ramsey that just about every manager and coach at every level of football copied his tactics. Alf had chosen a system he believed would win the World Cup for England, and he was proved right. Irrespective of whether such a system suited a certain team or players, many managers and coaches slavishly adopted 4–4–2 or 4–3–3 thinking it was the road to success. After all, what better example was there to follow than that of the world champions?

The tectonic plates of English football shifted seemingly overnight; the emphasis changed from scoring goals to not conceding them. In the season immediately prior to the staging of the World Cup, the one in which Liverpool won the Championship, 1,458 goals were scored in the First Division. The season after England's success the number of goals scored in the First Division was marginally down at 1,387; thereafter there was a season-on-season decline. In 1969–70, 346 fewer goals were scored in the First Division than during the season immediately preceding the 1966 World Cup.

To be fair, teams had already started to become better organized and the number of goals scored in the First Division and in the Football League gradually decreased throughout the sixties. But England's World Cup success, which inadvertently implied the success of 4–4–2, served to hasten the move towards less adventurous football. It is something of an irony that a World Cup Final that produced six goals should be partly influential in bringing about a more defensive-minded approach to the game.

Still, the winning of the World Cup was unquestionably the greatest event in the history of English football. It was the staging of the World Cup, however, that was to have the greatest impact on the game in this country. The final of 1966 was the first to be globally broadcast on television, the first to have a structured commercial and marketing strategy. The seeds of football's commercial potential had been planted, and gradually the clubs themselves began to take tentative steps towards this new land. In the World Cup's wake even matchday programmes changed. The World Cup produced glossy editions full of photographs. Supporters' expectations rose as a result, which marked the demise of the simple eight-page programme that easily fitted into your coat pocket and contained few, if any, photographs.

The patriotic and fervent support England had received also seemed to influence young supporters. Supporting your club became more tribal. After the World Cup singing on the terraces began to take on a more sinister tone. This was not simply down to football, of course. Society rapidly changed in the sixties, and by 1966 the decade had already taken on an identity of its own. Life in the sixties was not, as current makers of TV documentaries of the period would have you believe, all about peace, love and harmony. Those of us who lived in the sixties can testify that very few people were hippies. There was, however, rebellion by the young in the form of rejection of most things traditional. People's expectations rose, as did their standard of living and disposable income; consumer goods became readily available and, more importantly, affordable. No one unquestioningly trusted the pillars of society any more; the establishment, particularly Government and Church, had been shown to be just as fallible as and certainly no better than the man in the street. In general a more cynical, harder attitude began to prevail, which became more pronounced in the 1970s. Football reflects society, so the culture of the game began to change too. Come the end of the sixties, for example, those Liverpool fans who had congregated on the Kop in 1964 wearing collar and tie to the match and happily singing 'She Loves You' and 'You'll Never Walk Alone' were something of an anachronism. What's more, the days when opposing supporters happily mingled together on the terraces were over.

I'm not sure how much Liverpool the football team was affected by all these changes, though. Led by Shanks, respect, integrity and hard work remained the watchwords; and during the late 1960s, when the art of the winger became nigh on extinct, Liverpool proved an exception to the rule. In Cally and Thommo we continued to play with two wingers, albeit Cally would, in time, evolve into a midfield player. That is not to say we ever stood still, though. On the contrary, Shanks and Bob Paisley were forever introducing new ideas, some of which, however inconsequential they might have appeared to other managers, they considered of vital importance.

Our pre-match preparation was certainly always very important as far as Shanks was concerned. He had us stay in a hotel on a Friday night prior to home games, usually the Lord Daresberry in Warrington. I might eat an early evening meal with Sue and

Darren, join the team at Anfield, and we would set off for the hotel around eight p.m. At the hotel there would be tea, toast and honey for those who wanted it, then it was off to bed. We of course stayed in a hotel for away games too, but for some time our results in London had not been brilliant, which caused Shanks to look for possible reasons. One conclusion he arrived at was the amount we ate on the train journey down to Euston. As I said, I always played on an empty stomach and was even careful about what I ate the day before a game, but when travelling to London some of the lads would take afternoon tea on the train, then dinner at our hotel in the evening. Shanks was of the mind that this was too much food. To combat this Shanks devised a new routine. We began to take a later train on which we only had a cup of tea. The menu for our evening meal at the hotel was set by Shanks, and for years it never varied: a starter of tomato soup, followed by a choice of a main course comprising boiled fish, steak or chicken with a choice of green vegetables, no potatoes or chips allowed; for pudding we had fresh fruit either straight from the bowl or in the form of a salad – no cream. It was a menu not dissimilar from what top players eat today before a game, which to me shows again that Shanks was a man ahead of his time. There would be no more food until morning when a light breakfast was taken. Following our evening meal we were allowed to go out to catch the early evening showing of a movie at the cinema. On leaving the hotel, without fail Shanks would say, 'Hey, boys, no stomach scratches at the pictures.' Which meant no popcorn, ice cream or hot dogs. We would return to the hotel around 9.30 and had to be in bed for ten. Whether this new routine had anything to do with the fact that our results in London did improve I shall leave up to you, but improve they did.

When we were at home, Shanks wanted the opposition to feel uneasy about playing at Anfield, and he did all manner of things to ensure this happened. When leaving the dressing rooms you descended a flight of stone steps that led to the tunnel and the pitch. Directly above these steps Shanks arranged for a sign to be erected on the wall comprising the club badge and the simple message 'This Is Anfield'. Footballers tend to be a superstitious lot and we soon took to laying our hands on the sign as we descended the steps in the hope it would bring us luck; but that was not the reason Shanks had had the sign erected. He was well aware of the reputation of our supporters, particularly those on the Kop, and he wanted our opponents to read the sign and be in awe of Anfield, its atmosphere and the noise as they took to the pitch; he felt it might produce one or two nerves. Again, a very minor thing, but anything, no matter how small, that might give us some sort of edge was important to him, and he was never afraid to tinker with the status quo in order to gain that edge.

Shanks always tried to make a point of welcoming the opposition when they arrived. Of course his reasons for doing so had little to do with hospitality, more with winding them up or making a certain player feel uneasy. Shanks was highly respected for his knowledge of the game, in particular the worth of players, and he would play on this when greeting our opponents. Once he confronted Bobby Charlton.

'How're ye feeling, Bobby, son?' asked Shanks.

'Fine, Bill,' replied Bobby.

'Are you sure, son?' queried Shanks. 'Because you're not looking your normal self. A bit pale.'

Bobby assured Shanks he was fine.

'Good to hear you're OK, Bobby, because I was getting a little concerned about you when I saw those beads of sweat on your brow. You've been cooked up on that bus. God knows what germs circulate.'

'I think I'm OK,' said Bobby, now without great conviction.

'You think? Do you want me to get our doctor to check you over?'

Bobby declined and reiterated that he was feeling fine. Twenty minutes later Joe Fagan saw the United club doctor enter their dressing room.

On another occasion Shanks greeted Fulham's Johnny Haynes with the words, 'Johnny, it's an honour to welcome you here, you were a truly great player!'

On those occasions when he couldn't be there when the opposition arrived, Shanks would hand the door steward a box of toilet rolls with the instruction to hand one to each member of the opposition as they entered the ground. On hearing from the steward that this had been done, Shanks, Bob, Joe Fagan and Reuben Bennett would titter away, delighted at the effect their mischievousness might be having.

People talk about 'the Liverpool way of doing things' and there was once an article by football writer Frank McGhee in which he asked, 'What is the magic of Liverpool's enduring success as a team?' The short answer to that is there was no magic. It was simply common-sense football, attention to detail, and team effort. Shanks and Bob brought us up not to worry too much as individuals. Roger Hunt wasn't expected to win games on his own. Likewise I knew I wasn't expected to defend on my own. You may think that comes straight from John Cleese's 'school of the bleedin' obvious', but it's what I mean when I say we played 'common-sense football'. We all had individual jobs to do within the team, but Shanks expected us to share responsibilities as well as the ball.

One of the key things we tried to do was give every player a touch of the ball as soon as possible after kick-off. Shanks believed that if every player got an early touch and did it right, we'd all start on the right footing. We were encouraged to do the simple things and to be patient, especially if a goal hadn't materialized. The number of goals Liverpool scored in the final ten minutes of games was remarkable, testimony not only to our fitness and application but also to our patience. 'Be as patient as a graveyard,' Shanks once told us.

If we lost a game – and we didn't lose too many – there would be a discussion, but on Monday morning at Melwood, when everyone was relaxed, less emotional and more rational. These days the prevalent attitude is that you can only learn something after losing a game, but we had any number of lengthy discussions in the big lounge at Anfield during which we learned more from having won a game, such as how to play Roger Hunt in from a certain position, or how effective it was to have Geoff Strong hanging about outside the penalty area at corners so that he could pick up a loose ball or poor clearance to keep the pressure on.

Shanks and Bob wanted the players to be confident, but not over confident. As Shanks said on more than one occasion, 'Over confidence is a form of ignorance.' Above all we had confidence in one another as footballers. I would sit in the dressing room before a big game, look about and think, 'I'm glad we have Chris, Gerry and Big Ron. Roger Hunt and Saint are always likely to score. Cally and Thommo, I feel good with those on either wing . . .' and so I would go on. Roger Hunt told me he would do a similar thing, thinking along the lines, 'I'm glad Smithy is in this dressing room not the one next door.' We knew one another's strengths and patterns of play, we knew what was expected of us in certain situations, and we knew our individual roles within the team. There was no magic. When you know these things football is, as Shanks always maintained it to be, a simple game to play.

Like England in the 1966 World Cup, we had a simple system that enabled us to play. It was easily identified by other managers and coaches, but this never bothered Ramsey or Shanks. In fact, Shanks wanted our system and style to be readily identifiable as it acted as confirmation that we all knew what we were doing. The problem the majority of managers and coaches had was preventing us from carrying out our jobs successfully.

We began the 1966–67 League programme with a 3–2 victory over Leicester City at Anfield. Having scored the winning goal in the Charity Shield, Roger Hunt took all of ten minutes to open his League account, our other goals coming from Geoff Strong and Willie Stevenson. The following Wednesday summer was still very much in evidence, and on what was a sultry August night at Maine Road we went down 2–1 against Manchester City. Three days later Everton gained revenge for us having defeated them in the Charity Shield, winning 3–1 at Goodison. I scored our goal just before half-time but felt no sense of consolation. I hated losing at the best of times, but losing to Everton was worst of all. Defeat at their hands lingered in my system more than defeat against any other club. It seemed to affect me in all manner of ways. Normally I enjoyed reading the Sunday papers, for instance, but following a derby loss I could barely face them. I just had no interest in reading, even the non-sports sections, as I knew lurking elsewhere within the pages was a reminder of the match.

Whenever Liverpool lost, particularly to Everton, I couldn't wait for the next game to come along and the opportunity to rid my system of the taste of defeat. When Manchester City were beaten 3–2 at Anfield I felt a whole lot better, and that general feeling of well-being continued as Liverpool posted good results well into the New Year. In fact after that day when Everton beat us we lost only three of the next twenty-eight League matches. The highlight of this run was a 5–0 hammering of Leeds United at Anfield in mid-November before a crowd of 54,000. At this stage of the season Manchester United, Nottingham Forest, Spurs, Leeds and ourselves had formed a breakaway group at the top of the First Division. The 5–0 win did not, of course, decide anything, but it did give our title aspirations an extra lift. No one had inflicted such a heavy defeat on Don Revie's team since their return to Division One in 1964. Confidence in the camp was sky high.

In addition to the Championship and FA Cup we were also contesting the European Cup. Shanks saw these three competitions as 'priority', which is why we had once again not entered the League Cup. (Incidentally, only two teams declined to enter the League Cup in 1966–67, ourselves and Everton. As it was a relatively new competition, there was little incentive for the bigger clubs to enter as a matter of course. It was only when in 1966–67 it offered entry to the UEFA Cup that it really began to appeal.) First up we were drawn against the Romanian side Petrolul Ploesti. Little was known about them as a team, or Ploesti as a place, so Tom Saunders, a member of the training staff, was sent on a recce. Ploesti is in the heartland of Romania's oil and petrochemical industry, hence the 'Petrolul' part of the club's name. When Tom returned, Shanks asked him what sort of place Ploesti was. 'It's a bit like Ellesmere Port,' said Tom, 'but without Ellesmere's glamour.'

The first leg took place at Anfield. Gerry Byrne had sustained a cartilage injury in our opening match of the season against Leicester City, so his place was taken by Bobby Graham. Sadly Gerry's injury proved a very serious one that entailed a lengthy spell on the sidelines. Indeed we worried that he might never fully recover. Goals from Saint and Ian Callaghan gave us a 2–0 lead to take to Romania.

It was only my second trip behind the Iron Curtain, the first having been to Hungary when we played Honved in the Cup Winners' Cup. Shanks was always on his guard when we played in Europe, particularly so when we visited Eastern Bloc countries. To be blunt, he didn't trust them to be honest and upfront, often rightly so as it turned out. Prior to leaving Liverpool for Ploesti we were told only to drink bottled water or Coca-Cola, and, when dining, preferably to have the bottles opened at our tables. This was to ensure that the contents hadn't been tampered with, or in the case of water that tap water hadn't been used. When we sat down to dinner on our first night at our hotel, Shanks said he had ordered Coca-Cola for every player. Halfway through the main course he noticed there was no Coca-Cola on our tables, and came across to ask why we hadn't been served our drinks. Ron Yeats informed him that we had ordered Coke but had been told by the manager the hotel didn't have any. Shanks smelled a rat and immediately requested the presence of the manager, who repeated what he had told us. His hotel had no Coca-Cola. Shanks eye-balled the man, who began to shift uncomfortably and avert his gaze, which seemed to confirm Shanks's suspicions. Without saying another word, he pushed the manager to one side and made a beeline for the kitchen. Two minutes later he emerged carrying a case of Coke.

'What's this then?' demanded Shanks. 'No Coca-Cola? You're a cheat and a liar!'

Shanks placed the case of Coke on a table and said, 'Help yourselves, boys.' As he was saying this he caught sight of the hotel manager trying to slope out of the dining room and was on to him like a shot.

'Oh no you don't, I'm not finished with you yet,' he roared at the now quivering man, 'Telling my boys you had no Coca-Cola when it had been ordered and paid for. Now I'm going to make you pay for your cheating.'

The manager was literally shaking in his shoes.

'You're a disgrace to your party and you will be punished,' Shanks continued. 'I'm going to report you to the Kremlin!'

The second hint we had that Ploesti were not to be genial hosts occurred when we arrived at their ground, the Municipal Stadium. When we walked into the dressing room we found it had not been cleaned after a previous game. The room was littered with strips of bandage, elastoplast, lint, soiled towels, tea cups and clumps of mud. Shanks walked into the bath and toilet area and immediately ordered us back out to our coach, the reason for which became clear when he took the Ploesti officials to task. 'The toilets are clogged with human waste,' he told them forcefully. 'The dressing room is a disgraceful mess. What I have seen is degrading. It's totally unacceptable. Now, you either get some people in there to clean up or we are going home, and I shall report this club to UEFA and FIFA.'

We got back on the coach. Fifteen minutes later a very penitent Ploesti official boarded the bus accompanied by someone from UEFA. We were told that everything had been cleaned and disinfected and were asked to return to the dressing room. Shanks and Bob, still distrustful, went off to inspect their work. A few minutes later they returned, told us everything had been done to their satisfaction, and we disembarked for a second time.

Whether it was a genuine power cut or another ruse to try to unsettle us I don't know, but as we prepared for the game in our dressing room the lights went out and never came back on. Whatever the reason, this only served to convince Shanks further that any trip behind the Iron Curtain would result in Machiavellian behaviour on the part of the locals with a view to disrupting our preparations.

For this return leg Willie Stevenson replaced Bobby Graham at left-back, Willie's place in midfield being taken by a fit-again Gordon Milne. Otherwise the team was the usual suspects. Petrolul Ploesti proved to be far more difficult opposition on their own turf. Goals from Moldoveanu and Boc restored the tie to parity, and when Willie put through his own goal, things looked decidedly dodgy. We didn't panic, though. We remained patient and were rewarded for our endeavours on the night with a goal from Roger Hunt which made the aggregate score 3–3.

The following week we met again in a play-off in neutral Brussels. I sensed the Romanians believed they had missed their chance at home; certainly Ploesti proved to be far less potent away from home, and we were more dominant on the night than the 2–0 scoreline suggests.

On 7 December we travelled to Amsterdam to play Ajax. As I've already mentioned, Liverpool never paid too much attention to the opposition. We knew little about Ajax other than that they were an emerging team and a very talented one. This proved to be an understatement. That night, for the first time under Shanks's management, Liverpool hit a football juggernaut.

Fog as thick as elephant's phlegm engulfed the Ajax stadium. From the halfway line it was impossible to see either goal. We expected a postponement, but the game went ahead, only for the fog to become worse. The weather had nothing to do with our performance or the result, though. Quite simply, Ajax were outstanding on the night and we were blitzed 5–1. Their team featured Suurbier, Nuninga, Swart, De Woolf and a young player whose skills dazzled even on such a murky night, Johann Cruyff. They were a super side playing what would come to be known as 'total football'. From the start they never allowed us to pass the ball, and before we knew where we were, we were trailing 2–0.

We went all out in attack in an attempt to get back into the game, which produced an extraordinary sight. The fog was so thick by this stage that you couldn't see the touchlines, let alone our bench. As we pushed on I had moved up to the halfway line. I glanced across to my left and through the gloom could make out an approaching figure. At first I thought it was one of our lads, but as the figure got closer I was astonished to see it was Shanks on the pitch. 'Tommy, get Stevo and Geoff back here,' he shouted. 'We've got another game to play in Liverpool. It's not even half-time. Batten the hatches.' With that, he disappeared back into the gloom. The fog had rendered visibility so poor that the referee and linesmen didn't see Shanks running on to the pitch. I called for Willie Stevenson and Geoff Strong to drop back and we made a good attempt to batten the hatches, but to no avail. Prompted by Cruyff, Ajax set about us in no uncertain fashion and scored a further three goals. Chris Lawler managed to pull one back, but I can't tell you anything about it because I didn't see it. That night we underwent a unique experience: we trooped off the field as weary and defeated as characters in a Chekhov play.

In the dressing room after the game Shanks said, 'Haphazard play, boys. That's what it was, and it has cost us dear.' Then he added, 'Tonight we met a real class act. That boy Cruyff, he's some player.' It was unheard of for Shanks to compliment a member of the opposition. Due to the fog he couldn't have seen much of Cruyff, but what he had seen had impressed him greatly. Still, that didn't stop him being characteristically bullish during the post-match press conference. 'We have a tough job on our hands,' Shanks said at one point. 'Five-one down, but we will turn it around.' I think he believed it too.

A miracle was not forthcoming. In the second leg at Anfield Peter Thompson crashed a shot against the Ajax bar in the opening minutes but Cruyff again gave a peerless performance, scoring twice, a feat matched by Roger Hunt. The 2–2 scoreline was respectable enough, but the fact that we lost 7–3 on aggregate hit home hard.

As the shockwaves reverberated across Merseyside, we held a meeting to discuss what had gone wrong. Everyone had a say, but Bob Paisley summed it all up: 'Bottom line, we came up against what is going to be the best team in Europe. They played a type of game we haven't seen before. They didn't so much give us a football lesson as reinforce what we already know. To be successful, we have to keep learning and developing as a team. We're doing that, so we're on the right road.' We were on the right road, but it wasn't paved with gold, not yet.

Following our ignominious exit from the European Cup we concentrated on the League and FA Cup. In the latter, having disposed of Watford and Aston Villa we met Everton at Goodison in round five. A crowd of 65,000 were present, the atmosphere electric, as it always was on the occasion of a derby. There was little to choose between the two teams until Alan Ball pounced to score the only goal of the game and cement his reputation as the doyen of the Gladwys Street end.

That left the League, then, and thankfully the run of only three defeats from twenty-eight matches put Liverpool among the pacesetters in Division One. In mid-March we were second in the table, a point behind Manchester United with eleven matches remaining. It was then that we went off the boil, winning only two of those remaining games.

The injury to Gerry Byrne gave us a problem at left-back. Bobby Graham, who was really a winger, Stevo and Geoff Strong were all asked to play there, but when it had become apparent that Gerry was struggling with his knee, Shanks decided to go out and buy. In late February Liverpool paid £60,000 to Blackpool for Emlyn Hughes, the player whose voice sounded like a bowl of Rice Krispies. Ours was a happy dressing room, everyone got on, but only a matter of days after his arrival I had an uneasy feeling about Emlyn. I hadn't taken to him, and I wasn't the only one. There was something about Emlyn's personality and character that didn't rest easy with me. He came across as being full of cheer and bonhomie, but something inside told me it was all a front.

Emlyn played in ten of our final eleven matches, but it was purely coincidental that his presence in the team saw us winning just two of those games and, as a consequence, falling away badly in the race for the title. Easter is always crucial so far as trophies and relegation issues are concerned, and in 1967 three games in four days sorted the men out from the boys. Our programme began with the visit of fellow title contenders Manchester United. What should have been an exciting near-climax to the season proved something of a damp squib, the game ending in an uneventful goalless draw. We then met Arsenal in the first of a 'double header' and fared no better. After another disappointing 0–0 draw at Anfield we went to Highbury the following day and could do no better than 1–1. On the plus side we had remained unbeaten over Easter, but the reality was that three points from a possible six lost us ground to United, Forest and Spurs. More daylight was put between us and the Championship in our next match when we were beaten 2–1 at White Hart Lane – that man Greaves yet again with both goals. Victories over Newcastle and Sheffield United did little to restore our title credentials as sandwiched between those results was a surprising 1–0 defeat at home to West Brom. Two defeats and a draw in our final three matches saw us slip to a final position of fifth, which was respectable, but given that we had at one time been very much in the frame it was seen as a disappointing finale to the season.

Football was changing, as I have said. It was gradually becoming a more cautious game, but free-flowing, cavalier football was still alive and well in some quarters. Interestingly, it was the teams of those four good friends and revered figures in the game Bill Shankly, Matt Busby, Jock Stein and Bill Nicholson that continued to play attacking football when many sides appeared happy for matches to become a battle for midfield domination. When Celtic beat Inter Milan to win the European Cup, no one was more pleased than Shanks: the Scottish club's victory was a triumph for attacking football. Shanks, Busby and Nicholson were guests of Stein at the final. After the game Shanks went up to Stein and said, 'John, you're immortal.' In football terms, that is exactly what Stein had become. In time, so too would Bill Shankly.

6

SO NEAR YET SO FAR

AS PART OF OUR PREPARATIONS FOR 1967–68 LIVERPOOL RECEIVED invitations to play pre-season matches from both West Germany and Romania. For some reason Shanks wasn't keen on the latter, and he declined. It was an unwritten rule that politics and religion were never spoken of at the club, as Shanks and Bob believed such talk would always lead to problems. As Shanks once said, 'The word "politics" is derived from two words, boys. Poly, meaning many, and tics, meaning small blood-sucking insects.' Over the years, though, I gained the impression that Shanks was a socialist, but also that his idea of socialism was far removed from that practised in Iron Curtain countries. As Liverpool established itself as one of the leading lights in football, the club received many invitations to tour Eastern Bloc nations, but we only ever went there when we had to.

All our hard work was done pre-season. Training at Melwood was intense and physically demanding. Once the season got underway, due to our busy fixture list daily training was light as Shanks believed we would only need a rigorous session every four to six weeks in order for us to maintain maximum fitness and stamina.

Training over, we set off for West Germany where we were to play three pre-season friendlies. This was a time when clubs played such matches purely and simply as a way of getting players match-fit for a new season. Unlike today there were no commercial reasons for these trips, other than the fact that the club received a fee based on the gate money. The West German clubs provided us with testing opposition, which was good preparation for the season ahead. Some clubs began their pre-season by playing Scandinavian teams, which invariably resulted in walk-over victories. Shanks never saw the point of these games. He and Bob were always keen for us to play top-quality Continental teams, not only because the experience might be useful to us in European competition, but also because they hoped to learn something new in the way of tactics or preparation. Shanks and Bob preferred us to play in West Germany if possible not only because of the quality of the opposition and the facilities on offer, but also because the Bundesliga had been underway for some three weeks. Playing against teams that were match-fit was considered the ideal way for us to achieve our required level of fitness. The tour was deemed a success.

We began the season with a new signing: Tony Hateley (father of Mark) joined us from Chelsea for a fee of £96,000, at the time a record for Liverpool. Tony was a tall, powerful centre-forward who was a tremendous header of a ball. We opened with a goalless draw at Manchester City, followed three days later by a 2–0 victory over Arsenal at Anfield. The following Saturday we entertained Newcastle United, who themselves had a great header of the ball in Wyn Davies. We set out to play to Tony's strength, hitting high crosses and long balls, and it paid off handsomely: we beat Newcastle 6–0 and Tony scored a hat-trick, our other goals coming from Roger Hunt (two) and Emlyn Hughes. We again played the long ball up to Tony at Highbury in our next match but it didn't produce the goods. Arsenal's central pairing in defence, Ian Ure and Terry Neill, had the measure of him and we suffered our first defeat of the season, losing 2–0.

As the 1967–68 campaign unfolded I began to have doubts about the way Tony's playing style fitted in with the team. We were a passing side, but he needed deep crosses and high balls. We tried to persevere with this, and I'm not saying it was always unsuccessful; in fact Tony scored two hat-tricks for us that season. But, as one Liverpool fan put it, 'Like Douglas Bader, brilliant in the air but no good on the ground.' I felt that we might be compromising the entire team's style to get the best out of one player, but we got on with it and waited for Shanks's verdict.

In 1967–68 we played a total of sixty-three competitive matches and I featured in all but four of them. The ones I missed were due to injury, fortunately nothing serious. All told, Liverpool used seventeen players during the course of the season. The performances and versatility of Emlyn Hughes meant that Willie Stevenson played just one league game, against Wolves in November, in which he scored. Three weeks later he was sold to Stoke City for £48,000. It was very unusual for Shanks to sell a player to a rival First Division club. That he sold Willie to Stoke was, I think, not so much because he felt Willie could no longer do a job for us – indeed, Willie went on to make another 108 appearances in the First Division in Stoke's colours – but that the job was being done better by Emlyn Hughes. Shanks liked Willie as a man and appreciated what he had done for Liverpool; he wouldn't have denied him an opportunity of continuing to play First Division football once Stoke showed an interest. Shanks could be ruthless at times, but he was not so mean or small-minded as to sell a player who had given him and Liverpool sterling service only to a lower division club rather than a rival in the First Division.

Having entered the League Cup, the fact that we were also contending the Inter-Cities Fairs Cup meant that Liverpool were in pursuit of four trophies. I didn't think it possible for us to win all four, but I was hopeful of at least one.

For the duration of the season we were very much in contention for the League title. It evolved into a battle between Merseyside,

Manchester and Leeds. The two Manchester clubs, the two Merseyside clubs and Leeds slugged it out at the top, pole position exchanging hands from September until the penultimate game of the season. The First Division proved very competitive that year. Following our 2–0 defeat at Arsenal in late August we put together a run of four or five good results only to lose after that. Our best sequence of results was in mid-winter when we went ten games without defeat, although five of these were drawn. It was a pattern replicated by the other pacesetters. No one appeared able to string a lengthy run together, all of which made for a dramatic tussle at the top of the table.

We continued to chip away at points but endured a harrowing time of it at Easter, traditionally the time when title aspirations are enhanced or conceded. We went into the Easter programme of three games in four days on the back of three successive victories: Burnley had been beaten 3–2 at Anfield, Sheffield Wednesday 2–1 at Hillsborough, and then we recorded what we believed was a crucial 2–1 win at a packed Old Trafford, courtesy of goals from Ron Yeats and Roger Hunt. That victory knocked United off the top. They were replaced by Leeds, whom we trailed in second place by a single point. Then, what was seen by our fans as an easy start to the Easter programme on Good Friday proved anything but. Sheffield United were struggling at the foot of the table and in real danger of relegation, but we contrived to lose the game 2–1. It was not only a shock result, it dented our title hopes. The following day we overcame dogged Sunderland resistance at Anfield, winning 2–1 thanks to two goals from Roger Hunt in between which a teenaged Colin Suggett scored for the visitors. On Easter Monday we could do no better than a 1–1 draw at Sheffield United after having taken the lead courtesy of a penalty from Geoff Strong. Three points from six saw us lose ground to Manchester United, who enjoyed 4–0 and 3–0 victories over Fulham, and a 2–2 draw at Southampton. Manchester City also slipped up, winning only one of their three games and suffering two defeats.

Leeds looked strong: they beat Coventry and Spurs, although they lost at White Hart Lane (dare I say it, Greaves again), while Everton hung on to everyone's coat-tails.

With six games remaining it was anybody's title, but we stuttered and stumbled towards the finishing line. We received a massive setback to our Championship hopes on 20 April when we lost 1–0 at West Ham, only to bounce back to beat Fulham 4–1 at Anfield. One-nil up at home to Spurs on the 29th, Jimmy Greaves got out of our sight for just a few seconds, but you know Jimmy, that's all he needed, and a 1–1 result saw United and City draw away at the top.

We gave it our all at Leeds on 4 May and it proved good enough, goals from Chris Lawler and Bobby Graham effectively ending their title hopes and keeping ours alive. We now had two games remaining, at home to Nottingham Forest and away to Stoke City, whereas both United and City had one each. Our final match, at Stoke, was due to take place on the Wednesday following the final Saturday of the season, but chances were it would all be sorted before then.

On that Saturday morning it was, as usual, very tight at the top. Manchester City on fifty-six points headed the table on goal average from neighbours United, with Liverpool third on fifty-three but with that game in hand. In order to take the Championship we had to win our remaining two matches and hope that both City and United lost. For United to secure a second successive title they had to beat lowly Sunderland at home and hope City did no better than a draw at Newcastle United.

Our destiny was not in our hands, but stranger things had happened in football so we set about Nottingham Forest in no uncertain terms. Ian St John gave us the lead just after the half-hour mark and Tony Hateley made it 2–0 three minutes later. An excited buzz ran around Anfield as the terrace's jungle telegraph spread the news that both United and City were losing. We may have been two goals to the good, but it wasn't our style to sit back at home and protect a lead. We went for the jugular and beat Forest 6–1.

The City and United games were featured that night on *Match of the Day*, but I doubt many United fans tuned in. In what was a sensational result at Old Trafford, Sunderland beat the home side 2–1. No less sensational was the fact that Manchester City had stormed back at St James's Park to beat Newcastle 4–3 to become champions. The best we could hope for now was the runners-up spot, but on the Wednesday night at the Victoria Ground the drive was missing from our game and we lost 2–1. It had been a case of so near yet so far, something which was to epitomize Liverpool's fortunes during this period.

Manchester United compensated for missing out on the Championship by beating Benfica to win the European Cup, thus ensuring that the trophy stayed in Britain. United had a wonderful team containing the 'Holy Trinity' of Bobby Charlton, George Best and Denis Law. I was particularly pleased for Bobby. He was a good friend, and still is. United's success was a personal triumph for Bobby as he was one of the survivors of the Munich disaster. Shanks was delighted for his pal, United manager Matt Busby. The pair came from the same coalfield country in Lanarkshire, as did Jock Stein. The trio had an affinity with one another: they were managers who paid attention to detail but who could also view a wide horizon. When referring to this trio people invariably recall the great players they had in their teams. One of the great strengths they shared, however, was the ability to magnify the talents of what otherwise might have been quite ordinary players by the standards of their respective clubs. Geoff Strong and Tommy Lawrence at Liverpool; the full-back pairing of Tony Dunne and Shay Brennan at United; Ronnie Simpson, John Hughes and Bertie Auld at Celtic, to name but a few. Shanks, Busby and Stein had patience and faith in players prepared to slave away at their good points and work tirelessly to improve the weaker aspects of their play – that is, those players who were prepared to listen and learn – and they

reaped the benefits of that. The flair they shared for making footballers understand and accept the rightness of what they said and
then discover a new belief in themselves is, to my mind, one of the
hallmarks of a great manager.

Football writers claimed it was the most exciting end to a title
race for years, and they weren't wrong. After congratulating
Manchester City, some offered sympathy to Liverpool and United
for having been denied glory on the final day. I didn't quite see it
that way. Championships may be clinched on the final day of a
season, but they are won or lost back in November, January or
whenever. We had done well in the so-called 'crucial' games
against our fellow title contenders City, United, Leeds and
Everton. Of those eight games we lost just two, at home to United
and away to Everton. Our downfall was dropping points against
teams who were struggling near the foot of the table.

A meeting was held and various reasons put forward as to why
we had dropped 'silly' points. Gerry Byrne had come back and
played twenty-seven matches, but his presence in defence was
missed while he was recovering from injury. Though nobody said
as much, I think everyone felt Gerry was now not the same player
he had been prior to his injury; there were occasions when he
appeared to be struggling to get through ninety minutes. On
medical advice, he reluctantly retired prematurely from the game.
Gerry was a superb full-back, a key member of the team, and his
absence from the side was to prove a big loss. Tony Hateley had
finished as second leading goalscorer in the League with sixteen,
behind Roger Hunt (twenty-five). He had done well, but Shanks
and Bob were now of the mind that his style wasn't for us, and as
I stated earlier, I agreed with that. We had persevered with high
crosses and long balls into Tony, but often that led to us losing
possession, not least because Tony wasn't great at holding the ball
up and laying it off. As Tommy Docherty, who had been his
manager at Chelsea, remarked in his 2006 autobiography, 'Tony's
passing should have been labelled "To whom it may concern"'.

Against Sheffield United at Anfield such a situation had resulted in United breaking and scoring. The same had happened at Leicester when high balls into their penalty area were won by John Sjoberg which resulted in their winger, Mike Stringfellow, breaking and scoring both their goals. Nobody blamed Tony because we were a team and we shared responsibilities. Likewise no one was looking for excuses, only for reasons as to why we had come unstuck in certain games, particularly against lowly opposition.

Tony is a decent guy, but I did have a run-in with him that season, during a five-a-side at Melwood. What's more, my dusty with him occurred when I was trying to act as a peacemaker. I played a one-two with Saint, who subsequently scored. Tony retrieved the ball and, somewhat peeved that his side had conceded a goal, whacked it upfield. Saint was walking back towards our half and the ball hit him on the back of the head like a house brick fired from a cannon. I can't remember if Tony laughed or we all laughed, but Saint's Scottish blood boiled over. He would still have gone mad if Tony had been his best mate, which he wasn't.

'You idiot!' he shouted. 'It's a pity you can't be as accurate with the ball at ya feet on a Saturday!'

Tony, possibly believing that his size (and that of his fee) was the only thing that mattered in a situation like this, countered by saying, 'Who the hell do you think you're talking to?'

Saint didn't wait to give him an answer. He was straight in there, and the two began to wrestle.

I knew I had to put a stop to it before the situation escalated, so I got in between them and pushed them apart, saying, 'Hey, come on, it's only a five-a-side between team-mates.'

Tony suddenly turned his aggression on me. 'Who do you think you're pushing around?' he snarled, squaring up to me.

'If you want to find out, I'll show you,' I told him.

I was bigger than Saint but still short on inches on Tony. When he made for me, I lunged forward, or rather I jumped up, and nodded him. Saint and some of the other lads then jumped in and pulled us apart before it went any further. I turned away just in time to see Bob Paisley walking towards us. Satisfied that the confrontation had died down, Bob stopped in his tracks and returned to the group of players he was working with.

In my opinion the big fee that had been paid for him had given Tony an inflated sense of self-importance. He felt he could do what he liked. It took that ruck on the training ground to put him right. Don't get me wrong, though: I still see Tony from time to time, we always get on, and we have a laugh about that dusty. He realizes now that such overheated confrontations were part and parcel of life at Liverpool. Shanks, as I said, didn't frown on them, he encouraged them. When Bob returned to the Melwood building where Shanks was waiting, Shanks asked, 'Everything all right out there?'

'Yes,' Bob replied. 'Just another quiet day at the office.'

Shanks offered Bob a knowing smile.

To be honest, Tony did OK at Liverpool. He scored sixteen goals in thirty-eight League matches and twenty-seven in total. This included a hat-trick in the 6–1 win over Nottingham Forest and four in the fourth-round FA Cup replay against Walsall. In the third round we'd been drawn away to Bournemouth. A crowd of over 24,000 packed into Dean Court and witnessed what was almost one-way traffic. We battered the Third Division side, but an inspired performance from their defence, in particular goalkeeper Roger Jones, frustrated us and the game ended goalless. Over 54,000 attended Anfield for the replay, and Tony opened the scoring with an archetypal soaring header. As Cally said, 'When he came back down to earth there was snow on his head.' Further goals from Thompson, Hunt and Lawler saw us comfortably progress.

After disposing of Walsall we travelled to Spurs for what the newspapers referred to as a 'plum tie'. Again Tony was on the scoresheet in an exciting 1–1 draw (do I have to tell you who scored the Spurs goal?). The replay at Anfield produced another cracking match. Roger Hunt gave us the lead, Cliff Jones equalized, then, in the 78th minute, we were awarded a penalty. I had scored twice from the spot earlier in the season and had no qualms about stepping up to take another. Happily, I sent Pat Jennings the wrong way and Liverpool into round six.

West Bromwich Albion had a very good team at the time. In Jeff Astle they boasted a centre-forward who was every bit as dangerous in the air as Tony Hateley. The difference was that Jeff could do a bit on the ground as well. A goalless draw at the Hawthorns was followed by a 1–1 draw at Anfield (Hateley). Nigh on 57,000 attended the second replay at neutral Maine Road. Again Tony scored, but West Brom ended our cup dream, winning 2–1. They went on to beat Everton in the final.

In spite of his goals, Shanks and Bob reluctantly came to the conclusion that Tony was not quite right for Liverpool, and that the following season we would be better off reverting back to the three Ps – passing, possession and patience. Tony was soon on his way.

It was after that West Brom game that I became involved in a post-match farrago involving the police, or rather a certain policeman. We were all very disappointed to have lost to Albion and I was sitting disconsolately in our dressing room when there was a knock on the door. One of the lads answered and said, 'There's a copper wanting to see you, Tommy.' I had a cousin, Lawrie, who was a policeman. I assumed he had been at the game and wanted to have a word about the match, so I stepped out into the corridor. I was confronted instead with a policeman I didn't recognize, helmet under his arm and his bike leaning against the wall. I asked if I could help him and his reply astonished me.

'At around 9.15 p.m. this evening I was patrolling the perimeter track when you came across to take a throw-in,' he said in a dead-pan voice. 'You were heard to shout, "Chris, give me the fucking ball." I am cautioning you for use of foul and abusive language in a public place.'

I thought it was a wind-up arranged by one of the lads, and replied, 'It's a good job you weren't in earshot when their second goal went in.'

I smiled, but he wasn't smiling.

'You are Tommy Smith?' he asked.

I confirmed the fact.

'Mr Smith, I am arresting you for use of foul and abusive language.'

'To a team-mate?' I enquired incredulously.

This was no wind-up, the guy was serious. I had taken my boots off but was still wearing my strip, so when the officer made to take me by the arm I ducked my head back into the dressing room and shouted for Shanks.

'What's going on?' he asked when he joined us in the corridor.

I told him.

'Who are you?' asked the policeman rather curtly, shooting himself in the foot in the process.

Shanks took a step back, a look of amazement, surprise and indignation on his face.

'Who am I? Who am I? I'm the manager of this football team. But never mind who I am, who the fucking hell are you?'

'Are you in charge of Tommy Smith?' asked the constable. 'Because I've just arrested him for using abusive language during the game.'

'You've what?' roared Shanks.

The constable began to repeat his story but didn't get very far.

'You listen to me, son,' said Shanks through gritted teeth, the forefinger of his right hand wagging furiously, 'if you don't fuck off, I'll . . . I'll . . .'

I was on tenterhooks, eager to hear what drastic damnation might befall this pettifogging policeman.

'I'll let the tyres down on ye bike!' said Shanks eventually.

It wasn't exactly the retribution I had been hoping for.

'Stop making a fool o' yoursel' and go about proper police

business,' he continued, aware that in light of his letting-down-tyres comment the situation was in need of some gravitas.

It was then that the Manchester City manager, Joe Mercer, appeared in the corridor. Joe calmly walked up to us and asked the policeman to step outside for 'a word'. It transpired that the City winger Mike Summerbee had been through the same farce a few weeks earlier with the very same constable. Shanks knew the assistant chief constable in Manchester and was all for ringing him up and taking the matter further, but Joe told him it wasn't worth it as the situation could become protracted. Instead he proposed a simpler solution, one he felt would put an end to the matter there and then. I had to go outside, apologize to the constable, and say, 'I didn't realize the pitch was deemed a public place.' That sated him, and after advising me to be more careful in the future with my language to team-mates, with a nod of his head he took hold of his bike and wheeled it away.

'Policemen, bloody useless!' said Shanks when I returned to the dressing room. 'They have two on the door of Ten Downing Street and that Prime Minister still gets out!'

Our hopes of winning the Fairs (UEFA) Cup were also dashed. Having disposed of Malmö in round one, we thrashed 1860 Munich 8–0 at Anfield, rendering the 2–1 defeat in the second leg somewhat academic. We had high hopes of progressing further, especially when we were pitched against Ferencvaros of Hungary in round three, a decent side but hardly one of Europe's heavyweights.

When I travelled abroad with Liverpool I would often look to buy a little present for Sue and my mum, but, as on the occasion of our visit to Romania, this proved easier said than done in Budapest. I went out for a walk around the shops with Ian St John and Ian Callaghan, but buying a gift proved impossible as the shelves were nigh on empty. What few items were in the shops were food basics. I remember thinking, 'If this is communism, it doesn't work.'

During our walk we got chatting to a local guy. We were talking about the situation in his country, and at one point he said it was better now than in the past. 'A few years ago, after the uprising, if I was seen talking to you, I would be arrested and shot, but not now. They don't shoot citizens now.' When we got back to our hotel, we bumped into Ron Yeats and some of the other lads who had also been for a walk.

'The shops have nothing in them,' remarked Ron.

'It's even worse than that,' replied Saint. 'They've run out of bullets as well.'

The Ferencvaros team included Hungarian internationals such as right-back Novak (how we wished the left-back had been called 'Good': would anyone have feared the footballing abilities of Novak 'n' Good?), Havasi, Szucs, Szoke and Varga. They were an experienced side in European competition and displayed as much, beating us 1–0. I wasn't too upset, though, confident that we had too much quality for them to cause us problems at Anfield. But on the night the Hungarians shut up shop, content to soak up all our pressure. What's more, we fell for a sucker punch when Branikovitz scored following a breakaway. To lose 2–0 on aggregate was hard to take, particularly as we had totally dominated the second leg. Once again shockwaves reverberated across Merseyside.

Pipped for the Championship and unsuccessful in the cups – not the season we had hoped for, but at least it had its lighter moments. As long as I live I will never forget Tony Hateley scoring against his former club, Chelsea. The ball came across the edge of the six-yard box some nine inches off the ground. From where Tony was it would have been a simple matter of extending a leg and guiding the ball into the net with a boot, but he chose to dive and head the ball. He scored, but Anfield didn't know whether to cheer or laugh.

Another humorous moment at Anfield took place during our 2–0 win over Leeds United in December. Roger Hunt had put us ahead in the match, and a minute or so before half-time a bout of pressure ended when Gary Sprake gathered a cross from Cally. We fell back and Leeds pushed forward as Sprake, with the ball in his hands, prepared to throw it out to his full-back. But as he arched his arm behind him, he appeared to change his mind. He brought the ball towards his chest, lost grip of it, and the ball sailed behind him and into the net. I couldn't believe what I had seen, and neither could Anfield because for a moment there was silence before the ground erupted with a mixture of cheers and laughter. I remember Jack Charlton looking up wondering why on earth the crowd was behaving this way. He then spotted a disconsolate and embarrassed Sprake retrieving the ball from the back of his own net, and asked, 'What the hell happened?' Jack really didn't have a clue. He raced up to the referee, Jim Finney, and asked, 'What are you giving?'

'Goal,' said Jim. 'No other decision to give.'

Jack was fuming, but not with Jim. He made a beeline for Gary, only to be stopped by Norman Hunter, who grabbed him by the arm and pulled him back before he could do his goalkeeper any harm. As Norman told me some years later, 'I'll never forget that game. There was the most bizarre goal I ever experienced in my career, and I saved Gary Sprake's life!'

Within a minute of this bizarre incident the Kop struck up with a rendition of Des O'Connor's 'Careless Hands', which was the cue for the match officials and both teams, with the exception of Gary, to burst into laughter. The incident was captured for posterity on TV. As one would expect, it has subsequently been shown countless times, which served to give Gary a reputation among supporters as the clumsiest of goalkeepers. To be fair, he was a very good goalkeeper who in addition to turning in many fine performances for Leeds won thirty-seven caps for Wales. Gary learned to live with the consequences of his faux pas, and even to laugh about it too. His autobiography is entitled *Careless Hands*. Now there's a guy who faced his demons and stared them down.

Following our draw at Anfield against West Brom in the replayed FA Cup tie, Ian Callaghan gave a post-match interview for the BBC during which Kenneth Wolstenholme asked for his view of the game. 'It was a typical cup tie which produced some super football from both sides,' replied Cally. 'The supporters really got value for money tonight. I really enjoyed it.' We *did* enjoy the match. It was a cracking game of football. At the time we were involved in a battle for the League title, we'd been involved in Europe, we'd played eight FA Cup ties and now had to play another, but note, Cally never bemoaned the fact that a second replay against West Brom was an irritating addition in what was a very hectic season. Quite simply he, like the rest of us and every player of this period, loved playing football. We would rather play games than train, the more games the better. Even in a period when goals were fewer in number than in previous seasons, players still went out to entertain and derived enjoyment simply from playing the game.

I can't help but wonder if current Premiership players would give the same answer. For all their riches, how many of them do you see appearing to enjoy themselves on the pitch? How many do you see laughing during a game? I wonder what sort of reaction a mistake such as the one Gary Sprake made at Anfield would induce in today's players. When the Kop sang 'Careless Hands' we were laughing, but so too were the likes of Billy Bremner, Norman Hunter, Paul Reancy and Jimmy Greenhoff; even Jack saw the funny side eventually. I can't imagine Premiership players laughing in response to the crowd singing a funny song. When I was playing there was an affinity between players and supporters. Even top players lived in the same road as fans of their club. To take a dive when a goalkeeper came out at your feet would bring a rebuke from your own supporters as well as those of the opposition. Cheating was anathema to the majority. Shanks pilloried anyone he even so much as suspected of trying to gain an advantage by cheating. 'It's a stain on your ability as a footballer,' he once said.

'It tells me you don't have the skill and technique to overcome opponents in accordance with the rules of the game. So to me, anyone who cheats is not a quality player.'

I didn't earn a fortune when I was a player; even at this stage of my life I still have to work. But I'm glad I played in the era I did. The game was more physical, but even the artisans never complained; they accepted tough challenges as part and parcel of football. They were certainly OK by Shanks, as long as they were fair. My game was more physical than most, but what endeared me to Shanks and Bob, and many supporters, was the fact that I could also play, and without exception I always played for the shirt and the true enjoyment of the game. Of course I took my football very seriously, but there were times when I also laughed, not only at the expense of opponents but, on occasion, at myself. I remember once against West Ham trying my luck when the ball was cleared out of their penalty box. My shot sailed so high over the bar it nearly cleared the stand. I stood staring at the trajectory the ball had taken and chuckled at my own ineptitude. Bobby Moore walked past me and said, 'Typical centre-half's effort. In the same situation, I usually knock the hands off the town hall clock.' We laughed together. It saddens me that for all the wonderful players that grace the game today, that rarely happens now.

As was always the case, pre-season training at Melwood in the summer of 1968 was hard work. I was looking forward to the new campaign, determined to continue the good partnership I had formed with Ron Yeats in the heart of our defence. As part of our training, Shanks asked a sprinter to come down to Melwood and pass on some tips and technique (his tips were useful, but somewhat wasted on me as I had never been blessed with pace). I can't recall this guy's name: what I do remember was him being knackered at the end of one of our sessions. The training he underwent for sprinting was totally different to how we prepared for football. Our training was intense and had a lot to do with running, twisting and turning. The sprinter couldn't cope with it, which proved to me that when it comes to training for sport, it's a case of 'different strokes for different folks'.

A relatively recent addition to our squad was goalkeeper Ray Clemence, whom Liverpool had signed from Scunthorpe United for £18,000 the previous summer. Ray was brought in as understudy to Tommy Lawrence and would have to wait until 1970 before establishing himself in the first team. Though he had only been at the club for a year, I sensed Ray had all the makings of a top-class goalkeeper, though when he first saw him Shanks had had his doubts. Having been alerted to Ray by one of our scouts, Shanks and Bob had taken a trip to Scunthorpe to see the young man in action. Bob was keen, but Shanks noticed that Ray kicked the ball with his left foot and threw it with his right hand. For some reason Shanks found this disconcerting, but he was eventually convinced by Bob that such an idiosyncrasy would not affect Ray's development.

In keeping with other clubs at the time, Liverpool did not have a specialist goalkeeping coach. Ray began to learn his trade at Anfield by working with the man he hoped he would one day succeed, Tommy Lawrence, and occasionally Bob and Reuben Bennett. Ray learned from Tommy how to look after himself as a goalkeeper: this was a time when a forward had greater licence to 'let the keeper know he was there'. Tommy also taught Ray how to deal with one-on-ones. Tommy was one of the very best in those situations; he was rarely beaten when having to come off his line to deal with a rampaging opponent, and his timing was spot-on. He always stood and made himself as large as possible, which was easier for Tommy to do than Ray! Ray proved an excellent pupil, and in later years he proved himself adept at one-on-ones.

Once again we made a good rather than spectacular start to the season, with two victories, a draw and one defeat from our opening four matches. On 24 August Sunderland visited Anfield; we were sixth in the table with our visitors one place above. (Incidentally the match programme for this game referred to the last reserve team game, at Anfield against Leeds United, and made an appeal for fans to get along and lend their support as the attendance for the Central League fixture was a mere 6,812!) The team that faced Sunderland was, by and large, as it had been for some years, the exceptions being Peter Wall at left-back for the still-injured Gerry Byrne, Emlyn Hughes for Willie Stevenson, and Tony Hateley at centre-forward, Saint having assumed the number ten shirt from Geoff Strong (in the event Tony left the club a couple of weeks later and Geoff returned to the fold).

Football may have changed in the sixties, but not the composition of teams. Managers picked what they believed to be their best eleven and, barring injury or suspension, stuck to it, not only on a weekly basis but often for a number of seasons. That is not to say that there were limited opportunities for emerging players though; if anything there were more opportunities for homegrown youngsters than there are today, yours truly being a case in point. Patience was the key. A youngster had to exercise it, buckle down and continue to learn. If he was deemed good enough, his chance would eventually come, and when it did he had to seize it with both hands. Managers might have been reluctant to chop and change the side but that is not to say they would not take a risk on a youngster. In keeping with just about every team, if Liverpool weren't in contention for the Championship at the end of the season Shanks would play one or two youngsters in the final games to give them some experience and a chance to show what they could do. Today, when Premiership clubs receive millions of pounds according to where they finish in the table, managers are naturally reluctant to take such risks at such times. Hence, unless you are a young player of exceptional talent such as Wayne Rooney, first-team opportunities are fewer. At Arsenal Arsène Wenger offers opportunities to youngsters, but the majority are foreign players which to my mind does more harm than good to English football in the long term. The argument often voiced today is that cream will always rise to the top. That's true, but there is also a case for young players to be given a platform to flag their potential. Not everyone has the skills and presence of Wayne Rooney at the age of seventeen; the majority develop into fine players over the years, but in order for that to happen they have to be playing first-team football. Chris Lawler, Roger Hunt, Ian Callaghan and I were but four youngsters whom Shanks blooded and persevered with and who became cornerstones of the Liverpool team for many years.

Our game against early title pacesetters Sunderland (it's not often you see those words in the same sentence) got off to a flying start. Cally danced past Len Ashurst, his cross was beaten out by Jim Montgomery, and I followed up to drill it into the net. There were a mere fifty-seven seconds on the clock, the hands of which I had not knocked off! Chris Lawler made it two after half an hour, and Cally three just before half-time. To all intents and purposes it was game over. Tony Hateley added a fourth – his last for Liverpool – and though Colin Suggett scored late on for Sunderland it was very much a consolation goal. The following week we achieved a goalless draw at Everton to move to third in the table. Once again we were on the trail of the Championship and we were doing it by playing our preferred passing game of attacking football. After the Sunderland game Shanks sold Tony Hateley to Coventry City for £60,000.

In February 2007 Manchester United scored four goals within the first seventeen minutes of their game at Reading. The FiveLive commentator asked if any team in the top division had ever before scored four goals in the opening twenty minutes of a league game. The answer is yes. On 21 September 1968 we were four goals to the good against Leicester City after only twelve minutes. As you will know, when a team races into a commanding lead early in a game one of two things will happen: the team will go on to create some kind of record score, or the opposition will concede the game and concentrate on damage limitation. In the case of our game against Leicester it was the latter, and it finished 4–0.

Our goals that day came from Ron Yeats (two minutes), myself (four), Alun Evans (ten) and Cally (twelve). Alun Evans was making his Liverpool debut following a £100,000 move from Wolverhampton Wanderers. He was only nineteen so the size of his fee made headlines: he was Britain's first six-figure teenager. Alun had signalled his potential with some outstanding performances for Wolves and England Youth and under-23s. With his shock of blond hair he cut an unmistakable figure on the pitch and his move to Anfield was seen by the newspapers as the start of a glittering career that would eventually see him become an England regular.

I wouldn't say Alun was an archetypal Liverpool player, but he buckled down at the club and worked hard to fulfil the hopes people had of him. He certainly made a contribution – we never had to carry him – but I sensed the burden of expectation was too much for him. Shanks bought Alun hoping he would turn out to be a replacement for Roger Hunt, but it wasn't to be. Alun suffered a traumatic incident during a night out in a Wolverhampton club. Some thug picked on him, there were words, and the thug pushed a glass in his face. Alun suffered permanent scarring, but I think the psychological scar was worse. He also suffered from a troublesome back injury, and the combination of these things seemed to drain his confidence and his performances suffered as a result.

Alun topped a century of games for Liverpool (111), which was no mean feat, but he was eventually sold to Aston Villa for £72,000. A change of club did little to help get his career back on course. From Villa he went to Walsall, from there to the USA, and then he joined South Melbourne in Australia. He settled in Australia for a number of years, working as a painter and decorator, before returning to the north-west. He's still involved in sport, though not football: he was also a decent cricketer and in 2007 was playing for Lancashire Over-50s as a wicketkeeper-cum-batsman.

At the end of September we thrashed Wolves 6–0 at Molineux and achieved another terrific result away from home a week later, beating Burnley 4–0 at Turf Moor. To me, fourteen goals in three League matches, two of them away from home, offered ample evidence of our zest for attacking football as well as signalling our title aspirations. Those victories over Leicester, Wolves and Burnley formed part of a run that saw Liverpool lose only once in sixteen League matches, the only reverse a single-goal defeat at Manchester United, who in the wake of their European Cup success were experiencing a mediocre season and would eventually finish in mid-table.

The only other fly in the ointment during that run was an exit from the Fairs (UEFA) Cup. I use the term 'exit' purposefully because, in essence, Atlético Bilbao didn't beat us. Following a 2–1 defeat in Bilbao we reversed that scoreline in the return at Anfield. With the aggregate score at 3–3, the tie was decided on the toss of a coin. On this occasion Ron Yeats called it wrong, and we felt what the Cologne players had felt when we had progressed in the Cup Winners' Cup in similar fashion – heartbroken. There was, however, one light moment in that night of sour disappointment. As we dejectedly trooped into the dressing room, Shanks asked Ron what he had called.

'Tails,' Ron replied.

'No wonder!' cried Shanks. 'Jesus Christ, big man. Don't you know? You should never call tails!'

Another incident I remember that season concerned Gerry Byrne, who was at the time still struggling to get his career back on course. After training at Melwood on a Friday morning, Shanks would hold a team and tactics meeting in the home dressing room at Anfield. In the centre of the room was a table, and on that there was a board covered in green baize on which Shanks had marked out a pitch. He would use tiddlywinks to denote players when outlining the gameplan, blue for the opposition and red, naturally, for Liverpool. On one particular Friday we gathered round this table listening intently as Shanks held court.

'See here, I want our two full-backs to push on like this when we are in possession,' he said, pushing two red tiddlywinks along the baize. 'That way when we have the ball—'

Shanks stopped dead. He had glanced up, and his eyes were now affixed on Gerry, who was in the stages of growing a beard.

'Gerry, Gerry Byrne, what the hell is that on your face, son?' Shanks asked, slack-jawed.

'A beard, boss. I'm growing a beard.'

'There are no beards at this club, son,' announced a bristling Shanks, hitching his shoulders like Cagney and letting the syllables curdle, 'No beards. Ever!'

'Why not?' asked Gerry – a not unreasonable question.

'Why not? Why not?' repeated Shanks in astonishment and with not a little indignation. 'Jesus Christ, son, never cultivate anything around your mouth that grows wild around your arse!'

We players fell about laughing. Characteristically, Shanks had got his message over without Gerry feeling he had been carpeted and humiliated in front of his team-mates. Shanks had a unique way with words and that allowed him to have a unique way of handling us players. And, yes, Gerry did shave off his beard.

The title race of 1968–69 developed into a battle between Leeds United, Everton, Arsenal and ourselves, with Chelsea and Spurs hanging on to our coat-tails for much of it. Like Manchester United, near neighbours City, the reigning champions, had a mediocre time. City's final position of thirteenth was the second lowest of any post-war reigning champions, the lowest being that of Ipswich, who followed their Championship season of 1961–62 by finishing seventeenth. Having lost to United in mid-December, we then lost only two of our remaining eighteen League matches. Three defeats in thirty-four League games is the form of champions, but there was, quite literally, a sting in the tail of that sober fact.

With four matches remaining the title race had boiled down to ourselves and Leeds, with Leeds the favourites. As had happened the season before, lowly opposition proved a stumbling-block: in the first of these four games, on 22 April, we drew 0–0 with Coventry City who would avoid relegation by only a single point. From our point of view the Coventry result was disastrous. Our next game was against Leeds, who now only had to gain a draw to clinch the title. If Liverpool won, it would all depend on the final two games.

The Kop gathered in anticipation of one of Anfield's great nights. The atmosphere was electrifying, even by Anfield standards, and we set about Leeds from the kick-off. Geoff Strong, Emlyn Hughes and I lent support to every attack, and we launched many. The Saint, Cally and Thommo were buzzing, but Norman Hunter, Jack Charlton and Gary Sprake were outstanding, Sprake producing a superb performance to belie the sobriquet laid upon him by the Kop. The game was physical, it was unflinching, and it was frenetic. If anything the pace quickened in the second half and the football, desperate at times, was accompanied by an unrelenting din from our supporters. We threw everything at Leeds whose resolution proved absolute. When the final whistle sounded I put my hands on my hips and stared down at the turf, panting like a racehorse. I couldn't believe it. We had bombed Leeds for almost the entire ninety minutes and had nothing to show for our efforts. More to the point, the draw gave Leeds the Championship.

The Leeds players were so exhausted that they didn't jump for joy at the sound of the final whistle. Jack Charlton appeared to be the first to acknowledge what they had achieved: tentatively, he raised an arm. Billy Bremner clapped his hands and then went across to embrace Gary Sprake. Having regained their breath, gradually the Leeds players began to congratulate one another. We went up to them to tender our congratulations, and then a wonderful thing happened. Like a rumble of thunder, the Kop gave its salute to the new champions and the rest of Anfield followed suit. Don Revie later said, 'It was simply fantastic. What

a great gesture from the Liverpool supporters. Their sportsmanship will remain with me for ever.' Shanks too was generous in his
comments. 'The League Championship is the greatest prize in the
game,' he told the press after the game. 'I'm glad they've won it at
last. I'd like to offer my congratulations, particularly to Don. His
team are deserving champions.'

We still had two games to play, and we went about them in a
professional manner; Shanks wouldn't have had it any other way.
We lost 1–0 at Manchester City, however, and drew 1–1 with
Newcastle. We went out to win both games, but there is no doubt
in my mind that with the Championship gone our performances
lacked the usual potency. Following that final game at St James's,
Emlyn Hughes happened to remark, 'Well, I'm disappointed we
never won the League, but runners-up isn't bad.' Bob Paisley
overheard this and was on to him like a flash. 'First is first and
second is nowhere,' he said, borrowing the remark Shanks had
made to us at the Christmas party all those years ago when I was
a groundstaff lad. Bob was right to reprimand Emlyn; no other
Liverpool player would have said such a thing. Again, it told me
something about Emlyn, something that didn't rest easy with me.

Our record of three defeats in thirty-four League matches was
admirable enough, but credit to Leeds, they had produced even
better, only two defeats throughout the entire season. To me, however, their success epitomized the way football had gone since the
World Cup. Liverpool still went out to entertain and attack, but a
more cautious style of play with an emphasis on not conceding
goals had proved profitable. Leeds won the Championship by
securing more points (sixty-seven) than they scored goals (sixty-
six), and this at a time when only two points were awarded for a
win, remember. For all that we went out to attack, however, we did
not forget our responsibility to defend. In conceding only twenty-
four goals that season we created not only a club record but, along
with Leeds and Arsenal, broke the record for the fewest goals conceded in a season, which had been twenty-eight by Huddersfield

Town in 1924–25, the season before the offside law was changed. The decline in the number of goals scored was evident throughout all four divisions. In 1968–69 Halifax Town won promotion from Division Four having scored fifty-three goals, only one more than Terry Bly of Peterborough managed to score by himself in Division Four in 1960–61. It would be churlish of me not to commend Leeds for maintaining a consistent level of performance from the first game to last, but there was good evidence of the growing trend of teams to rely on defence in the statistics that emerged from their Championship season.

On the plus side, the game still had plenty of individuals for whom spectators would part with hard-earned money just to see. Jimmy Greaves, Best, Law and Charlton, Bobby Moore, Roger Hunt, Gordon Banks, Dave Mackay, Billy Bremner, Alan Ball, Peter Osgood, Derek Dougan and Howard Kendall to name but a few – all were crowd pullers as well as crowd pleasers. Yet again Jimmy Greaves finished as the First Division's leading goalscorer, but Jim's total of twenty-seven was his lowest tally barring 1961–62, when he spent part of the season at AC Milan, and 1965–66, when he missed much of the season after contracting meningitis.

Perhaps the most telling words on how the game had become too reliant on defence came when Matt Busby announced his retirement. Speaking to the press in January 1969, he said, 'The way things are going alarms me deeply. What is new and frightening about the game is that you now have sides whose main assets are physical hardness and the ability to smother fluid, expansive football. They use strength and fitness in the name of professionalism to neutralize skill, and the unfortunate truth is that all too often it can be done. Of course, there are still really great players who cannot be subdued all the time, but increasingly their talents are seen in flashes and they have to live dangerously. It's true there are still teams who believe the game is about skill, talent, technique and imagination – Liverpool, Tottenham Hotspur,

Everton, West Ham and this club [United] spring to mind – but for any one in the Football League, you'll now find ten who rely solely on runners, hard men and a smothering midfield and defence.' We at Liverpool were not to be swayed from our belief that we could still go out and play attacking, entertaining football and be successful.

On a personal note, it had been another very good season for me. For some time now Shanks and Bob had seen me as one of the cornerstones of the team. I had formed a solid partnership in the centre of defence with Ron Yeats, and when asked could also do a job at full-back or in midfield. Family life had got better and better too. In January 1968 Sue had given birth to Janette, and Darren was now coming up to four. Sue and I revelled in parenthood. We survived the birthday parties and made Christmases magical. We were menders of broken things, suppliers of needs, givers of rewards, singers of songs, devisers of games, readers of stories and tellers of tales of our own childhoods. We taught our children to look and listen, to think, to question and to explore. Most of all, we gave our children love. We loved every minute of it.

That summer of 1969, as we prepared to go off on a family holiday, I received some very good news. Sir Alf Ramsey contacted me. He had drawn up an initial squad of forty players for the 1970 World Cup Finals in Mexico, and I had been included.

7

LEADERSHIP IS ACTION NOT POSITION

I WAS LOOKING FORWARD TO THE 1969–70 SEASON IMMENSELY, which due to the World Cup in Mexico the following summer proved to be the shortest on record. Liverpool had established itself as one of the top teams in the country, and I was confident that at least one major trophy would arrive at Anfield. I also had that added incentive of having been selected for Sir Alf Ramsey's initial squad for the World Cup. It was early days, an entire domestic campaign lay ahead, but I was determined to produce the sort of performances that would lead to my making the final squad for Mexico. My inclusion in Alf's squad was a fillip for me, but I was realistic about my chances. I was very much aware I was but one of forty players who would, in time, be whittled down to twenty-two, and England were well served as far as central defenders were concerned. The imperious Bobby Moore was the cornerstone of England's defence, Jack Charlton was still very much in the frame, and Everton's Brian Labone had emerged as a central defender of true international class. England were reigning world champions and, along with Brazil, widely considered as the best in the world. Breaking into the final party would be tough, but the fact I had made the initial group was proof that I was in Alf's thoughts.

Liverpool usually reported back around the first week of July, but because the season was kicking off early (on 9 August), training was moved forward by ten days. This threw us out of kilter as far as touring the Continent was concerned, so Liverpool's 'warm-up' programme consisted of a trip to Belfast to play Linfield (2–1), a short trip up the north-west coast to Blackpool (1–1) and just the one match on the European mainland, a 1–1 draw with Feyenoord. Then the real business of the season began. We set about things in no uncertain fashion, remaining unbeaten in our first eleven League and cup matches and scoring thirty-four goals in the process. Liverpool were not following the trend for ultra cautious football.

Our season had got off to a cracking start with a 4–1 win over Chelsea at Anfield. Once again the team comprised the familiar faces, though Gerry Byrne was absent. Little did we know at the time, but due to his troublesome cartilage Gerry had played his last game for Liverpool. In his absence, Geoff Strong started the season at left-back. Emlyn Hughes continued in the left of midfield with Bobby Graham in the number nine shirt, playing alongside Roger Hunt and Saint upfront. Otherwise it was much the same Liverpool team as it had been for some four years. Our desire to attack was exemplified by the fact that both our full-backs, Chris Lawler and Geoff Strong, found themselves on the scoresheet, our other two goals coming from Saint.

In those first few weeks we also made progress in cup competition. A trip to Watford in the League Cup produced a 2–1 victory. In goal for Watford that night was Bob Slater who was making his first appearance of the season. It wasn't the happiest of nights for Bob: under pressure from Roger Hunt he palmed a cross from Cally into his own net, and Liverpool enjoyed the rare experience of progressing in the League Cup, which had really grown in popularity, not only with clubs but also the supporters.

The fact that the final was now held at Wembley and the winners gained entry into the Fairs (UEFA) Cup had given the competition real kudos. After a tentative first few years, when Liverpool had declined to enter, attendances for League Cup matches had risen year on year; in 1969–70 they hit a record 2,300,000. Popular as it had become, Liverpool's connection with the League Cup continued to be tenuous: following our victory at Watford we exited the competition in the next round, losing 3–2 at Manchester City.

Yet again we were involved in Europe, and as in the previous season it was the Fairs Cup. The first round pitched us against Dundalk of the Republic of Ireland. Dundalk comprised part-time players, and it was a tie we were expected to win handsomely. The first leg took place at Anfield in mid-September and we showed no mercy, crushing the Irishmen 10–0. We took the lead as early as the first minute through Alun Evans, after which we were lining up to score, yours truly netting two of our goals. After the game, Dundalk's 'Paddy' McConville voiced a wonderful piece of optimism and defiance during an interview with a reporter. Responding to the suggestion that the tie was over, McConville replied, 'Well, we have a big task on our hands, that's for sure. But there is another leg to come, so it's really only half-time.'

The side for that first leg against Dundalk showed a number of changes. Ray Clemence had been making good progress in the reserves and he was given an outing in goal in place of Tommy Lawrence. It was nigh on impossible for Ray to show our supporters his mettle as a keeper that night; such was our dominance he found himself with little to do. The other new face was that of Alec Lindsay, whom Shanks had signed from Bury for £35,000. Some Liverpool supporters are of the mind that Alec was signed as a replacement for Gerry Byrne, but that was not the case; Alec was originally brought in as a left-sided midfielder. But there is a twist to that story. Alec's arrival at Anfield had been pure serendipity.

One Friday morning before training at Melwood I was sitting on the grass next to him. The pair of us were lacing up our boots when I saw Shanks and Bob walking towards us. Shanks was pointing in our direction; it seemed ominous.

'You been up to anything?' I asked Alec, knowing that some sort of confrontation was in the offing.

'No,' he replied. 'Have you?'

I told him I hadn't, but I knew from Shanks's demeanour there was a problem with one of us.

When they reached us it was clear from Shanks's facial expression that he was not best pleased.

'Hello, Tommy, son, how are you this morning?' asked Shanks.

'Fine, boss, raring to go,' I replied guardedly.

'That'll do for me, son,' said Shanks, much to my relief. 'And how are you, Alec?'

'Great,' said Alec, not looking up from his boots.

Shanks bristled. 'You might think you are, son, but you're not!'

That made Alec look up.

'I've watched you playing for our reserves on the left wing. You were crap. We tried you upfront. To be honest, son, you were hopeless there. We tried you on the left in midfield. You did little better. You lacked the pace to get away from players, and that's not all you lack. You lack the necessary to be a Liverpool player.'

Alec was shaken by Shanks's brutal honesty. I felt embarrassed for him, but not having seen him in action for the reserves I knew better than to question Shanks's assessment of him.

'What's going to happen?' asked Alec, seemingly fearing the worst.

'We paid Bury good money for you, son, and you're not delivering,' Shanks repeated. 'You want to tell me why?'

'OK, fair enough, but when your scout saw me playing for Bury I was at left-back,' Alec replied, quite literally in defence of his reputation and career. 'You've never played me there.'

'No, son, don't you lie to me. We don't have liars at this club.'

'But I did,' Alec insisted. 'I only ever played left-back at Bury.'

'Are you certain?'

'Yes, boss. I should know, I was there.'

Shanks cast a glance at Bob.

'Then who's the fella who played left midfield in the Bury team, same blond hair and cut as you?' demanded Shanks.

'Jimmy Kerr,' replied Alec.

'Hell, Bob, we've signed the wrong player!' said Shanks in total disbelief. 'I want that scout in here, now!'

Liverpool really had signed a player they had not intended to sign, but in time Alec turned out to be the right player. Bob's insistence that Shanks try Alec at his more natural position of left-back, rather than move him on immediately, produced dividends. Alec was given his opportunity in the first team to show what he could do, and after two years of trying various players in the position in which Gerry Byrne had excelled, Liverpool at last found a suitable replacement.

Shanks liked a big, powerful man in the centre of defence, and in April 1969 he had made another acquisition, paying Bristol Rovers £50,000 for Larry Lloyd, initially as cover for Ron Yeats but with a view to one day replacing him. Larry made good progress in the reserves. He made his first-team debut in a 2–2 draw at West Bromwich Albion at the end of September but immediately reverted back to the second team. I think he expected to see the season out in the Central League team, but as things turned out his elevation came sooner than expected.

We suffered our first reverse in mid-September, losing 1–0 to Manchester United at Old Trafford. That defeat apart, we continued to post good results until November when we suffered a hefty 4–0 loss at Derby County. November was a month in which we won just one League match from five and exited the Fairs Cup. After such a sensational start to the season, things were becoming a little flaky.

We'd been drawn in round two against Vitoria Setúbal and lost the first leg in Portugal by the only goal of the game. Yet again I felt that would not prove too mountainous to climb when back at Anfield. On the night, however, what was seen as only an uphill task suddenly did become mountainous. Against the run of play Setúbal took the lead when we gave away a needless penalty and Wagner scored from the spot. The scoreline remained 0–1 until the second half when, on the hour mark, we were awarded a penalty. I stepped up to level the scores on the night and give us hope, but it proved short-lived. Almost from the restart Setúbal mounted an attack and their second goal had, should I say, a familiar ring to it. Wagner tried his luck again and Geoff Strong, in attempting to block the effort, could do no more than turn the ball past Tommy Lawrence.

Minutes after that I went in for a fifty-fifty ball with their winger, Jacinto. I went to play the ball, but Jacinto raised a boot and went over the top. His studs crashed into my right kneecap and I felt a searing pain shoot up my leg. I never liked to stay down when injured as I never wanted the opposition to sense I was not 100 per cent, so I took to my feet almost immediately. I carried on playing but, rather than easing, the pain in my knee gradually became worse. I knew something was wrong, but at the time I didn't think the injury was anything serious.

Undaunted by Setúbal's second goal we pushed forward and laid siege to their penalty box. The Portuguese keeper, Vital, lived up to his name, producing vital saves from Cally and Thommo. Eventually concerted pressure paid off when Alun Evans, who had come on as a substitute for young Steve Peplow, struck with two minutes to go to set up a dramatic finale. From the restart we gained possession, poured forward, and Roger Hunt – who had been out of the side due to injury but had come on as late sub- stitute for Bobby Graham – made it 3–2. It was a comeback, of sorts. The final scoreline made the tie 3–3 on aggregate and Setúbal went through on the new away-goals rule – a great improvement on the toss of a coin.

After the game Shanks gave an interview to football writer Bryon Butler in which his prickly, defiant response to the defeat failed to mask his disappointment. Butler began by asking Shanks how he felt about having lost the tie.

'We beat Setúbal tonight and we didn't lose the tie as such, we simply ran out of time,' replied Shanks. 'We won one game, they won one. They have gone through. The rules say we scored the same number of goals, but as a team we scored more: we scored their second for them tonight.'

It was improbable logic but typical of Shanks when faced with defeat.

'Are you saying the rules have to be looked at?' Butler then asked.

'No, no, we know the rules when we enter. It's not the rules that need to be looked at.'

'What then?'

'We're always looking at ways to improve as a team. We'll continue to do that.'

No one attached much, if any, significance to what Shanks said, but looking back, perhaps Shanks was already contemplating an overhaul of the team. Roger Hunt was fit again, but the word around the dressing room was that Shanks thought his age was against him and he was willing to let him go.

After the Setúbal game I had a restless night. The pain in my knee intensified and I was up and hobbling around just after six a.m. Bob Paisley always arrived at Anfield between eight and eight-thirty to give treatment to those players with injuries. When he arrived that morning I was waiting for him.

He asked me to sit on the treatment table and set about examining my knee.

'Tommy, you'd better ring Sue,' he said. 'Ask her to come to the ground to collect your car. We're going to the hospital.'

I still didn't know the extent of my injury, but I knew it wasn't good news.

The doctor at the hospital told me that part of my right kneecap had been sliced off. 'I don't know how you managed to carry on playing football with your knee like this,' he said. 'Usually such an impact shatters the kneecap like glass. Yours has been sliced. I should imagine you'll not be playing football for some five to six months. Good news: the bone has been sliced clean. We can put the kneecap back together by operating. You've had a stroke of good luck.'

I thought to myself, 'If this is what good luck is, I dread to think what it must be like to have bad luck.'

They operated on my knee the following day and I stayed in hospital for some four days before returning home. To my great relief the surgeon told me the operation had been a success. All that was left for me to do was to rest and recuperate before beginning the slow build-up to optimum fitness.

As we entered December, Everton led the table by eight points from Leeds, with Liverpool in fourth place. Everton were playing exceptionally well, and when we crossed Stanley Park for the first derby of the season, few football pundits fancied our chances. We went into the game off the back of a 1–0 home defeat against Arsenal and a 1–1 draw at Leeds. I was very disappointed and frustrated to be a spectator during this period; I simply loved playing and couldn't wait to get back into the fold. My place in the centre of defence was taken by Geoff Strong, who had a simple philosophy as far as football was concerned: 'Play me anywhere, boss, as long as you play me.'

I was delighted to see Liverpool produce an exhilarating display at Goodison. Following a goalless first half, Emlyn Hughes gave us the lead two minutes after the interval. Little over five minutes later a cross from Cally was met by Everton full-back Sandy Brown who bulleted a header past his own keeper Gordon West. Even to this day Sandy's own goal is talked about on Merseyside. It was an absolute belter, and it entered derby folklore – and not for that reason alone. The game was featured on TV and a camera had been positioned near the touchline from where Cally made the cross. As the ball entered the Everton penalty box, the camera captured a burly policeman patrolling the perimeter track in front of the Gladwys Street end. As he passed behind the goal the policeman turned his head towards the pitch just in time to see Sandy make contact with the ball. I can only think he must have been an ardent Liverpool fan, because as the ball ballooned the Everton net and Sandy fell to his knees in despair, the portly policeman was seen throwing his head back and roaring with laughter. Had Sandy's stunning o.g. not been captured on camera it would still have entered the folklore of Merseyside derbies, but thanks to TV, the abiding image has been not so much Sandy's header but that of the 'laughing policeman', who looks as if he has stepped straight from Charles Penrose's classic old song.

Again, when was the last time you saw a policeman laugh at a football match, or for that matter at any time when on duty? Should such a thing happen today, no doubt some idiot would complain, questioning the impartiality of the police. There would be the suggestion that sensibilities had been offended; the police-man's superiors would have the constable in to remind him of his responsibilities – you know how it is now. Back then the incident was simply viewed as a great bit of fun – and by Evertonians too. It was also seen as showing policemen to be human, just like the rest of us, and I suppose the TV people saw it as a great piece of telly, which it was.

The 3–0 derby victory – our third goal was scored by Bobby Graham, who in my estimation never received the plaudits his efforts deserved – was a tremendous boost to the players as well as our supporters. After an indifferent set of results many believed we had turned a corner, and in light of his comment after the game against Setúbal, perhaps Shanks did too. If he had been planning a shake-up, our great victory at Everton proved to be, for some, a stay of execution.

One player who did leave Anfield that month, however, was

Roger Hunt. Shanks's predecessor, Phil Taylor, had signed Roger from local junior side Stockton Heath in 1958. After eleven years at Anfield in which he had made 492 appearances and scored 286 goals – and acquired a World Cup winner's medal along the way – Roger joined Bolton Wanderers on a free transfer. He had been a tremendous servant to Liverpool, a great club man and a good friend. I was sorry to see him go but understood Shanks's reasons for releasing him.

I continued to watch frustrated from the stands as results remained fitful. The very next game saw Liverpool beaten 4–1 at Anfield by Manchester United; on Boxing Day we notched up a record 5–1 win at Burnley; then into the New Year draw followed defeat followed draw. But while we stuttered and spluttered in the League, we had high hopes of doing well in the FA Cup, and slowly but surely our progress in this competition began to gather momentum. Coventry City were beaten in round three after a replay. We then enjoyed a comfortable victory over Wrexham at the Racecourse Ground, and in round five overcame our *bête noire*, Leicester City, though it needed two games. By February I was back in action for the reserves; my recovery programme had gone very well and I felt no problem with the knee. So I was delighted to be declared fit and included in the side for the replay. A capacity crowd of 42,100 crammed into Filbert Street and what they saw was a tight, evenly contested cup tie. With the game goalless, Peter Thompson, struggling with an injury, was replaced by Alun Evans, and it was he who swung the tie in our favour, scoring two late goals. Manchester United, Chelsea and Leeds United accompanied us into the velvet bag for round six, but the draw was benevolent to Liverpool: we booked a visit to Watford, struggling near the foot of Division Two.

I had got through the Leicester replay without any discomfort, but in the following match, a goalless draw in the League against Newcastle United, though I felt no pain, I noticed the knee was a little swollen. Prior to the tie at Watford I received treatment throughout the week from Bob. I was desperately keen to play, and come Thursday morning I thought I would. That afternoon Shanks asked Bob what my chances were. 'His knee's a little swollen,' Bob replied. 'As a precaution I think it best to rest it for a week.' My heart sank, but deep down I knew he was right. It was better for me to rest than to play and possibly incur further damage, which would result in another lengthy spell on the sidelines.

I listened to a radio commentary of the Watford game while sitting at home; Peter Thompson, who had failed to recover from the injury he sustained at Leicester, also listened to the game at home. The team Shanks picked included Peter Wall at left-back, Geoff Strong alongside Big Ron in the heart of defence, Ian Ross and Emlyn Hughes in central midfield, Cally and Bobby Graham on either flank, and a strike force of Alun Evans and Saint. It was a grey, murky day with the sort of thin but constant rain which appears so slight that you wonder if you will need a coat, and the radio commentator said the weather was depressingly similar at Watford. Little did I know as I sat down to listen that within ninety minutes my mood would match that of the weather.

The Watford team included Mike Walker in goal (later to manage Norwich and Everton), Duncan Welbourne, Stuart Scullion, Ray Lugg and Barry Endean, a centre-forward Watford had signed from Sunday football in County Durham. It was Endean who proved to be Liverpool's nemesis: he scored the only goal of the game some ten minutes from time. When the final whistle sounded, I was stunned. It was not only the shock result of the sixth round, it was the cup shock of the season. Without taking anything away from Watford, it had been possibly the worst performance by a Liverpool team since I joined the club. No sooner had the game ended than my telephone rang. It was Peter Thompson. 'Thank God that didn't happen on our shift,' said Thommo, the tone of his voice exuding both shock and despair. In footballers' parlance, it had been a good one to miss.

I was told that Shanks didn't berate the team in the dressing room after the game, which was typical of him. Even on Monday morning he held back. That he barely made reference to such a terrible result and performance convinced me that he was planning something. Big changes were afoot. The Watford result hammered home to Shanks that certain players had reached the tipping moment in their careers, while others simply didn't have what it took to play for Liverpool. Shanks was upset and angry, not solely because we had lost in the FA Cup to a side struggling to avoid relegation to Division Three, but because some of the great players he believed could go on well into their thirties had given evidence that this was not the case.

The cull began immediately. For the next game against Derby County, Ray Clemence replaced Tommy Lawrence in goal, and, having rested, I replaced Ron Yeats in the heart of defence. Thommo was also fit and he came back. There were no places for Ian St John and Ian Ross. The Watford debacle effectively ended the Anfield playing careers of Tommy Lawrence, Big Ron and Saint. Though all three were still part of the set-up the following season their appearances in the first team were limited. Peter Wall was sold to Crystal Palace, and Ross and Bobby Graham were also destined only to play bit parts before they too moved on. As the season unfolded Larry Lloyd was introduced into the heart of defence alongside me. Roy Evans (later to manage the club) made a number of appearances at left-back, as did Big Ron, and Doug Livermore was tried upfront alongside Alun Evans. In addition to ringing the changes, Shanks and Bob were out and about watching games at every given opportunity in search of players they felt could help take Liverpool into a new era of success. The team was being dismantled and rebuilt. Everyone would now have to be patient. I felt it would be some time before Liverpool emerged again as a real force in the game.

It was little consolation that we won three of our final four League matches. I particularly remember the penultimate game, a mid-week match at Sunderland. No matter what happened in our final two matches we were going to finish fifth or sixth. Sunderland, however, were playing their final game for their First Division lives: they had to win to stay up at the expense of Crystal Palace. Liverpool went out to win every game, even if it was a pre-season friendly. That night, however, probably because it was a fag-end game with nothing really at stake for us, we lacked our usual edge. For some reason Shanks and Bob seemed a little sub-dued too. Sunderland would never have a better opportunity to beat us, but they were so poor they couldn't do it. Four minutes from time Chris Lawler cut in from the right and drilled a low shot past Jimmy Montgomery. There were over 33,000 inside Roker Park but you could hear the clunk as the ball hit the stanchion in the back of the goal. Sunderland were down; but given the season we'd had, we weren't exactly on a high.

Liverpool had not won a major trophy now for four years, since winning the championship in 1966. In the intervening years we had always been in contention for the title, but not this time. Having finished as runners-up to Leeds the previous season we finished fifth in 1969–70, fifteen points adrift of champions Everton. A number of First Division clubs might have settled for that as it did, after all, afford entry into Europe, but for Liverpool, fifth place represented failure. Shanks believed the team was going backwards and he slammed on the brakes, with a view to then going through the gears.

My disappointment with the club's mediocrity was compounded when I was left out of Sir Alf's final twenty-two for the World Cup in Mexico. Throughout 1969–70 Sir Alf held a series of England 'get togethers' which I attended. The first took place at Bisham Abbey and comprised a training session, a practice match and a series of meetings. Curiously, the main talking point of one of these meetings was teeth. We were told we would be playing foot-ball at high altitude in Mexico and as part of the acclimatization programme each player had to report to his dentist to ensure his teeth were in 'A1' condition. Apparently, at high altitude minor problems with teeth can be exacerbated. I always looked after my teeth, but a few of the lads had to undergo major dentistry.

The second 'get together' took place at FA headquarters at Lancaster Gate. This meeting provided us with further information about the conditions and climate we were to encounter, the culture of Mexico, what we might expect from the press, and what was expected of us in the way of discipline and behaviour. I remember proceedings being delayed because Bobby Moore wasn't present. Sir Alf strutted up and down impatiently, checking his watch every thirty seconds, seemingly reluctant to begin until his skipper was present. Eventually Bobby strode elegantly into the room and took his seat. At first Alf didn't say anything. Then, with Bobby seated, to everyone's astonishment Alf said, 'Hello, the prize prick has arrived at last. May I remind you, Robert, someone has to be last, but no one need be late.' Suitably admonished, Bobby apologized to the room.

I thought I was knocking on the door of an England place when Alf included me in the squad for the game against Scotland at Hampden Park in April. The annual Home Championship match between the 'auld enemies' was the highlight of the international calendar, and having announced the team, Alf then said that either Alan Mullery (Spurs) or I would be the substitute. I was disappointed when Mullers was named, but reasoned that my inclusion in the final thirteen for such an important fixture was proof positive that I was close to making the final squad for Mexico. For the record, the game ended goalless before a crowd of 137,438 and Mullers played a part, replacing my Liverpool team-mate Peter Thompson.

The Scotland game was England's final match before leaving for a series of 'acclimatization' matches in South America. I genuinely did believe I would make the final squad when it was announced at the beginning of May. I was walking through Liverpool city centre on the day itself when the 'headline board' of a newspaper seller's stand caught my eye. The headline read, 'Hughes In, Smith Out for Mexico'. I bought a copy of the *Liverpool Echo* and read of my omission from the World Cup party while standing on the street. I was very disappointed not to be going, doubly disappointed that Sir Alf hadn't rung me to give me the news in person, or at least written. Among the other 'hopefuls' to be omitted were Peter Shilton and Cally. A few days later I met Cally who told me he had learned of his fate on the radio. 'Typical Alf,' I told him. 'Do anything to avoid having a phone bill.'

Another instance of Alf curtly severing contact with a player concerned none other than Jimmy Greaves. Following the injury Jimmy sustained during the group stage of the 1966 World Cup Finals which resulted in him being replaced by Geoff Hurst, Alf recalled him to the England team in 1967, only to then leave him out of the side. Jimmy told Alf that if he was not to be a part of the England team any more he would prefer to be told rather than continue to turn up for training with no hope of being included in the side. Alf assured Jimmy he was still very much in his thoughts, and asked him to await a call. In 2007 I rang Jimmy to verify this story. At one point in our conversation he said, 'Actually, Tommy, when I heard the phone ring, I thought it might be Alf. I'm still waiting for him to call!'

Sir Alf and Shanks were both great managers; I would put them up there with the very best British football has ever produced. Both, however, rarely, if ever, took a player aside and gave a reason for having dropped him from a team. Bob Paisley was totally different. Bob had missed out on a place in Liverpool's 1950 FA Cup Final team; he understood how a player felt when omitted from a team and, unlike Sir Alf and Shanks, always made a point of talking to the man in person. Bob wouldn't go into detail, but at least the player in question was given some sort of reason for why he was out, and didn't feel that he'd been cold-shouldered.

Like most other people, I watched the World Cup in Mexico on television at home. I felt for Alf and the boys when we lost to West

Germany in the quarter-final, a game I felt we could and should have won. I knew how bitterly disappointed the lads would be, particularly Bobby Charlton, it being his last World Cup. I watched the ITV coverage of the England party preparing to leave for home; rarely, if ever, have I seen such a sad and dejected group of players. The ITV commentator, Brian Moore, remarked, 'After all the meticulous preparation and planning and the Herculean efforts of the team, the players now return home with nothing to show from having been in this World Cup.'

Which wasn't exactly true. They all had lovely teeth.

To the neutral observer the Liverpool side that kicked off the 1970–71 season at Burnley must have had a very unfamiliar ring to it: Ray Clemence, Chris Lawler, Ian Ross, me, Larry Lloyd, Emlyn Hughes, Ian Callaghan, Alun Evans, Bobby Graham, John McLaughlin (a product of the youth team) and Peter Thompson (sub: Jack Witham). We won the game 2–1, the goals coming from Emlyn Hughes and Alun Evans. It was a very proud day for me. During the summer Shanks had called me into his office and given me some fantastic news. He had appointed me captain of the team. I had skippered the side on previous occasions when Ron Yeats wasn't available, but this was different. Shanks was of the mind that I had 'qualities of leadership', and when he asked if I would accept the captaincy on a permanent basis he barely got his words out before I said yes. I felt it a great honour and privilege to captain Liverpool. It was not a nominal position, the role carried with it real responsibility, and I was determined to carry out my duties to the best of my ability.

One of the first to congratulate me was Ron Yeats. Ron had been skipper since joining the club and I took the opportunity to ask for his advice.

'Always remember this,' Ron told me. 'Whatever goes wrong during a game, it's not your fault, even when it is.'

'How come?' I asked, in all sincerity.

'Because you're the captain,' ventured Ron. 'If the team concedes a goal, look about for the player who is looking most guilty, and blame him.'

I was flabbergasted to hear this, but on recalling those times when we had conceded a silly goal, I could remember Ron getting verbally stuck in to one player or another.

'Does it work?' I asked.

'Well, it worked for me for nine years,' he said.

We remained unbeaten for the first eight League matches of the season, but deep down I knew this current Liverpool team wasn't of the strength of previous sides. The run included five draws, two of which were at home, to Crystal Place and Manchester United. Following our first defeat in the League at Southampton at the end of September, there were wins over Chelsea and Burnley but also defeats at Ipswich and Spurs. I felt we were in for a season of not so much being there as thereabouts.

Uncharacteristically for Liverpool, we were having a problem in front of goal. We were putting teams under pressure but not putting the ball in the back of the net with anywhere near the regularity we had once achieved. In part this was due to the fact that we were now coming up against sides with defensive game-plans. Many teams were happy to stay back in numbers, as was the trend of the day, and it frustrated the hell out of us. Faced with blanket defences we found goalscoring opportunities were fewer. That's not to say opportunities were not created, though, but whereas previously we had been clinical in front of goal now we were, at times, profligate – a problem that had evolved because Liverpool now lacked a good finisher, a twenty-goal-a-season striker. Alun Evans ended the season as our leading scorer in the League with just ten goals; our second leading marksman was John Toshack with five. Four years earlier our full-backs had scored more than Tosh. In saying that I mean no disrespect to Tosh. He was a victim of circumstances. A striker won't score goals if he's not receiving good service, and for a time he wasn't. In the event we scored only forty-two League goals in the entire season, an average of one per game, by far the lowest by any Liverpool team in the history of the club. I was left thinking how much had changed in the space of a year: the previous season we had scored thirty-four goals in our first eleven games. I knew we were far from being a mediocre First Division outfit. Throughout 1970–71 we always featured in the top six, but I was acutely aware I was captain of a team in transition. Curiously, rather than making me anxious, that filled me with hope.

As the season progressed, so did we as a team, though we encountered setbacks prior to Christmas. Ignominious exits from the League Cup had become something of a Liverpool speciality, and after having overcome Mansfield Town after a replay, we were beaten 2–0 at Swindon Town. That night Shanks tried Alun Evans upfront with Jack Witham, who had been signed from Sheffield Wednesday. Playing behind that pair was Doug Livermore. It made little difference: we were still ineffective in front of goal.

Our League Cup replay against Mansfield Town marked the debut of Steve Heighway. Steve is a Sheffield lad. He had done particularly well at his school, High Storrs, and having acquired good A-level qualifications he gained a degree in Economics at Warwick University. Steve combined his studies with playing non-League football for Skelmersdale United in the Cheshire League, and it was while playing for Skem that his talent was noticed by a Liverpool scout. Steve was not the only graduate to join Liverpool: Shanks also signed Brian Hall, who obtained a degree in Mathematics at Liverpool University. When both Steve and Brian made the first team, Shanks roomed them together as he believed that being on a similar intellectual level they would get on. Shanks once said in an interview with John Keith of the *Daily Express*, 'If only one had made the first team, the alternative would have been to room that boy with Tommy Smith,' which I took to mean that he thought I too might have something in the way of grey matter.

Steve and Brian may have been intellectually compatible but

they were two entirely different types of player. Steve was tall, lean and lightning quick, not a physical type of player at all; Brian, on the other hand, was small, compact and fiercely competitive, especially when contesting the ball. Both, however, possessed good football brains and were real workhorses. We soon nicknamed them 'Big Bamber' and 'Little Bamber', after Bamber Gascoigne, the presenter of *University Challenge*, which they both loved to watch. They competed with each other to see who could amass the most points. One evening at a hotel prior to a game they arrived in the TV lounge but too late to catch *University Challenge*.

'As you pair weren't here, Jack Witham took on Ian Ross,' I told them.

'How'd they get on?' asked Steve.

'Drew nil-nil.'

Incidentally, Steve Heighway must have created some sort of record when he made his Liverpool debut against Mansfield on 8 September as the very next day he made his international debut for the Republic of Ireland against Poland in Dublin. Two debuts in two days is some going, and to the best of my knowledge is a unique feat in top-class football.

As we entered the New Year Liverpool had played twenty-two League matches of which only eight had been won. On the plus side we had lost on only four occasions. Without doubt the outstanding result during this run, in all probability of the entire season, was the one we gained at the expense of Everton on 21 November. On that day I led out Liverpool for my first derby as captain. As we left the home dressing room it was as if the corridor had been filled with the noise of dozens of worn car-engine tappets as our studs click-clacked along the floor. I remember saying to myself, 'I'll kill to win this game.' That is how much captaining Liverpool to victory over Everton meant to me. The game is so ingrained in the memory I can still rattle off the teams: Ray Clemence, Chris Lawler, Alec Lindsay, me, Larry Lloyd, Emlyn Hughes, Brian Hall, John McLaughlin, Steve Heighway, John

Toshack and Ian Ross; and for Everton, Andy Rankin, Tommy Wright, Henry Newton; Keith Newton, Brian Labone, Colin Harvey, Alan Whittle, Alan Ball, Joe Royle, John Hurst and Johnny Morrisey.

Anfield was packed to the rafters with a capacity crowd of 54,000. The mood and atmosphere inside the ground made a heady cocktail of expectation, nervous tension and high-voltage partisanship. Up in the main stand the directors of both clubs puffed away on cigars the size of rolling pins. As I led the team out on to the pitch an ear-splitting roar made the hair on the back of my neck stand on end. I won the toss and chose to attack the Kop in the second half, as was the tradition at Liverpool, irrespective of the opposition.

When the game got underway, bedlam broke loose and what seemed like the sound of a tornado swept down from the terracing and stands. As the first heated exchanges were witnessed the supporters seemed to up the ante. Anfield filled with a cacophony of noise, an alarming, volatile, collective sound that encouraged the players to fly into tackles with greater intensity and, occasionally, dubious intent. In those first few minutes bush-fires of anger flickered all around the pitch. It was no match for the faint-hearted, it was a match of gleaming steel, mostly of the broadsword, which was used with impunity by both sets of players and allowed to be used by a referee who would have had a short career today. There were plenty of tackles that made even the most seasoned players wince, several moments when the football was as rare as uncooked meat. I was slamming into tackles too, but by no stretch of the imagination was I the only perpetrator. The crowd regularly displayed their anger at the other team's perceived guilt.

As the watery November sun dipped out of sight behind the Kemlyn Road stand, a fast and furious first half ended goalless. Shanks appeared satisfied with the game and how we were applying ourselves. 'Keep a hold of that ball, be patient, a goal will come,' he told us.

He was half right. The second half was some ten minutes old when Everton found their tidemark. Alan Ball made progress down our right-hand side and deep into our half. Chris Lawler should have come short to close Bally down, but didn't. I went across to do that job, only for Bally to exchange passes with Johnny Morrisey and for the ball to be whipped across to our far post. Everton's young centre-forward Joe Royle was a superb header of the ball. He rose like a Delia Smith sponge cake, met the ball with the meat of his forehead, and Ray Clemence found himself clutching at thin air. The Blue contingent on the terraces erupted.

Mindful of the advice given to me by Ron Yeats, I looked around for the most guilty face among my team mates. Chris Lawler was walking away, hands on hips, head bowed. I ran up to him and gave him a verbal onslaught.

'You never went short! You never shouted you were gonna hold back! Shout, ye bugger!'

True to character, Chris never said a word. He merely carried on walking and took up his position for the restart.

Ten minutes later the Everton supporters must have thought they had died and gone to heaven. Everton were on the attack when I won the ball from Joe Royle some thirty-five yards from our penalty area. I was looking for options when suddenly Alan Whittle slammed into the back of me and got a foot on the ball. I turned to give chase but Whittle sprinted a few yards and then, seeing Ray Clemence off his line, chipped him. As chips go it was nigh on perfect. The ball sailed over Ray's head, quickly descended, passed under the bar and slithered down the back of the net. Once again the Everton contingent in Anfield went berserk, and again I looked around for someone to blame. The goal had been my fault really, but I should have had a call of 'Man on!' I might have been able to take evasive action then. Chris Lawler had the most guilty face; in truth, he was the nearest team-mate to me.

''King hell! You shudda shouted "Man on!"'' I bellowed to his face, ''King hell, Chris, open your mouth and shout for it, God's sake!'

Chris didn't say a word. After a deep intake of breath, he shrugged his shoulders and went across to take up his position for the restart.

My first Merseyside derby as Liverpool captain was turning into a nightmare. Two-nil down to Everton, and at home! I felt shame, and I was angry. I glanced across to our bench. Shanks had his eye on me. He clenched a fist and gritted his teeth, a gesture I took to mean 'Get them going', which is exactly what I did. I began to shout, even scream, driving my team-mates on to even greater efforts.

Some eighteen minutes from time we were thrown a lifeline when the 'bookworm' Steve Heighway booked his place in the history of derby matches. Receiving the ball on the left wing, though policed by Tommy Wright, Steve turned his marker in the space of a hearthrug and cut inside. Henry Newton barred his way, but Steve dropped his left shoulder, Henry went that way, Steve the other, and he fired low past Andy Rankin at his near post. Anfield erupted, or at least the red faction who were by far in the majority did. We were back in the game.

Steve's goal lifted the side and we took the game to Everton. To their credit, Everton defended manfully and played their part in a game that had now become one of suffocating tension. Again it was Steve Heighway who proved the thorn in their side. He jinked his way past Colin Harvey and in all probability couldn't believe his luck when Tommy Wright laid off him. Steve had pace, and now space. He lofted a forty-yard ball to the far post where John Toshack emulated Joe Royle by heading powerfully past Andy Rankin. Our supporters tumbled down the terraces, Everton were rattled, and I felt the game had swung in our favour and was now there for the taking. I urged us to keep the pressure on. We poured forward and laid siege to Rankin's goal. The Liverpool supporters waited in anticipation, those of Everton in trepidation. It was as if the Kop sensed our time was coming. This feeling hardened into conviction with less than five minutes remaining. I exchanged passes with Steve Heighway who then took on Tommy Wright, beat him, and advanced with the ball to a point about a yard from the Everton byline, right in front of the swaying massed ranks of the Kop. His way barred by the Everton defenders, Steve played the ball back to Alec Lindsay who whippd it into the Everton penalty area. Tosh jumped a fraction too early; when the ball reached him he was on the descent and couldn't get above the ball to head it towards goal. Knowing that he couldn't execute a goal-bound header, he went for the only other option. He glanced the ball back with the top of his head in the direction of the angle of the six-yard box in the hope that a team-mate was following up in support.

The ball began to descend just beyond the angle of the six-yard box. Steaming towards it was Chris Lawler, who met the ball on the volley and rifled it past a thicket of blue shirts and into the roof of the net. Anfield convulsed in mass hysteria. From 2–0 down we now had a 3–2 lead. I couldn't believe it, and in all probability neither could the 54,000 people present in the ground that day. We all made a beeline for Chris, and I was one of the first to throw my arms around him.

'What a goal! What a 'king goal, Chris! I love ya! You met it brilliant!' I screamed into his ear.

Cool as a cucumber, Chris turned towards me. 'Yeah,' he said in an unemotional, matter-of-fact of voice, 'and I didn't shout for that one either.'

Despite victories such as this, we had become the draw specialists of Division One. Having drawn ten matches prior to New Year our first two matches of 1971 against Blackpool and Manchester City also ended all square, but as the new blood in the team began to make its mark, results improved, just in time for both the FA and UEFA Cups.

With Ray Clemence in goal, and Chris Lawler and Alec Lindsay in the full-back positions, I had begun to form a half-decent partnership in the centre of defence with Larry Lloyd. It wasn't the same as playing alongside Big Ron, who to my mind was the superior pivot of the two, but as the season progressed we gained an understanding. We began to post good results in the New Year not least because Steve Heighway, John Toshack, Brian Hall and, when selected, Phil Boersma had also settled into the team and were making a really positive contribution. Peter Thompson and Cally were both struggling with injuries, but we now had suitable replacements in Heighway and Hall. Shanks, however, still had the problem of finding a foil for Tosh. At times Alun Evans, Bobby Graham, John McLaughlin and Jack Witham were all tried, but the results were, at best, mixed.

We got off the mark in the Fairs Cup by laying a ghost to rest when we beat Ferencvaros of Hungary. Another trip behind the Iron Curtain saw us dispose of Dynamo Bucharest (4–1 on aggregate), and then we enjoyed double-bubble victories over Hibernian which set up a quarter-final tie against favourites Bayern Munich. It was another European night of electricity at Anfield when we took on Bayern. The atmosphere was terrific, and we played up to it. Alun Evans, recalled to the team, had a night of nights, scoring a hat-trick to give us a 3–0 win and, to all intents and purposes, put an end to the tie. In the return a fine goal from Ian Ross gave us a 1–1 draw and a 4–1 aggregate victory.

Having removed the favourites from the cup, I thought we could go all the way and win it. The stumbling-block was Leeds United, whom we met in the semi-final. Everyone had been hoping we would be kept apart in the draw, but we came out of the bag together, which at least meant one British side would progress to the final to meet either Juventus or Cologne. The first leg took place at Anfield and yet again we encountered a resolute Leeds defence. A goal from Billy Bremner gave Leeds the advantage, and try as we might, we couldn't produce an equalizer. We went to Elland Road confident we could turn the tie around, and we nearly did too.

Cally, who had been struggling with a cartilage injury throughout the season, twanged the Leeds bar in the first half and Tosh rapped a shot against the foot of Gary Sprake's left-hand post in the second. Leeds too had their chances, but the goalless draw was enough to see Don Revie's team progress to the two-legged final, where they overcame Juventus to become the fourth English club to win the Fairs Cup in successive seasons. Not that that was a great deal of consolation for me.

In tandem with our progress in the Fairs Cup we also enjoyed a terrific run in the FA Cup. Aldershot, Swansea City and Southampton were all accounted for at Anfield before we met Spurs in the sixth round, also at Anfield. That game ended goalless, but a solitary goal in the second leg from Steve Heighway before a White Hart Lane crowd of 56,283 took us through to a semi-final at Old Trafford against Everton.

Liverpool had met Everton in an FA Cup semi-final way back in 1950, at Maine Road. It was part of Mersey folklore that Liverpool won 2–0, that Bob Paisley scored the first and my childhood idol Billy Liddell the second. Bob had then suffered a terrible blow: he was left out of the team for the final, which Liverpool lost 1–0 to Arsenal. So Bob had more reason than most for us to beat Everton and go on to Wembley, especially as there was the prospect of playing Arsenal who were up against Stoke City in the other semi-final.

It was Everton who suffered the blows this time round. Their manager, Harry Catterick, was absent having contracted bronchial influenza in Greece where Everton had played a European Cup tie against Panathinaikos. Everton were led out by coach Wilf Dixon. Then further bad luck beset them when their influential centre-back Brian Labone limped off injured and was replaced by full-back Sandy Brown. There is no doubt in my mind that Everton missed Labone (it would in fact turn out to be his last derby appearance as his great career was drawing to a close). Still, Everton took the lead through Alan Ball, prompting us to go in search of an equalizer. I played a long ball to Steve

Heighway who drew the Everton defence before slipping a pass to Alun Evans, who restored parity. Ten minutes later John Toshack challenged Andy Rankin for a high ball. The Everton keeper spilled it, and as players from both sides took to their toes to reach the ball first, not for the first time Brian Hall provided a sharp answer to a starter question.

We had made it to Wembley. I took particular pride from a post-match quote from Shanks, who said, 'If Tommy Smith isn't named Footballer of the Year, then football must be stopped and the men who pick any other player sent to the Kremlin. I understand it isn't a very sociable place!' I wasn't. Arsenal's Frank McLintock won the honour. On hearing of the news, Shanks said, 'They say no news is good news. No football journalists is even better!' I now set my heart on captaining Liverpool to FA Cup Final glory and clearing Bob Paisley's head of his disappointment from 1950.

As League champions, our opponents Arsenal were hoping to achieve only the second Double of the twentieth century, matching the feat achieved by their near neighbours Spurs in 1961. Needless to say, I was convinced they wouldn't do it. We had conceded only one goal in the cup and a club record low of only twenty-four League goals. I felt confident that our form in 1971 was such that we would overcome Arsenal, but I also knew it would be a tough, tight final.

I felt immense pride as I led the Liverpool team out at Wembley. To captain Liverpool in an FA Cup Final was another dream come true. I had been the youngster in the team when we won the cup in 1965, now I was a seasoned pro at the head of a young side. Arsenal, on the other hand, largely comprised experienced players who knew what it took to win at Wembley.

It wasn't a classic final, and after ninety minutes neither defence had been breached. Wembley once again witnessed extra time, as it had done on our last visit back in 1965. The extra time was only two minutes old when Steve Heighway broke away down the left, cut inside and put us in the lead with a shot that beat Bob Wilson at his near right-hand post. We were the younger team and I thought we'd be strong enough to hold out, but Arsenal showed their experience and didn't panic. Eddie Kelly, a substitute for Peter Storey, took advantage of a rare slip in our defence and toe-poked the ball goalwards. George Graham may or may not have applied the finishing touch, but it didn't matter to me; Arsenal were level a minute before the change-around. It was one of the softest goals Wembley had ever witnessed, but, as you know, they all look the same in the football record books. Both teams went in search of a second, and eight minutes from time disaster struck for us. There appeared to be little danger when John Radford played the ball to Charlie George some twenty-five yards from goal. Charlie touched the ball forward before unleashing a shot that took a deflection off Larry Lloyd which was enough to deceive Ray Clemence. The tag of 'lucky old Arsenal' held true. If it had not been for that deflection, Clem would, I am certain, have saved Charlie's effort.

For many, the abiding image of that final was the reaction of Charlie George to what proved to be the winning goal. Having seen his effort hit the net, Charlie flopped back on to the Wembley turf, arms outstretched in readiness for the congratulations of his team-mates. Some saw it as arrogance; I didn't see it at all. When the ball hit our net, in despair and desperation I focused my eyes on Wembley's turf rather than witness the joy of the Arsenal players. The cup and the Double went to Arsenal. Credit to them, they had won through after having been drawn away in every round, and had come from behind not only against us in the final but also against Stoke in the semi-final.

It was another very disappointing end to a season for Liverpool. I felt gutted, but after a few days of coming to terms with our defeat at Wembley I managed to put things into perspective. Of twenty League matches in 1971 we lost just four – a marked improvement. All told, we lost four in twenty-eight. The damage had been done prior to Christmas. Along with Arsenal we laid claim to the only unbeaten home record in the division, but ten draws at Anfield was a significant factor in our finishing fourteen points adrift of the champions. Shanks might have removed much of the old guard, but he had introduced younger players whose potential was clear to me. We had finished fifth in the League, reached the semi-final of what had now become the UEFA Cup, and the final of the FA Cup. As disappointed as I was, I sensed we were getting back on track, that a new, vibrant Liverpool team was in the making. This heartened me more than I can tell you.

Little did I know it, but at Wembley that day was another Liverpool new boy. Shanks had signed the twenty-year-old Kevin Keegan from Scunthorpe United a week before our appearance at Wembley. To be honest I knew nothing about Kevin, other than having seen his name in the Scunthorpe line-up when reading match reports in the newspapers. Understandably a £30,000 signing from Scunthorpe had failed to excite the Liverpool supporters, but very soon Kevin's presence and talent would play a key role in what was to be an unprecedented period of success for Liverpool Football Club. At last, Shanks had found the perfect partner for John Toshack.

8

PURSUIT OF GLORY

AFTER HEARING FAVOURABLE REPORTS ABOUT HIS PERFORMANCES, Shanks had sent Bob Paisley and Joe Fagan to check Kevin Keegan out. They watched him for only twenty minutes before heading home. The following day Shanks asked Bob, 'What do you think?' Bob's answer was swift and simple: 'Sign him.'

Ian Callaghan was struggling to regain fitness after a problematic cartilage operation and Kevin was initially bought as a stop-gap replacement. But he was never going to be a 'stop-gap' anything. The first time I saw him I knew he possessed the talent, drive and hunger to make it at Liverpool. As for Cally, happily he recovered, and he went on to play for Liverpool for another six years.

At Scunthorpe Kevin had played as a right-sided midfielder, which is where he first played in a practice match at Melwood. Bob noticed that during the game Kevin often veered to the left. This was an unexpected bonus. Most players are naturally right-sided when they run and play; right-footed but left-sided players don't come along often, and it is good to have one in a side as it helps give a team all-round balance. Every player worked hard in training at Liverpool, but rarely, if ever, have I seen anyone put as much into it as Kevin did. He wasn't a naturally gifted player like George Best or Kenny Dalglish; to all intents and purposes he was manufactured. Shanks, Bob and Joe Fagan spent countless hours working with him on his game and technique. As captain I was responsible for play on the field during games, and what I liked about Kevin was that he listened and picked up things quickly. For a guy of only five foot eight he compressed a lot of strength into a small frame. He wasn't a great ball-playing artist, far from it, but there is an old adage in football that it is not how, but how many – how many goals you score, how many goals you help create, how many opponents for whom you make things difficult, how many times you win the ball in the air irrespective of your height, how many times you take a man on and beat him, how many times you tackle and win possession of the ball, how many times you make a telling pass or cross, or simply pass to a guy with the same coloured shirt, how many times you take defenders away to create space for attacking team-mates. Kevin ticked all those boxes.

In his first months at the club I watched him work tirelessly at his game. For a guy of modest height and physique he developed into a player tough enough to take the knocks. He was also quick, a good striker of the ball with either foot and, for his size, decent in the air. Reuben Bennett worked wonders in improving his strength and stamina while Bob helped him become more tactically aware. In the striking partnership he formed with John Toshack, it was the latter who possessed the greater football nous and acumen, but Kevin had the edge in speed and mobility.

I knew he was knocking on the door for a place in the first team as soon as the 1971–72 season kicked off for us against Nottingham Forest. I thought that if Kevin played it would be on the right in midfield, but Shanks had a surprise in store. When the team was announced, Kevin was upfront alongside Tosh. It was another masterstroke by Shanks. He had decided Kevin would be better employed as a striker because of his speed, agility and eye for goal, and also because Cally had made rapid progress and he was by far the better player on the right of midfield.

A crowd of 51,000 turned up to see us take on a Forest side that included Peter Cormack, the former Sunderland centre-forward Neil Martin and Ian Storey-Moore. I doubt if many Liverpool supporters were expecting much of Kevin, it being his first game, but his performance was such that he won our fans over straight away. After some twenty minutes Tosh headed down a cross from John McLaughlin and Kevin made it a scoring debut. I added a second from the penalty spot, and though Storey-Moore repeated that feat for Forest the half-time scoreline of 2–1 belied our superiority. Forest made a fight of it in the second half, but when Emlyn Hughes added a third, our season and Kevin's career at Anfield were off to a flyer.

The following Tuesday night, Wolves were beaten 3–2 at Anfield before another bumper attendance of 52,000, our goals coming from Tosh, Heighway and yours truly, which made me, to date, Liverpool's leading goalscorer! I knew that wouldn't last. It didn't, and neither did our explosive start to the new season. Following victory over Wolves, we won just three of the next ten League games, which included successive draws against Manchester United, Stoke City and Chelsea – a wobbly period which coincided with another spell on the sidelines for me due to an injury I sustained in the European Cup Winners' Cup, a competition Liverpool qualified for because of Arsenal's Double (they entered the European Cup).

In early September I missed our Cup Winners' Cup first leg against Servette in Geneva due to a niggling injury; Emlyn Hughes took my place alongside Larry Lloyd in defence with Ian Ross in midfield for Emlyn. Liverpool lost 2–1 but everyone was confident we would overcome what was skilful though moderate opposition at Anfield. In the event we did exactly that, goals from Hughes and Heighway giving us a 2–0 win on the night and 3–2 on aggregate, though I have cause to remember this match for other reasons.

The severed kneecap I sustained against Setúbal was a particularly nasty injury, but against Servette I suffered an injury that was equally debilitating. Some minutes from time Chris Lawler forced the Servette winger Barriquand down the line and I came across to execute a sliding tackle to finish the job. I took the ball cleanly but Barriquand went over the top, in so doing raking his studs down my right leg from the shin bone to the ankle. The referee awarded us a free-kick and cautioned Barriquand – this was a time when it seemed the only way a player could be sent off was if he took a gun on the pitch and shot someone. As I have said, it was never me to stay down when injured, so although I felt a stinging pain in my right leg I simply took to my feet, content that we had been awarded the free-kick. As I walked to take up my position I was aware of wetness on my right shin. Thinking it was just evening dew from the pitch on a late summer's night, I didn't look down. Instead I looked at the man I was marking, the Servette striker Desboilles. He wasn't making eye contact with me; his eyes were fixed on my right shin. What's more, he was looking aghast. I found that a tad disconcerting, so I too looked down at my right leg and noticed that my sock was completely ripped. I used to strap my ankles with bandages for support and secure them with tape, but I never wore shin-pads. I should have done that night. On examining my leg I saw that Barriquand's studs had ripped the support bandage and tape apart, but that wasn't all. The cut down my leg was so deep I could see my shin bone protruding through ragged skin.

I turned to Larry Lloyd. 'Shit! I'm going to have to go off,' I said to him, and signalled to the bench to get Ian Ross stripped. I then caught the attention of the referee, pointed to my right leg, then to the tunnel. The referee turned as white as the shirts Servette were wearing and indicated that I should leave the field immediately. Joe Fagan came out to attend to me, took one look at my leg and said, 'Let's go, Tommy.'

Ian Ross was a good footballer who had played against the likes

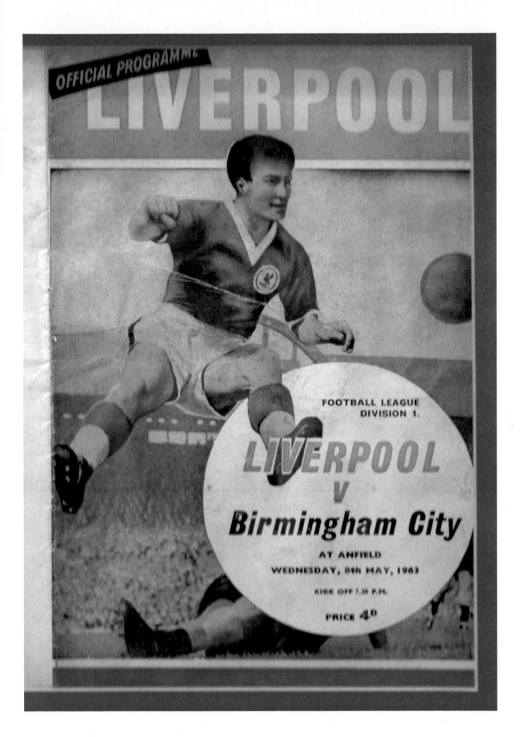

The match programme that means the most to me – my debut for Liverpool against Birmingham City. After the game I walked the streets around Anfield reliving every moment of the game in my mind.

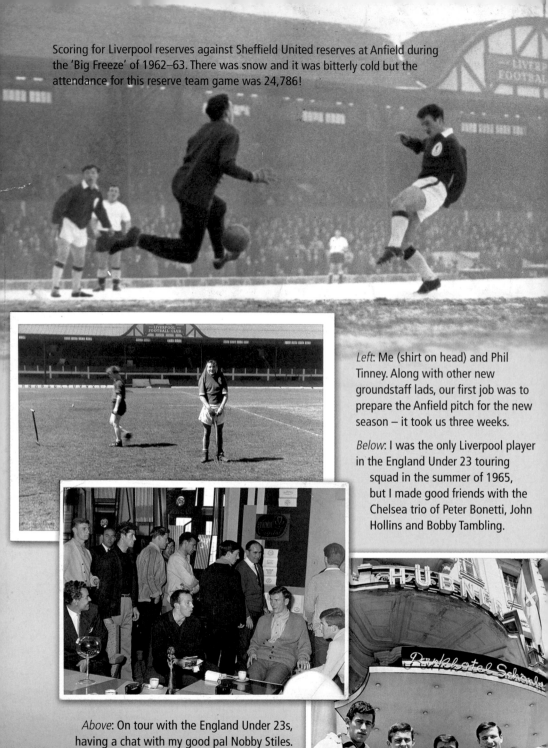

Scoring for Liverpool reserves against Sheffield United reserves at Anfield during the 'Big Freeze' of 1962–63. There was snow and it was bitterly cold but the attendance for this reserve team game was 24,786!

Left: Me (shirt on head) and Phil Tinney. Along with other new groundstaff lads, our first job was to prepare the Anfield pitch for the new season – it took us three weeks.

Below: I was the only Liverpool player in the England Under 23 touring squad in the summer of 1965, but I made good friends with the Chelsea trio of Peter Bonetti, John Hollins and Bobby Tambling.

Above: On tour with the England Under 23s, having a chat with my good pal Nobby Stiles. Among those in the background queueing for their grub are Bobby Thompson (Wolves), Peter Bonetti (Chelsea), Paul Reaney (Leeds), George Armstrong (Arsenal) and manager Alf Ramsey.

Above: Liverpool on tour in the USA in 1964. Alan A'Court is third from left, front row. I had to dig him out of a hole – literally.

Below: We celebrate winning the Championship in 1964. On the table is the papier mâché trophy made by someone in the club office. Holders Everton insisted they had to 'go by the book' and return the actual trophy to the Football League for presentation at a later date, so we improvised.

Above: I complain about Billy Bremner acting up in the 1965 FA Cup Final, whilst the referee admonishes Ron 'The Colossus' Yeats who is just out of shot.

Below: A dream come true for me. Liverpool celebrate winning the FA Cup for the first time in 1965. My mum predicted this would happen one day.

Opposite page, insert top: The match programme from the 1965 FA Cup Final – the first FA Cup Final to feature two Scots as team captains, Ron Yeats and Bobby Collins.

Opposite page, insert bottom: We fill the FA Cup with milk. After having covered every blade of grass at Wembley, Geoff Strong (far right) feels the effects of the first drag of his roll-up!

Opposite page, main picture: Parading the Cup before thousands of fans in Liverpool city centre. The fans were probably thinking, 'We've waited hours for a bus, then three come along together.'

THE FOOTBALL ASSOCIATION CHALLENGE CUP COMPETITION

FINAL TIE

EMPIRE STADIUM

WEMBLEY

LEEDS UNITED
VERSUS
LIVERPOOL

SATURDAY MAY 1st 1965, Kick-off 3 p.m.

Official Programme
One Shilling

LIVERPOOL

LAWRENSON'S

LIVERPOOL F.C.
CUP WINNERS 1965

CRN 992

POLICE

CLICKETY CLICK - OUR YEAR

1966

The year of The Great Double!

EVERTON
F.A. Cup Winners

LIVERPOOL
League Champions

Below: Liverpool on holiday in Spain in 1966. (*L to r*) A local fan, Tommy Lawrence, Gerry Byrne, Chris Lawler, another local and (*foreground*), Roger Hunt and me. There is a space next to me as Cally had gone off to get a round in.

Bottom: Ron Yeats carries the Championship trophy, Everton skipper Brian Labone the FA Cup and Roger Hunt and Ray Wilson the World Cup, as Liverpool and Everton players combine on a lap of honour following the 1966 Charity Shield at Goodison.

LIVERPOOL
FOOTBALL CLUB
ANFIELD

WEMBLEY 1965

FOOTBALL LEAGUE — DIVISION I
**LIVERPOOL v.
SHEFFIELD WEDNESDAY**
SATURDAY, 2nd APRIL, 1966   Price **4**ᵈ

Kick-off 3 p.m.

OFFICIAL PROGRAMME

Above: Liverpool players enjoy a night out at the Empire Theatre to see – and meet – Shirley Bassey. With most players on a basic salary of £35 a week, we were hardly in the class of 'big spenders'.

Left: I pose proudly before my second car – a Triumph. The suit is from John Collier – the 'window to watch'.

Above: I was so excited to appear on *Match of the Day* for the first time that I took a photograph of our TV as Liverpool kicked off the game. I'm with Saint and Roger Hunt.

Below: With Saint, Shanks, Emlyn Hughes and Peter Thompson, having inspected the City Ground pitch prior to playing Nottingham Forest in 1969. From my puffed-out cheeks you can tell it was a bit parky.

of Franz Beckenbauer and Bobby Charlton and done well against them. He wasn't, however, what I would call sharp. When I approached the bench Ian shook my hand as he stepped on to the pitch, glanced down and asked one of the dumbest questions I have ever been asked.

'Is it your leg?'

'No,' I said, 'I've got a slight headache.'

The club doctors were brothers, Bill and John Reid. Bill was the younger sibling and he didn't care for stitching, so that was left to John, who attended me in the treatment room. John was a good old boy who enjoyed the hospitality afforded to him at games and invariably would have a brandy or two at half-time. Which prompted us players to joke, 'If anyone gets injured, make sure it happens in the first half before the doc has a drink.' Joe told me to lie down on the physio bench and gingerly removed my right boot. I could tell from his intake of breath that he thought the injury a bad one. Then John Reid arrived, and his prognosis hardly filled me with hope.

'Smithy,' he said, 'that's the worst cut I've seen without being in the operating theatre. You're going to be out for some time.'

At which point Bill arrived on the scene.

'What're you gonna do, doc?' I asked.

'I'll clean it and try to stitch it,' John said.

It was the word 'try' that worried me.

John peeled away my ragged sock and deftly cleaned the shin and ankle in preparation for the stitch-up. Having got his needle ready, he seemed to take a long time looking at the wound; eventually the hand holding the needle approached my shin, only for him to suddenly retract it. He wiped his brow with the back of his hand and turned to his brother.

'Bill, go get Tommy a brandy, and get me one as well – a large one!'

What ensued was like some scene from a Western film in which a doctor removing a bullet from a cowboy orders whisky, which you think he is going to administer as a makeshift anaesthetic for the patient but he ends up swigging it himself for Dutch courage. Bill duly returned with the brandies. I declined mine so John downed them both as if Courvoisier urgently needed the bottle back. Suitably fortified, he then set about my leg.

He filled the whole wound with Cicatron, a penicillin powder, before beginning the job of closing it up. The stitches clearly needed to be tied tighter because halfway through the job Doc Reid turned to Joe Fagan and asked, 'Are your hands clean?'

'No,' replied Joe.

'Oh well, never mind,' said the doc. 'Put your finger on that knot while I tighten it.'

The job done, I looked down at the stitching. Each stitch was about an inch apart.

'That's never right, surely?' I said, pointing at the gaps between the stitches.

'Tell you what, I'll pack the gaps with more penicillin powder,' said the doc, and he duly did just that.

I gained a reputation for being a hard man, but I was only cautioned twice in my entire career and sent off just the once. The dismissal was for taking issue with referee Clive Thomas – not that I was unique in having done that. My sending off occurred some years later during a game against Manchester City. I was so incensed that City's Tommy Booth had continually kicked Phil Thompson and got away with it that I called Clive a cheat, which was wrong of me, I know. I had to go for that, but when I reflect on some of the despicable and dangerous treatment I received for which the perpetrators went unpunished – a sliced kneecap and the baring of my shin bone, for instance – I do sometimes wonder how some officials see the game. Yet again I was left to contemplate the fact that some players with no reputation for hard play often did more damage with one callous challenge than I ever did with dozens of hard but fair tackles.

My spell on the sidelines coincided with Liverpool struggling to win, but on my return in mid-October we recorded what was only our second victory in seven games when we beat Nottingham Forest 3–2 at the City Ground. I was delighted to be back in the team, even more so because I scored the winner. Our form improved in the run-up to Christmas and there was only one defeat in ten League matches, albeit at Everton. Unfortunately, during this period we were knocked out of the Cup Winners' Cup, beaten by a very good Bayern Munich side. The first leg at Anfield ended goalless, but a Bayern side that contained Franz Beckenbauer, Sepp Maier, Paul Breitner, Uli Hoeness and Gerd Muller, all of whom went on to help West Germany win the World Cup in 1974, proved too good for our youngsters. Bayern deservedly won the return 3–1 but, given the quality of the opposition, I didn't feel there was any disgrace in that. With so many top-quality players in their ranks I was sure Bayern would go all the way and win the competition. As it turned out they were beaten in the semi-finals by Rangers, who went on to defeat Moscow Dynamo in a final that, sadly, was besmirched by the puerile behaviour of a section of their fans.

Keegan, Heighway, Hall, Tosh and Clem were all relatively young, inexperienced players, so we were doing well to be among the leading clubs in Division One as we entered the festive period. However, at that point the wheels came off the wagon. After a 3–2 defeat of fellow title contenders Derby in mid-December, we failed to record a single victory in our next five matches. What's more, we failed to score a single goal. Having disposed of Oxford United in the FA Cup, we also exited the competition when beaten by Leeds United after a replay.

We were missing Larry Lloyd, and more importantly Tosh, both of whom were injured. Their absence had a not inconsiderable effect on the way we were playing. Without Tosh, Kevin Keegan wasn't as effective as a striker. Shanks tried him alongside Jack Witham and Alun Evans but to no avail. Kevin needed Tosh, whose physical presence was problematic for defenders and whose positional play created any number of openings for Kevin. I knew that once Larry and Tosh returned to the fold things would once again look up for us.

That happened against Crystal Palace in late January. We had slipped to sixth, but with both Tosh and Larry back in the side we immediately got back on the pace. Kevin scored, Cally helped himself to a brace and Chris Lawler also got himself on the score-sheet in a 4–1 win that did wonders for our confidence. It marked the beginning of a run that saw us lose just once in sixteen matches, with thirteen wins. There were some handsome wins too: 5–0 against Newcastle United, 3–0 against Manchester United at Old Trafford, and 4–0 against Everton at Anfield. I remember the Everton victory, of course, and for good reason. The game was only twenty-five seconds old when my pal from my days with Liverpool Schoolboys, Tommy Wright, put through his own goal. Ten minutes into the second half, John McLaughlin (not the one of the same name on our books) did the same. Two-nil up against Everton, and they had scored both for us. Such a unique event couldn't go without comment from the Kop. No sooner had McLaughlin scored than the Kop struck up with a chant of 'TV commentators, will think you're impersonators, of Sandy Brown, of Sandy Brown!' On hearing this I burst out laughing, as did most of the Liverpool team. Needless to say, the Everton players didn't see the funny side of it, particularly when Emlyn Hughes and Chris Lawler added to their misery.

As I said, I was good friends with many of the Everton players, and I joined them for a drink after the game. I made a point of chatting to Tommy Wright and told him not to feel so bad, that own goals happen for most players. 'Putting through my own net after only twenty-five seconds – I'll never hear the last of it,' said Tommy. 'Still, I guess it's a once-in-a-lifetime experience.' It wasn't. In Everton's very next match, against Manchester City, Tommy put through his own goal again after only thirty-five seconds, which must be some sort of record.

Our tremendous form in the New Year saw us going head-to-head with Leeds United, Derby County and Manchester City for the title. For a time Manchester United and Arsenal were also in the frame, but United's slim hopes were all but ended when we defeated them 3–0 before a packed Old Trafford, a game which produced yet another verbal gem from Shanks.

After training at Melwood on the Friday morning prior to meeting United we returned as usual to Anfield for a team talk. The players gathered around the table as Shanks began to go through the United side, in so doing casting aspersions on the ability of almost every one of their players. 'His distribution is terrible, couldn't pass wind,' he said of one; 'Useless in the air, can't direct the ball, has a head like a sheriff's badge,' he said of another; and so Shanks continued. 'They're an overrated team. Go out tomorrow and play them off the park.' At which point it occurred to me that he had omitted to mention three United players.

'Boss, you've never mentioned Best, Law and Charlton,' I ventured.

Shanks took a step back, and his jaw dropped. 'Jesus Christ, Tommy, son,' he said in amazement, 'you telling me we can't beat a team with only three players in it?'

Shanks knew that the team had now gelled. Having dismantled one great Liverpool team, he was well down the road towards creating another. In essence we had been in transition for five years. In that time we'd had quality players but not enough of them to win titles and cups. Now, however, I felt Liverpool were on the verge of success. Ray Clemence was becoming a terrific goalkeeper, and having such a good man at the back took some pressure off us as defenders. Chris Lawler, Alec Lindsay, Larry and I were more relaxed in our play, secure in the knowledge that should one of us slip up the chances were it would not result in a goal. Cally was excelling on the right of midfield, Emlyn Hughes and Brian Hall were outstanding in the centre, and Steve Heighway was flying on the left. Tosh and Kevin had developed a great understanding with each other; what's more, they had begun to score goals. That was the regular side, in addition to which Shanks could call up, among others, Bobby Graham, Phil Boersma and John McLaughlin, whose versatility enabled them to fill various positions.

We went to the Baseball Ground for our penultimate match of the season off the back of eight consecutive victories in which we had scored twenty goals; we had conceded only three in our previous fifteen matches. The situation at the top of Division One was tight to say the very least. Manchester City led the table on fifty-seven points but had completed their season. We were just a point behind City with two games to play. Derby too had fifty-six points but their remaining game was against us. In fourth place came Leeds on fifty-five points with two games to play. We were all confident that we had the wherewithal to win the title, me more than most. Derby, under Brian Clough and Peter Taylor, included Colin Todd, Roy McFarland, Alan Durban, John McGovern, Kevin Hector, Archie Gemmill and John O'Hare in their ranks, so I knew it would be tough for us, but I was convinced we could take them.

Back then we played on what were basically four types of pitch. The season began on lush playing surfaces that resembled bowling greens, which would gradually deteriorate as the season unfolded. Winter produced two types of pitch, either frozen solid or like a Christmas pudding. Come the end of the season, the winds of late March and April dried out the pitches, which were almost devoid of grass except on the wings, leaving them bone hard and bumpy. Most pitches in the Football League were slaves to this cycle, but by far the worst sufferer was the Baseball Ground. The pitch there was a notoriously bad drainer. I had played there in mid-winter when the mud was so thick and gluey it all but sucked the boots off my feet; now, on 1 May, it was as hard as pine knot, the surface bare and uneven, the sort of pitch that makes the ball appear overly light, always bouncing around knee height.

The football writers predicted a tense, tight game, and for once they weren't wrong. The first half was goalless, and as the second progressed I felt a point was ours. Late on, however, John McGovern popped up to score what was the only goal of the game to send the majority of the capacity crowd of 40,000 wild with delight. After playing so well it was a bitter disappointment to journey back pointless to Merseyside. Our only consolation was that our final game at Arsenal was now anything but pointless. Our title hopes rested on a victory at Highbury, and how Leeds fared at Molineux.

Derby's victory over us elevated them to the top of the table on fifty-eight points, but their season was now over so things certainly weren't straightforward. Manchester City were now out of the frame, but Leeds had beaten Chelsea which meant that Don Revie's team had fifty-seven points, with one game to play, at Wolves. Leeds were the favourites, needing only a point from their last game to win the title, but if we beat Arsenal by two clear goals and Leeds lost at Molineux, the title would be ours as we would pip Derby on goal difference. Derby had to hope that Leeds lost and we didn't win in order for them to be crowned champions, but there was nothing they could do now, so Brian Clough took his players on holiday to sunny Majorca. We and Leeds were to work up a sweat in other ways.

Don Revie was furious when the Football League insisted his side play Wolves on the Monday night following their appearance in the FA Cup Final against Arsenal on the Saturday. That was the same evening we were playing Arsenal. In the event Leeds travelled to Molineux as the cup holders, having beaten Arsenal 1–0 at Wembley, which meant that not only the title but the Double was theirs for the taking. Even allowing for their exertions two days earlier, Leeds were expected to gain the point they needed at Wolves to win the Championship. It was an extraordinary climax to the season, but one that was to leave a very sour taste of disgust in my mouth, and not because of anything to do with Leeds or Derby. Unbelievably, it was all down to one of my Liverpool team-mates.

One of the things I have discovered from writing this book is that an autobiography is the perfect vehicle for telling the truth about other people. So before I go on to offer my recollections of the events of the evening of 8 May 1972, let me state that Emlyn Hughes and I never got on.

When Emlyn first arrived at Anfield I had no cause not to welcome him, as I would do any new player. Very quickly, however, I began to take a dislike to him. Initially this was down to certain characteristics he displayed which I felt were not in keeping with the Liverpool way. Prior to Emlyn arriving I'd had the privilege of playing for a number of years with a bunch of players I considered not only team-mates but good friends. When a manager creates a team, if he has anything about him as a manager, he will know that not all players will get on with one another like a house on fire. Shanks was lucky in this respect: the likes of Saint, Big Ron, Chris Lawler, Roger Hunt, Gerry Byrne, Tommy Lawrence, Geoff Strong, Gordon Milne, Cally, Thommo and I all gelled and enjoyed one another's company immensely. Many people think that's the norm in a professional football team; on the contrary, it's rarely the case. Generally speaking, players do get on with one another. Some will make strong and lasting friendships with team-mates; with others they will be matey within the working environment, but they won't see them socially. Think of your own working environment. How many of your work colleagues would you say are close friends? How many do you simply 'get on' with? Is there the odd individual you don't warm to? It's the same in football. A team comprises all manner of different personalities and characters. When two players don't hit it off, all a manager can expect of them is that they respect each other as footballers. That's how it was for Emlyn and me.

As I mentioned earlier, no sooner had Emlyn arrived at the club than I began to notice small character traits that were not in keeping with how the other players conducted ourselves. Shanks had brought us up always to be polite and respectful to people, for example to the staff of the hotels in which we stayed. When we sat down for a bite to eat at a hotel, Emlyn always chose to sit at the end of the table nearest the kitchen door. When a waiter emerged carrying two plates of food, Emlyn would intercept him, cast an eye over the food and choose whichever one appealed. On one occasion he wanted some more steak. Rather than asking the waiter politely, he pointed to the remaining meat on his plate and said, 'Oi, you, over here! Get me some more of this, will you?' Now I am well aware that is a minor indiscretion on his part, but no other Liverpool player ever spoke to hotel staff in such an inconsiderate way. The fact that Shanks and Bob were at the far end of the table meant they never heard the way Emlyn spoke to waiters, otherwise I am sure one of them would have had something to say. When I was made captain I did comment on the often curt way in which he addressed hotel staff. All he said by way of reply was, 'You are joking, aren't you?'

Minor unsavoury character traits apart, in my opinion Emlyn often displayed behaviour that belied his chirpy, cheerful public persona, antics which resulted in him becoming disliked not only by myself but by many of the Liverpool players. For the best part most players didn't let Emlyn's irritable behaviour get to them, but the tide seemingly turned over an incident involving his car.

As part of a commercial deal struck by the FA, every member of England's squad for the 1970 World Cup Finals was given a Ford Mexico car, a version of the Escort. In return for the car, each player consented to attend a certain number of Ford promotions throughout the year. At the end of the twelve months, the players had the option of purchasing the car for a peppercorn sum, or returning it to Ford. As a member of Sir Alf's final squad, Emlyn had one of these Ford Mexico cars. At the time he was living in lodgings with a family by the name of Firth. Mrs Firth had a teenage son called Kenny, whom I knew to be a decent lad. One

Friday prior to an away match at Manchester United we were staying, as usual, at the Lord Daresberry Hotel in Warrington. Apparently that weekend Kenny Firth had a problem with his own car and rang Emlyn to ask if he could borrow his, for which Emlyn gave permission. Unfortunately, on the Saturday night Kenny was involved in an accident on the A580 East Lancs Road. No one was hurt but the police were involved. It transpired that Emlyn only had third party, fire and theft insurance, which meant Kenny wasn't insured to drive the car. Emlyn now had a problem. He should never have allowed Kenny to drive the car, knowing he wasn't insured.

On the Monday morning, a solicitor I knew, Bill Twidale, rang me. Bill was not a happy man. He told me that Emlyn had been down to the police station and made a statement to the effect that Kenny Firth had stolen his car. There was little I could do other than try to have a word with Emlyn, which as team captain I attempted to do. I also suggested to Bill that he might have a word with Emlyn's dad, Fred. I was told that Fred travelled down to Merseyside, had a meeting with Emlyn and Bill at Bill's office, and in no uncertain terms told his son to retract his statement. Bill informed me that matters were subsequently sorted out and Kenny faced no charges. But the incident left a sour taste. I was not alone in the dressing room in thinking that Emlyn had behaved in a despicable way.

I could list all manner of things Emlyn did that evoked ire not only in me but other people. Suffice it to say his behaviour and character were such that I increasingly grew to dislike him. When the players were allowed a beer – at a hotel, say – we would break into groups of four and one person in each group would offer to buy a round. The buying of the rounds was always shared out. If, for example, one night Kevin, Tosh, Cally and I each bought a round, the next time we had a beer Clem, Chris, Steve Heighway and Bobby Graham would get them in, and so on. Emlyn always hung back and would only join us when everyone had had a beer.

Only then would he say, 'Anyone having a drink, lads?', to which, of course, we would all reply that we were OK. One night Larry Lloyd took Emlyn to task on this, saying he always bought himself a beer but never anyone else. 'Hey, you can't say that, big fella,' replied Emlyn. 'I always offer.' Which was true, but I think you get my point.

In all my time as a club player I roomed with only two players, Chris Lawler from the early 1960s to 1974, and Ian Callaghan from 1974 to 1980 (which included the spell we spent together at Swansea City). In his first five years at Liverpool, Emlyn roomed at one time or another with every player but me and Chris. When we stayed at the Lord Daresberry on a Friday night prior to a home game we always took thirteen players: the chosen eleven, the substitute and a reserve who was on stand-by in case anyone suddenly took ill. Thirteen is an odd number. For a number of years whenever we stayed at the Daresberry, Emlyn roomed alone. Make of that what you will.

As for Shanks and Bob, well, Shanks couldn't have cared less if players didn't get along as long as they performed well together on the pitch. To him, football was all that mattered; personal relationships between players were simply not an issue for him. Both Shanks and Bob were at pains to keep a respectful distance from all players, but Bob was somewhat different from Shanks in that he admired Emlyn as a footballer and respected his knowledge of the game. But he, too, never warmed to him as a person.

And so to the events of 8 May, the night we had to beat Arsenal by two clear goals and hope that Leeds United lost at Wolves in order to win our first League Championship for six years.

Our team bus arrived early at Highbury, some ninety minutes before the kick-off. I was standing in the corridor outside our dressing room when Emlyn approached me and said, 'I want a word.' This was unusual in itself, as we rarely spoke to each other except during games.

'We're not out on the pitch, yet,' I informed him.

'Yeah, right, but I want a word now.'

'What about?'

Emlyn looked up and down the corridor as if to assure himself he would not be overheard.

'I've been chatting to a couple of the Arsenal lads,' he informed me. 'If we pay them fifty quid a man, they'll throw it.'

'You are kidding?' I said, for want of anything more purposeful to say while my mind grappled with the immensity of what he was apparently proposing.

'Look, Arsenal will finish fifth no matter what happens tonight,' Emlyn continued. 'We pay each of them fifty quid and the game's ours. If I go in that room and ask each of the lads for fifty, they'll tell me to sod off, but they would give it to you.'

I was totally taken aback. For once I was unsure of what to do. I stepped into the dressing room and asked Cally to come out. But when Cally and I stepped back into the corridor, Emlyn was gone. When I told Cally what Emlyn had proposed his eyes widened to the size of Doulton dinner plates. We exchanged the sort of looks miners exchange on hearing a heavy beam creak and crack.

'And what's your take on this?' asked Cally eventually.

'No way,' I said, unable to control what was nervous laughter.

'Good,' said Cally. 'That's what I'd expect you to say. Listen, Tommy, you don't like him and he doesn't like you. But he's asked you to go in there and put this to the lads. He says he's done that because they might say yes to you but not to him. I know you won't go in and put this to them, but you know the lads as well as I do, they'd say no to whoever went in there with such a proposal. Have you thought of this? That he might not have spoken to the Arsenal lads and is trying to set you up, to create trouble for you?'

That got me thinking. What Emlyn said had come as such a shock to me I hadn't been thinking clearly and objectively. But what Cally said made sense. Over the years I have pondered this matter a lot and come to the conclusion that in all probability Emlyn hadn't spoken to the Arsenal lads of this sordid proposal. I knew the Arsenal lads; I couldn't imagine them agreeing to such a thing.

I led Liverpool out at Highbury struggling to put the matter to the back of my mind and concentrate on the task in hand, that of trying to win the game and, hopefully, the Championship. The game was played at break-neck speed, but not to the detriment of skill. The tension in the stadium throughout was of the piano-wire variety. Emlyn rattled the Arsenal bar from thirty yards, and from the rebound Kevin Keegan's overhead kick cleared the same spot by a whisker. Two minutes from time, having received a message that Leeds were losing, we scored through John Toshack, only for his effort to be adjudged marginally offside. It was agonizing. When the final whistle blew it was if my heart had sunk to my boots. For all that it ended goalless, it was rated as the best game seen at Highbury all season. Needless to say, that was no consolation for us.

When we trudged wearily into the dressing room, a radio conveyed the news from Molineux. Wolves had sensationally beaten Leeds 3–2 in what had been another dramatic and controversial game. By all accounts, Leeds had had two good penalty appeals turned down, and Peter Lorimer had hit the bar with a header in the last minute of the game. Derby County, out in Majorca, must have been going berserk.

I looked around the changing room and noticed that Emlyn was crying. 'All that effort, all season, now this. We've lost the Championship.' I couldn't be doing with it. I was too disgusted with him.

Immediately after the game we travelled back to Merseyside. Inside the coach it was as if someone had placed a coffin on the back seat. When I arrived home – and Sue will vouch for this – I was so angry and upset about the Emlyn incident that I shed tears of bitter frustration. At the time I was still unsure if his aim had been to set me up; all I knew was that I felt I had been used and, to a degree, abused. Prior to the incident Emlyn and I had disliked each other; now I struggled to define what my feelings were towards him. It wasn't hate, but it was pretty darn close to it. The other problem I had was that Emlyn was a superb player and a key member of the team. I had to face up to the fact that I would have to carry on playing alongside him and temper my dislike of him for the good of the team, the club and our supporters. Given how I was feeling that night, it was some ask.

There is an ironic postscript to this story. The *Sunday People* subsequently printed an article alleging that certain Leeds United players had tried to bribe Wolves in the other game. The Leeds skipper, Billy Bremner, was named. He was so incensed about these claims that he went to court to refute them, and won substantial damages from the newspaper.

I like to think that in my own way I too won. I hadn't for one moment contemplated complying with Emlyn's proposal, even if it was true. If, as I now surmise, it wasn't, then I didn't fall for his set-up. More to the point, I had the strength of character not to seek any sort of retribution; for the good of the team and the club, I never alerted Shanks or Bob to the matter. Had I done so at the time it would eventually have become public knowledge, and the very thought of such a scandal within the club would have devastated Shanks. I simply couldn't allow that to happen to the man.

For all the sourness of the final act of 1971–2, I was looking forward to the 1972–73 season with great optimism as I felt Liverpool now had a team capable of winning major trophies. Younger players had gained in experience, while senior pros such as Cally, Chris and, dare I say it, me appeared to be playing better than ever. During the summer Shanks sold Alun Evans to Aston Villa and bought Peter Cormack from Nottingham Forest; he also took a flyer on Tranmere's Trevor Storton. Those transfers apart, it was the same playing staff that had seen the club through the previous season. I took that to mean that Shanks was more than happy with what he had, and I trusted his judgement. I felt he too believed we had sufficient quality to win silverware.

The team that began the season against Manchester City was comfortingly familiar: Clemence, Lawler, Lindsay, me, Lloyd, Hughes, Keegan, Hall, Heighway, Toshack and Callaghan. With the exception of the introduction of Peter Cormack for Brian Hall, barring the odd injury this team saw out the season. And what a season it turned out to be. Nigh on 56,000 spectators crammed into a sun-kissed Anfield to watch our opening game. We made a perfect start, goals from Brian Hall and Cally giving us a 2–0 victory in a game that saw Larry Lloyd and City's Wyn Davies sent off after clashing when contesting a high ball. Larry later had his red card rescinded. I can only imagine this was because the Football League couldn't understand how the referee had seen the incident accurately at such an altitude.

City's neighbours, United, visited Anfield on the Tuesday night and a crowd of nearly 55,000 saw goals from Tosh and Steve Heighway replicate our 2–0 success of the opening day. Our first visit was to Selhurst Park, where an Emlyn Hughes goal earned a hard-fought 1–1 draw. The Palace goal, scored by Peter Taylor, resulted from a mistake by Steve Heighway. The following Monday, during Shanks's talk about the game, he laid into Steve, admonishing him for having dwelt on the ball.

'It was you, Steve Heighway, who cost us the two points,' said Shanks. 'You dawdled on the ball, lost it and never chased back. Have you no pride, son? Have you got no legs? The guy played a one-two and Alec was sold down the river!'

'I'm not a defender,' said Steve, which for such a cerebral guy was not the most intelligent thing to say to Shanks.

'No, son, but you belong to a team. I'll tell you what, if you saw your next-door neighbour's house on fire, would you go and get a bucket of water?'

'What does that mean?' asked Steve.

Shanks was immediately taken aback. He was very much aware

of Steve's intellectual credentials but he wasn't going to let him denigrate his homespun philosophy.

'I am asking you to provide me with an answer to my question,' said Shanks.

'I'll provide a sensible answer when you ask me a sensible question,' retorted Steve.

That did it. Shanks bristled. His face went puce and the veins on his temples turned as thick as biros. 'Get him out! Take him out now, before I . . . Tommy, Chris!'

In what had suddenly turned into a very tense and uncomfortable atmosphere, Chris and I went across to Steve and gently guided him out into the corridor.

'He's blaming me for costing us a point. I'm not accepting that. And what have I said?' pleaded Steve.

'Listen,' I told him, 'just take it. If he blames you, say nothing. Accept it and he'll accept it. By taking issue with him you do yourself no favours. You just inflame the situation. Now get in there and say you're sorry. No one is bigger than Liverpool Football Club, and to all intents and purposes Shanks is Liverpool Football Club. He built this.'

That's how you had to react to Shanks. The vast majority of the time he spoke good football common sense, wisdom even. Occasionally there was a touch of Samuel Goldwyn to his words, and he often picked out someone to carry the can. But we had all been subjected to that; it wasn't personal. Just because Shanks had a go at you, it didn't mean you wouldn't be in the team for the following game. Positive or negative words from Shanks were in fact an indication that you were very much in the frame. The time to worry was when he ignored you. Shanks was a formidable character and manager. He had a burning enthusiasm for Liverpool, a fanatical devotion to the game, almost to the exclusion of everything else. He spent so much time at the club, his idea of a good night out was a good night in. I have never come across anyone so single-minded. What Steve had failed to realize was that Shanks was totally dedicated to his players, even if he did occasionally single someone out for what that player believed was unfair criticism. To Shanks, everything about Liverpool was the 'gggrrreatest' – his players, his team spirit, his backroom staff, the supporters, the groundsmen, the tea ladies. The only people he wasn't keen on at the club were the directors.

Sure enough, Steve Heighway kept his place for the 2–1 victory over Chelsea at Stamford Bridge, which we followed with a 3–2 win against West Ham. Successive defeats on the road at Leicester (our bogey side) and Derby County knocked us out of kilter but we bounced back and beat Wolves 4–2 at Anfield. A point at Arsenal in our next game was followed by a 5–0 thumping of Sheffield United. That victory over Sheffield United on 23 September took Liverpool to the top of Division One, and that was where we intended to stay.

In tandem with our excellent form in the League we also enjoyed unprecedented success in the UEFA Cup. Six British teams had qualified for the competition: Spurs (the holders), Manchester City, Stoke City and Liverpool from England, while Aberdeen and Partick Thistle represented Scotland. Our campaign began on 12 September with a tie against Eintracht Frankfurt, whom we beat 2–0 at Anfield. A goalless draw in West Germany was good enough to see us progress to the next round, where we came up against AEK Athens. In those days it was always thought beneficial to play the first leg away from home and to attain the sort of result that would enable you to complete the job on home turf; but we weren't really bothered if we played home or away in the first leg. We had confidence in our own ability to beat teams and saw the job as one that had to be done whatever the circumstances. As it turned out, again we were drawn at Anfield in the first leg, and we comfortably dispatched the Greeks with goals from Phil Boersma, Peter Cormack and me. The atmosphere in Athens was heated in more ways than one. When we took to the pitch the crowd was very volatile but we seized the initiative from the outset and scored through Emlyn Hughes. Later in the game Boersma got a second and Emlyn a third to make it 3–1 on the night and 6–1 on aggregate. The change of atmosphere in the stadium in the course of the ninety minutes was remarkable. When the final whistle sounded there were still around 30,000 home fans in the ground but you could have heard dust settle. Dynamo Dresden were beaten in the quarter-finals, and when the draw for the semi-finals was made only two British teams remained, ourselves and Spurs. Everyone hoped we would avoid each other to set up the prospect of a second successive all-British European final (Spurs had beaten Wolves in the final the previous season), but it was not to be.

An Alec Lindsay goal was all that separated the two sides in the first leg at Anfield on 10 April 1973, and in light of that Spurs must have really fancied their chances back on home territory. In a thrilling game at White Hart Lane, Martin Peters scored twice for Spurs, but the telling goal came from Steve Heighway. His effort was good enough to put Liverpool through to the final on the away-goals rule. The Spurs manager was Shanks's good friend Bill Nicholson. After the game Nicholson came into our dressing room to offer his congratulations, which was typical of the man.

'Have you heard who you'll be playing in the final, Bill?' Nicholson asked Shanks.

'Aye, Borussia Mönchengladbach,' replied Shanks.

'Yes, well, just as well you went through and not us,' said Nicholson wistfully. 'I can't pronounce it.'

By the latter stages of the 1972–73 UEFA Cup, this new Liverpool team Shanks had created was truly galvanized. I have mentioned the contribution and effect of the Toshack–Keegan partnership upfront, the presence of Clem, and how the other players, Emlyn included, gave their all for the cause. We were, however, playing in a slightly different style to previous Liverpool teams I'd had the privilege of playing in. In previous seasons we had laid siege to opponents only to be frustrated more often than not by a well-organized blanket defence. Shanks and Bob had become aware of the limitations of pounding away at sides that deployed ten, sometimes eleven players behind the ball. Our play had now become more subtle. The new philosophy was that goals were easier to come by through counter-attack than continuous pressure.

One way we did this was to have Clem instantly throw the ball out to one of our full-backs, or to someone in midfield, as soon as he collected a cross or executed a save. As soon as Clem had that ball in his hands, Chris or Alec would make space and move forward, making themselves available for a quick throw. Bob had pointed out that a team is at its most vulnerable the moment it loses possession. Our intention was to take possession quickly and attack as quickly as we could. That way we would stand a better chance of scoring a goal than if we took a minute and a half to work the ball upfield, by which time our opponents would have fallen back. The prime aim was to pass the ball quickly, to get it up to Tosh and Kevin a.s.a.p. If the opportunity of going for goal was denied to that pair, then they knocked it back to our midfield players who would be tanking up from deep. Cast your mind back to old *Match of the Day* footage of Liverpool games, if you can. How many times did you see Tosh knock the ball back, or a cross come from out wide to a Liverpool player marauding up from deep who then shot from the edge of the opponents' penalty box, or just outside it? So effective was this counter-attack it was carried on into the days of Dalglish, Souness and McDermott. Remember a Spurs side containing Ossie Ardiles and Ricardo Villa being walloped 7–0 at Anfield in 1978, and McDermott racing from deep to thump home a header from the edge of the box with hardly a Spurs player in sight?

Should we not be able to pass the ball quickly, the alternative was to keep possession and work an opening, usually courtesy of the intelligent off-the-ball running of Tosh or Kevin. The mantra was that every player must feel comfortable on the ball in all areas of the pitch, whether at pace or not. Passing and movement were the keys, and in this respect Shanks, Bob, Joe Fagan and Ronnie Moran would have quiet words with players to enable them to become more adept at this. They might have a chat with someone one day and make another suggestion the following week. You never noticed things were getting better on a daily basis; it was only when you looked back that you suddenly became aware that the team, and every player in it, was part of a constant process of improvement. After a number of seasons in which Liverpool had been a 'nearly team', by 1972–73 we had, at last, emerged as a true force in domestic and European football.

It was also emphasized to us that what we players did off the ball was as important as what we did when the ball was at our feet. In the course of a ninety-minute game, even the busiest of midfield players will have the ball at his feet for a total of no more than two and a half minutes, so it stands to reason that what a player does in the other eighty-seven and a half minutes is crucial to proceedings. As a central defender I was as much involved in the game when play was fifty or sixty yards away as I was when in the heat of battle. Cally and Steve Heighway on the flanks got through as much work as anyone. They were mobile all the time, dropping back when we were on the defensive, and moving to create space or to make themselves available when we broke from the back. Unlike my early days at Liverpool when wingers hugged touchlines, Cally and Steve played from the wings, not on the wings.

Peter Cormack, who came into the side in September 1972, did a great job for us. He was a player of craft and stealth who was not dissimilar to Saint in his defensive work behind the front line. For the meat of the season Peter kept Brian Hall out of the side, which believe me took some doing. This was also the season when Phil Thompson first appeared for Liverpool. He deputized for me in defence when I sustained an injury in December; he also appeared at left-back, and on one occasion in midfield. Such were his performances, Phil was soon to establish himself as a regular.

★

Come January 1973 we had been sitting on top of Division One for nigh on four months, with Arsenal, Leeds and Ipswich Town (under Bobby Robson) doing their best to keep with the pace. On 6 January we travelled to West Ham, who were lying fifth in the table and going well. Kevin was up against Bobby Moore – a truly great player of course. Shanks seemed to feel Kevin was a little apprehensive about facing Bobby, so prior to the game he indulged in a little psychology. As we were about to get changed, Shanks entered the room and walked over to Kevin. 'Son,' he said, 'it's tragic. I've just seen Bobby Moore come in. He's been in them nightclubs again, son. He's got baggy eyes. Must have an injury because he was limping. He looks awful, son. It wrenches at my heart, it's tragic, because he was once a great player. He's gone, but show him no mercy. Do your job, son, massacre him.' As we were about to leave the dressing room I looked across at Kevin. He was taking deep breaths and continually jutting his chin out. He thought he was up against a geriatric and was going to do exactly what Shanks had demanded.

West Ham were difficult opponents, but we played exceptionally well as a team. Kevin was outstanding, and he scored the only goal of the game to consolidate our position at the top of Division One. Back in the dressing room Shanks was buoyant, complimenting every player. Eventually his attention focused on Kevin. 'Jesus Christ, son,' said Shanks, beaming, 'you'll never play against a better or fitter player than Bobby Moore. He's a master, but you had the beating of him today. Grow in confidence, son. You were up against world class and you ran rings around him!'

Another game I remember well was Spurs at the end of March, a game which had an early kick-off due to the running of the Grand National. They came to Anfield off the back of five successive victories; they were in the top half of the table with an outside chance of making Europe (sounds familiar, does it not?). The game is particularly memorable for an outstanding performance by Spurs' goalkeeper Pat Jennings. Had it not been for Pat we would have won by five or six goals; as it was, Pat earned his side a 1–1 draw. He produced an unbelievable save from Peter Cormack, who met a cross on the edge of the six-yard box and blasted the ball goalwards only for Pat to palm the ball away. On another occasion he managed to hold a point-blank header from Brian Hall. Minutes later he flung himself to his right to tip away a thirty-yard blaster from Emlyn that seemed destined for the top right-hand corner of his net. He also saved two penalties, one from Kevin, the other from me.

I usually took our penalties, but when we were awarded one some seven minutes before half-time, Kevin asked if he could take it. As he appeared confident, I had no hesitation in saying yes, only for Pat to save his effort. Five minutes from time, with the score at 1–1, we were awarded another penalty. This time there was no way I was going to allow Kevin to take it, and to be honest, he didn't offer. My success rate was very good; I felt sure I could tuck it away and win the game. On this occasion, however, though I hit the ball right, Pat flung himself to his left and held it. I fell to my knees and beat the turf with my fists in frustration.

As I did so, I was suddenly aware of laughter. I glanced up towards the goal. Pat was holding the ball to his chest with his right hand, his left hand was clenched, punching the air in triumph, but he wasn't laughing. I quickly glanced behind me. The referee, Mr Raby (Leeds), was holding his arms aloft to signal play on, and it was he who was laughing. 'Play on! Play on! This is wonderful stuff!' he cooed. I took to my feet and, for all that I was frustrated at having failed with the penalty, I found I too had a smile on my face. It was indeed wonderful stuff. It never occurred to me to take issue with the referee for enjoying the moment of Pat saving a second penalty. Sure I was annoyed I hadn't scored, but I too appreciated that Pat had capped an unbelievable performance with the saving of yet another penalty. It was quite remarkable, something that would provide a conversation point around hundreds of pub tables and energize talk on factory floors. Intent as I was on winning personal battles and games, football was also fun. Sadly, if a referee in today's Premiership reacted in a similar fashion to such an incident he would be chastised and in all probability hauled over the coals.

I am only too aware that some reviewer of this book, not old enough to have watched football back in the early seventies, may adhere to the stereotypical view that the seventies produced rough-house, cynical football in which there was no place for fun and humour. No doubt such a reviewer may feel compelled to write something along the lines of: 'There goes another old pro, writing his memoirs of how the game was better in the old days and romanticizing incidents.' I'm not saying football was better back then, it was just different. Nor am I romanticizing, and to validate this, in this book I reproduce a photograph from my personal collection: Pat Jennings is punching the air in celebration, I'm on my knees beating the ground in frustration, and the referee, hands aloft, is laughing and enjoying the moment.

On Easter Monday we met our old adversaries Leeds United at Anfield in what was our penultimate game of the season. Only Arsenal could deny Liverpool the Championship, and only then if we lost our final two matches and Arsenal won their remaining games by substantial margins. Anfield lay flooded in goldleaf sunshine. There was every just cause for celebration among the 56,000 spectators who thronged the terraces and stands, but we knew we had to make certain of victory to secure Liverpool's first Championship for seven years.

Leeds, as ever, were doughty opponents, but on this occasion we had more than the measure of them. Following a goalless first half, they came out and gave it a go in the second period. During an early bout of pressure I intercepted a pass from Peter Lorimer, fed the ball to Cally and he was away. With Leeds players chasing back, Cally made tremendous progress down our right and crossed the ball to Tosh; he nodded it back to the on-rushing Peter Cormack who, from the edge of the area, smacked it past David

Harvey. Anfield erupted, and I could almost feel the Championship trophy in my hands. Five minutes from time Kevin Keegan made it 2–0. When the final whistle blew, someone relayed the message that Arsenal had only managed a 2–2 draw at Southampton. To all intents and purposes we were champions. I was elated and very, very proud to have captained Liverpool to the title. For me, this was momentous. I had seen the changes at the club, been part of the initial renaissance, contributed to a very successful period, then one of transition. Now Liverpool were riding high once more, the best team in England. Only Chris, Cally and I remained from the last Liverpool team to have won the Championship. I was deeply moved.

It was still mathematically possible for Arsenal to overtake us, but to do that we had to lose our last game against Leicester and they had to win their remaining two games scoring thirty-one goals in the process – no way. The following Saturday we played out a goalless draw against Leicester City. The fact that we hadn't won mattered not one jot. When the final whistle blew, 57,000 supporters joined us in what was party time. I was presented with the Football League Championship trophy, the real one, and Shanks, resplendent in a dark grey suit, red shirt, tie and pocket handkerchief, joined us as we paraded the silverware around a jubilant Anfield.

As we did our lap of honour, Shanks's feeling for the club and our supporters was vividly illustrated. As we stood before the Kop, a supporter threw a Liverpool scarf down on to the perimeter track. A policeman stepped forward and flicked it to one side with his boot. Shanks was on to him like a flash.

'What do you think you're doing? That scarf is someone's life you're grinding in the dust!'

You know, I think he was right.

Back in the dressing room, the champagne flowed. It was the sweetest of moments, yet at the same time it was a weird feeling to have won the Championship. You have to be confident as a player.

I was always confident that we would win every game we played, and throughout 1972–73 I had remained confident we would win the Championship, but somewhere deep down inside was a little voice saying, 'Can this really happen for you? You've got a wonderful family, a good life and career. That's the reality of it. Do you really think you're so blessed your dreams can also come true?'

I shut the voice up that day.

On 9 May, a week after we celebrated our title success, we played the first leg of the final of the UEFA Cup at Anfield. On the day two surprises were in store. The first involved the selection of the team: to everyone's surprise, Shanks dropped John Toshack to the bench and opted for Brian Hall. The second surprise was the weather. That evening as our coach made its way to Anfield from Liverpool's Holiday Inn where we had stayed for the afternoon, a rainstorm straight out of the book of Genesis descended on the city. I'd never experienced anything like it. Thick, low, bible-black clouds turned a late spring evening to night. The rain lashed out of them in torrential streams. As a great howling wateriness enveloped the city, the drains couldn't cope. Down-pipes gushed like fire hoses; roads and streets soon took on the appearance of ponds and lakes. Before long our coach was creating a bow wave as the driver gingerly steered it towards Anfield.

'What's the forecast for tonight?' asked Alec Lindsay.

'Dark,' I replied, and everyone laughed nervously.

As we entered Anfield the rain was still coming down as mercilessly as our ambition to win the cup. Once inside the dressing room I forgot all about the weather because my mind was totally focused on the game. We were unaware as we prepared for the match that officials from both clubs and UEFA were meeting with the referee to discuss whether it was possible for the match to go ahead. The pitch was waterlogged and the game should have been postponed, but as this was the UEFA Cup Final, it was being broadcast on television and all the spectators were already gathered, the decision was made to go ahead.

When I emerged from the tunnel at the head of the Liverpool team and looked around Anfield I instinctively said ''King hell!' as I couldn't believe the sight that greeted my eyes. The rain was still falling and the pitch was totally saturated, great pools of water sitting on the surface. It later transpired that the torrential rain had caused damage to one of the drains, which had broken. A piece of it had been flushed into the pitch's major drain release and wedged there, causing a blockage which had resulted in all the surface water.

The game, such as it was, was a farce. It was like trying to play football in a two-inch deep paddling pool. Conditions were so bad that neither ourselves nor the German lads could kick the ball further than two yards across the surface. Players were constantly overrunning the ball. After less than half an hour of pantomime play, the referee summoned me and the Mönchengladbach skipper, Gunter Netzer, and informed us that he was abandoning the game. Neither Gunter nor I protested. UEFA asked the respective clubs what they would prefer to do about restaging the game. Thank heavens they did, because the officials from both clubs were decisive: they had no hesitation in suggesting the game should take place the following night.

In those twenty-four hours, Shanks had a major rethink. He surprised Mönchengladbach by recalling Tosh upfront and relegating Brian Hall to the bench. He knew the Germans had pre-pared meticulously to deal with a particular Liverpool attacking plan, and changed it. Even from the shambolic half-hour of the night before, Shanks had seen that the Germans were not particularly comfortable in the air at the back. If anyone could exploit that perceived weakness, it was Tosh. Shanks's instincts proved spot on. We gained a tremendous advantage by beating Mönchengladbach 3–0 with two goals from Kevin and one from Larry Lloyd. Tosh caused havoc in the air, and although he didn't get among the goals himself, he was instrumental in our victory.

The return leg in West Germany was always going to be tough, but it proved to be more problematic than even Shanks had envisaged. We certainly needed that three-goal advantage because Mönchengladbach totally outplayed us in the first half. Netzer, Bonhof, Vogts, Wimmer, Danner and Rupp were outstanding. Twice the latter made goals for Heynckes, and at one point we seemed to be hanging on by the merest of threads. In the second half Shanks told Tosh and Kevin to play deeper, replaced Steve Heighway with Phil Boersma, and played Phil as a lone striker. Believe me, such was the pressure from the home side he was very much alone. Shanks turned to me. 'Keep it tight. Tight!'

I did my best to ensure we did just that. I rallied the troops and attempted to lead by example, calling upon all our expertise and resources of character. At crisis moments in any match you often have to look beyond your own game and think of the team. I knew I had to drive the lads on to an even greater effort, to redeploy them, keep up their morale and organize both in defence and midfield. Gradually the game began to turn our way. When the final whistle sounded, such was my sense of relief that for a few moments I couldn't bring myself to celebrate.

The UEFA officials carried a large table on to the pitch and the UEFA Cup was placed in the centre. By this time our supporters were swarming all over the pitch, but happily it was all celebratory and good-humoured. When I was presented with the trophy I did wonder why two UEFA officials handed it to me. When I took hold of it, I found out. The UEFA Cup must be the largest major trophy in world football; what's more, it has a heavy marble base. I was exhausted with the sheer effort of the match, but felt I had no option but to lead the lads on the traditional lap of honour. The UEFA Cup has no handles either, so it is difficult to hold at the best of times. We hadn't gone far when I turned to Cally and handed him the trophy so he could brandish it for all our supporters to see. Cally carried it for about six yards, then handed it back, saying, 'I can't carry this, it weighs a ton!' No one else fancied carrying it either, so I held it aloft for the duration of the lap. As if that wasn't bad enough, at one point a very large Liverpool supporter ran up and jumped on my back. 'Smithy, Smithy,' he screamed in my ear, 'we've won the UEFA Cup!' Over my shoulder I shouted back, 'If you don't get off my back, you'll have it over your head!'

There is a postscript to this story of the supporter jumping on my back. In 2005 Sue and I were shopping in a supermarket when a lady approached me. She asked if I remembered the 1973 UEFA Cup Final and a supporter jumping on my back as I paraded the trophy. 'That was my husband,' she informed me. 'And he's over there, by the baked beans.' I made my way over and had a chat with the lad and we laughed about the incident. I returned to Sue, thanking my lucky stars it had been some thirty years ago that he had jumped on my back and not now. He was some size!

When I entered our dressing room still carrying the UEFA Cup, I saw Shanks sitting down, mulling over his first European trophy.

'Here you are, boss,' I said, handing him the cup. 'It's all yours.'

To be honest, I was glad to be rid of the thing. I don't think I could have carried it another yard.

Shanks and Joe Fagan later said that my performance that night was my best in a Liverpool shirt. I don't know about that, but I admired and respected both men immensely and their words were much appreciated. It had been a terrific season for the club. Liverpool became the first English club to win the Double of a League Championship and a major European trophy. In the course of the season we played sixty-three competitive matches and called upon the services of just fifteen players. As Sue and I prepared to take Darren and Janette on summer holiday, I recall thinking to myself, 'When my career is over, I'll look back on this time, and these will be the great days.' In the event, even better days were to come, for the club and for me.

9

DROPPING THE PILOT

IT WAS A JULY MORNING AND WARM AT NINE A.M., A SURE SIGN OF A blistering day to come, one of those rare English summer days when you have a shower first thing and two hours later feel in need of another. I arrived at Anfield prior to joining the rest of the lads for the short trip to Melwood for training. Everything seemed perfectly normal. The banter rattled, quips were made in response to newspaper articles being read. Nothing was untoward, or so it seemed. Just as we were about to leave, Shanks got hold of me and asked if he could 'have a word'. The three words that always precipitate trouble.

I followed Shanks into his office. He indicated that I should take a seat. I did.

'Tommy, son, I've decided to make Emlyn captain. You'll still be club captain, of course, but from now on Emlyn will captain the team. OK?'

It wasn't OK, but what the hell. The decision had been taken.

That said, Shanks took to his feet and began to walk across to the door.

'OK, Tommy, son, thanks for coming in. See you at Melwood.'

Within three-quarters of a minute of having entered his office, I found myself outside in the corridor again.

Body language and posture are good indicators of how someone is feeling. As I walked down the corridor I must have looked as if I'd been stuffed by an incompetent taxidermist. Stuffed being the apposite word. Given my record at the club and the way I had applied myself to the role of captain, initially I felt I had been treated shabbily by Shanks. But the very fact that he had called me in and spoken to me in person about this I saw as a mark of his respect for me. Ask any Liverpool player who played under Shanks about being left out of the team and he'll tell you that Shanks never gave a reason, he just totally ignored you. The same applied when you were injured.

Having got over the initial shock of the news, I found I was OK about having been relieved of the team captaincy. Like my predecessor, Ron Yeats, I had taken my responsibilities as captain very seriously. The amount of work I had undertaken off the field was considerable. Organizing visits to local hospitals and schools; answering letters of requests for autographs and personal appearances at charity functions, golf days and cricket matches; dealing with players who, for whatever reason, had a grumble – the tasks were daily and endless. In addition to which, at Liverpool the captain was responsible for matters on the pitch. Pardon the pun, but I did feel relieved to be left with an ostensibly nominal position. But I wondered why Emlyn had been chosen. As I have said, I respected Emlyn as a player but not as a person, and he wasn't exactly Mr Popular with the other players. For the good of the team, and because he did make a very positive contribution to the side, in my opinion Emlyn was 'tolerated' by many of the lads. The only player he seemed to get on with was Tosh. I couldn't see him commanding the total respect of the players.

It was three years later when I finally discovered the reason why Emlyn had been appointed captain. I was having a chat with Bob and he told me that Emlyn had gone to Shanks and said he would leave the club unless he was made captain. Shanks didn't want to lose a player of Emlyn's calibre, especially not to a rival club such as Everton, Manchester United, Leeds or Arsenal, so he had complied with Emlyn's demand. I wasn't surprised to hear of this. To my mind Emlyn knew he wasn't Mr Popular, but as captain he knew he could command the ear of the players. Whether their reaction to what he had to say went any further than merely listening remained to be seen.

I had now been at the club long enough to know when Shanks had decided to drop a player from the team. During his team talk on a Friday, if he didn't mention a name with reference to a specific shirt number when detailing tasks, experience had taught me that the player who had worn that shirt in the previous game was out.

The 1973–74 season opened with a home game against Stoke City. On the Friday after training at Melwood we assembled around the green baize pitch on the table in the centre of the home dressing room.

'Aye, goalkeeper has to feed the ball quick to full-backs, OK, Clem?' Shanks began. 'Number two, always be making yourself available, Chris, and push on at every opportunity. Number three, likewise, Alec, son. Number four, we play one-up, one-round at the back. Geoff Hurst will be up front for them. Good in the air. Number four and five, Larry, might think about taking it in turns to mark Geoff. That way you get a rest and he doesn't. Number six . . .'

I looked across the room to Bob and Joe Fagan. They were looking down at the floor, anywhere but at me. That clinched it. I would not be wearing the number four shirt for our opening game, which resulted in a 1–0 victory. I also missed the following two games, a defeat at Coventry and a draw at Leicester City. I was restored to the team for the fourth match of the season, a 2–0 victory over Derby County. Naturally I was delighted to be back, but just as no reason had been offered for my omission from the side, no reason was given for my return.

Looking back, our League form up to October was of the ominous variety, though no one saw it that way at the time. Ten League matches produced five wins, three draws and two defeats, in addition to which we enjoyed what I can only describe as an unconvincing success in the European Cup against Luxembourg part-timers Jeunesse Esch. Then, after a 2–1 win over Newcastle United on 6 October, we suffered successive 1–0 defeats at Southampton and Leeds United. The latter were enjoying an unbeaten start to the season that would continue for twenty-nine League matches, at the time one match short of the all-time un-defeated run set by Burnley way back in 1920–21. Leeds opened a sizeable gap at the top of the First Division, but it was October so we players didn't consider a six-point lead to be insurmountable.

In round two of the European Cup we were expected to over-come Red Star Belgrade without too much difficulty. Red Star were a decent team, but we had beaten better in Europe. No alarm bells were ringing when we went down 2–1 in Belgrade, even though we were impressed with the way Red Star, managed by Miljan Miljanic, had played. Theirs was also a passing game, but essentially from the back. I firmly believed we would overturn the 2–1 deficit at Anfield, but I was not to be part of our efforts: Phil Thompson took my place in the centre of defence. Red Star played even better at Anfield and their 2–1 victory sent shockwaves rever-berating around the club. As holders of the UEFA Cup we had been expected to do well in the European Cup. To exit in round two, and, with all due respect, to a team not considered to be one of the European heavyweights, prompted many an inquisition in the press. What we didn't know at the time was that Shanks was holding an even more thorough inquisition in the boot room.

You never stop learning in football, not least because the game is forever developing as people introduce new ideas. You might wonder how such a simple game in which the basics never change can constantly be in a state of flux, but just as there are only so many musical notes in existence yet people continue to write new songs and music, football too lends itself to perpetual creativity. What was evident from the games against Red Star was that football was undergoing another change. The game was becoming more expansive and fluid. More thoughtful play, high on technique, produced more effective play. Red Star had shown that building from the back was the way forward. They had centre-backs who were as comfortable on the ball as the most creative midfield players. Shanks and Bob sensed that the age of the big stopper centre-half was over. They wanted defenders to be creative as well as destructive, initiating attacks from the back, bringing the ball out of defence, coming forward to all intents and purposes as a central midfield player might. I was a casualty of that home defeat against Red Star, which was somewhat ironic given that I hadn't played. After the Red Star game I found myself out of the side for another four matches, none of which, I have to say, Liverpool lost. To bring about this more fluid style to our play, Shanks had replaced me with Phil Thompson, who initially played alongside Larry Lloyd, only for Larry then to be displaced by Emlyn.

We were due to play Arsenal at Highbury. I knew Shanks was not happy with our recent performances and had the distinct feeling that he was going to leave me out. As he discussed our visit to Highbury, he began talking of what he expected from each position. 'Our number four must be ready for any sharp breaks,' he said – not the usual 'Tommy, son, make your presence felt in there.' So I instinctively knew I was not in the team, but having been named in the squad I was prepared to travel to London later that day, although I would have preferred to stay behind and play for the reserves rather than make what from my point of view was a futile trip. As we prepared to set off I did ask Shanks if I had a shirt. 'I haven't made my mind up, Tommy,' he told me, which to me belied his dictum about the importance of truth at the club.

'I'm not going,' I told him. 'I'd rather stay and play for the reserves than sit in a stand.'

'You'll have to go, I've told the press,' he replied.

In order not to place Shanks in an awkward position, then, I agreed to travel.

As we journeyed to London on the Friday afternoon, I grew more and more agitated. We usually left our bags on the bus when we travelled to away games, but on matchday I carried mine into Highbury. When we got into the dressing room I dropped it by the door. I went to the loo, and Peter Cormack followed. Peter had also been subjected to the numbers game and I told him that if I wasn't to receive a shirt I was going to catch a train home rather than sit in the stand.

'If that's what you're doing, I'll come with you,' Peter said.

We returned to the dressing room, Shanks announced the team, and sure enough I didn't get a shirt. Peter was named as substitute. I stood up and walked towards my bag, picked it up and said, 'Good luck, boys. See you in training tomorrow, Joe.' Joe Fagan looked at me knowingly.

Suddenly I was outside Highbury, among hundreds of supporters. One Liverpool fan came up to me and asked, 'Where are you going, Tommy?'

'Home,' I said. 'I'm not playing and I'm not watching. I'm not a good spectator.'

'If you're not playing, I'm not watching either. I'll come home with you.'

'No, son,' I said, 'stay and support the team.'

Then I headed for the tube station, made my way to Euston and caught a train back to Lime Street.

It seemed a long journey, one during which I gave my situation considerable thought. I was far from happy, but I decided to report to the ground on the Sunday morning to do a bit of training and hopefully prove a few people wrong.

When I arrived at Anfield the following day, Joe Fagan was already there. Joe knew exactly how I was feeling, and I believe he was sympathetic to my cause. I walked past Shanks's office. The door was open. He spotted me and called me in.

'Listen, Tommy, son, I know how disappointed you are,' he began. 'I don't blame you for walking out and going home. Tell you the truth, son, I would have done exactly the same if it had been me.'

If that was an attempt to pacify me, it didn't. It was Shanks playing familiar mind games. As I said, I was left out of the team for the rest of the month.

I'd told Shanks I was injured. Joe Fagan collared me and asked what was up with me. I told him I was not happy to carry the can for the defeat against Red Star when I hadn't even played. Joe told me I wasn't seeing the big picture, and asked if I was really injured. I was upfront and told him, 'No.'

'Then why won't you travel?' he asked.

'What's the point? He won't play me. I'd rather turn out for the reserves, Joe.'

Towards the end of November, the Stoke City manager, Tony Waddington, made an enquiry about me. He rang me at home and informed me that he had spoken to Shanks about the possibility of my joining Stoke on loan. Once again I was miffed because no one at the club had spoken to me about Stoke's interest and the possibility of a loan move. I left it with Tony.

I went into training on the Monday morning as normal. Eli Wass, our head groundsman, came out and said, 'Tommy, there's a phone call for you, the guy says it's urgent.'

I went to take the call. It was Tony Waddington.

'Where are you, Tommy?' he asked. 'Didn't Bill Shankly tell you to report to Stoke this morning?'

I informed Tony that I had received no such instruction and that I wanted to discuss the matter with Shanks. I was fuming. I was an established Liverpool player with my career on the line, and nobody could bring themselves to discuss what was going on with me. I found Shanks and in no uncertain terms told him that I was angry with the situation as it stood.

Eli agreed to take me back to Anfield to get my car. Even that was somewhat demeaning: he drove a Reliant Robin three-wheeler with a top speed of twenty miles an hour, and he was having trouble with it. After what was an excruciatingly frustrating journey, I collected my car and drove down to Stoke with my mind in a tizzy. Tony Waddington issued me with the papers for a month's loan, and paid my expenses and a week's wages in advance. But being away from Liverpool instantly felt like a terrible wrench. I couldn't believe how this had all happened. It was as if I had no control over my own situation. Still, at least I was now with a club that wanted me.

I drove back to Merseyside and that very night received another call from Tony. He sounded shell-shocked as he informed me that the loan deal was off.

'Why, what have I done?' I asked.

'Nothing,' said Tony. 'Shanks told me he wanted the option of recalling you at a minute's notice should he have any injury problems. That's no good to me.'

Tony's words took on a clearer meaning when I reported back to Anfield the following day. It transpired that Chris Lawler had a cartilage problem. Shanks informed me that he was restoring me to the team for the game at West Ham on 1 December.

'Lovely to see you back, Tommy, son,' he said. 'I want you to play right-back for me.'

I was still angry with the treatment I had received, so I informed him, 'I'll play right-back for the team, the club and our supporters, but it won't be for you!'

'Whatever,' he replied.

Once again I was taking the advice Shanks had given me as a groundstaff lad, not to take shit from anybody. The trouble was, you never knew with Shanks. He liked to wind you up and get your blood boiling. In my case he knew I would channel my aggression into games, towards opponents. When I left his office he was smiling; he knew I would be in growling mode come matchday. We beat West Ham 1–0 and then defeated Everton by the same score.

I was happy to be back in the team. Shanks was happy too. But I still felt he had treated me shabbily.

My delight with the recall was tempered by the news that Chris would be out for some time. As it turned out, the injury ended his Anfield career. Chris was the first person I'd made friends with when I joined the club as a fifteen-year-old. We had roomed together throughout my career to date, we were really good friends, and I admired and respected him both as a player and as a man. I did not hesitate to get on with the job I had been asked to do, but my joy at being restored to the team was tinged with regret. Now only Cally and I remained from the 'old guard'.

Yet another era for Liverpool was beginning, and it brought with it another position for me to play in the team. I settled down to the role of right-back and, in the parlance, made it my own. During my time at the club I had played centre-forward, inside-left, on the right and in the centre of midfield, centre-half, sweeper, and now right-back. I thought about what Shanks had said when he bought Geoff Strong from Arsenal, that he had signed him not to fulfil any specific role but as a footballer, 'like they did in the old days'. I convinced myself that was how Shanks saw me now.

Leeds were still going great guns at the top of Division One, but we gave them more than a run for their money. In a run of twenty-two League matches from the autumn of 1973 to April 1974 we lost just the once, at Burnley. In addition to which we were also enjoying a very successful run in the FA Cup.

As I made clear earlier, as a competition I love the FA Cup. Sometimes the law of the jungle is overturned and the small can for once devour the large. I was never reminded of this more than in our third-round tie against Doncaster Rovers at Anfield, a game I missed due to injury. Doncaster were scrubbing about at the foot of Division Four, but the FA Cup galvanized them. At half-time the nation's reporters must have sensed a major story in the making: Doncaster were leading at Anfield by two goals to one courtesy of Michael Kitchen and the towering Brendan

O'Callaghan. In the second half we drew on our bruised pride, our attacks acquired more purpose and Kevin Keegan equalized – in so doing scoring his second of the match – but Doncaster held out for what was a highly creditable if somewhat incredible draw. A crowd of 25,000 filled Belle Vue for the replay in which a more logical pattern of play prevailed. Goals from Heighway and Cormack produced what in the end was a comfortable 2–0 victory.

In the main, Carlisle United had goalkeeper Alan Ross to thank for a goalless draw at Anfield in round four. Ross produced a string of excellent saves to bolster a Carlisle team that battled from start to finish. Carlisle can boast the best average home attendance in the country per capita, and back in 1974, despite a population of some 80,000, a crowd of over 21,000 thronged Brunton Park in the hope of seeing an upset. I can't say I was sorry we disappointed them with a 2–0 win over a side that included John Gorman (later Glenn Hoddle's assistant when Hoddle managed England), Ray Train and Chris Balderstone, who also played county cricket for Leicestershire and later went on to become a Test match umpire.

The referee for that game at Carlisle was Jack Taylor, who refereed the 1974 World Cup Final. Jack and I had a little history. It went back to my days as a player in the Liverpool youth team. When we played West Ham in the FA Youth Cup Final we beat them at Anfield but lost heavily in the return at Upton Park. I felt that Jack made several mistakes in the second leg, and as I left the pitch I told him in no uncertain terms what I thought of him. The Brunton Park pitch was very icy that day, and during the second half United's Joe Laidlaw was bearing down on our goal when he slipped and fell. I was a good two yards from him when this happened but Jack came running up and booked me. We subsequently appealed, and Joe was called as a witness. When he told the Disciplinary Committee he had slipped on the icy pitch and I was nowhere near him, the faces of the committee members dropped.

In round five we came across more familiar opposition in the form of Bobby Robson's Ipswich Town. Goals from Hall and Keegan provided what was now becoming a familiar scoreline. A single-goal victory at Bristol City in round six took us into the semi-finals where we came up against Leicester City; the other semi-final was contested by Newcastle United and Burnley. We dominated the tie at Old Trafford but could not beat a Peter Shilton-inspired Leicester. The contest produced no goals until the second half of the replay when a scrambled effort from Brian Hall was wiped out minutes later by a Len Glover equalizer. Then, with Shilton's goal coming under increasing pressure, Tosh created an electrifying goal for Kevin and then scored one himself to turn a Liverpool v. Newcastle final from expectation into reality.

As April unfolded the race for the title boiled down to a two-header between Leeds and Liverpool, with Stoke City and Derby County still in the frame should either team court disaster. In the event Stoke and Derby went off the boil, though Leeds and ourselves didn't exactly pull up trees. We contrived to win just one of our remaining eight League matches, a 4–0 success over Manchester City at Anfield. We drew five and lost at Sheffield United, but by far the most crucial result proved to be our single-goal defeat at home to Arsenal on the 24th. Leeds had surprisingly lost three successive games at the end of March, but we were unable to capitalize. The loss to a mid-table Arsenal, courtesy of a goal from Ray Kennedy, was our only home League defeat of the season. As a result we could no longer overtake Don Revie's side, and not for the first time during my Anfield career, Liverpool finished runners-up. Leeds were not in action that day, and having been so often the 'bridesmaids', missing out on silverware when success was in their own hands, I couldn't help but think it ironic that they should win their second title in six years when the players were sitting at home. But credit to them, they had led the table from the start and had come within a whisker of creating a new record for the longest sequence of unbeaten games.

Another big name was languishing at the other end of the table: this was the season when Manchester United were relegated to Division Two under Tommy Docherty. In truth, Tommy had inherited an ageing team. He rang the changes, and promotion was achieved the following season at the first attempt. At the time several United players had passed the tipping moment in their respective careers, and George Best was being, well, George. Tommy had to wield the axe and rebuild, just as Shanks had done. Shanks was very good friends with the Doc and appreciated the deficiencies of the United team he had inherited. Following one game at Anfield, Joe Fagan, who had been listening to the radio, informed us that United had lost again and slipped to the bottom of the League.

'Aye,' said Shanks, 'and they'll take some shifting!'

Due in the main to his debilitating injury, Shanks was of the mind that time had to be called on Chris Lawler. Another casualty of Liverpool's new style of play was Larry Lloyd. Having lost his place in the side in the New Year, Larry moved on to Coventry City. One manager who felt Larry still had a role to play in the modern game was Brian Clough, who later took Larry to Nottingham Forest, where, of course, he not only won a League Championship medal but helped his club to success in the European Cup. As I say, one of the intriguing aspects to football is its unpredictability!

You might be wondering how I was getting on with Emlyn. I am at pains to point out yet again that I respected Emlyn as a footballer and for what he did for Liverpool, but that is as far as it went. We never talked, except on the pitch. He kept his distance from me, which suited me fine. I got on well with the rest of the lads and, for want of a better word, tolerated Emlyn. To be honest, I might have thought a good part of the problem with Emlyn rested with me but for the fact that he wasn't exactly popular with the majority of the team. With Chris out of the frame, I roomed with Cally, and for all that Emlyn was now captain, Cally and I assumed the role of senior pros at the club. None of the lads ever got out of order, but when we were allowed a few beers, such as on a close-season tour, and certain individuals became overly exuberant, it was Cally and I, not Emlyn, who would say, 'That's enough, lad, calm your nerves. We have a responsibility to the club and our supporters.' Such was the common sense displayed by everyone, and such was the respect players felt for the club and our fans – and, I would like to think, the seniority of Cally and me – our advice was always taken.

In the build-up to the FA Cup Final some of the Newcastle players tried to indulge in a little psychology, but it didn't work as far as we were concerned. Newcastle's young full-back Alan Kennedy appeared on television and during the course of an interview said that I was now too old to get through ninety minutes at Wembley, and too old to take him on. I'd only just turned twenty-nine so I did wonder what exactly he meant. Did he mean I could get through ninety minutes at any ground other than Wembley? His words did nothing more than gee me up to prove him wrong. The Newcastle centre-forward, Malcolm Macdonald, was particularly boastful, saying he was going to do this and that to the Liverpool defence. Malcolm had scored a hat-trick on his debut for Newcastle against us. Ten minutes from the end of that game he was injured and carried off the field. The game was featured on television and I remember watching it (painful as it was) and the commentator saying, 'How sporting of the Liverpool players who are offering words of condolence to Malcolm Macdonald as he is taken from the field.' What a number of us were actually saying was, 'You'll never score against this club again as long as I'm playing', and words to that effect. For the record, he never did. Malcolm was a terrific, rampaging centre-forward out of the old mould, but again, his words prior to the final served only to make us determined to make sure he didn't get so much as a sniff of the ball on the day.

On 4 May, as the clock ticked round to three, the teams walked out at Wembley: Ray Clemence, me, Phil Thompson, Emlyn Hughes, Alec Lindsay, Brian Hall, Peter Cormack, Ian Callaghan, Steve Heighway, John Toshack, Kevin Keegan and Chris Lawler (our substitute) alongside Iam McFaul, Frank Clark, Pat Howard, Bob Moncur, Alan Kennedy, Jim Smith, Terry McDermott, Tommy Cassidy, John Tudor, Malcolm Macdonald, Terry Hibbitt and Tommy Gibb (their sub). Throughout the first half Newcastle matched our tireless running and desire to attack. There were precious few chances, but what chances there were fell to us. As planned, Malcolm Macdonald wasn't getting a sniff. I sensed it would be only a matter of time before we turned our dominance into goals. In the second half I thought we had broken the deadlock when a stunning twenty-five-yard shot from Alec Lindsay flew past Iam McFaul. Alec was beside himself with joy, jumping and punching the air, only to be metaphorically and literally brought down to earth when the refereee, Mr Gordon Kew, ruled offside.

'Who was offside?' asked Brian Hall.

'Someone sitting up in Row G, I think,' I replied. 'It certainly wasn't one of us.'

Apparently Mr Kew, who had a very good match, thought Kevin was offside.

Undaunted, we continued to take the game to Newcastle. In the 57th minute I made progress down the right and crossed the ball into the half-circle on the edge of the Newcastle penalty area. Brian Hall's gymnastic attempt to connect with it failed, but he drew Bobby Moncur from Kevin. Before the gap could be sealed, Kevin controlled the ball with a single touch and rifled it high to Iam McFaul's left. Iam managed to get his fingertips on the ball but not enough to divert it away from goal. The red contingent in Wembley erupted, and I felt in my bones that we were on our way to victory.

There was not enough resilience in Newcastle to bounce back. From the restart we took control again. Tosh's dominance in the air was forever problematic to the Newcastle defence, and he sent Steve Heighway clear to make it 2–0. It was then, and only then, that Malcolm Macdonald demonstrated that he was still on the field: two low drives of his were comfortably fielded by Clem before once again he settled back into relative obscurity. With the red ribbons in all probability already tied to the handles of the cup, Kevin notched his second and our third. An eleven-pass move began with the intention of keeping possession of the ball, but when I was sent clear once again down the right I looked up to see Kevin steaming towards the Newcastle penalty area. I played a one-two with Steve Heighway, and though close to the byline when receiving the return, I pulled the ball back to an unmarked Kevin who side-footed home.

With seconds remaining and the final won, once again I received the ball wide on the right. Alan Kennedy came towards me I nutmegged him on the line, played the ball to Steve Heighway, then turned back and sarcastically applauded. 'You're right, son, I'm too old to take you on,' I told him. OK, that was un-professional of me, but Alan's pre-match comments were still very much in my mind. On hearing the whistle, the first person I shook hands with was Alan Kennedy. When the final whistle sounds, it's over, and personal battles are forgotten, which is how it should be.

Our supporters sang Shanks's name, and a couple of them raced on to the pitch and prostrated themselves before him. 'While you're down there, would you mind giving my shoes a quick polish?' quipped Shanks, forever the purveyor of the comic one-liner. He was also full of brio and sparkling wit during our post-match banquet where, flanked by his players, he gave a 'live' interview to Jimmy Hill for *Match of the Day*.

'How does this cup win compare with the club's first in 1965?' asked Jimmy.

'This game was very one-sided,' replied Shanks.

To everyone's surprise, Jimmy then asked Shanks about me, saying that I served as a good guide to footballers who, confronted with disappointment, often give up and ask for a move.

'Tommy and I had our differences during the season, but we're not like many of the politicians, you know – we don't harbour ill feeling,' Shanks began. 'If we had behaved like many a politician and continued our grievances, Liverpool would have dropped down. Many politicians carry on their grievances and the country falls down. But Tommy and I put it all behind us. And you saw Tommy today. Magnificent.'

'We're sleeping together now!' I piped up.

'Hear that? Tommy's almost as fast as me,' retorted Shanks.

'If the walls in your office could only talk,' said Jimmy.

'How boring they'd be,' said Shanks.

'What I mean is, you always seem to pass on good advice to your players,' Jimmy continued.

'It's the only thing to do with it,' replied Shanks, quick as a flash.

At which point Jimmy, realizing he had elicited some gems from Shanks, and being the pro he was, decided to get out on a high note and handed back to the studio.

An estimated half a million people thronged the streets of the city to see us parade the FA Cup from an open-top bus. As the bus approached St George's Hall I was standing next to Brian Hall when Shanks came over to us.

'You two boys know about these things,' he said. 'What's the name of that Chinaman, the one who has all the sayings?'

'Confucius?' I suggested.

'No, no, the leader who has the little red book.'

'Chairman Mao,' Brian informed him.

'Aye, that's the fella, thanks,' said Shanks, and he disappeared back down the bus leaving the pair of us none the wiser.

When we arrived at the hall we assembled on the balcony. The noise generated by the thousands of people gathered on the streets below was deafening, but when Shanks stepped forward and raised a hand they immediately fell silent.

'Even Chairman Mao has never seen a greater show of red strength than this!' announced Shanks.

The streets erupted.

In the summer of 1974 the Football League met to discuss the future of the game. To the best of my knowledge the only change to come from this summit was the decision to change the ante-diluvian system of goal average to goal difference. On hearing this I thought to myself, 'Well, that's going to bring the crowds in at Doncaster and Rochdale.' I remember there were also calls for the domestic season to have a more defined beginning and end as it was thought this would replenish the supporters' appetite for the game during the summer break. There were also calls for less football on television as it was thought a constant diet of 'highlights' conditioned supporters to think that every match was electrifying, and they would be put off by the reality of football when actually attending a game.

I had been involved in football long enough to know that any change to the game always met with opposition. Twenty years on from Hungary's watershed victory over England at Wembley, for all that football had developed as a game, the sport itself was still entrenched in tradition, too accustomed to simply muddling through to accept changes without misgivings. In 1974 the game had never before found itself in quite the same economic plight. Many clubs were living hand to mouth. Many grounds had changed little since the Edwardian era, Anfield being a rare exception. The muddling through was to continue. Hooliganism in the form of criminals using football as a theatre for their puerile behaviour was on the rise, but thankfully, generally speaking the football was getting better. George Best continued his pained disentanglement from the game, but there were other players who, while they did not possess the football genius of George, nevertheless proved crowd pullers, Kevin Keegan being a prime example. Bobby Moore was coming to the end of what had been an illustrious and imperious career, but the game could still boast Peter Osgood, Charlie George, Franny Lee, Colin Bell, Tony Currie, Alan Ball, Alan Hudson, Martin Buchan and Howard Kendall, and there were new, exciting kids on the block: Steve Heighway, Steve Coppell, Dennis Tueart, Billy Hughes, Lou Macari, Steve Kindon and Gordon Hill. So, despite the dire financial situation and the administrative muddling through, there was still much to be positive about, and nowhere was this dynamic positivism more evident than at Liverpool.

After a summer holiday in Spain with Sue and the children, I reported back for pre-season training. It was 12 July 1974, seemingly just an ordinary day at the Melwood training ground. We were all looking forward to what we believed would be another successful season, having just finished runners-up in the League and won the FA Cup with a comprehensive victory over Newcastle United.

At the start of every season you reassess your strengths with a view to making further progress. No one at Liverpool ever looked back, although Shanks had every reason to be proud of what the club had achieved in the previous thirteen seasons. Under Shanks, Liverpool had won the Second Division title and then proceeded to become one of the most consistent sides in the First Division, year in, year out. In successive seasons we had finished eighth, champions, seventh, champions, fifth, fifth again, third, champions and runners-up. No other club could boast such a record in the same period. In addition to the Second Division title and three First Division championships, Shanks had led us to two FA Cup Final victories, and we had been beaten finalists on another occasion; we had also been runners-up in the European Cup Winners' Cup, reached the semi-finals of both the European and Fairs Cup, and won the UEFA Cup. This added up to seven major trophy successes at home and abroad, in addition to which our reserve team had won the Central League on several occasions. Liverpool had not been out of the top six in the First Division for nine seasons, which ensured regular appearances in Europe. Not surprisingly, Shanks had become a football legend in his own life-time. He was respected as a manager and a man throughout Europe, idolized by Liverpool supporters, and respected by those of all other clubs, including Everton. He had assumed control of a club that was a mediocre Second Division outfit with a dilapidated ground and turned it into a major force in football with a stadium to match. He had created not one but three great teams. His hunger and enthusiasm for the game and for Liverpool Football Club appeared to be as great as ever.

So when Shanks gathered all the playing staff together that July morning I thought he was about to give us a pep talk for the season ahead. He wasted no time in getting straight down to the point.

'Boys, I've got a big meeting at Anfield this afternoon,' he informed us. 'I have decided to retire. My time here is done.'

Like every other player in the room, I sat there absolutely stunned. I felt my forehead prickle as adrenalin rushed to my head. No one had expected this.

Shanks didn't say much more. He simply told us that he'd wanted to tell us first before his decision was made public. He didn't talk of a successor, he simply thanked us for all our efforts and wished us the best of luck for the future.

We all sat silent and dumbfounded, all except for one player. When a manager departs, particularly one of the stature of Shanks, players look to their captain for calm leadership and objective words. Emlyn Hughes began to cry. In between sobs he managed to say, 'But you can't retire, boss. You just can't.' The rest of us players were only concerned about Shanks, and many a withering look was directed at Emlyn. It encouraged me that the boss appeared calm and in control, as one would expect. Shanks didn't look upset, and I should imagine the last thing he needed at such a moment was his skipper wailing.

'Give it a rest,' Alec suggested to Emlyn.

Sensing that an awkward moment was becoming even more awkward, Shanks once again seized the initiative.

'I've simply done enough and had enough,' he told us. 'I've been in this job a long time. I want to spend some time with my family. I have to think about my health and my wife, Nessie.'

I sat there thinking, 'You can't do this, boss,' but I knew better than to question him on such a monumental decision. I realized he must have given the matter considerable thought, and I knew him well enough to know that once he had made his mind up there would be no retraction. That is why Emlyn's tears were inappropriate and failed to move me or anyone else in that room. I surmised that Shanks had been thinking about this for months, running the whole scenario through his mind time and again before arriving at his decision; after all, he was now sixty-one. Not that any of this made it easier to accept, of course.

As Shanks prepared to leave, my mind flashed back to the day when he kindly agreed to see my mother and me before inviting me to join the groundstaff. I owed him a lot. We all did. He had turned the club around, restored pride to our supporters. His retirement was indeed a watershed moment.

The press were summoned to a noon conference. Shanks was flanked by chairman John Smith, vice-chairman Jack Cross and directors T. V. Williams, Eric Sawyer and Syd Reakes. Even hardbitten sports journos gasped in astonishment when John Smith delivered the news. This only a matter of weeks after Shanks had been awarded the OBE for services to football. It emerged that Shanks had turned down the offer of a new contract, and the offer to take a sabbatical. 'Coming to my decision was like walking to the electric chair,' he told the press, characteristically resorting to a Cagneyesque image. His retirement was indeed as dramatic and unexpected an event as a scene from the gangster movies he loved.

Later that day I managed to have a word with him. I sincerely thanked him for all he had done for me as a kid and senior pro. I had spent a decade and a half under his tuition. It was as if a part of me had died. I took some consolation from the fact that he was getting out at the top. 'Managing a football club is like drowning,' he told me at one point. 'Sublimely peaceful and pleasant once the struggle is over.' Unlike the poet Stevie Smith, he had spent his time not drowning but waving, but I understood his point.

Many great things have since been said and written about Shanks as a manager, all of them totally justified. His genius as a manager apart, for me one of the greatest things about him was that he captured what it was like to be human. He spoke directly to his players and his public and defied football convention. In an era when caution and defence and playing to a rigid system were of paramount importance to many teams, he offered emancipation by encouraging a sense of freedom in our play. He wanted his players to express the talent they had been blessed with, and Liverpool as a team to play attacking, entertaining football. He was the manager who launched a thousand quips and spoke much wisdom; he was never given to pithy soundbites, whinging or denigrating other managers. When I now look back, I feel that our loss, and football's, is that we no longer live in an age when a manager can become a legend, popular and respected by supporters of whatever hue, and we understand why.

One of the things I recall about that day was the evening news on TV. A crew had gone on to the streets to obtain reaction from Liverpool supporters to the news of Shanks's retirement. One young Liverpool fan was asked, 'What do you think about Bill Shankly retiring?' He had obviously not heard the news and looked straight into the camera with a shocked look on his face. 'Shankly?' he said disbelievingly. 'Bill Shankly?' The camera stayed fixed on his face. The lad just shook his head. Tears welled, and he couldn't speak another word.

The vox-pop ended with a Liverpool supporter of around seventy years of age, who simply remarked, 'The king of Anfield is dead.'

'Long live the king,' I found myself saying to my TV screen.

10

GIANTS AMONG MEN

AS A MANAGER, SHANKS WAS IN MUCH THE SAME MOULD AS HE WAS as a player – outrageous, obsessed, ironic, totally focused, honest, passionate, funny, a stickler for discipline and fine detail, compassionate though at times ruthless. Football and Liverpool were to have more successful managers, but the game has never produced such a complex character who at the same time could come across as straight-talking and uncomplicated.

Shanks spanned the two great ages of football. His playing days in the 1930s were those of Brylcreemed short back and sides, heavy boots with bulging toe-caps and baggy shorts. When he enjoyed pre-eminence as a manager, it was an era of permed hair, tight-legged Gola tracksuits and the first of the player's agents. One good team can make a manager's reputation, but it is continuity of high achievement that proves his worth beyond doubt. Shanks spanned successive decades in football with all the presence of the Severn Bridge, which is why even today our recollections of him are still strong.

We all know what Shanks said about life and football. When he said it, it was not some sharp quip to win him publicity in newspapers. He never had to do that; just about everything he said was eminently quotable. He even made a request to the Anfield milkman for extra pints sound like a humorous but profound philosophy on life. When he said football wasn't a matter of life and death, it was much more important than that, it was Sam Goldwyn meeting Bertrand Russell. In essence, that was what Shanks was – part football manager, part stand-up comic, part philosopher, common sense embedded in the barbs thrown at you to see how you coped. I knew Shanks well, but millions of others who had never met the man also felt they knew him. I believe this is because it was not in the man to appear before a TV camera or radio microphone and offer bland answers to questions, or to indulge in insipid superlatives about players or a team's performance. He was passionate about football and life, and when he spoke, he spoke from the heart. In public Shanks openly displayed passion and emotion a-plenty, angst and frustration too, and because such traits are common to us all, people felt they knew and understood him.

I have mentioned how on the day he announced his retirement I managed to have a word with him, and told him that I owed him a lot. I still do. I was fourteen years old when my dad died; less than a year later I joined the Liverpool groundstaff. In my first years at Anfield, Shanks became a father figure to me. He was not one for mollycoddling, but in his own way he looked out for me and gave me 'fatherly' advice, particularly on how to survive in football. 'Football is a simple game made unnecessarily complicated by coaches,' he once told me. Given that he has signed good players, which Shanks invariably did, a manager's success depends on how well he motivates his playing staff. Shanks was the elemental expression of this unwritten law. Few managers, if any, have ever been able to motivate players as Shanks did. He made you feel like a world beater. His basic rules for playing the game were simply 'common-sense football': 'Pass to the nearest team-mate', 'Don't be afraid to improvise out there on the field', 'Chase and get the ball back when you lose it', 'Move up into attack when we have possession', 'Display the skill and speed you have been blessed with', 'Give them no respite; chase, challenge, harass and run at them.' He demanded a lot from his players, but nothing that he did not give himself.

When foolish people questioned his credentials for being a manager – he had no coaching certificates, grades or badges – he had one answer: 'Bill Shankly! They're my qualifications, the way I was born. And that's all the qualifications anyone needs in the game I'm in.' In 1960 Bob Paisley attended Walter Winterbottom's FA coaching school at Lilleshall and was in the same class alongside Tommy Docherty, Peter Taylor, Dave Sexton, Don Revie, Billy Bingham and Malcolm Allison. When I was on the Liverpool groundstaff, Bob persuaded Shanks that he too should attend the FA coaching course. 'I'm not going to be a better manager because I have a piece of paper,' Shanks told him. 'Chamberlain came back from Munich brandishing a piece of paper. Worst piece of paper we've ever had. But I'll go because there's always something you can pick up, even from the most stupid people.'

Shanks never saw the course out. Some years later he told me, 'I was there with Ronnie Moran and Joe Fagan. Peter Doherty, Jimmy Hagan and Raich Carter were also on the course. We had this schoolteacher trying to tell us how football should be played. One morning this schoolteacher toe-poked the ball to me. I told him, "I'll show you how to kick a ball. How do you want it? Stabbed, stroked, hit, a follow-through or driven?" I took over the class. Before the day was out, Ronnie and Joe were working with one group, Raich, Jimmy and Peter with another. The FA coaches just sat it out at the side of the field.

'No, no, Tommy, son, you don't need a piece of paper or a badge to be a manager or to play this game. The practical thing is everything. If a boxing coach is teaching you how to hit a punch-bag or dodge a punch, and Muhammad Ali comes along and shows you the professional way, you don't look at the other fella. It's Ali you listen to and follow.'

Shanks's tactical talks were always positive. In the main they consisted of what Liverpool could do to exploit weaknesses in our opponents. I've given examples of how he would build confidence and morale by way of a humorous catalogue of our opponents' frailties, often deriding their talent. Having met the opposition off their coach, he would say something to one player or another to make him feel unsettled. He would then come back into the dressing room where he would recount the nervous looks, wariness and idiosyncrasies of our visitors. All of which was purposefully designed to amuse, relax and build our confidence.

I remember Newcastle United arriving for a game and their players walking out to check the state of the pitch. As the players descended the steps leading to the tunnel, Malcolm Macdonald's eyes alighted on the sign that read 'This Is Anfield'.

'Well, at least we've come to the right place, gaffer,' said Malcolm to his manager, Joe Harvey.

'Oh yes, son, you'll soon find that out right enough,' retorted Shanks.

That day we beat Newcastle 5–0.

For a game against Leicester City, I was up against their centre-forward Allan Clarke. Shanks told me that part of my role was to bring the ball out of defence when I had won possession. 'But be mindful, Tommy, son. Clarke will be there to try and stop you doing that.'

'Should I go inside or outside him?' I asked.

'Oh, don't waste energy running round him, just go straight through the bastard.'

On another occasion Shanks said to Roger Hunt, 'Their goal-keeper's mother is a relation of mine. She's terrified that you'll break her son's wrists with your powerful shooting. I've promised her you'll not hit him, that you'll put the ball in the corners of the net and out of his reach.' Roger was only too aware that in all probability the goalkeeper's mother had never met Shanks. Nevertheless, he still felt lifted by his words.

Shanks's ability to enthuse players was obvious from their response. I have explained how Geoff Strong lived up to his name once he arrived at Anfield. Tosh wasn't exactly an all-out grafter at Cardiff City, nor Peter Cormack at Nottingham Forest, but Shanks had them running their socks off for Liverpool. Scouts from major clubs had not recommended Kevin Keegan after seeing him at Scunthorpe as they felt he lacked strength and, believe it or not, bravery. Bob and Joe saw in Kevin what others had not seen, and he went on to become one of the best players in Europe. As I said, to a large extent Kevin was a manufactured player, by Shanks and his backroom staff.

Alec Lindsay, albeit bought by mistake, Ray Clemence and Kevin Keegan all arrived at Anfield from clubs in the lower reaches of the Football League. Steve Heighway and Brian Hall came out of non-League football. That's getting on for half a team, one which won the Championship, the FA Cup and the UEFA Cup. Clem, Kevin and Steve also went on to help Liverpool win the European Cup; Alec wasn't in that side, his place having been taken by Joey Jones, who was signed from Wrexham. Shanks had his scouts comb the Third and Fourth Divisions and non-League for talent when other managers ignored that level of football. Such players were far from the finished article when they arrived at Anfield, but the time and expertise Shanks and his staff invested in them ensured that they went on to become top-quality footballers. I doubt if Liverpool or any top Premiership club of today combs the lower reaches of the Football League for emerging gems. They should do, because they will be there. Perhaps today's top clubs have had their heads turned by agents. Perhaps they are of the mind that talent lies abroad, not in the lower leagues within our shores. Maybe certain managers, under pressure to produce continual success, don't wish to invest time and expertise in honing a rough diamond. Shanks was willing to do all that, and more.

Before he signed a player he would discuss with his backroom staff and scouts every aspect of the man's ability, personality, character and personal life. If he thought the player ticked all the boxes, he would sign him. On one occasion Shanks was on the point of signing a player from a rival club. The footballer in question could be a little wayward, but that didn't bother Shanks; he knew he could handle him. The player arrived at Anfield but during his medical it transpired he had contracted a sexual disease. Shanks slammed the door shut on the move immediately. 'I'm not having a philanderer here. This is a family club. Send him back!' The press was told the move had fallen through because the medical had revealed the player to have high blood pressure. It was Shanks who had the high blood pressure that day.

A team reflects its manager. Cities and towns also respond to certain types of manager and their particular brand of football. Liverpool and Shanks were totally in tune, sharing the same vivacity and whole-hearted approach to life and football, often believing the two to be one and the same. Shanks loved the Liverpool supporters and they loved him. In part the supporters loved Shanks for the success he brought to the club, but also because they knew he understood them. How many top managers can one say that about today?

He may have had little time for theoretical coaching, but he was the epitome of the tracksuit manager, imparting all his considerable knowledge of the game to his players. 'We have a free-kick outside their box and they line up their wall,' he once explained. 'The player taking the free-kick flicks the ball in the air. If the shooter gets his head over the ball and volleys it halfway down on its descent, that ball will clear the wall. Then physics will play its part. The ball will suddenly dip. Aye, dip, dip under the bar and into the net.' And that's exactly what happens. It works. On another occasion, 'Stan Matthews could cross the old leather laced-up ball to Stan Mortenson so the ball always arrived at

Morty's head with the lace facing the other way. That way, when heading the ball Morty didn't have to make contact with the lace with his forehead, which hurt. Now, you show me the coaching manual that taught Stan Matthews how to do that.' And this was also spot on: 'When you're moving down the wing looking to cross the ball, don't push the ball in front of you and just bring your foot around the ball then cross. Arc your body around the ball, so you're facing the way you want the ball to go, then cross it. That ball will fly into the penalty area.'

I think much of his decision to retire was down to the fact that he simply wanted to remove himself from the strain of managing a club that had rarely been out of the limelight in all the time he had been associated with it. Without a doubt his decision to retire had much to do with his feelings for his wife, Nessie. He was beginning to feel tired and ragged, and I think he felt the constant pressure of management had been unfair to Nessie. Such was his devotion to the club and football, they never went out to the cinema or the theatre. He had devoted fifteen years to Liverpool, and prior to that had managed Carlisle United, Grimsby Town and Huddersfield Town. I believe he felt he had achieved his goals and had now reached a stage in his life when he should be devoting his time to Nessie.

I had my differences with Shanks. For a manager who enjoyed a reputation for being quotable, curiously his articulation deserted him when it came to leaving a player out of the team or moving him on. I was angry with Shanks when he arranged for me to go on loan to Stoke City, angry because although I had served him and the club for thirteen years he hadn't thought fit to discuss the matter with me. The lack of compassion he showed to players in such circumstances had, I am sure, much to do with his roots and upbringing.

He was born in 1913 and brought up in the Lanarkshire coalfields where poverty haunted every family. At the age of fifteen he began work in the pits. There was a special bond among miners.

They relied on one another not only to get the job done but to stay alive. Down a pit, phoneys and cheats didn't last for long, they simply weren't tolerated. It was an attitude Shanks took with him into football. He played his football in the thirties when frugality was a byword for working-class life, when players earned little more than those who stood on the terraces to watch them. Then came the Second World War, during which he served in the RAF, a war in which he told me many of his pals were killed. His generation was a hardy generation, they had to be. They had been through a lot and were not given to showing their emotions. Little wonder that he had no time for players upset at being left out of the team.

Players invariably point a finger at the manager when left out of the team, but I don't think Shanks saw himself as being responsible. As far as he was concerned, a player was left out because he had a better option. Towards the end of his reign at Anfield, Larry Lloyd was out of favour. One morning at Melwood, Larry took Shanks to task on the matter of his omission from the team. 'If you want to get in the side, get in! I'm not stopping you, you are!' retorted Shanks.

He didn't bear grudges. When words were exchanged, that was it; both parties had got it off their chest and the following day he expected you to get on with the job. I had my run-ins with him, he made me angry at times, but such anger was fleeting. I served under him for thirteen years; it was only natural we should have the occasional spat. But those confrontations never tainted the love, respect and gratitude I had for the man.

He was, of course, supremely entertaining. In the mid-sixties, before there was a Holiday Inn in Liverpool, prior to a European home game we would stay at a hotel in North Wales. This was a time before every hotel room had its own TV set. The night before our game Shanks told us we could go into the hotel's TV lounge to watch a world championship boxing bout, and that he and Bob would join us later. When Shanks arrived he was taken aback to see us watching *Coronation Street*. He went up to skipper Ron Yeats and asked what was going on. Ron pointed out two elderly ladies sitting watching the TV and explained that they were in the lounge when we'd got there watching *Coronation Street* and no one had felt it right or proper to ask them to change channels.

Shanks marched to the front of the lounge and bid the two women good evening. 'Ladies,' he continued, 'there is some fine boxing on the television tonight.'

The two elderly ladies explained that they were watching their favourite soap, which they never missed.

'It's not me who wants to watch the boxing, it's these young boys,' said Shanks, pointing us out. 'That's the trouble with young people today. They expect to get everything too easy.'

The ladies were in full agreement.

'Not like when we were young, eh? Young people today don't realize what we went through. Hardship and depression in the 1930s, then a world war.'

The ladies continued to nod in full agreement.

'Aye, and what did we lay our lives on the line for, ladies?' he asked before answering his own question. 'So people like these young boys here could have freedom, live lives free from persecution, in an honest and open democratic society.'

The old dears looked at Shanks, wondering what on earth he was getting at.

'You do believe in democracy, don't you, ladies?' he asked.

'Yes, of course we do,' the pair chorused.

'Good!' said Shanks, clapping his hands together. 'Then let's have a vote on whether we watch the boxing or *Coronation Street*!'

For a man who poured scorn on pieces of paper that stated someone was a top coach, when it came to his own paperwork he answered all his mail by doing his own typing. On his last day at the club he typed a note to Bob Paisley, his successor, and left it on the desk in the manager's office for Bob to find the next day. The note, meant as a confidence booster for Bob, simply said, 'Bill

Shankly says Bob Paisley is the best manager in the game.' The following morning, when Bob entered the office on his first day as manager of Liverpool, he found Shanks's note and read it. He added two commas to it and arranged for it to be posted to Shanks's home. The amended note read, 'Bill Shankly, says Bob Paisley, is the best manager in the game.'

Initially, Bob was a reluctant successor to Shanks, as he told us when he first gathered the players together. 'I don't particularly want the job,' he said, 'but someone's got to do it.' To a man we all said he must take the job and that he would have our full backing and support. 'Thanks, that's gratifying to know. Well, I suppose that's it then. We'd better get on with the job.'

Along with Cally, I was the senior pro at the club. I remember talking in confidence to our secretary, Peter Robinson. Peter intimated that the board were of the mind that should Bob fail to win trophies and keep Liverpool at the forefront of English football in his first season as manager, they would be looking for a replacement. As far as I was concerned, I was determined to do my bit to ensure that would never happen.

Bob had his own ideas and ways, but unlike many a new manager he opted for evolution rather than the upheaval of revolution. He had the common sense not to try to change the culture of the club, a culture that had been set in place by Shanks, but he proved more astute at selecting players and getting the best out of them by emphasizing their individual strengths and working to improve any weaknesses, a perfect example being Ray Kennedy.

Ray could be forgiven for thinking that no one cared one iota about him signing for the club from Arsenal for what was then a club record fee of £150,000. He had the misfortune to sign for Liverpool on the day Shanks announced his retirement, and as a result his record transfer was afforded only a few column inches on the inside back page of newspapers when in normal circumstances it would have been headline news. Ray had been bought as a centre-forward, but, having watched him in action, Bob was of the mind that he would be best employed elsewhere, and switched him to the left-hand side of midfield. It was in that position that Ray developed into one of the best midfield players in the country.

Bob possessed an incredible knowledge of the game and players. In truth, he was more tactically astute than Shanks, and his man-management was also superior. Often this never came across when Bob spoke to the media, but you knew instinctively that he had a tremendous grasp of the game. Shanks had introduced certain ideas into our training that ensured we never forgot the basics. Bob continued that. For example, if someone scored against you in the five-a-sides, the ball might end up thirty yards beyond the goal. You wouldn't just retrieve it, you had to go with a team-mate, and on your return play one-twos with each other. No time was wasted on the training field; there was an opportunity to nurture good habits and practices at all times. People used to say that Liverpool's passing was superior to that of other teams. This had much to do with the work Bob had us doing on the training ground. If you found yourself hemmed in by the corner flag with the ball at your feet, there would always be two, sometimes three team-mates supporting you on the ball. I look at some Premiership teams now and I see players under pressure when in possession with no team-mate within twenty yards. That never happened at Liverpool. Bob was at pains to emphasize that we had to provide good options for the man on the ball. Of course, doing that necessitates players being very fit. Again, our work in this respect was done at Melwood; that's where the gruelling work at 'the boards' paid dividends. Similarly, should you make a twenty-yard pass to a team-mate, the rule was you had to follow it up by running six to eight yards to support the man you had passed to.

Bob's first competitive game in charge of Liverpool was the Charity Shield match against Leeds United at Wembley on 10 August 1974. It was the first Charity Shield game to be screened live on television, but rather than being a showpiece for the game it was a shabby and ugly match in which charity was in short supply. From the very start both teams went at each other hammer and tongs. After some fifteen minutes a game of football broke out, but it was fleeting. There were off-the-ball incidents, niggling fouls, late tackles and the occasional flare-up. After an hour Kevin Keegan and Billy Bremner had a set-to. Billy had been subjecting Kevin to a series of fouls and the pair eventually clashed. The referee, Mr Matthewson, dismissed both for fighting and they compounded their ignominy when leaving the field. His frustration got the better of him, and Kevin took off his shirt and cast it aside as he made his way down the touchline. For whatever reason, Billy followed suit. I still have the image in my head of the linesman casually kicking Billy's shirt to one side so that its presence would not be a hindrance to him when running up and down the line. It was a shoddy climax to an unsavoury incident in what had been a travesty of a Charity Shield match, one that did English football no favours. Kevin and Billy were subsequently hauled over the coals for their antics: both were fined £500 and banned for eleven matches. I felt sorry for Kevin as he had had to put up with a lot of provocation, but the severity of their punishment had much to do with the fact that their fracas had taken place at Wembley before the TV cameras.

Phil Boersma had given us a first-half lead only for Trevor Cherry to equalize for Leeds with twenty minutes of the game remaining. Given the fare that had been on display, few would have wanted further helpings, but as there had to be a winner on the day the game went to penalties. Both teams scored their allocated five, one of which I converted. Surprisingly, Leeds nominated their goalkeeper, David Harvey, to take their sixth; he fired the ball high, wide and handsome over the bar. Cally then thumped home his spot-kick to give Bob his first major trophy in his first competitive match as Liverpool manager. From that day on it was as if the trophies just kept on coming for Bob and Liverpool.

Our opening League game of the 1974–75 season was at Luton Town. As usual the team assembled on the Friday for a team meeting.

'What are these meetings about?' Ray Kennedy asked me.

'Oh, Bob will just highlight one or two things about Luton. He'll allocate us specific tasks. Just a routine pre-match meeting.'

I remember Bob being somewhat nervous as he spoke to us. He wasn't the best at public speaking.

'Well, boys, we start at Luton tomorrow,' he told us. 'They have whatcha-me-cally on the wing. Has some speed, but can't cross a ball. But the lad who's marking him has to be alert. Don't be wandering around like a miner without his lamp. Tommy, I want you to keep an eye on thing-me-bob.'

Bob offered a nod in my direction as he placed a blue tiddlywink on the green baize cloth. I didn't have a clue which Luton player he was referring to, but I knew better than to say anything as I knew it would make Bob feel even more uncomfortable.

'Now then, I want you to keep an eye on you-know-who,' Bob said to Brian Hall. 'You keep him quiet and we'll have no problems.'

'Who're you talking about, boss?' asked Brian.

'You know, what's-his-face,' said Bob, becoming a little irritated at the fact that he had been unable to conjure up the names of the Luton players.

'Yeah, right,' said Brian, himself none the wiser about whom Bob was referring to.

'Ah, bollocks!' Bob suddenly exclaimed. 'Just go out and beat them!'

With that, he turned and casually made his way out of the room, humming a little song to himself.

Ray, who as it turned out hadn't made it into the team for the Luton game, turned to me and said, 'What was all that about?'

'Listen, Ray,' I told him, 'we've done all the right things in training. Everyone knows their job. If we want to know which Luton players the boss was talking about, we'll just look in the match programme tomorrow.'

Ray looked rather unsure, but he was soon to discover that though Bob could not match Shanks's articulation and ready wit, he was the shrewdest judge of a player in the game. For the record, we beat Luton 2–1. I managed to score our first goal of the season. Steve Heighway got our second when he rounded what's-his-face after Brian Hall had intercepted a pass from thing-me-bob.

Bob's inability to remember names of opposing players was simply down to the fact that, other than noting their general formation, he was never bothered about the opposition. He never set one man on another in all my time at Anfield. Like Shanks, Bob had complete confidence in the team he had created and felt that if there was any worrying to be done it should be done by the opposition. It wasn't Bob's style to come into the dressing room, talk up an opponent and ask one of us to concentrate on him. In the late seventies Nottingham Forest winger John Robertson was running teams ragged. He was terrific with the ball at his feet and a pin-point crosser of it. We contained him without ever having a man mark him closely. If the opposition had a lively, young, inexperienced player in their side, I would lay off him because if I went diving in he might beat me instinctively and would gain in confidence from having done so. I would hang off such players and say something like, 'All right, son, what are you going to do now?' It planted a seed of doubt in the mind of my opponent. That was the way Bob wanted me to play it. Simple things like that may appear inconsequential, but to Bob they were of vital importance to winning games. I gained something of a reputation for hard tackling, but you wouldn't believe how many times I won the ball through interception. That was Bob's style. He saw defence as the core of the team but deployed central defenders who were mobile, bright, comfortable on the ball and adventurous. The fact that players such as Phil Thompson, Alan Hansen and, later, Mark Lawrenson were not sledge-hammer tacklers was not an issue for

Bob. He liked defenders who could spring from defence to attack by virtue of their ability to read a game and intercept a pass from the opposition. 'That way,' he once told us, 'it not only cuts down on injuries, because the more physical contact the more the chance of an injury, it also means you can use the ball better because you've won it cleanly, you're not at full stretch, and you're in space.' Bob would also tell us to watch the opposing goalkeeper take two kicks. Having done so, he expected us to be able to gauge where the ball was going, and for one of us to position himself a couple of yards from that spot. Applying these little things in games enabled Liverpool to become all-conquering.

Bob was at Liverpool for forty-four years, longer if you include his directorship and advisory role when Kenny Dalglish was manager. I doubt we will ever again see someone connected to a club for such a period of time. Like Shanks, Bob came from the sort of background where football offered an almost magical release from the drudgery of the coal face, shipyard, factory floor or, in his case, the building site. Like Shanks and the other paid-up members of that old school, Matt Busby, Jock Stein and Bill Nicholson, Bob never forgot the blessing bestowed upon him – that of being paid for doing something he loved. He saw football as something of a triviality when set against war, which he had experienced as a member of the Tank Regiment, or social deprivation. As he once told us, 'Football gives meaning to many people's lives, not just those of you lucky enough to play the game for a living but also those who watch from the terraces and pay our wages. Never forget the responsibility we have to those people.'

In comparison to Shanks, Bob was low key, but his achievements in the game were to be monumental, and he was cherished by players and supporters alike. He was the unpretentious embodiment of John Lennon's 'working-class hero'. No one could mistake him for a saint, yet he was a man of unyielding integrity and laudable principles. There was never the remotest danger of his being contaminated by the materialism and publicity that envelop many who find prosperity through football. He remained loyal throughout to his roots and to himself. At the height of his success with Liverpool I'd see him wandering around the corridors of Anfield wearing a cardigan with leather elbow patches and carpet slippers on his feet. He'd produce a bag of toffees from his pocket and offer me one. More like the Werther's Originals idea of a granddad than the mastermind behind one of the greatest teams in the history of British football.

Shanks rebuilt Liverpool Football Club, but Bob's role was vital. Their relationship wasn't a case of Mozart and Salieri, a jealous rival scheming against his talented, charismatic colleague. Theirs was one of the truly great partnerships of football management: Shanks with his drive, infectious belief and great motivational skills, Bob with his profound knowledge of tactics and the strengths and weaknesses of players.

Bob also possessed an in-depth knowledge of injuries, whereas Shanks had no time for genuinely injured players. Chris Lawler was unswervingly loyal to the club and his team-mates. Like the majority of us, he would not let on when he was carrying a knock for fear of missing a game and losing his place in the team. As a result, he missed only three games in seven seasons. On the occasion when Chris did succumb to injury, he was being treated by Bob when Shanks popped his head round the door to enquire whether he would be fit for the game on Saturday.

'No chance,' Bob replied. 'His injury's a bad one.'

'Bad injury? Rubbish!' snapped Shanks. 'The boy's a malingerer!'

Shanks might have retired, but he still turned up at Melwood, almost on a daily basis. On seeing Shanks, the players instinctively referred to him as 'Boss'. I understood why Shanks could not keep away. Liverpool had been everything to him, a great love of his life. As with couples who decide to split up, the decision to part is invariably easier than the actual mechanics of separation. So it proved for Shanks. Though everyone was pleased to see him, the consensus was that his constant appearances were unfair on Bob. In an attempt to keep himself fit, Shanks began to join in the five-a-sides, and it wasn't long before he started to offer advice. I am not saying that Shanks was there to undermine Bob's authority, far from it; Shanks's ties with the club were so strong he was invariably drawn to it the moment he awoke of a morning. In the end Bob and Joe Fagan took him to one side and diplomatically pointed out that his presence was having an unsettling effect. Bob explained that he had to be able to run the training in his own way. That must have been one hell of a difficult thing to do, but it had to be done, not just in the interests of Bob as our new manager, but for the players, the team and the club too. Shanks obviously understood, because he then kept his distance. Ironically he began to go to the Everton training ground for his daily work-out. Shanks's house overlooked Bellefield, and he was made very welcome there by Everton. It's hard to think that in some respects he was made to feel more welcome by our fiercest rivals, but I fully understood why Bob took the stance he did, and their relationship was not affected in any way.

I felt for Shanks. He was a legend at Liverpool, *the* legend. But his time was now over, a new era was underway, and Bob had to be allowed to exercise his judgement as a manager unfettered by the influence of his great pal. Personally, I feel Shanks should have been made a Liverpool director. He never liked the directors but he would have made a positive contribution to the board and the club, and even that level of contact would I am sure have satisfied him to some degree.

Though Liverpool were to be denied success in both the FA and League Cups, for much of the 1974–75 season we were one of seven clubs that fiercely contested the Championship, along with Derby County, Ipswich Town, Everton, Stoke City, Sheffield United and Middlesbrough. I doubt whether we shall ever again see the top division title contested by a bevy of provincial teams, but in 1974 the First Division and football in general was far more democratic as far as the distribution of honours was concerned. Just how democratic was evidenced when the first League tables of the season were published: the early leaders at the top of the First Division were newly promoted Carlisle United!

Up to the end of October things had gone well in the League for Liverpool and Bob. A Steve Heighway goal gave us a 1–0 victory over Leeds and a one-point lead at the top of Division One, only for us then to hit the buffers. Our next six matches provided us with not a single victory. Two defeats and four draws saw us slip to fifth, but the title race was so tight and open I knew a consistent run would put us right back in the frame. One of those draws was a 0–0 at Everton before a Goodison crowd of nigh on 57,000. Ironically, on the day a Merseyside derby produced no goals, forty-four goals were scored in the other ten First Division matches. What's more, the entire Football League programme that day resulted in nearly 140 goals being scored, the highest for some time. Slowly but surely, the ultra-cautious defensive game that had bedevilled the sport in the late sixties and early seventies was giving way to a more adventurous style of football.

Ray Kennedy had come into the side and, after initially starting as a striker, was beginning to make his presence felt on the left side of midfield. Big Tosh had struggled with an injury and then struggled to get back in the side, so much so that at one point he was on the verge of joining Leicester City, only for City to pull out of the deal on medical grounds. That said, Tosh still emerged as our leading scorer in the League. Phil Neal contested the position of left-back with Alec Lindsay; Terry McDermott, whom Bob had signed from Newcastle United in mid-season, started to make his mark; and youth team product Jimmy Case was introduced to a variety of roles by Bob and never let us down when called upon. The team was playing well, and barring a five-match spell I spent on the sidelines in the New Year as the result of an injury, I continued to give my all at right-back.

I returned to the team in mid-February in a goalless draw at West Ham. Prior to this game Liverpool had lost 4–1 at Newcastle, and though the draw at West Ham was satisfactory in that we got a point and kept a clean sheet, it signalled the beginning of a run that would see us draw six consecutive matches. We may have emerged as favourites with pools punters, but those six draws didn't help our credentials as possible champions. The tabloid press were writing Liverpool off, some even questioning whether Bob had it in him to succeed Shanks as manager. Bob couldn't say profound things with the regularity of Shanks, but his response to the stinging criticism of the team and his management was worthy of the great man himself: 'Always remember, the football press is like a swimming pool: all the noise is at the shallow end.'

The final run-in saw us win six and lose two of our remaining eight matches and we fell just short of giving Bob his first League title in his first season in charge. Amazingly, the lead had changed hands on twenty-one occasions, which was a record for the First Division. Curiously, Derby County didn't top the table until mid-April, but credit to them, they hung on in there. In 1972 Derby, managed by Brian Clough, had won the title while holidaying in Spain; on this occasion they again clinched the Championship without having to kick a ball: although Dave Mackay's side still had a game to play, our defeat at Middlesbrough in our pen-ultimate game of the season and the fact that Ipswich Town could only manage a draw at Manchester City made Derby champions. Liverpool, again, had to settle for the runners-up spot.

Not for the first time, we were also bundled out of European competition at the hands of opposition we were expected to beat comfortably. The competition was the Cup Winners' Cup and the opposition Ferencvaros of Hungary. It was a tie that embroiled me in a little controversy.

Liverpool's quest for the Cup Winners' Cup had begun on 17 September against Stromsgodset from Norway, which proved to be a mismatch of a tie. We won the first leg at Anfield 11–0, and it's easier for me to tell you who didn't score on the night than who did – Clem and Brian Hall. The second leg was a formality, but such was the desire of the Norwegians to see Liverpool in action, a capacity crowd of 17,000 packed into Stromsgodset's compact but tidy Marienlyst Stadium in Drammen to see Ray Kennedy score what must have been one of the most superfluous away goals in European competition history.

Round two paired Liverpool with Ferencvaros. All appeared to be going to plan when Kevin gave us the lead midway through the first half, but Ferencvaros were not to be overawed or overrun. As the game progressed they began to assert themselves and eventually secured the draw they had come to achieve when Mate proved himself to be anything but a mate when he equalized in the second period.

In that game, some of the Ferencvaros players indulged in a little gamesmanship. Whenever I got near one of their number he went down like a bag of hammers. On more than one occasion a forward bursting into our penalty box launched himself skywards in the hope of being awarded a penalty. We were subjected to much of the same in Hungary. With the game at 0–0 Takacs went to ground while I was a good yard from him; fortunately the referee was having none of his antics. With the tie still goalless I went across to take a throw-in. As I was waiting for the ball to be thrown to me, something else was thrown – a bottle. I managed to get my head to one side and it hit me on the shoulder. A second passed, then I thought to myself, 'Two can play at this game,' so I fell to the ground. The Ferencvaros players surrounded the referee, apparently saying that I was play-acting and that I had not been injured by the projectile – which was true.

We drew 0–0 on the night, which meant Ferencvaros went through on the away-goals rule, but the story of the tie does not end there. Having watched footage of the incident, I was taken to task by UEFA who said my delayed response to the bottle-throwing incident was 'elaborate, over-the-top play-acting designed to deceive the match official', and I was given a European suspension. The bottle thrower was traced by the Hungarian police, and he eventually appeared in court and was given a jail sentence. While I accept that two wrongs do not make a right and my reaction to the bottle throwing was over the top, the fact remains that I was struck by a bottle. Should such an incident occur today, irrespective of whether the player was hurt or not he would not be hit again with a suspension and it would be the home club that got punished.

The incident brought a moment of levity to our next training session at Melwood. My reaction to the bottle throwing and the news that UEFA were to act against me had made headlines in the newspapers. After training I was walking towards the Melwood pavilion when, thump!, something hit me on the back of the head. Instinctively I ducked and quickly moved away. On turning to see what on earth it was that had struck me, I was greeted with the sight of all the lads laughing at Alec Lindsay brandishing a plastic bottle some six feet in length and four feet in circumference. Where he had got this large plastic bottle from I don't know, but I saw the joke and joined in the laughter. That's how it was at Liverpool: we took our jobs seriously but we didn't take ourselves too seriously. As my mum once told me, 'You grow up the first day you laugh at yourself.'

It had not been a bad first season for Bob as manager. The Charity Shield was in the Anfield trophy cabinet and runners-up in Division One meant qualification yet again for Europe. But he wasn't satisfied, far from it, and neither were we players. We all wanted true success, and I felt Liverpool were once again on the way to achieving it. As the season progressed Bob had become more assured and confident in his new role as manager. He had signed two very good players in Phil Neal and Terry McDermott and had been largely instrumental in the signing of Ray Kennedy. As the new players Bob had signed – and, in the instance of Jimmy Case, brought into the side – began to make their presence felt, so

I was made to realize that another new era was indeed beginning for the club.

I mentioned earlier that the number of goals scored on a particular Saturday in November 1974 was the highest for some years. Managers and coaches were indeed beginning to respond to the call for more open, attacking football. The evolution was slow, but football needed this more expansive and fluid approach as in 1974–75 the game, in keeping with other sports, had not been immune to the social and economic pressures of society. The energy crisis was still prevalent. Problems with the oil supply from the Middle East were exacerbated by a dispute between miners and the government, resulting in an energy crisis for the UK. Not only were oil and petrol in short supply, but power stations were also affected and they could not produce enough energy to meet demand, so the nation was placed on a three-day working week. We players at Liverpool were reminded to turn out lights when leaving rooms, and not to use electricity unnecessarily, for example for hair dryers. Even copying a single-page document on the club photocopier involved more form filling than a three-year club contract. Clubs of the stature of Liverpool could cope with such prudence, but it was little wonder that many other Football League clubs were experiencing an even more precarious existence. Portsmouth, for example, said that if it had not been for a rock concert staged at Fratton Park the club might have gone into administration.

For too long English football had drifted along, accepting band-aid solutions to what was a major problem – a lack of finance. The solution had been to play more games, as matches generated gate money. But with the honourable exceptions of Liverpool, West Ham, Manchester United, Everton, Ipswich and, let it be said, Leeds, the football served up by many clubs in the late sixties and early seventies had hardly been entertaining or dramatic. Several clubs – fortunately, Liverpool was not one – had been blighted by hooliganism too, which was on the increase. Yet when radical solutions were put forward, such as in 1974 the call for smaller divisions, more seats in grounds (no one called them stadiums back then), shirt advertising and points for goals, these were dismissed by the powers that be. The general feeling was, however, that something had to be done, and soon.

11

THERE NOT THEREABOUTS

WITH NOTHING MUCH HAVING RESULTED FROM THE FOOTBALL League's summit the previous year, the FA met in similar fashion in the summer of 1975 and introduced a new disciplinary code to begin in 1975–76. Any player accumulating twenty penalty points either by way of dismissal or cautions would receive an automatic ban, and tackling from behind was outlawed – not that I had ever perpetrated such a thing. The FA went on to say that any player sent off would not be able to contend the referee's decision but instead of receiving a three-match ban would miss only one game but also collect twelve penalty points. Clubs whose players accumulated a hundred penalty points would be censured by the FA. To all intents and purposes this was the sum total of the FA meeting to, as they put it, 'Improve English Football'. There was, however, one other innovation: numbered boards were to be used to signal substitutions. Clubs such as Rochdale and Doncaster Rovers must have been clapping their hands with glee at the action taken by football's administrators to resolve the financial problems that riddled the game.

I have made a point of mentioning the FA's disciplinary

clamp-down not only to illustrate that little was being done to solve the financial problems besetting English football, but also because I have seen it written that these measures taken against rough-house play more or less signalled the end of players such as me, Norman Hunter and Ron Harris. To be perfectly frank, the FA's new disciplinary code didn't affect me one iota, simply because I never went in for tackles from behind. To quote Jimmy Greaves, I was hard but fair. Nor was I one of those players who amassed disciplinary points. I was only dismissed once in my career, for dissent, and booked on only three occasions, in a playing career that lasted for nigh on two decades. For someone to write that the FA's new disciplinary code brought an end to hard players such as Ron, Norman and me is nonsense. Our careers were coming to an end because of the noiseless footsteps of time.

The 1975–76 season did not start well for me, or for Liverpool. Our first match was at Queens Park Rangers and I was very disappointed when Bob named the team, and me as substitute. Alec Lindsay failed to get a shirt: the full-back positions went to Phil Neal and Joey Jones. In the first half a mistake by Emlyn resulted in Gerry Francis giving Rangers the lead, an advantage they held to half-time. If our supporters expected the team to turn things around in the second half they were to be disappointed. We hadn't played well in the first period, and if anything our play deteriorated after the interval. With some twenty minutes remaining Emlyn rampaged forward, was dispossessed, and Rangers broke away with more or less a clear run on goal. The ball was crossed to Mick Leach who made it 2–0.

Immediately the ball hit the net, Bob turned to me in the dugout and said, 'Get warmed up, Tommy, you're going on.'

I was in the process of doing just that when Joe Fagan approached me.

'Take your boots off, Tommy,' he said, his disenchantment obvious to me.

'You what?' I asked, somewhat perplexed by this instruction.

'Take your boots off,' repeated Joe. 'I'm not letting you go on and be associated with this shit. Go and sit back down in the dug-out.'

I did as I was told.

As I have said, neither Shanks nor Bob thought it appropriate to remonstrate with players immediately a game had ended, but such was Bob's anger at this performance and the result, to everyone's surprise back in the dressing room he let rip, and the subject of his wrath was Emlyn.

'You bastard, you bloody bastard!' roared Bob. 'You cost us that game. I should never have listened to you when you came to me saying we needed more pace in both full-back positions, that I should change things. It's the last time I listen when you come calling.'

Emlyn didn't say a word. He just stared down at the floor.

I couldn't believe what I had just heard. It was patently obvious to me that Emlyn had been in to see Bob to encourage him to leave me and Alec out of the team in favour of Phil Neal and Joey Jones; no other interpretation could be placed on Bob's words. I had nothing against either Phil or Joey, both of whom I got on really well with, but for Emlyn to actively try to have me removed from the team filled me with anger. I too couldn't hold back. I stepped towards Emlyn.

'You bastard!' I snapped, giving vent to my anger. 'I should knock the living daylights outta you!'

A hand gripped my arm. 'Oh no you don't.' It was Alec Lindsay. 'You'll wait in the queue, Tommy, and I'm at the head of it. If any-one's going to knock the living daylights out of the bastard, it'll be me.'

There were calls for calm and, not wanting to fuel what was a volatile atmosphere, I walked over to a corner of the dressing room to simmer, as did Alec. The pair of us kept our eyes trained on Emlyn though, who was at pains not to make eye contact with either of us, or anyone in that room.

For the next four matches Bob stuck with Phil Neal and Joey Jones. At the end of September, Liverpool having won two from five League matches, Joey picked up an injury in a 1–1 draw at Leicester City and Alec was recalled at left-back. In the following game an injury to Phil Thompson resulted in me being recalled against Aston Villa where we recorded a 3–0 victory courtesy of goals from Tosh, Kevin and Jimmy Case. I thought my performance had enhanced my case for a place but I found myself overlooked for our next match against, of all teams, Everton, a game that ended in a goalless draw. Up to the second week in December I made only two appearances in the League and two in the UEFA Cup. In the meantime I turned out for the reserves, giving my all in the hope of being recalled and resurrecting my Anfield career which, to be perfectly frank, I thought looked decidedly fragile.

Late November and early December saw Liverpool go four games without a victory. On 13 December we were due to play at Spurs. I had returned to the team in the previous game in the UEFA Cup against Slask Wroclaw and was delighted when Bob took me to one side and informed me that he was going to stay with me at right-back against Tottenham, with Phil Neal continuing at left-back.

The team hit the high gears at White Hart Lane. Kevin gave us a first-half lead and further goals from Jimmy Case, Phil Neal and Steve Heighway gave us what was an emphatic win over the home side. I retained my place in the side for our next match, a 2–0 win over QPR, after which there was no looking back for me or for Liverpool – not that anyone at Liverpool ever did do that in the literal sense. We were little over halfway through the season, but of our remaining twenty-two League games we lost only two, with fourteen victories, the pick of which was a 5–3 win against Stoke City in our third but last game of the season. We followed this by beating Manchester City 3–0. QPR, having completed their season, led the table, a single point ahead of Liverpool. We had one game left to play. Another Championship was there for the taking.

Liverpool's quest to win the UEFA Cup had begun when I was out of favour. Having beaten Hibernian 3–1 on aggregate the team recorded a fine 3–1 first-leg victory over Real Sociedad in San Sebastian. I featured in the second leg at Anfield, where we blitzed the Spaniards 6–0 to make the score 9–1 on aggregate. Following this convincing win I again found myself out of the side in the League, but I played in our 2–1 win against Slask Wroclaw in Poland, and in the return leg on 10 December, when a Jimmy Case hat-trick gave us a convincing 3–0 win. By the time Liverpool met Dynamo Dresden in the quarter-finals in March I was once again established in the team at right-back.

Along with Hansa Rostock, Dynamo Dresden were regarded as one of the best teams in East Germany. Later, the pair would be the only two East German clubs admitted to the Bundesliga. Financial difficulties subsequently resulted in Dynamo having its professional licence withdrawn and the club was expelled from the Bundesliga. Nowadays they play their football in a semi-professional regional league, but in 1976 they were a force to be reckoned with. In reaching the quarter-finals they had accounted for, among others, Honved and Moscow Torpedo. They were top of the East German League with a side containing six current East German internationals.

Iron Curtain countries were never the best places to visit as we were never afforded the hospitality we received in other European countries, basically because the hotels in which we stayed were comparatively spartan and there was always the unwelcome presence in the hotel lobby and lounge of men wearing black leather overcoats, which in Dresden I took to be members of the Stasi. We did a job on the night and the game ended goalless, but had it not been for both goalkeepers the scoreline would have been different. The Dynamo goalkeeper, Boden, pulled off two superb saves from Kevin and Cally, but the real turning point came when Clem brilliantly saved a late penalty. In the event it required goals from Kevin and Jimmy Case for us to progress in the return at Anfield and set up a plum semi-final against Barcelona.

British teams did not boast good records in Spain, particularly against Barcelona. We always adapted our game when playing on the Continent, more content than ever to retain possession and look for an opening. To go out and take the game to a team of the calibre of Barcelona, which included in its ranks Johann Cruyff and Johan Neeskens, would have been foolhardy because they were very good at soaking up pressure and hitting you on the break.

I remember us staying in what must have been the biggest and most salubrious hotel in Catalonia. The pile of the carpets was so thick you could just about walk across them without the aid of snow shoes, and the Anfield pitch could have fitted into the dining room. It was a very popular venue for conferences, and the night before the game we were unable to acquire a room for a team meeting. So, after we'd had a bite to eat, Bob spread the green baize on a table in the corner of the dining room and we all gathered round as the hotel staff cleared the other tables.

'We're playing Barcelona tomorrow night,' began Bob, as if we didn't know. 'What can I tell you about them?' He placed a blue tiddlywink in the centre of one of the marked goal areas. 'Their goalkeeper, what's his name?'

'Mora,' said Joe Fagan,

'Aye, that's the fella. He's a flapper. So let's get the crosses going in. Look for Tosh.'

Another blue tiddlywink was placed on the green cloth.

'Their right-back . . .'

'Tome,' said Joe.

'That's him,' said Bob. 'He's crap. All right peg and all over the place. No positional sense. Easily wound up, so you know what to do. Now, their left-back.'

Bob looked up at Joe as he placed a blue tiddlywink on the left side of the cloth.

'Miguell,' announced Joe.

'Aye, him. He's not fast, but he's quick.'

We all chortled with laughter. Bob suddenly realized what he had said and began laughing too. He threw the remaining tiddlywinks across the cloth.

'Ah, bollocks to them,' he said. 'Just play them off the park and beat them. That's what we're here to do.'

We played a patient game, and it paid off handsomely. We worked to create an opening and Tosh scored a wonderful goal that silenced the 90,000 crowd in the Nou Camp. It was the only goal of the game and, credit to him, it was a beauty. After the game Tosh told the press, 'When my playing career is over and I look back on the goals I scored, this one will probably stand out more than any.' All these years on, I wonder if Tosh still feels that way about the goal he scored that night?

Though Rexach scored for Barcelona in the return at Anfield to set the nerves of our supporters on edge, Phil Thompson then popped up to score, which was good enough to take us through to what was Liverpool's second UEFA Cup Final. Our opponents were Bruges, who had beaten West Ham in the other semi-final as well as accounting for AC Milan, Roma, Ipswich and Lyon in earlier rounds. Bruges had endured the more difficult passage to the final and the quality of the teams they had beaten left us in no doubt that they were a force to be reckoned with.

In the event I was taken aback by their fearless approach to the game. Opposing teams usually approached matches at Anfield with due caution, but not this one. Having dealt with our initial assault, Bruges went on the attack and kept on attacking. Such was their support play that we found ourselves unable to break out of defence. A packed Anfield was stunned into silence when Lambert gave his side the lead after only six minutes. Not content to sit back and defend that lead, Bruges continued to take the game to us and five minutes later went 2–0 up courtesy of Cools.

At half-time I sat in the dressing room not quite believing what had happened, but as ever, we remained resolute. 'You haven't started playing yet,' Bob told us. 'Go out and play. Take the game by the scruff of the neck and boss it.' Which is exactly what we proceeded to do. It was the epitome of the old phrase 'a game of two halves'. Having been shell-shocked by the Belgians in the first half we asserted ourselves in the second. On the hour Jimmy Case pulled a goal back, side-footing home following good work from Steve Heighway on the left. By now the atmosphere in Anfield was fizzing, reminiscent of our most memorable European nights. With our supporters urging us on, we continued to pen Bruges back in their own half of the field. Kevin put Ray Kennedy clear, only for Ray's low drive to smack against the foot of Jensen's left-hand post. Ray, however, was not to be denied. Minutes later I played the ball across the field to Steve Heighway, he played a one-two with Kevin, and the ball was laid into the path of Ray Kennedy whose drive from twenty-five yards put us back on equal terms. Steve was giving Bruges all manner of problems, and when he cut in again from the left and was sent tumbling the referee did not hesitate to point at the spot. Kevin elected to take the penalty, and it was a good one, hard and low to Jensen's left, the keeper going the wrong way. Even by past standards the game was considered one of the best European ties witnessed at Anfield. To have come from 2–0 down to win 3–2 against such quality opposition earned us plaudits from supporters and press alike. The job, however, was still far from done.

After that first leg of the final on 28 April we had to turn our minds once again to the Championship, specifically to Wolves at Molineux, a game that was crucial for both clubs. QPR had been sweating at the top of the First Division for ten days prior to us playing our final League match. Quite simply, if we won at Molineux we would be champions, at the same time condemning Wolves to relegation.

Molineux was filled to its capacity of 49,000 with an estimated 5,000 locked out. Those lucky enough to gain entrance witnessed a thriller. After twelve minutes Steve Kindon raised the hopes of the home supporters, and those of QPR, when he gave Wolves the lead. Tosh and Kevin began to create chances but they went begging, and come half-time many minds must have gone back to 1972 when Leeds were denied the Championship at Molineux in similar circumstances. During the interval Bob remained calm, however. He told us to be patient, to keep playing the football, as he believed Wolves would eventually crack. We didn't panic and we continued to play a passing game, but Wolves held firm. With twenty-five minutes to go Bob brought on David Fairclough for Jimmy Case.

David had already gained something of a reputation for being a 'super-sub'. Unable to command a regular first-team place he had found himself on the bench towards the end of the season, and when introduced late in games his speed had resulted in him scoring vital goals for us, up to this point seven in our previous seven League matches. I like David, he's a nice lad, he could have been a very good player, but in my opinion he didn't quite have it to play consistently at the top level. He was incredibly quick and his direct running unsettled defenders, but the thing about him was that should he play for ninety minutes you'd get two great runs out of him; should he play for ten minutes you'd still get two great runs out of him. Hence he was often substitute. I remember once discussing David with Bob and Joe. The three of us were in agreement that David had tremendous potential, but that his mental attitude was not quite right for the full game. Bob remarked that when on the bench, David appeared to be as keen as mustard to play, and when introduced he made a whirlwind contribution as if hell-bent on proving a point. 'However,' said Bob, 'play him from the start and it's as if he's in a comfort zone. Almost as if he's of the mind, "This is my rightful place", and he feels he doesn't have to give the sort of effort he musters when coming on for twenty minutes as sub.'

I remember once playing for the reserves with David against Manchester United reserves. I had been brought up by Shanks to give my all for any Liverpool team, irrespective of whether the game was a final, a reserve game or a friendly. In the first half David contributed virtually nothing. At half-time I berated him for his lacklustre effort, at one point saying, 'If I was up against you today, I'd be able to bring a bloody deckchair on to the pitch and sun myself.' In the second half it was as if David was a different player entirely. He caused United all manner of problems and scored a hat-trick. As we left the field at the end of the game, he turned to me.

'Are you happy now, Smithy?' he asked.

'It worked though, didn't it?' I said. 'I get on to you, you get worked up, and you take it out on the opposition.'

Which was a ploy often used by Shanks.

Though he did not get on the scoresheet against Wolves, without doubt David's speed and direct running upset their defence.

When you are chasing a game it is amazing how quickly time seems to pass. As we continued in our attempts to breach Wolves' rearguard the minutes seemed to fly by. Conversely, I know that when you are under pressure, defending a slim lead, as Wolves were doing, every minute seems to last an age. There were only some twelve minutes remaining when Tosh rose to knock the ball into the path of Kevin, who rifled it past the Wolves keeper Gary Pierce to send our travelling support wild. Having held out for so long, the despondency among the Wolves players was palpable. I looked at them and just knew they didn't believe they could score another. What's more, I also thought they wouldn't be able to prevent us scoring a second. In the last five minutes Tosh conjured up that second goal; Ray Kennedy got a third to put the issue beyond doubt. Liverpool were champions for a record ninth time in what was Bob Paisley's second season in charge. Rarely can the reaction of two sets of supporters have been so marked. Ours were wild and joyous; the Wolves fans were silent in despair. Even though I was delighted, the contrasting emotions of the crowd were not lost on me.

With the press after the game, Bob was characteristically modest and at pains to mention Shanks. 'Bill Shankly set such a high standard for this club,' he said. 'Liverpool have been geared to this sort of thing for fifteen years. All I have done is to help things along a little.'

Once again I was left to ponder how unpredictable football can be, a fickle mistress to say the very least. The season had begun for me on a sour note. I hadn't managed to regain my place in the team on a regular basis until mid-December. Now I was to collect yet another Championship medal and to take to the pitch of the Olympia Stadium in Bruges hopeful of helping my club win another UEFA Cup.

The team showed one change from the side that won the first leg: David Fairclough was on the bench, his place in the side taken by Jimmy Case, who had been the substitute for that first leg. We knew our task would be anything but easy and so it proved, especially when Bruges took an early lead through a penalty by Raoul Lambert after I had a rush to the head and got my hand on the ball. After a quarter of an hour Phil Neal was fouled some three yards outside the Bruges penalty area. It seemed the Belgians were expecting Emlyn to float the free-kick towards Tosh and Phil Thompson, but he tapped it to Kevin who hit a rasping right-foot drive high into Jensen's net as I and Jimmy Case bore down on goal ready for a rebound.

Bruges had to take the game to us, and they did; our plan was to soak up the pressure and hit them on the counter-attack. As the game progressed so did the intensity of the Bruges attacks. In the second half such was the pressure that Jensen was almost a spectator. Lambert thumped a drive against the foot of Clem's right-hand post. Heads, midriffs and legs conspired to block a succession of shots. I managed to head an effort from Sanders off the line, and Clem produced an acrobatic save from Van Gool. But we didn't falter. When the final whistle put an end to the hostilities I punched the air in relief more than joy.

Liverpool had repeated their Double success of League Championship and UEFA Cup, and Bob had another two trophies to savour as manager. As Emlyn went up to collect the cumbersome and weighty cup I was consumed, not for the first time, by an overwhelming feeling that Liverpool had embarked on a new and exciting era under the management of Bob Paisley. We were now at the forefront of English football, and any trace of doubt that Bob could not only continue but build on the success Shanks had brought to the club had been removed. It had been a roller-coaster season for me, but now I was on top of the world. I took particular pride in the fact that it was the UEFA Cup we had won as I believed this competition harder to win than the European Cup. There was only one entrant from each country in the European Cup. Of course there was the possibility of coming up against, say, Real Madrid or Inter Milan, but should you overcome such opponents you knew you were unlikely to encounter opposition of that quality again. The UEFA Cup was different. England, Italy, Spain and West Germany were invited to enter four teams – that's sixteen of the top clubs from four countries considered to have the best leagues in Europe. Should you beat, for example, Roma, there was the possibility of facing AC Milan, Juventus or Napoli in the next round – and that was just the Italian teams. Ask any player or manager of the time and I'm sure they'll agree that it was harder to win the UEFA Cup than the European Cup.

Emlyn and I still only talked to each other when on the pitch. The ploy he had pulled before the season started had only served to make me more wary of him, but the sense of professionalism and dedication to the cause instilled in me by Shanks overrode any personal differences between us. Emlyn was an excellent player who made a significant contribution to the team. I recognized this fact, though it didn't make me warm to him in any way. We got on with our respective jobs, which Bob expected us to do.

To cap what had been a memorable season for the club, Kevin Keegan was voted Footballer of the Year, only the second Liverpool player to have been afforded this honour by the football writers, the other recipient having been Cally two years earlier. I felt the award was deserved, and I told Kevin as much. He had arrived at Anfield as something of a rough diamond, but he had worked very hard to improve his game, so much so that he had developed into one of the finest players in the game. I was pleased for him.

That summer, Sue and I took Darren and Janette to Florida, and we also moved house. For a number of years we had been living in a lovely house on the outskirts of Ormskirk, but we decided to move to the Blundell Sands area of Liverpool, in part because Sue and I liked the area, but also because of our children's schooling. Following our move Darren attended St Mary's School and, later, Janette went to Merchant Taylor's, both considered to be very good schools.

The trip to Florida was part holiday, part business. Throughout my career I had always started training two weeks before official pre-season took place at Liverpool, keen to keep myself as fit as possible during the summer. So when a pal of mine who was living in Florida rang to ask if I would be interested in spending part of the summer playing for Tampa Bay Rowdies, I talked the matter over with Sue, got back to him and said yes. The only problem was that Liverpool didn't want me to go. Bob was OK about it, but the directors, in particular chairman John Smith, didn't agree.

I telephoned John at the brewery he was connected with, explained how beneficial the trip would be for me, and was somewhat taken aback by his terse and intransigent response. John was adamant: he would not let me go to Tampa. I was in the process of explaining again how playing part of the summer would aid my fitness levels when he put the phone down on me. I was furious. I immediately rang back, only to discover that John was 'unavailable'. His secretary told me he was on his way to Lime

Street station as he was attending the England–Wales international that weekend. I thanked her, and headed for Lime Street.

When I caught up with him I told him in no uncertain terms that I didn't like the way I had been treated by him. I made mention of all the years of service I had given the club and the fact that Bob was OK about me going to Florida.

'If you go, you'll find yourself out of the pack,' he informed me, 'the pack' being the first-team squad of sixteen players.

I reminded John that he didn't pick the squad, that was the remit of Bob. He never budged an inch.

'OK, then, stick the squad,' I told him, and set off for home.

I suspect John subsequently spoke to Bob because a couple of days later the club granted me permission to go to Florida.

1976 was the US bicentennial year. Due to the celebrations the number of matches teams played in the US Soccer League was reduced, in the main to accommodate a Bicentennial Festival Tournament which involved teams from the United States, Italy, Brazil and England. Due to the fledgling nature of American football (or soccer as they called it) at the time it was agreed the USA national team could contain guest players. I was asked if I would guest for the USA, and I readily agreed.

I played in the 2–0 defeat against Brazil and in the 1–0 defeat against Italy. Those losses meant the USA were out of the tournament, but it was then announced that an 'unofficial' international would take place against England. Having played for England in 1971 against Wales, my only cap, I now had the almost unique distinction of also playing against my country. I say almost unique because another footballer played for and against England, the legendary Blackpool centre-forward Stan Mortenson. All home internationals that took place during the Second World War were deemed 'unofficial' and players were not awarded caps. Mortenson was named as reserve for a game against Wales at Wembley, but following a first-half injury to the Welsh inside-forward Ivor Powell, during the half-time interval it was agreed

Mortenson could take Powell's place in the second half. My circumstances were altogether different, but Stan Mortenson and I still share the distinction of being the only two players to have played for and against England, albeit unofficially. The England team included goalkeeper Jimmy Rimmer (Aston Villa), Mike Doyle (Manchester City), Trevor Brooking and my Liverpool team-mate Phil Thompson, and they proved too good for the USA, England triumphing 2–0.

I enjoyed my short period with Tampa Bay. One of the highlights was a game against New York Cosmos in which I had the unenviable job of trying to mark Pele. He had always been a hero of mine and it was an honour and a privilege to play against the great man. Cosmos beat Tampa 2–0, and when the final whistle sounded I was delighted when Pele came over to me and embraced me. After the game we had a good chat, which proved the beginning of what I am happy to say has been a lasting friendship. Pele told me he was aware of my 'reputation', but that I had not fouled him. I told him the so-called reputation was not to be believed.

'I don't,' he said. 'You're a footballer, like me.'

'I wish,' I replied. Pele was now in his mid-thirties but still a giant of football, still possessing the physical prowess, fitness and array of skills that had bedazzled for two decades. One of the problems I had when playing against the great man was actually getting near him. Pele almost invariably was a first-touch player; on those rare occasions when he did hold on to the ball, he twisted and turned and shielded it with every part of his body, including his backside. This made it almost impossible to get a foot on the ball.

Tampa reached the play-offs and had high hopes of defeating Toronto in the semi-finals until the quixotic policy of US soccer at the time played its part. It was announced that the clubs that had reached the semi-finals could sign additional players for this stage of the tournament. Tampa never took up this option, but Toronto did: they went out and signed Eusebio, his fellow countryman

Simões and the Italian international Facchetti. Tampa lost the game and Toronto went on to win the play-off final, a success that was greeted with much chagrin by those involved in US soccer: a Canadian team being crowned champions hardly provided the game in the USA with the sort of publicity they had hoped for.

Sue and the children had headed back to England prior to the play-offs as arrangements had to be made for Darren and Janette's schooling. Also, Sue wanted to see how the house we were having built in Blundell Sands was progressing. In the event, when she returned home she discovered, much to her dismay, that there had been no progress on the new house. It was going to be another two to three months before our new home was habitable, so Sue now had the job of having to find a flat for us to live in. Needless to say, this involved a lot of conversations between Sue and me. What money I did earn playing for Tampa I think I must have spent on transatlantic phone calls.

Prior to Sue and the children returning to England I can recall sitting on the beach in Florida and taking time once again to reflect on how good life had been to me. I had a wonderful and loving family. I was at the top in my career as a footballer, and Liverpool were enjoying unprecedented success. I was far from rich, but we had a few quid in the bank, enough to make you feel confident in life. It's funny what a difference a little money makes. I recalled the time after Dad died, prior to my joining Liverpool, when Mum's financial situation was perilous. Unless you have been in that situation you can never know just how fragile life is. You have just about enough to live on, but should anything go wrong, such as the washing machine breaking down or an unexpectedly large bill dropping through the door, life becomes immediately problematic. As I lay on that beach I was mindful of how fortunate I had been; should any unexpected expense occur now, I knew I could meet it.

As I thought about my career at Liverpool, it also occurred to me that quite often when I had helped the team win trophies and enjoyed a superlative end to a season, the following campaign began with some sort of problem for me. For example, having helped Liverpool to lift both the Championship and UEFA Cup in 1973, the following season saw me out of the team for a time; likewise, 1975–76 began with me not being picked. I am not a pessimist, far from it, but having helped Liverpool to yet another Double success I did wonder what might be around the corner for me, football being, as I always say, a very unpredictable business.

Sue took Darren and Janette on a short holiday to Devon, accompanied by her sister and brother-in-law, while I reported back for pre-season training in preparation for 1976–77.

Pre-season went well, but a week or so prior to Liverpool's opening match against Norwich City I happened to notice a small lump, about the size of a pea, on the back of my right knee. I referred it to Bob and Joe, who didn't think it was anything to worry about. Because I felt no discomfort, neither did I. With the opening day approaching, however, I began to feel a little stiffness in my right knee which as the days went by gradually became worse. I was ruled out for the Norwich match, received treatment, and didn't return until our fifth match of the season, at Derby County. We beat Derby 3–2, Liverpool's fourth victory in five, the only defeat having occurred at Birmingham City. I played in the following two games as well, a 2–0 win over Spurs and a single-goal defeat at Newcastle, but after the Newcastle game the stiffness in my knee returned. Again I received treatment which seemed to ease the problem, but the worrying thing was the lump on the back of my leg appeared to have grown.

Throughout the autumn I continued to receive treatment. Hindsight is the only exact science, and I should have asked to be referred to a specialist, but after each session of treatment the stiffness eased and I was hopeful that one day it would clear up and disappear completely. I was unable to cope with the rigours of playing week in, week out, but because the problem flared up only to dissipate following treatment I played the occasional game. Bob was of the mind that my experience would be useful in the European Cup, so he decided to play me in European rather than domestic matches.

Liverpool's involvement in the European Cup began in mid-September with a tie against Northern Ireland champions Crusaders. I partnered Emlyn in the centre of defence and we had little in the way of difficulty against a plucky Crusaders side, goals from Phil Neal and Tosh giving us a 2–0 victory and, I suppose, Crusaders some hope for the return leg. Such hope was quickly banished when David Johnson, whom Bob had signed from Ipswich Town, gave us the lead on the night. Thereafter it became something of a stroll as we clocked up another four goals without reply to win 7–0 on aggregate.

To be honest, my experience was not needed against Crusaders, but I like to think it came in handy in round two when we travelled to Trabzon in Turkey. It was decided that we would stay in Istanbul as the club felt the quality of the hotels in the capital city would be superior to those in Trabzon. Well, that was the theory. For those of you who have never been to Istanbul, the city comes as something of a shock to the system. You may still be in Europe, but a trip through the streets is enough to convince you that you are in the midst of a totally different culture. As our coach picked its way through the streets of Istanbul I gazed out of the window and took in the sights. Men and boys with handcarts, old men with bundles of goods on their backs that were so heavy their bodies were bent double, beggars and shoeshine boys populated every street. The bars and cafés seemed to be patronized by men only, the women seemingly scurrying about their business, many of them wearing the veil. The coach lurched and bumped as it negotiated the pothole-strewn streets off which shot bazaars bustling with life and activity. Mosques jostled for position alongside buildings ancient and modern in the only city in the world to have played host to consecutive Christian and Islamic empires. This confusion of sights and sounds initially I found very alienating, yet at the same time I was fascinated by it.

To be honest, from the outside our hotel looked fine. It was only when we assembled in the foyer that I first began to have – pardon the pun – reservations. No matter how warm the welcome, foreign hotels – particularly those in Eastern Europe, and Istanbul is as east as you can get – always contrived to alienate. For me it was the decor. The carpetless foyer, the intricate wrought-iron banisters on marble, or in this case stone, staircases, and shuttered rather than curtained windows served to reinforce the fact that you were a stranger in a strange land. I had done enough travelling not to be disconcerted by this, but this hotel I did find disconcerting.

When Cally and I arrived at our room, I put the key in the door, stepped inside, then stepped back out into the corridor again so that Cally could enter. It was that small. Such a tiny space would have been pushed to accommodate two single beds, and they hadn't attempted it: alongside one wall were rackety wooden bunk beds. The room carried the odours of spiced food, car exhausts and humanity going about its business on a boiling hot day, and somewhere on the air the smell of a river assailed the senses. I opened the shutters to find, less than fifty yards away, a large mosque. Nothing wrong with that, of course, except we were to discover that they did a lot of praying at this mosque, and people were called to prayer by a muezzin in a minaret whose voice was amplified through loudspeakers. An inspection of the en suite revealed that there was no toilet tissue. I rang down to reception only to be told that the hotel didn't have any. Cally and I subsequently discovered that the Liverpool *Daily Post* can be put to a variety of uses. By this stage Liverpool travelled with a chef when abroad. He brought with him all the food we needed, but he had trouble being accommodated in the hotel's kitchen which resulted in what I can only describe as basic meals being prepared.

I had a fitful night's sleep. Every turn resulted in the bunk beds creaking and groaning; together with the sounds of the city outside it was a wonder I got any sleep at all. Having managed a few hours of it I was awoken at dawn by the call to prayer. Cally and I didn't go. To compound our misery we found that the shower wasn't working. We visited the rooms of some of the other lads only to discover they too had the same problem. It transpired that there was a fault with the water supply. I can't say I was sorry to leave the hotel and head for the airport. I can't tell you anything about the flight to Trabzon and I doubt whether any of the other lads could: we spent the journey catching up on our sleep.

Against Trabzonspor, Bob moved me to right-back with Phil Thompson pairing Emlyn in the centre and Joey Jones at left-back. The crowds in Turkey were often volatile towards English clubs, and this night proved no exception. The Avni Aker Stadium only had a capacity of 25,000 but it sounded as if twice that many were in the ground as the home side went in search of an early goal. The pitch was problematic for us. The grass had been allowed to grow to some four to five inches in length. It was as if we were playing football in water, and it made it difficult to chip and float passes. Every touch of the ball by a Liverpool player was greeted with cat-calls and whistles, but with our minds totally concentrated on the job in hand we never let that get to us. When Cemil scored the only goal of the game from the penalty spot after Emlyn had handled, the home supporters went berserk, believing that the breakthrough would herald further goals. It never happened. We played the possession game, and though we never managed to capitalize on what few chances we created, I knew from the relatively muted sound that greeted the final whistle that the home fans shared our belief that their team had not done enough to survive at Anfield.

After the game Bob said we could catch a flight back to London that night or travel back to the hotel in Istanbul, have a look around the city in the morning and catch a flight later in the day. As intriguing and as interesting a city as I found Istanbul to be, I don't have to tell you what the response to that was.

The second leg against Trabzonspor took place a fortnight later, but my knee had not recovered sufficiently for me to be included in the side. As expected, we accounted for the Turks at home, goals from Steve Heighway, David Johnson and Kevin Keegan giving us what in the end was a comfortable 3–0 victory. I continued to receive treatment in the days that followed, but the knee only got worse. The stiffness was such that I could hardly bend it. More worrying was the fact that the lump continued to grow, until it was bigger than a large egg. Further treatment was considered futile, so I was referred to a specialist. He examined my knee and told me I had what was called a Baker's cyst. I asked if it was a simple matter of an operation to cut the cyst from my knee and was somewhat taken aback when he told me, 'No.' In normal circumstances he could remove the cyst by means of a simple operation, but because this cyst had been allowed to go untreated for so long it had attached itself to the muscle at the back of my knee. Had the matter been referred to him earlier, the operation would have been quite straightforward; now there were complications.

'How long, doctor?' I asked.

'Three to four millimetres,' he told me.

'Not the attachment to the muscle; how long before I will be able to play football again?'

'Oh, I'd say you'll be back in four months.'

'Four months!' I repeated out loud. I had been expecting him to say three to four weeks.

The specialist knew his stuff, thank heavens. I was admitted to hospital and had the operation which, fortunately, was a success. The timescale of the healing was all down to the muscle, which needed time to recover. I took things easy and slowly started my recuperation. Once the muscle had recovered sufficiently to allow me to play again, it was then a matter of working towards achieving match fitness, and to help me do that I played a number of games for the reserves. At the end of February 1977 I was considered fit and strong enough to play competitive football again, almost four months to the day after the original diagnosis.

Bob recalled me to the side for Liverpool's European Cup quarter-final against St Etienne on 2 March. I was named substitute, only this time I had no qualms about being on the bench. I was just so relieved to be fit again and back in the fold. St Etienne were a very talented side; many European football writers felt they could go all the way and win the European Cup. In their tight, compact ground, roared on by an enthusiastic home crowd, St Etienne set about us from the start. Their star players were Rocheteau, Larque and Bathenay, and it was the latter who gave the home side the lead. With the score at 1–0 and with some twenty minutes remaining, it seemed Bob was happy to settle for the single-goal deficit. But our defence was coming under increasing pressure from the home side. He turned to me in the dug-out and said, 'I'm bringing you on, Tommy. Rally the troops, keep them calm, and make sure we don't concede another.' I did my best to do just that. There was no further score and everyone seemed happy enough to return home trailing by the one goal.

I did wonder if Bob was still of the mind only to call on me for European games, especially as Liverpool were riding high at the top of Division One, but I was included in the team for our very next League match, a 1–0 defeat at Spurs. As so often happens in football, one man's misery provides another with an opportunity. Phil Thompson was having trouble with a cartilage and Bob asked if I would continue to play in the heart of defence alongside Emlyn. No problem with that.

Liverpool consolidated their League Championship position on 12 March with a victory at Middlesbrough, and four days later we faced St Etienne in the return at Anfield. All appeared to be going well when Kevin Keegan gave us the lead in the first half to restore the tie to parity. All appeared to be going well for us in the second half too, until Bathenay produced a piece of true class. In all the years I played football I have been privileged to witness many fantastic goals, and the one Bathenay scored for St Etienne that night is right up there with the best of them. There seemed to be no danger when he picked up the ball some five yards from the centre circle in our half of the field. He advanced – still no danger – then from fully forty yards out unleashed a tremendous thunder-bolt of a drive that beat Clem all ends up. Unbelievably, the ball was still on the rise when it ripped into the back of the net. Clem was a top-class goalkeeper; it took something very special to beat him from that distance, and that is exactly what Bathenay produced. It truly was an incredible strike. It was a wonder Clem didn't catch a cold from the draught created by the ball as it bulleted past him.

With St Etienne 2–1 up in the tie and having scored an away goal, we now faced a real uphill task. The goal pepped the French side whose play immediately took on greater authority and assurance. I had been around long enough to know that when players played like that they believed they were going to win a game. We battered them, but to no avail. St Etienne coped with everything we conjured up.

Some twenty minutes from time, Bob brought on 'super sub' David Fairclough for Tosh. If not exactly enjoying his night of nights, it was certainly a memorable twenty minutes or so for David. St Etienne found his speed and direct running difficult to cope with and it was he who set up Ray Kennedy for our second goal. That made the tie 2–2 on aggregate, but with Bathenay's away goal St Etienne were still in the driving seat. Minutes from the end David set off again on one of his bullet runs, kept his cool and slipped the ball past Curkovic to secure the all-important third goal. I remember glancing up at the Kop. It was as if thousands of rugs had suddenly been pulled from under the feet of our supporters as they tumbled forward en masse. It was a memorable night not only for David but also for Liverpool. I had only known such an atmosphere at Anfield at night on one other occasion, when we beat Inter Milan back in the mid-sixties. When the final whistle sounded the stadium erupted.

I'll be the first to admit that Liverpool enjoyed a comparatively easy passage in Europe that season. Crusaders and Trabzonspor were European lightweights. St Etienne were a class outfit and provided us with our most difficult tie, certainly more difficult than our semi-final opponents, FC Zurich. The Swiss champions were the surprise package of the semi-finals. They had beaten Glasgow Rangers, Turun Pallesuera from Finland (once heard of, never heard of again) and Dynamo Dresden, who in all probability had provided them with their toughest challenge. The cup holders, Bayern Munich, together with Real Madrid, Torino, Bruges, Benfica and PSV Eindhoven, had, surprisingly, fallen by the wayside. I couldn't see us having trouble against FC Zurich, and so it proved. A 3–1 success in Switzerland effectively ended the tie, but just to make sure we beat them 3–0 at Anfield.

I had been at Anfield for sixteen years but my enthusiasm for the club and football was as strong as ever. Liverpool were contesting three major trophies, the Championship, the FA Cup and the European Cup. In my salad days, when Liverpool were chasing three trophies I believed we could win all three. I was thirty-two years old now with a lot of football experience under my belt, but the optimism of my youth remained undiminished. I believed Liverpool could win a unique Treble.

We had assumed top spot in Division One in October and, but for a brief hiatus of a few days prior to Christmas, had remained in pole position. Manchester City were hot on our heels with Ipswich Town, Aston Villa and Newcastle in with not so much a shout as a slightly raised voice. Following the defeat at Spurs which marked my return to League action, we embarked on an unbeaten run of eleven matches which took us to the penultimate game of the season.

Sidelined with the knee injury I had missed Liverpool's early successes in the FA Cup, against Crystal Palace, Carlisle United and Oldham Athletic, but I returned to cup action in mid-March when we faced Middlesbrough in round six. Boro were ensconced in mid-table in the First Division and managed by John Neal.

Above: With my team mates, following my appointment as captain in 1970.
I am very proud to have been the first Liverpool captain to raise a major
European trophy – the UEFA Cup in 1973. I also held aloft the League
Championship that same season.

Below: Shanks presents me with the club's 'Player of the Year' award in 1971.

Top: I thump the ground in frustration after Spurs' Pat Jennings saves a penalty taken by me. Pat had also saved an earlier penalty from Kevin Keegan. I heard someone laughing and looked up – it was the referee, Mr Raby from Leicester. 'Play on, this is wonderful stuff,' he laughed. It was, and I laughed too.

Above: Pre-season training in 1973. I am next to Kevin (front row), doing the old trick of moving your arms quickly up and down to suggest you are running fast.

Right: With the FA Cup in 1974. It is

I must have had a rush of blood to the head. I'm trying to out-run 'Nijinsky' – Colin Bell of Manchester City.

Above: I feigned injury when hit by a bottle whilst playing against Ferencvaros in Hungary. The following day at Melwood, Alec Lindsay made much of the incident!

Below: With the Tampa Bay Rowdies line-up in the summer of 1975. I am front row, centre. Far left, back row, is Clyde Best (then of West Ham) who now runs a successful dry-cleaning business in Portland, Oregon. Middle row, third from right, is Rodney Marsh.

Below: Doing a bit with the weights. Pre-season at Melwood was when all our hard training took place.

Left: Celebrating European Cup success in 1977 with Ronnie Moran. I'd given my front teeth to Ronnie, who'd kept them in a handkerchief in his pocket. Such was our joy, the press lads took their shots before he gave me my teeth back.

Below: That goal – against Borussia Mönchengladbach, European Cup Final 1977. The move that did not go to plan!

Above: Sue and I proudly display the European Cup as we fly back from Rome.

Right: We assemble on the balcony of the Walker Art Gallery following Liverpool's European Cup success. The celebration was spoiled by a crass interlude on the part of Emlyn Hughes, who managed to upset everybody.

Winning the European Cup really went to my head.

Below: With my great pal Bobby Charlton following my Testimonial at Anfield in 1977. And you never thought you'd see Bobby in a Liverpool shirt.

Leeds United's Allan Clarke asks me how long there is to go and I tell him, 'Two minutes.'

Above: Liverpool proudly display the European Cup, European Super Cup, League Championship trophy and Charity Shield, lining up with star player and captain Kenny Dalglish (back row) and Kenny Dalglish (middle row) with manager Bob Paisley and his coaching and medical staff.

Below: Liverpool in League Division 1 in the 1980s, together with the coaching and backroom staff with two of the groundsmen. Bob Paisley, one of the greatest Liverpool managers, takes the centre stage in the picture.

Their side included my old team-mate Phil Boersma, the ex-Leeds and England full-back Terry Cooper, David Armstrong, the centre-forward who looked fifty when he was twenty-one (when he passed fifty he never looked any older than he did when twenty-one), and a midfielder who was to greatly impress Bob that day, Graeme Souness.

Prior to the match a local band did their stuff before a good-natured crowd of 56,000. I joined the rest of the lads in inspecting the pitch, and while I was out there I noticed both sets of supporters wearing rosettes complete with a little tin cup in the centre of the red and white tissue paper as neatly folded as hospital bed sheets attended to by a diligent nurse. It was as if we were harking back to the heady days of the early sixties and it gave me a real sense of the tradition of the FA Cup.

Boro were a club that had become twitchingly obsessive about winning something. They had been thought of as 'unfashionable' for too long. Though Boro had acquitted themselves well in the First Division under John Neal's predecessor, Jack Charlton, they had gained a reputation for being one of the most defensive-minded teams in the land. Neal had introduced a more positive style to their play, but their strength was still defence.

From the start we never allowed Boro to settle, and if they thought a long ball down the middle would embarrass us, they were soon disillusioned. It was meat and drink to Emlyn and me. Graeme Souness got through a tremendous amount of work in midfield, most of it in the nature of defence, but at no time did Boro present a picture of being potential cup semi-finalists. Individually they had their moments, but collectively such moments were rare. Following a goalless first half the deadlock was broken when David Fairclough, on from the start, showed John Craggs a clean pair of heels and rifled home past keeper Pat Cuff. Having taken the lead I sensed we were home. Kevin Keegan, who had been characteristically irrepressible all after-noon, popped up in the Boro penalty area to notch a second, and it was all over bar the shouting, which was now all being done by our supporters.

As fate would have it, we were drawn against Everton in the semi-final, the other semi-final being contested by Leeds and Manchester United. Whatever the outcome of either tie, it was going to be what the press dubbed 'a heavyweight final'. At Maine Road 53,000 Merseysiders witnessed a match that was clouded in controversy. It was one hell of a game to play in, pulsating from start to finish. Terry McDermott put us in the lead only for Duncan McKenzie to equalize before half-time. The second half ebbed and flowed, and the capacity crowd seemed to cherish every moment. Jimmy Case restored our lead, and with only minutes remaining it seemed we were Wembley bound. Then Bruce Rioch equalized. Following a spell of intense pressure from Everton, and with the game into injury time, the ball was played into our penalty box from the Everton left wing by Ronnie Goodlass. McKenzie helped the ball on and Bryan Hamilton, a substitute for Martin Dobson, seemingly appeared from nowhere on the edge of our six-yard box to side-foot the ball past Clem. The Everton players and their supporters went berserk, and my stomach turned over.

The referee that day, Clive Thomas, was no stranger to controversy. In the previous season he had sent off three players in a European Championship semi-final and had gained a reputation in our domestic game for being somewhat unpredictable. Playing to type, Clive disallowed Hamilton's late effort and Liverpool breathed again. The reason why the strike had been disallowed was a source of mystery to many. Clive probably didn't help himself after the game when the press asked him to explain himself. He replied, 'Watch the TV tonight, you'll see it then.' Clive had ruled Bryan offside. Being fair to Everton, I felt the decision debatable to say the least. I watched the incident on TV that night, and as soon as Bryan put the ball in the net I noticed the linesman, Colin Seel, begin to run back towards the halfway line. He obviously thought the goal was good. In his autobiography, Clive stated that he'd also disallowed Bryan's effort for handball. It may well have been, but I didn't see it.

You will be only too aware, regarding such decisions as the one delivered by Clive that day, that these things are often a case of swings and roundabouts, and that they tend to level out over the course of a season. I can remember Liverpool having what I believed to be a legitimate goal disallowed at Stoke that season in a game that ended goalless. Going back to September of that season, Newcastle's Paul Cannell scored the only goal of our game at St James's Park. There was nothing wrong with Cannell's effort, other than that I had been fouled in the build-up and we had not been awarded the free-kick. Against Everton it was our turn to get the rub of the green. The thing was, Everton were still very much in the cup after the goal was disallowed; they had it all to play for. But I sensed their deep feeling of injustice, together with the possible notion that they had 'missed their chance' to beat us and didn't feel they could take us a second time. We swept them aside in the replay, which again took place at Maine Road. Phil Neal gave us the lead from the penalty spot, and second-half goals from Jimmy Case and Ray Kennedy emphasized our superiority on the night. Once again Liverpool were at Wembley, and our opponents on this occasion were Tommy Docherty's Manchester United.

Three days after that replay with Everton, on 30 April, we beat fellow title contenders Ipswich Town 2–1 at Anfield in what was a stormy and tempestuous game. Steve Heighway was carried off with an eye injury following a clash with Mick Mills. As Steve lay prostrate on the ground with blood streaming from a cut around his eye, Mick claimed he had never made contact with him. 'We'd better keep an eye on the referee then,' I told Ray Kennedy, 'because someone's knocked the living daylights out of him!' I had a running battle with Paul Mariner, and Kevin with Brian Talbot. As the robust tackling continued unabated and unpunished, players resorted to taking retribution themselves, which is always a bad sign. It was very unusual for Bob to comment on the performance of a referee, irrespective of the result, but he did on this occasion. He said to the press after the game, 'Tension often affects managers and referees, but this time it was the referee [Peter Willis] and his linesmen who were affected. Their performance today could have cost us the Treble.' Bob also went on to suggest that teams of referees and linesmen should be kept together for an entire season so they could develop an understanding with one another. He was widely quoted, but perhaps it was a sign of those times that he was never subsequently taken to task by the authorities for his comments.

On 3 May we triumphed over Manchester United in the League courtesy of a goal from Kevin Keegan. All we had in our minds was the possibility of the Treble, and with every game the dream grew closer to reality. Successive draws against QPR and Coventry City strengthened our position at the top of the League, so much so that we only needed a point from our final two games to become the first club to win successive Championships since Wolves back in 1959.

West Ham had the dubious distinction of having to come to Anfield on the day we went in search of that point. West Ham were embroiled in a fight to avoid relegation and, credit to them, they battled from start to finish, contesting every ball. We went out to win the game, as we always did, but one of our chief aims was not to concede, as achieving that would land us the title. The West Ham keeper Mervyn Day must have cursed the fact that he didn't have a clause in his contract paying him extra for piece work, because he would have picked up a bulging pay packet that week. He produced a string of saves; two in particular from Cally and Jimmy Case were out of the top drawer. Trevor Brooking and 'Pop' Robson gave evidence that they might threaten at the other end, but West Ham appeared more than content with the point earned from a goalless draw, though of course not as happy as we were.

It was Liverpool's tenth Championship success, which set a new Football League record. I wasn't too bothered about records, but I was very proud of the fact that we had retained the Championship, which I regarded as a remarkable achievement. It's difficult to win the Championship in the first place, but more difficult to retain it. A team has to be consistently good throughout an entire season in order to stand any chance of winning the Championship. To replicate that form the following season takes some doing, and I believe that any side that does so touches greatness. The second season is also harder because you are the reigning champions; every team, irrespective of their position in the League, raises their game in the hope of achieving kudos through having beaten the title holders. A team might also be fortunate regarding injuries and suspensions in a title season; such good fortune rarely continues for a second season, so you need good-quality players in reserve, which is what Liverpool had.

Of course it would be remiss of me to refer to Liverpool's second successive Championship without paying due respect to the work of Bob and his lieutenants Joe Fagan, Reuben Bennett, Ronnie Moran and the rest of the backroom staff, which included Roy Evans and chief scout Geoff Twentyman. They had carried on the work of Shanks and achieved what few thought possible: they had improved on the work of the great man, which arguably was the greatest achievement of all.

These were heady days for Liverpool, and for me. Having begun the season troubled by injury and out of the team, I couldn't believe how much things had changed. I would have been happy just to be back in the team, but I'd won another Championship medal and there was the possibility of the FA Cup and European Cup as well. I had known some great seasons in my time at Anfield, but 1976–77 was shaping up to be the best of all. I was determined to enjoy every moment of it, aware that I was nearing the end of my playing career at Anfield. The prospect of helping Liverpool achieve a unique Treble at this stage in my career I found totally incredible. I remember thinking to myself, 'These will be the great days, Tommy, just you wait and see.'

Standing in Liverpool's way were Manchester United and Borussia Mönchengladbach, who had beaten Dynamo Kiev in their European Cup semi-final. The Borussia team boasted Vogts, Klinkhammer, Bonhof, Stielike, Heynckes and Schaffer, all West German internationals, and West Germany were the current holders of the World Cup. Borussia also had in their ranks the Danish international Alan Simonsen, rated at the time as one of the best players in Europe. They would prove a stiff test of our European credentials; indeed a number of English bookies had them down as favourites to beat us. I never took umbrage at that. But the FA Cup and European Cup Finals respectively represented our 67th and 68th competitive matches of the season, and they were to take place within four days of each other. What Liverpool were now seeking to achieve seemed barely credible.

12

HOME ARE THE HUNTERS

THERE ARE A NUMBER OF UNWRITTEN RULES IN FOOTBALL WHICH curiously apply to the game irrespective of the period, and over which no administrator or manager can exercise control. For example, no matter how poorly a certain player has performed and how few goals he has scored for a club, following a transfer, when he returns with his new club he'll score against his old club. A team previously unable to put a win together will, following relegation, suddenly start to win matches. When a team enjoys a good spell of results, a regular supporter who persuades his pal, a fair-weather supporter, to attend the next match summons fate. The team will play poorly and lose, prompting the fair-weather fan to say something along the lines of 'It's been two years since I last went to a game and from what I saw today it'll be another two years before I come back.' And when two teams from the same division meet in a cup competition, the team that enjoys success in the League will lose the cup match.

The latter applied to Liverpool and Manchester United in 1977. In our Championship season we had drawn at Old Trafford and beaten United at Anfield. They had failed to score against us in either of those two matches. The previous season, Tommy Docherty's side had lost in the FA Cup Final to Second Division Southampton. The bookies made Liverpool odds-on favourites to defeat United at Wembley. With so much going for us, I should have known nothing would go to plan as we went in search of the magical, and at the time never-done-before and seldom-contemplated, Treble.

The scenes inside Wembley on 21 May, with both sets of supporters decked out in red, were magnificent on a day of bright sunshine. There were 100,000 inside the stadium. Liverpool and United were the country's two best-supported teams, yet each club received just 25,000 tickets. As usual, half the tickets for the final had been distributed by the FA to, well, the usual suspects. We players even found tickets difficult to come by. Each Liverpool player was allocated only eight, a far cry from the sixties when we had received twenty-five per player. My set extended to immediate members of the family only, but I could have no gripes about that. Liverpool's average attendance at Anfield was around 50,000, which meant that half of our regular support would have to go without or try to obtain a ticket from elsewhere. The ingenuity of Scousers being what it is, many managed to do just that. I dare say the same applied to many United fans.

The previous year, United had made the mistake of swaggering in the days leading up to the final against Southampton. Rather than being confident of victory, United seemed convinced they could not lose and underestimated Southampton. It proved their undoing. Though the bookies' favourites, I can honestly say that though we too were confident of victory against United, we certainly didn't underestimate them. Whenever we enjoyed a good run of results, before a game Bob would say to us, 'Don't go out with your big heads on,' a gentle reminder that we had to give nothing but 100 per cent irrespective of the opposition. He never had cause to say that prior to our meeting United; we knew they would provide difficult opposition.

Sportsmanship prevailed prior to the start of the game when both sets of supporters sang the traditional Wembley hymn, William Monk and Henry Lyle's 'Abide With Me', with soul-stirring passion. The refrains penetrated the tall glass windows of the Wembley changing rooms, giving one the sense of being in church.

As is often the case when two big clubs meet in a Wembley final, the media were expecting a classic encounter. I don't have to tell you that more often than not such a meeting of football giants fails to live up to expectation. In truth, that was the case for this game, but it did go some way to restoring faith in football at a time when hooligans were besmirching our beautiful game. Both teams enjoyed a reputation for attacking football, with United exuding a more cavalier touch to their play. We had scored seventeen goals on our way to Wembley, United ten, though they had been involved in fewer replays. One thing all the pundits agreed on was that the final would produce goals.

A Liverpool side featuring Ray Clemence, Phil Neal, Joey Jones, me, Emlyn Hughes, Ray Kennedy, Kevin Keegan, Jimmy Case, Steve Heighway, David Johnson and Terry McDermott began the game with confidence oozing out of its pores. We dominated the first half without ever turning our dominance into goals. The nearest we came to breaking the deadlock was a header from Ray Kennedy minutes before half-time that thumped against Alex Stepney's post. When the second half got underway I still expected us to score, but United got in there first. In the 50th minute there appeared to be little danger when Jimmy Greenhoff received the ball some twenty-five yards from our goal. We seemed to have plenty of cover on, but Greenhoff flicked the ball over Emlyn Hughes, and Stuart Pearson raced clear to hammer the ball unerringly past Clem.

Determined to bounce back at the first opportunity we immediately set about United once more. Within two minutes of Pearson's opener, Jimmy Case controlled a centre from Joey Jones on his thigh, turned on a penny and drove the ball high past the flaying arms of Stepney and into the roof of the net. It was one of the most spectacular Cup Final goals in years. One-all, nothing decided, all still to play for.

Having dominated proceedings, three minutes later we again found ourselves chasing the game. Following a scramble reminiscent of the fight to get on the last bus home, I got a foot on the ball but felt I was unfairly impeded by Jimmy Greenhoff. The referee thought otherwise and the ball broke to Lou Macari, who advanced, tried his luck and was granted it. Initially Macari's shot appeared to be going wide, but the ball deflected off one of Emlyn's legs, then off the back of Jimmy Greenhoff and over Clem. Rather than bounce into the net the ball appeared to drag itself exhaustedly over the line. I don't think it even reached the back of the net. It didn't matter, United had the lead, and try as we did we couldn't salvage the game. Our luck was out on the day, and so too was that of Ray Kennedy who with minutes remaining hit the woodwork for a second time when he rifled a shot against the United crossbar with Stepney in a tizzy as to the whereabouts of the ball.

To their credit, United remained calm and resolute; what's more, they held firm. When the final whistle blew my heart sank. In such circumstances you have to force yourself to shake the hands of your opponents, not because you begrudge them their victory but because your disappointment is so great you would rather not speak to anyone. We were all hugely deflated, but to a man we heartily congratulated the United players, in so doing adhering to a maxim of Shanks and Bob: 'Be dignified in victory, be gracious in defeat'.

One man's meat is another man's poison. Ask a United supporter of a certain age for his or her comment on the game and no doubt they will tell you, 'It was a great final, full of fast, exciting football.' Ask a Liverpool supporter for an opinion and you will be told, 'It was an awful game.' The bottom line is we lost, and the result stood as an insuperable obstacle to Liverpool making English football history. We were devastated. We had dominated the first half, and without taking anything away from United, we were, generally speaking, well under par. Lou Macari's goal had had more than an element of luck to it. It was what in football parlance is called a 'scruffy goal'. Even Lou said it was a fluke. As I told the BBC after the game, his shot, 'appeared to hit everything bar the back of the net, but they all count – in our case, in this instance, for nothing'.

It was a shattering experience, but we knew we had to pick ourselves up straight away. Little time to rest, no time for reflecting on what might have been. We travelled back to Liverpool on the Sunday afternoon. The players spent the night with their families before flying out to Rome the following day. Many a modern team might complain about such a tight schedule, particularly as it was coming off the back of a long and arduous season; but after experiencing a numbing defeat, players want to get it out of their systems as soon as possible, and the best way to do that is by playing another game. The fact that we had a European Cup Final four days after losing the FA Cup Final, rather than being a negative thing, was to my mind a great positive. To have had that defeat at Wembley swilling around in your system throughout the summer would have been disorienting to say the least. We now had an opportunity to expunge the black memory of Wembley, and that thought alone was a great fillip for everyone.

One of Liverpool's strengths as a team was its collective spirit. During the post FA Cup Final banquet, to a man we vowed we would not be bowed by the defeat. We agreed we had enough strength, motivation and conviction to bounce back and win the European Cup, not only for Liverpool, but for England. I wonder if such an attitude – of winning the Champions League, as it is now erroneously called, for England – prevails in the dressing rooms of, say, Stamford Bridge or Old Trafford? I would like to think it does, but I doubt it.

Incidentally, after the FA Cup Final I had a little chat with one of United's former players, my good pal Denis Law. It transpired that Denis had seen Borussia Mönchengladbach on a number of occasions during the season. He told me he thought they were vulnerable in the air at the back, particularly from set pieces. I locked that little nugget of information away in my mind.

The word was out that Kevin Keegan was about to leave Liverpool. Since his arrival from Scunthorpe Kevin's contribution and impact at the club had been nothing short of remarkable. He had played his part in three League Championships, two UEFA Cup wins and an FA Cup success. The Kop adored him and he was popular in the dressing room, but he had shocked Liverpool supporters by saying that he was seeking a move to the Continent. Kevin is a grand lad, he was a great player and as honest a professional as you will find, but I think he made a mistake when he said that he wanted to leave Anfield to enhance his career. We were the club that had finished the season looking to achieve the Treble of League Championship, FA Cup and European Cup. Where on earth was he going to go to do better than that? Possibly he was looking for that extra financial security for his family that comes with any big transfer move. For sure, any number of top clubs in Europe paid better wages than Liverpool, but we were on the verge of becoming the best team in Europe. Perhaps it might have been better if he had said he was looking for financial security, as many Liverpool fans could only see one of their idols about to walk out on a winning club. Kevin's decision did not unsettle the team, neither did his desire to get away affect his performances for Liverpool. He gave his all in every game.

I too was uncertain about what the future held for me. I was thirty-two and I'd been at Liverpool for seventeen seasons. Bob was seamlessly creating another great Liverpool team and, given my age, I didn't know how many days I had left at the club. As a result I was doubly determined to finish with the European success that had so long eluded the club. I knew Kevin felt exactly the same way.

Under Shanks we learned a lot. Under Bob we took it further. We had developed into a team of greater tactical awareness, one that controlled matches a lot more; we had learned how to retain possession of the ball rather than lay siege to the opposition; we had learned to subdue our opponents and gradually impose ourselves on the game. We were, arguably, the fittest team in Europe. We could outrun, outfight and in the majority of cases outclass any team you could care to mention. In 2007 Jimmy Greaves appeared in a TV documentary that reviewed football in the 1970s. At one point he was asked if the current Manchester United, Liverpool or Chelsea teams would have beaten the Liverpool side of the seventies. Jimmy replied, 'Who can say? What I do know is, the first problem those teams would have would be getting the ball off that Liverpool side of the seventies.' I was confident that we could outplay and outpower Borussia Mönchengladbach too. I was also aware we had another advantage over the Germans: our fans and their fervent support.

When we arrived at Rome airport a posse of press photographers and reporters from all over Europe were there to meet us, if not exactly to greet us. The press scrum was assembled behind metal crush barriers as we made our way to the airport terminal. As we did so, one of their number called out to Bob, asking if this was his first time in Rome.

'No, I've been here before,' replied Bob. 'The last time I was here, I was in a tank.'

Bob was a down-to-earth guy who never thought anything untoward of any nation and its people. He never meant his comment to be in any way insulting to our hosts, but Cally, Jimmy Case and I immediately cringed. Bob was simply stating a fact, but I had been around long enough to know how such an innocent reply could be interpreted by the press, our own included. Bob too had been around a long time, longer, but his reply emphasized to me how naive he was when dealing with foreign journalists.

Having noted Bob's comment, the press then went in search of a player for a reaction. We had only been in Rome for a matter of minutes but we were already facing a potentially tricky situation with the Italian press. For whatever reason the lads felt I was best suited to speak, so before leaving the airport I found myself facing a gaggle of Italian journalists. I was mindful of the advice Shanks once gave me: 'Keep it brief, then get out.' I said something to the effect that Bob had made his comment in light of the fact that he was proud to have been a part of the Allied forces that liberated Italy and its people, with whom Britain had always enjoyed close ties. I don't know if my comment had any effect but, happily, nothing subsequently appeared in the Italian press to suggest that they had taken exception to Bob's well-meant reply.

The incident did not scupper our usual pre-match preparation. We were all relaxed and totally focused. Bob didn't emphasize how important the game was – he didn't have to. In his team talk he simply told us to play to our strengths, to keep hold of the ball and 'boss it'. He told us to watch out for the speed of the Danish international Simonsen and to clamp down on Stielike, because if we didn't 'he can play a bit', but that was the sum total of his notes on the opposition. His final words were, simply, 'Just go out and beat them.' As I said, it was our usual pre-match preparation.

Prior to leaving our hotel Bob received a telegram wishing us good luck and every success in the final. It was from Tommy Docherty.

The Olympic Stadium in Rome boasted a capacity of 60,000 and it was estimated that some 50,000 of the supporters that night were Liverpool fans. How on earth they managed to get tickets I don't know, but somehow they did. I remember, when the teams took to the pitch, looking up around the stadium and seeing Liverpool fans everywhere. It was like a home game. There were so many of them I was pushed to spot any Mönchengladbach fans in the stands, though obviously a number of them were there.

Bob made one change to the team that had lost the FA Cup Final to Manchester United: Cally replaced David Johnson, which meant a 4–4–2 formation with Kevin having the job of pulling their defenders from central positions and Steve Heighway stretching the German defence from wide. Bob was later to confide to me that he felt we would have won the FA Cup the previous Saturday if he had played the same team at Wembley as he did in Rome. Who am I to argue with Bob, but I don't think he made a great mistake in playing David Johnson instead of Cally at Wembley. He chose what he felt was the team that would do the job on the day. That we didn't was largely due to the way United applied themselves, and of course to us players for not producing the goods.

We adapted our game when playing in Europe. We played a more patient game, preferring to keep possession of the ball and not attack teams with the verve we applied in domestic games. We were only too aware that should we commit men forward in numbers, Continental teams were very good at hitting you on the break. Also, their technique was very good; should we allow a top team too much of the ball, they could demonstrate that they really could play and would grow in confidence. A team plays as well as it is allowed to play, and we were determined not to give Mönchengladbach an opportunity to show how good a side they were. When competing in Europe we blended technique, sophistication and possession with the archetypal English ethic of runners and workers. You never saw a Liverpool player pass the ball and trot forward; our game was all about supporting the man on the ball. In Europe this allowed us to preserve our 'steamroller' qualities, but also to pace ourselves more economically and use the ball to good effect.

The European Cup Final marked my 600th senior competitive game for Liverpool. But I wasn't bothered by personal statistics; all I was focused on was playing my part in helping us win the European Cup for what would be the first time in the history of the club. It had been nine years since Manchester United had become the first, and they remained the only English team to have lifted the trophy. I had a feeling in my bones that we would match the feat.

Any doubts about the effect of the numbing defeat we had suffered at Wembley four days earlier were allayed in the first quarter of an hour. Jimmy Case, Ray Kennedy, Cally and Terry McDermott were all using the ball proficiently and running with good purpose into space. We took control of the midfield from the start, which is what we knew we had to do, and gradually we became dominant in all areas of the field. Which was no mean task, given that Mönchengladbach contained several players who had featured for West Germany in the 1974 World Cup, which they won, plus Simonsen. Within the first ten minutes or so I had a good feeling about the game. We were playing much better than we had done at Wembley. Upfront Kevin and Steve Heighway looked much sharper than they had done against United, and we felt comfortable and in control across the back. Our desire to be positive without being reckless paid off after twenty-eight minutes. Terry McDermott saw a gap and raced into it, latching on to a perfectly timed pass from Steve Heighway. Another gap appeared, to the left of keeper Kneib, and Terry exploited it calmly and clinically. The Olympic Stadium immediately erupted as 50,000 Liverpool supporters aired their tonsils and gave vent to their joy. We continued to harass and hassle Mönchengladbach into making mistakes, but our industry was not to be rewarded by further goals. During the half-time interval Bob and Joe just told us to 'keep it going'. Everything was going to plan. Mönchengladbach had shown commitment to match their undoubted skill, but had made few inroads into the game.

We took to the field for the second half with our heads up. Our supporters were simply magnificent. As we started the second period, the frenzied atmosphere on the terraces seemed to cut into the sultry night air. I thought to myself, 'There is no way we're going to lose this.' But Mönchengladbach began the second half with much more purpose. They buzzed, snapped into tackles, closed us down quickly, played the sort of game we had played in the first period. We all knew they were a top-quality side that would not roll over, but we were confident of containing them.

With only six minutes of the half having passed, however, we were rocked. We won possession in midfield, but Simonsen intercepted a raking pass from Jimmy Case. We were caught pushing on and treated to the sight of Simonsen's backside as he sprinted towards an isolated Clem. Emlyn, Phil Neal and I gave chase, we really dug in, but he was away. Simonsen was so fast he made the Olympic qualifying time for 100 metres. If having a ball at his feet slowed him up, it didn't show. The Dane sped into the box, glanced up, then fired a fierce low shot past the advancing Clem. As the back of the net billowed I ground to a halt. Simonsen wheeled away, arms aloft in triumph. You could have heard a pin drop. Jimmy was mortified, his face riddled with angst. He began to apologize, but I told him to forget it and to 'get buckled down to the job', which to his credit is exactly what he did.

The higher the level you play at, the fewer mistakes are made during the course of a game; the better the quality of the opposition, the more these few mistakes will be punished. We had made one mistake and had been punished for it. Simonsen's goal lifted Mönchengladbach and we found ourselves enduring a very nervous ten-minute spell in which we lost our way a little. It was during this spell that Clem made what to this day he maintains were the two most important saves of his career. The first was from Stielike who found himself just yards from our goal with the ball at his feet, only Clem standing between him and glory. Clem did what he'd done so many times before when faced with a one-on-one situation, which he had learned from his days understudying Tommy Lawrence. He took up the correct position and tried to make himself look as big as possible. Then, when Stielike was about to strike the ball, he spread himself towards it in the hope of making a block save. Stielike's shot cannoned into and off Clem's body, and we managed to clear our lines. Minutes later Simonsen latched on to a great through-ball from Stielike and his electric pace did for us again. Clem reacted immediately, racing off his line to narrow the angle and Simonsen's view of the goal. In the few seconds that followed there was nothing I or my fellow defenders could do but watch. Clem stayed on his feet until the last possible moment. As Simonsen pulled the trigger, Clem went to ground, spread his body and palmed the ball away to safety.

We owed it to Clem, big time. If either of those efforts had resulted in a goal, our task would have been monumental as Mönchengladbach had proved more than adept at protecting a lead. As it was, we gradually began to reassert ourselves and the final developed into an open, end-to-end thriller as both sides went in search of what they believed would be the decisive goal.

With Tosh and Phil Thompson sidelined through injury we lacked height upfront, and in midfield too. By no stretch of the imagination can I boast a towering physique, but I am taller than Kevin, Cally, Jimmy and Terry Mac and had always been decent in the air for a player of my height (five ten). Throughout the season, due to our lack of height upfront, Bob and Joe had told me to go up for corners. The plan was for Steve Heighway to float the ball towards the near post and for me to flick it on and down towards the far post, where Kevin and Terry would be lurking with intent. When Steve Heighway won a corner on the left, the Mönchengladbach defenders gravitated towards Kevin and co. at the far post. I wandered forward. The plan was for me to hold off until the last possible moment, then, as Steve addressed the ball, time my run to get on the end of the cross. All went to plan, up to a point. I stayed deep, and seeing Steve address the ball I sprinted forward in the hope of flicking the ball towards the far post. No Mönchengladbach player picked me up; I suppose they never expected the 'old man' in the Liverpool team to burst forward. I continued to sprint forward into space, only for Steve to then surprise me. Rather than float the ball, as was the plan, Steve drove it as hard as he could to a point some ten yards from the near post.

The ball left his boot like a house brick fired from a cannon. I was on my way but had to dig in and up my pace to have any chance of making contact. I took to my toes, sprinted as fast as I could and took off.

It is amazing what flashes through the mind in a split second. Having gauged the speed and trajectory of the ball I knew that if I made contact there was no way I would be able to deftly flick it on with any accuracy towards Kevin and Terry at the far post. As I was making my run I glanced towards goal and saw that there was no defender guarding the near post. As the ball raced towards me I made the decision to go for goal. I met the speeding ball with the meat of my forehead, doing my best to direct it towards the goal side of the near post. The ball cut off my head almost at a right angle and shot off towards the goal. I never took my eyes off that ball as I made my descent. I saw it pass between the angle of the post and the crossbar and billow the net. Once again the Olympic Stadium filled with an eruption of noise, and I found myself smothered by red-shirted team-mates.

My goal not only took Mönchengladbach by surprise, but everyone else too. Even TV commentator Barry Davies took a second to realize it was me who had scored. Sue was sitting in the main stand with the wives and girlfriends of my team-mates. When the ball hit the net, they all jumped to their feet and screamed, 'Goal!'

'Who got it? Who got it?' Sue shouted.

'Tommy! It was your Tommy!' shouted Ray Kennedy's wife.

To this day I have never been able to bring myself to ask Steve Heighway why he drove the ball hard into the box rather than float it. All these years on so many people recall that goal vividly. It was the breakthrough we had been looking for and it set us on our way to winning the European Cup for the very first time, which I believe is why it seems to have a special place in the memory. That goal is also a cherished moment in my life, which I suppose is why I have never been able to summon the courage to ask Steve why he chose to drive the ball with such ferocity. I just fear he might say something that will spoil the memory for me.

The goal seemed to knock the wind out of Mönchengladbach. I sensed they didn't believe they could conjure up an equalizer, particularly as we didn't sit back and try to defend our lead. On the contrary, the goal proved a fillip to us and we penned our opponents in their own half of the field.

Kevin had led Bertie Vogts a merry dance throughout the game. Seven minutes from time, Terry played the ball to Kevin who went on a determined run that took him into the Mönchengladbach penalty box. Vogts was snapping at his heels, and as Kevin accelerated away his only riposte was to pull him down. Phil Neal stepped up to take the resultant penalty. I was on tenterhooks as I stood and watched Phil approach the ball. A little puff of dust rose from the pitch as Phil made contact with the inside of his right boot. Kneib moved to his left, the ball went to his right, and I knew we were home and dry.

When the final whistle sounded I flung my arms aloft in jubilation and not a little relief. There were beaming smiles from all of us as we hugged one another before we shook hands with the Mönchengladbach players. That done, as tired as I was, I danced a little jig before embracing Cally, along with me the last of the 'old guard'.

It was a very proud and happy moment for me when Emlyn lifted the European Cup aloft and our great supporters sang the old favourite 'Ee-aye-addio, we've won the cup!' At last Liverpool had translated domestic dominance into the ultimate European supremacy and we proved popular winners with supporters of whatever hue. Ever since we had beaten St Etienne in the quarter-finals I'd sensed that football fans across the country had entreated the gods to look favourably upon us. Now, in the presence of 60,000 frenzied spectators, the European Cup, with its unmatchable kudos and prestige, had returned to England for only the second time and after an absence of nine years. Best of all, from my point of view, it was going to Liverpool. I was pleased for our supporters and for everyone connected with the club, and I was also delighted for Bob and his backroom staff, particularly Joe Fagan. Bob's association with the club went back to the forties. I struggled to imagine what his thoughts and emotions were at this time.

Had it been difficult to win the European Cup? The fact that Liverpool were only the second English team and the third British team to have won the competition in its twenty-two-year history, I feel, is testimony to the fact that it was very difficult to win Europe's premier trophy. That said, I do recall remarking to Cally after the game that it had been easier to win the European Cup than the two occasions on which we won the UEFA Cup. Then again, I also think it was harder to win the European Cup than the current Champions League. I am not out to decry or denigrate the Champions League, far from it. The quality of football in the Champions League is top class, generally speaking superior to that of the European Cup in its old format. However, the league format of today's competition affords teams a better chance of progressing. In the old knockout system, should you not triumph over a two-leg tie, you were out. What's more, there was no consolation of a parachute into the UEFA Cup. For example, in 1998–99 Manchester United won the Champions League and did the Treble. Without taking anything away from what was a tremendous achievement, United remained unbeaten in their group but only won two of their six matches. Both United's games against Barcelona ended 3–3; had that been in the old knockout format, the tie would have been decided on penalties. United may well have won; then again, they may well not have. Likewise in 2003/04, in the group stage Porto lost 3–1 at home to Real Madrid and drew 1–1 in Spain, which in the old format would have seen José Mourinho's side out of the competition. Porto, however, progressed by virtue of finishing runners-up in their group and subsequently went on to win the Champions League.

Beating Borussia Mönchengladbach, a side containing several players who had helped West Germany win the World Cup, was certainly the high point of my career. To win a European Cup winner's medal with the club I loved meant more to me than I can say. It was a historic night for the club, a great night for the players and a highly memorable one for our supporters, whether they watched the game in the Olympic Stadium or at home on their TV sets. The irony was that Liverpool had at last conquered Europe without the guidance of the man who had always harboured the dream of turning Liverpool into undisputed European champions – Shanks. He was there on the night, he congratulated Bob, but I did wonder if alongside his obvious joy for the club there was also regret.

And when we are 'old and grey and full of sleep and nodding by the fire', I wonder what will be the most clearly defined memory of that night in the Olympic Stadium, 25 May 1977? The fact that we had shrugged off the fatigue and bitter disappointment of a Wembley defeat just four days earlier to give English football the biggest boost it had had in years? The wonderful vocal encouragement of our supporters? Clem's crucial saves at the feet of Stielike and Simonsen? Kevin running rings around a world-class player, Vogts? My goal perhaps? Or Bob Paisley, that most undemonstrative of managers, walking on to the pitch and shaking hands with the Mönchengladbach players before turning to his own men and hugging us like children for the simple fact that we had played so well when it mattered? Bob, the man who 'learned to labour and wait', sported a smile as broad as a melon slice as he watched us do our lap of honour. At one point I looked across and caught him gazing up at the night sky. I wondered what he was thinking. I know what I was thinking: 'This is for you and Shanks, Bob.'

There was no official post-match banquet. The club had hired the hotel dining room for what proved to be a very joyous post-final party, attended by the directors, management and players along with our wives and girlfriends, and selected members of the local media. Sue and I found ourselves sharing a table with Joe, Cally, Kevin, Steve, Jimmy and their wives. I didn't want to keep going up to the bar to buy rounds, so I made just one visit. I ordered a bottle each of brandy, gin and whisky, two bottles of lemonade, and two cases of Peroni. It was, after all, a very special occasion. The hotel provided a buffet of sumptuous Italian food: plates of prosciutto with rocket salad, antipasti platters, polenta with Parma ham, Tuscan chicken with black olives, seafood pasta parcels – you name it. About an hour into the party someone opened a fire door and about two hundred Liverpool supporters swamped the room. Within fifteen minutes what had been a sumptuous and largely untouched buffet was laid bare. It was as if a plague of locusts had descended.

I love Liverpool supporters and always welcome their company, but with so many ecstatic people in the room the atmosphere soon became a little too heady. We just wanted to enjoy the moment in one another's company, a fact recognized by Joe.

'OK, come on,' he said, taking to his feet.

'Where are we going?' I asked.

'To my room, and bring all that booze with you.'

We assembled in Joe's room, and as there were so many of us, we left the door open. We sipped our drinks and talked about the final and the season in general for some twenty minutes. Then we heard voices in the hall, and Bertie Vogts appeared in the doorway.

'Where are you lads off to?' I asked.

'Bed,' replied Bertie.

'No, don't do that, come and join us for a drink.'

Bertie disappeared back into the hall only to return accompanied by Bonhof, Simonsen, Stielike and Heynckes. We spent the rest of the night together drinking and talking, not exclusively about football but also about our lives, politics and all manner of things.

The following morning we assembled by the hotel pool where more Peroni was consumed. I was sitting with my feet up on a table on which stood the European Cup when a photographer asked if he could take a picture. I told him that would be OK, as long as he sent me a copy for my personal collection. He subsequently did. That morning various press lads came and went, but one in particular hung about. The reporter in question had often written less than complimentary things about me in his newspaper. Fed up with his criticism, before the final I told him that if he wrote another derogatory piece about me I would throw him in the hotel swimming pool. The article he penned prior to us playing Mönchengladbach was anything but complimentary to me, and that morning this reporter removed his clothes and sat by the pool in his swimming trunks. I figured his game: he was hoping I would carry out my promise and throw him in the pool so he could have an exclusive. I ignored him totally. When the time came for us to get ready to depart, he looked a tad miffed.

'My editor's expecting the story of you throwing me in the pool,' he said as I prepared to leave.

Again I ignored him.

'If I don't file, I might get the sack. It's not like it used to be. Journo jobs are hard to come by now.'

'You could try the *Echo*,' I suggested.

'Which *Echo*?' he asked.

'The one in the reading room at the British Museum,' I replied before heading into the hotel.

Sue and I sat next to each other on the flight back to Liverpool and for part of it we were entrusted with the European Cup, basically because given the size of the trophy no one else wanted to sit with it on their knees. Sue and I were more than happy to have its company. I just sat there staring at it. I thought about all the fine teams that had won it: the great Real Madrid side of the 1950s, AC Milan, Benfica, Celtic and Manchester United. I thought of the players, heroes of mine, who had lifted the very same cup that was now resting on my knees: Di Stefano, Rivera, Eusebio, Billy McNeill and Bobby Charlton. We were also happy to pose for a photograph when asked by one of the photographers from the *Liverpool Echo*. The guy took his picture and sent us a copy as a keepsake. I have many photographs of Sue and me which I treasure, but the one showing us with the European Cup is a particular favourite.

And I thought about Liverpool, how thirteen consecutive seasons of European competition had now resulted in us winning the greatest European trophy of them all. Home are the hunters, home from the hill. At last.

13

THE INAUDIBLE FOOT OF TIME

THE SUMMER OF 1977 SAW STREET PARTIES TAKING PLACE UP AND down the country as the nation celebrated the Queen's Silver Jubilee. There were also a few parties held in Liverpool, though not necessarily to mark Her Majesty's twenty-five years on the throne. It was football's close-season, but you wouldn't have thought it, so often was football in the news. What's more, it was making front-page news – always the mark of a game in trouble.

A matter of weeks after having guided Manchester United to victory over Liverpool at Wembley, Tommy Docherty was sensationally sacked. Even today I hear people erroneously say that he was sacked for having an affair with Mary Brown, the wife of United's physiotherapist. Tommy and Mary were unhappy in their respective marriages. They didn't have an affair, they fell in love, divorced their spouses and got married. Over thirty years on they are still together. Their children have borne them grandchildren. An affair it wasn't. At the time some newspapers referred to Tommy's situation as being 'a scandal'. They were partly right: the scandal was that Tommy was sacked by United for having fallen in love.

Tommy was replaced on the front pages by Don Revie, who resigned as manager of England and the following day told the *Daily Mail* he was to coach the United Arab Emirates at a salary of £60,000 a year plus bonuses, tax free. That story was to run and run, even when Revie's successor, Ron Greenwood, was appointed England manager later that summer.

Having helped Liverpool win the European Cup, and with 323 appearances and a hundred goals to his name in all competitions, Kevin Keegan left Anfield, as he said he would. He joined Hamburg for a fee of £500,000. Never again would *Match of the Day* viewers hear David Coleman utter the immortal and oft-repeated line, 'Toshack, Keegan, one-nil!'

And it was while playing against, rather than with, Kevin that I lost my cool – by and large a pretty rare experience. As part of the transfer deal, Liverpool agreed to play a friendly against Hamburg, who at the time were one of the top teams in the Bundesliga. Now I would growl and shout at opponents and I looked upon it as part and parcel of the game if they growled back. That's football. What I disliked, however, was an opponent flouting one of the pros' unwritten rules of the game, that is, trying to belittle another player – in this case, me!

Hamburg had a player who, if my memory serves me right, was called Magath. He was a very good player, but on this day he over-stepped the mark. I don't speak German, but I didn't need to to know he was having a go at me. Which was fine: you dish out the verbal and you take it in football. Seemingly aware that his verbal tirade was getting him nowhere, at one point Magath ran up to me and grinned right into my face, willing me to do something stupid. That got him nowhere either. Minutes later he was in my face again, grinning and laughing, nodding his head, urging me to have a go at him. Again I ignored him. During the half-time interval I guessed he must have been laughing in the dressing room, telling his team-mates that he was giving me a hard time. Kevin had just joined Hamburg and had yet to learn German; if he'd been a bit more proficient in the language I am sure he would have warned Magath off. As it was, Magath continued to rile me during the second half. At one point he grinned in my face and said in English, 'Hey, hard man, not so hard are you, yeah?'

Midway through the second half I went on a run down the line and crossed the ball, but it went out of play. As I was running back to take up my position in defence, Magath ran up to me with another mocking grin on his face. He said something in German which I didn't understand, but from his tone, I knew it wasn't complimentary. I'd had enough. Without breaking stride I let him have it and he went down like a bag of hammers. No one saw a thing, and by the time the trainer came on I was thirty yards away and back in position. I'm not proud of breaking his nose, far from it, but in a career as long as mine the red mist is bound to descend at least once. After the game Bob Paisley said, 'I saw what happened. He was asking for it, but for heaven's sake, don't do it again, Smithy.'

I never did.

One footballing story that made only a few lines in the national newspapers, if it was mentioned at all, was the signing of Alan Hansen from Partick Thistle for a fee of £100,000. You don't have to have me tell you that it proved to be one of the best signings of Bob's management career. Alan was what Liverpool called a 'flyer' signing. Before the end of every tax year, in order to reduce the amount of tax to be paid on profits the club would reduce its level of profit by spending £100,000 or so on a new signing. Rather than the player in question being one of undoubted quality who Bob knew could do us a job, he took a 'flyer' on a player unproven in the First Division but one who he believed had potential. Should the player in question make the grade at Anfield, all well and good; if not, then at least the club had reduced its tax bill.

A hundred thousand was a lot of money to a club like Partick Thistle which when selling a player to another Scottish club had become accustomed to the fee being paid in instalments. When

Alan arrived at Anfield to sign for Liverpool he was accompanied by the Thistle director, Scott Symon, who in addition to having managed East Fife, Preston North End and Rangers also had the distinction of being the only man to have played for Scotland at both football and cricket, a feat later equalled by Andy Goram. Prior to Alan signing on the dotted line, Symon asked our secretary, Peter Robinson, how Liverpool intended to pay for Hansen.

'Would a cheque be all right?' asked Peter, opening the club chequebook and reaching for a pen.

Symon's jaw dropped. Partick Thistle had never received so much money in one go. Alan later told me how, when travelling back to Glasgow on the train, Symon kept taking the cheque out of the breast pocket of his jacket to look at it – in disbelief.

The arrival of Alan Hansen and the departure of Kevin Keegan were testimony to the fact that for all we had won the European Cup and the League Championship, Bob was still in the process of developing and creating a new Liverpool team. That summer, David Johnson turned down a move to Leicester City. David was to stay at the club for the duration of 1977–78, but his appearances were limited. John Toshack's Anfield career was also coming to a close; midway through the season he accepted the offer of the job of player/manager at Swansea City.

I was also reassessing my position at the club. Since being removed from the 'pack' after spending part of the summer of 1976 playing for Tampa Bay Rowdies, I had spent the 1976–77 season not as a fully fledged member of the first-team squad, just being paid on a 'pay as you play' basis. I only received £150 a week if I played in the first team; should I not play in the first team and turn out instead for the reserves, I received basic reserve-team money plus a £2 victory bonus. Fortunately, having recovered from the cyst on my right knee, I regained my place in the first team. Unlike 'official' first-team squad players, I had to play to receive the win and crowd bonuses. Like every other player I did, however, receive the bonus paid for winning the European Cup, which was £5,000 less tax, plus a bonus of £5,000 for winning the Championship. Now I am well aware that in 1977 £150 a week was more than the average working person earned, but it was a low wage compared to the average First Division player of the time. Not that Liverpool were your average team, either: we had won the European Cup and League Championship. The players who were members of the first-team squad but who had not played many first-team matches still received the bonuses, whereas I didn't. My contract was due for renewal that summer and it was obvious to me that John Smith, Peter Robinson, Bob and I had some talking to do.

Prior to our meeting I talked matters over with Sue. I told her that if the club wanted to release me, it was fine with me, I'd go. It wasn't really 'fine with me', but I saw my situation as a Hobson's choice, and a laissez-faire attitude was my way of dealing with disappointment and sadness. Sue was with me all the way, but as usual she encouraged me to adopt a more rational approach. She told me, 'If you're not wanted, then you'll find another club or something else to do in life. But before making any decisions, wait and see what the club have to say, then give the matter considered thought.'

As had been the case with Shanks before him, as manager Bob was responsible for who stayed and who left the club. Bob told me that should I wish to leave he would not stand in my way, but he wanted me to stay. He felt I could still do a job for him and the team, and as such he was offering me a two-year contract. I didn't want to leave, I loved Liverpool, and I was delighted to be offered a two-year contract – to be honest it was better than I dared hope for – but there remained the subject of money, which I had to talk out with Peter Robinson and John Smith. I informed Peter and John that I was more than happy to sign the two-year contract that was on the table, but on condition that certain matters were resolved. Peter asked me what I wanted. I told him that I felt I had played my part in the success the club had enjoyed, and was informed that that was not in doubt. Reassured by this, I then told Peter and John that I wanted the bonuses I felt I was entitled to from the previous season paid into my pension fund. I sensed that Peter was sympathetic to my request. John sighed, but rather than being the signal for a protracted argument, I felt his sigh was one of resignation. The matter of the unpaid bonuses was agreed, so I signed the new contract.

I felt much better for having committed myself to the club. I was coming up to thirty-three. I knew Bob was still in the process of developing the team, that there would be more new signings, and that in all probability I would not have a regular place in the Liverpool first team. But then, who did? Liverpool-born Terry McDermott had made a tremendous impact since arriving from Newcastle United, but Terry never considered himself a regular in the side, even when he played week in, week out. I laugh when I hear players saying that they left a certain club because the manager couldn't guarantee them regular first-team football. No one at Liverpool ever considered themselves a fixture in the team, not even Kevin or Clem. In order to be selected we all knew we had to keep on producing the goods. Competition for places was hot; it always had been during my seventeen years at the club. We all knew we had to give of our best in every game and that anything less than that was unacceptable. What's more, none of us would have had it any other way. We were all of one mind when it came to issues like that.

That's not to suggest that there was never any disharmony behind the scenes at Liverpool, of course. That summer of 1977 there was a little unrest following the civic reception granted to the club for having won the European Cup and League title. As we gathered on the balcony of the Walker Art Gallery for the thousands of local folk who'd turned up the occasion was harmonious and jubilant. Suddenly, Emlyn seized the microphone and began to sing 'Liverpool are magic, Everton are tragic'. The mood immediately changed, and it deteriorated further when Emlyn repeated his 'message' while addressing local dignitaries inside the gallery. Emlyn was in the process of attempting to persuade everyone to join in when Bob stepped up and took the microphone from him. The atmosphere in the room was now a mixture of embarrassment and relief when it should have been joyous.

I was not alone in wincing when I heard Emlyn's tasteless chant. In fact I felt very uncomfortable. What he did was crass, thoughtless and insensitive, the very antithesis of what Shanks had preached to every player – 'Be dignified in victory, be gracious in defeat'. The two clubs were fierce rivals, but only on the pitch. Many of the Everton players were personal friends, and I knew a lot of people at the club. Emlyn's remark was ungracious, uncalled for and unsporting. You can imagine what Evertonians thought of it. At a time when the game needed every bit of good publicity it could receive, it was hardly conducive to fostering good relations. The Liverpool board were far from happy, and Bob took Emlyn to one side and expressed his displeasure. The incident was deeply embarrassing for the club, and Bob asked Emlyn to go on local television the following day and issue an apology. Emlyn dutifully did this, but in the minds of many the damage had been done. Retribution was swift: two days later Emlyn awoke to find that during the night someone had painted his house blue.

I had been granted a testimonial by the club, and it took place the following night. Many of my Evertonian mates were at Anfield as well as Liverpool supporters for what was the perfect opportunity to have a real party and revel in our European success in Rome, which guaranteed a full house for a match between Liverpool and a Bobby Charlton Select XI. It was a tremendous night, not only for me, but for a certain Liverpool supporter.

In the weeks leading up to my testimonial, the BBC had got in touch with me. Esther Rantzen hosted a programme that featured a strand where they tried to make a viewer's dream come true. One of our supporters, who played in one of the local Sunday leagues, had written in saying that his dream was to play at Anfield. The BBC asked if it was possible for this lad to play for Liverpool in my testimonial and I had no hesitation in saying yes. Apparently, when he received the news the lad did daily training in order to get himself fit enough to play alongside professionals. The BBC expressed a fear that even so the lad would in all probability be nowhere near fit enough to participate, so they asked if I would personally train him at Melwood. This I agreed to do. All went well, the supporter gradually achieved a reasonable level of fitness, and as the big day drew near I advised the lad to drink water and not beer over the preceding weekend. My advice fell on deaf ears. When he reported for training on the Monday prior to the game he had put on eight pounds. Rather than the drawing board, it was back to the training ground.

We brought him on in the second half, not revealing his identity to Bobby or his team. To his credit the lad played well enough for Bobby and his team-mates to take him for a reserve-team player. The BBC had asked if we would contrive for him to score a goal, as that would really be a dream come true. With minutes remaining the lad had come nowhere near to scoring, so on receiving the ball I ran into the penalty box and Bobby Charlton deliberately tripped me up. The lad stepped up for his big moment in front of the Kop. Rather than cheering a goal, however, for their own safety the Kop parted like the Red Sea as the lad drove his penalty into their midst. For a moment no one knew what to do, then the referee saved the day: he signalled that the goalkeeper had moved and ordered the penalty to be retaken. Again the lad stepped up, only to blast the ball wide of the goal. I glanced over towards the touchline and caught sight of someone from the BBC pleading for the kick to be taken a third time. I spoke to the referee, who then ordered the kick to be retaken because Jimmy Case had encroached into the area. For a third time the lad stepped up. An eerie silence befell Anfield as the lad ran up, and then a collective groan as he sent the ball high over the bar yet again. This time the BBC guy on the touchline raised an arm and let it drop, as if to say 'Forget it', before turning away in frustration. It must have been embarrassing for the lad, but at least we had been instrumental in making his dream come true.

At the end of the game we paraded the European Cup before our supporters. It was an unforgettable night for me. I received tremendous applause from the 50,000 crowd and felt very humble that so many people had turned up to say, well, 'Thanks.' I eventually left the field to a standing ovation.

That night we had another party at the Holiday Inn. Every player was there, wives and girlfriends too, and some of my old mates, such as Jimmy Tarbuck, Gerry Marsden, Stan Boardman and Kenny Lynch. The following morning I was a little groggy when I took an early-morning telephone call. A plummy voice said, 'Mr Smith, can you come down to reception? I have some very important news for you.' I thought it was Tarby up to one of his tricks, but decided to go along with the gag. I jumped in the shower, put on some clean clothes and went down to reception expecting Tarby to jump out from behind one of the sofas. Instead I was confronted by a very elegant-looking man in a pin-stripe suit. The man introduced himself and informed me that he was an equerry from Buckingham Palace. I thought to myself, 'Oh Tarby, you're good. This has almost got me going.'

'Mr Smith,' he continued, 'I have been sent to ask if you will accept an MBE from Her Majesty the Queen in recognition of your sterling services to English football.'

I glanced about the foyer, expecting Tarby to appear. He didn't.

'Is there a problem, Mr Smith?' the equerry asked, having had no reply from me.

'Can I ask you a question?' I said.

'By all means,' he replied.

'Is this for real?'

'Mr Smith, I can assure you it is indeed "for real".'

He showed me some identification and went on to explain that such an honour cannot simply be given; protocol demands that they ask if you will be a willing recipient. I was now convinced that this was no wind-up and I had no hesitation in offering my respectful acceptance.

Could it get any better? The Championship, the European Cup, my testimonial, and now Buckingham Palace.

Some weeks later I travelled down to London with Sue, Darren and Janette. The MBE meant as much to me as any football medal. To me, it signified that I had served my profession well. I felt hugely proud, not just for myself and my family, but for my team-mates, the management and all the Liverpudlians who had supported me down the years. I saw it as a salute to them as much as to me.

Throughout the previous season Emlyn and I had continued our strained relationship. We might never have spoken off the field, but on it we formed a good solid partnership in the centre of defence. When Emlyn was in trouble, I never hesitated to help him out. I'd arrive on the scene saying something like, 'Come on, Emlyn, give it [the ball].' To be fair, he always backed me up in similar fashion. We were both committed to the cause and neither of us let our frosty relationship be detrimental to the team.

But matters came to a head that summer. Emlyn was a fantastic player, and he seemed to get along OK with Tosh – they had gone into business together, opening a sports shop in Formby – but I can't say he had formed solid friendships with the majority of the other lads, far from it. Prior to every home match Emlyn continued to room alone at the Lord Daresberry, and I'd noticed how he gravitated towards every new signing at the club. Rather than this being a genuine effort on his part to make a new arrival settle in at the club and feel at home, I saw this as an indication that he knew he was not liked by many of the existing players – a notion that became, in my opinion, one of fact that summer.

As I have said, the Liverpool players, Emlyn included, devoted a lot of time to visiting schools, hospitals, youth and boys' clubs and the like. Just about every player was connected to a major sports manufacturer by way of a kit or boot deal – for example, I was with Gola, Clem with Adidas – and whenever any of us made a personal appearance on behalf of their manufacturer, rather than request a fee we asked if we could receive some items of sportswear in lieu of our time. The respective manufacturers were only too happy to comply and we would often be given a sack of sporting items, some of which we shared out for personal use but the majority we put to one side to hand out on those occasions when we made our visits. Should a manufacturer pay a fee to a player for making a personal appearance, or should one of us receive a fee for, say, opening a new car showroom, we put the money into a kitty; this was then used to pay for the players' Christmas party, covering the cost of food, drink and presents. We liked to celebrate Christmas at the club. There was also a club party attended by all the staff and their wives/husbands and children at which every child received a present. This arrangement regarding complimentary sports kit and personal fees had been in place among the players for a number of years and no one had ever abused it. I think you may by now be ahead of me on this one.

As a result of us winning the European Cup and the Championship, Adidas awarded Liverpool the accolade of being their 'Team of the Year'. The award was to be presented at a dinner held in Paris that summer, and Bob, John Smith, Peter Robinson and Emlyn, as captain, were invited to attend on behalf of the club. When Emlyn returned from Paris he said nothing about the awards dinner, and to the best of my knowledge no one asked him about it. Curious to know what had cracked off in Paris, Clem rang his contact at Adidas. During the conversation the Adidas executive happened to mention that when in Paris Emlyn had received two bags of sporting goods and a payment of £200. When the players discovered this we were not best pleased. We let the matter ride for a few days, but Emlyn never produced the bags or the money. We had no proof whatsoever, but the suspicion was that the sportswear had ended up in Emlyn's sports shop though no one ever went there to check.

We were due to fly out to Finland to play a series of friendly matches as part of our preparation for the new season. Emlyn had picked up an injury in pre-season training which meant he could not take part in any of these matches. As we were about to leave for Liverpool airport, Bob took me to one side. He told me that as club captain, in the absence of Emlyn he wanted me to take on the role of team captain for the trip to Finland, which I told him I was only too happy to do. It transpired that Bob had another job for me. The players were to receive a bonus for the trip, but as Emlyn was injured, Bob asked me to do a collection among the players to ensure Emlyn 'didn't miss out', and suggested I ask each player to donate £10. I wasn't enamoured by the thought of doing this, but I had a job to do so I complied with Bob's request.

I went to every player, and to a man they refused to make a contribution. When I asked Cally, he asked me what the other players had given. 'Excuses,' I told him. I never at any time tried to influence the lads, I simply did as I was asked by Bob. But no one was willing to give money on behalf of Emlyn.

When I informed Bob of this he was not best pleased. He summoned me, Cally and Steve Heighway and in no uncertain terms told us of his disappointment.

'You shower of bastards,' he said at one point. 'Not a penny for the lad from any of you. Like him or loathe him, he deserves a bonus.'

'Hold on boss, you don't know the situation,' I said.

I put Bob in the picture. I told him about the Adidas sportswear and the money Emlyn had received during his visit to Paris. As Bob listened, his attitude to the matter visibly changed.

'Are you certain about this?' he asked when I had finished my explanation.

The three of us told him we were.

'Then bollocks to him, leave him,' said Bob, and in saying that he left us.

The matter, however, was far from over. When we returned from Finland, Tosh confronted me about the situation one morning after training. 'It's a bit out of hand, Tommy,' he said. 'I didn't put anything in because it would have been pointless as no one else had. But it's not fair of you.'

'Hey, I didn't influence anybody,' I informed him. 'If the lads had all given, I would have handed the money over. Fact is, none of them gave anything and that was their decision.'

Tosh rumbled on.

'Tosh, I don't want you and me to fall out,' I said, 'but if you don't see yourself off, I'll see you off. Drop it, please.'

He did.

Later that morning I was just about to enter the showers when I heard Emlyn address me from across the changing room.

'Hey, Smithy, you're out of order you are!' he shouted.

I'd had more than enough. I walked over towards him.

'You only think of yourself, you self-centred, devious little shit,' I shouted. 'I don't want to hear from you again, because if I do hear that squeaky voice of yours I'll do time for you. And that's not a threat, it's a bloody promise. Now, shut it and keep your distance from me.'

I thought Emlyn and I were alone, but we weren't. Joey Jones walked into the room from out of the showers.

'Go on, hit him, Smithy, before I do,' said Joey contemptuously.

Confronted with both Joey and me eyeballing him, Emlyn gathered up his belongings and left the room.

Emlyn did indeed keep his distance, not only from me but from the majority of the other players. He still got on OK with Tosh, though, who in turn got on with the rest of us. Emlyn's public persona remained that of an affable, happy-go-lucky, jovial guy. He became popular with television producers and began to make more and more appearances on programmes; he also enjoyed popularity with audiences. On the pitch you would not have thought anything was untoward, but off it Emlyn found himself increasingly isolated.

He was made acutely aware of this when the FA asked clubs to form a working party to discuss discipline on the field and compile a dossier of suggestions. Liverpool decided that John Smith, the chairman, should speak for the board. Bob Paisley represented the management, and to ensure that every level of the club had a voice, reserve-team trainer Roy Evans was also invited to join the committee. The final thing to do was to select three players. It was decided that the best way to do this was to vote by secret ballot. Ronnie Moran acted as the adjudicator and subsequently counted the votes. Steve Heighway, Cally and I were elected, and when Ron read out how many votes the others players received, it was a little embarrassing. For all that he was team captain, Emlyn didn't receive a single one.

It genuinely saddens me to speak this way of someone who is now no longer with us, but that's how it was. Emlyn was a tremendous player and a great servant of the club, but that's as far as I can go in terms of serving him with personal plaudits.

When a player hits his early thirties what he hopes for from his club is a two-year contract. He knows he is coming to the end of his career, and should he not have a regular place in the first team, at least he has the security of two years' work during which time he can look for another club or begin an alternative career. That was my mindset as Liverpool prepared for 1977–78. I loved Liverpool and didn't want to leave the club, but I was conscious of the fact that I was in the autumn of my career as a footballer.

The season began with Liverpool contesting the Charity Shield against Manchester United at Wembley, a game which marked the debut of the player Bob had signed to replace Kevin Keegan, Kenny Dalglish, who was brought in from Celtic for a fee of

£440,000, at the time a record between British clubs. The match ended in a goalless draw, but from what little I had seen of Kenny in training, I knew he would do for me. I missed this game because I had picked up an injury during pre-season training, but Ronnie Moran very graciously presented me with the Charity Shield medal he received on the day. 'You deserve it, Smithy,' he said.

The following week Liverpool's League programme opened at Middlesbrough. I was named in the squad but didn't play. Kenny Dalglish, however, did, and he scored in a 1–1 draw. I wondered if I would ever play for Liverpool again. Phil Neal and Joey Jones had established themselves at full-back, and Phil Thompson and Emlyn appeared first choice in the centre of defence; my first-team opportunities were going to be limited. I thought about asking to go somewhere on loan, or perhaps moving on altogether. Wigan Athletic had expressed an interest in my becoming their player-manager, but as so often happens in the unpredictable world that is football I returned to the fold for our very next game. Bob took me to one side and informed me that Phil Thompson had sustained a bad knee injury at Ayresome Park and the likelihood was he would be out for some time. He asked how I would feel about playing alongside Emlyn again. I told him there was no problem between Emlyn and me on the pitch, that we both went out to do a job for him and the team. He smiled, nodded his head and told me I would be playing against Newcastle United on Tuesday night.

The game was Kenny's home debut. It's funny how the memory can play tricks. Many people think Kenny joined Liverpool when in his late teens or early twenties; he was, in fact, coming up to twenty-seven – a peak for most strikers. Kenny, as you know, would go on to scale even greater heights, not the least of which was replacing Kevin as the idol of the Kop. At the time I had begun to write a column for the *Liverpool Echo*. Prior to Kenny making his Anfield debut I wrote, 'You can't take a player of the calibre of Kevin Keegan out of your side and not suffer for it. It is essential that Liverpool win something this season to take the pressure off Kenny Dalglish, and off Liverpool for selling Keegan. I have seen enough of Kenny to know his pedigree is not in question. He is a player of grace, guile and strength, different to Keegan, who is all-action. Kenny's technique is excellent. His control and an ability to hold up the ball, shield it from defenders then bring team-mates into the game with a slide-rule pass will be invaluable to Liverpool. Kenny is a proven goalscorer and his positional sense and vision will, I am sure, create countless opportunities for team-mates.'

Many people see Kenny as being rather dour. I found him to be very sociable. He joined in with the laughter and banter, and once he settled in, quite often he instigated dressing-room pranks and jokes. Whether it was a grin or a grimace, Kenny exuded the look of a man who is not interested in coming second, which suited Liverpool down to the ground. He possessed the fortitude and presence of mind to cope with the great expectations people had of him and the pressures that come with being a top player at a top club. Such expectations were present from the start, no more so than on that Tuesday night when we faced Newcastle at Anfield. There were nigh on 49,000 present, and just about every one of them wanted to see if Kenny Dalglish was all the papers were cracking him up to be.

Considering it was only the second League fixture of the season, Newcastle arrived with a side ravaged by injury, and minus Malcolm Macdonald, who was now plying his trade with Arsenal. We knew their ploy would be to defend in numbers, and they didn't disappoint on that score. It was one-way traffic throughout the first half, but thanks to some sterling work by goalkeeper Steve Hardwick and a defence comprising John Bird, Aiden McCaffrey, Alan Kennedy and Irving Nattrass in the unaccustomed position of right-back, Newcastle absorbed all our pressure. The second half was less than two minutes old when I won possession of the ball and found Cally, who in turn found Ray Kennedy. Ray hit a long ball forward to Kenny who turned, beat John Bird for pace, then coolly lifted the ball over the head of the advancing Hardwick. Kenny walked towards the Kop and raised both arms and our supporters reciprocated in time-honoured manner. Their new king had been crowned.

Having conceded the lead, Newcastle embarked upon a damage-limitation exercise which was only partly successful. Kenny came within a whisker of adding to his tally when he fizzed a shot inches wide of Hardwick's left-hand post. Terry Mac, Phil Neal, Emlyn and Ray Kennedy too went close as the Newcastle defence struggled to contain our momentum. In a rare attack, Clem saved from Tommy Cassidy only for us immediately to regain the initiative. Three minutes from time, Emlyn played the ball to me. I played it forward to Kenny who picked out Steve Heighway with a tremendous cross-field pass. Steve made ground before slipping the ball behind John Bird and into the path of Terry Mac, who side-footed past Hardwick. Anfield erupted, and characteristically the Kop responded to Dalglish in imaginative fashion, singing 'Kenny's From Heaven' to the tune of the old standard 'Pennies From Heaven'. You don't hear singing like that at matches any more. Kenny was on the mark again in our very next match, a 3–0 win against West Bromwich Albion to continue our good start to the season. We remained unbeaten in seven, the first reverse coming in October when Manchester United triumphed 2–0 at Old Trafford.

It was during that game that I first felt a problem with my knees. Seventeen years of football were beginning to take their toll on my body. Apart from all the running, football demands a lot of twisting and turning. Though I didn't realize it at the time, my cartilage and ligaments were beginning to give out. If I had been in my early twenties I might have missed a game, maybe two at the most, but the older you get the longer it takes for your body to overcome injuries. I found myself sidelined for nigh on two months and missed eight League matches and Liverpool's initial defence of the European Cup, against Dynamo Dresden. In football, one man's misfortune results in an opportunity for another, and with both me and Phil Thompson injured, the man who benefited was Alan Hansen, who was given his opportunity in the first team.

Come the end of November the knees seemed fine and Bob recalled me for the 4–0 victory at Leicester City. It was a welcome win as Liverpool had slipped to fifth following a run of five matches which had not produced a single victory. I played in the game after that too, a 2–0 win against West Ham at Anfield, but the knee problem returned during our game at Norwich City on 10 December.

At 2–1 down we were chasing the game in the second half when I stretched for the ball and tore my right calf muscle. I tried to soldier on but the pain became so bad I knew I would have to leave the field. I signalled to the bench that they should get our substitute, David Johnson, warmed up. David was ready within two to three minutes, but such was the pain it seemed to me like two hours. Joe Fagan came on to the pitch to attend to me, and it was just as well he did. I could hardly walk without his assistance. I had left the field at a point which necessitated Joe and me walking down one side of the pitch then across the back of the goal, as the Carrow Road tunnel at the time was situated in one of the corners of the ground. Joe gave me a helping hand as I hobbled along the perimeter track behind the goal, and as I did so I became the victim of a torrent of abuse from a Norwich supporter. He was standing at the front of the terrace and must have weighed about eighteen stone. As we passed his bulky frame his words grew even more venomous.

'I'm not having this,' I thought, and I broke free from Joe's helping arm.

'No, no, don't, Tommy, ignore him,' pleaded Joe.

'I'm not going to do anything,' I assured him.

I hobbled on for a couple of paces as the vitriol continued, then suddenly broke rank from Joe and, ignoring the pain in my calf, made for the abusive supporter. I brought my head to within a couple of inches of his nose.

'Whaaaaaaaaaaaa!' I shouted at the top of my voice.

Filled with terror, his eyes and mouth opened wide and he shot back, taking half a dozen young Norwich supporters with him and ending up on his back. The Norwich supporters in the immediate vicinity burst out laughing. I turned to see Joe laughing too.

My injury, however, proved no laughing matter. I was out for another two months, which gave me plenty of time to ponder my future. I now had eighteen months of my contract remaining. I reasoned I could return to fitness but that the problems with my knees would be ongoing. I wanted to see my contract out at Liverpool though, and should that mean playing just the occasional game, or even spending my time helping the youngsters in the reserves, then so be it.

I spent most of December and January receiving treatment on my right calf and my knees, and towards the end of January I felt fit enough to have a run-out with the reserves. Liverpool were handily placed in the League in fourth place, with recently promoted Nottingham Forest the surprise pace-setters. We had exited the FA Cup at the first time of asking, suffering a 4–2 defeat at Chelsea, but for once we had made good progress in the League Cup, and in the European Cup there were the quarter-finals to come. The season held a lot of promise for the club, but I wasn't sure what part, if any, I would play in events. You never know what lies around the corner in life, but the trick is to walk down the street and have a look. Metaphorically speaking, I made my mind up that I would 'walk down the street'.

At the end of January I told Bob I was fit and ready, and I was selected for a run-out with the reserves against Preston. The Liverpool reserve team that day included goalkeeper Steve Ogrizovic, a recent signing from Chesterfield, Jimmy Case, David Johnson, Howard Gayle, Brian Kettle, Colin Irwin, Alan Harper and Sammy Lee. It was a line-up that proved far too powerful for Preston's second string, as the final scoreline of 8–0 suggests.

As I left the ground that day a couple approached me and asked if they could have a word. I agreed, thinking they were Liverpool supporters wanting to talk about the club. It transpired that they were not Liverpool supporters, but the parents of a teenager who had played for Preston reserves.

'We are aware of your reputation, Mr Smith, and we want to thank you for not kicking our son, or mistreating him physically during the game.'

I was taken aback. I thanked the couple for their sincerity but was at pains to point out that I never went around kicking opponents or 'mistreating' them physically. At which point the couple appeared somewhat embarrassed.

'Don't worry,' I reassured them. 'I do play the game very hard, but I also play it fair – at least I try to.'

'But you have such a fearsome reputation,' said the lady.

'Really? At Liverpool, the only time a player realizes he has a reputation is when Bob Paisley tells them they're not living up to it.'

The winter weather that had threatened finally arrived in February, snow and ice resulting in many matches being postponed. I was disappointed to be kicking my heels for a couple of weeks as fixtures fell foul to the severe weather. Thankfully, the weather then eased and I played for the reserves in a 4–0 win over Derby County. The following day I got up and went about the house as normal. It took ten or fifteen minutes for me to realise it, but when I did I was immediately buoyed: I felt no after-effects whatsoever from the previous day's game. I trained that day and felt great. My calf and knees were not giving me a problem at all. The combination of the treatment I had received and a prolonged rest seemed to have done the trick. I wasn't naive enough to think the knee problem was over and done with, that it would not return some time in the future, but I knew there was life, and games, in the old dog yet.

Liverpool were due to entertain Manchester United on 25 February, and one morning after training Bob took me to one side.

Apparently Ronnie Moran had told him I had played really well for the reserves. Joey Jones was injured, and Bob informed me I was back in the side to face United. Needless to say, this news delighted me.

I partnered Alan Hansen at the back against United, with Emlyn switching to left-back. We took the lead courtesy of another new signing, Graeme Souness, who had joined from Middlesbrough the previous month. Further goals from Ray Kennedy and Jimmy Case gave us a 3–1 victory to keep us in touch with League leaders Nottingham Forest.

Forest were on fire. When Brian Clough's side assumed pole position in mid-October, many football writers were of the mind that it would only be a matter of time before they were 'found out'. Far from blowing up, Forest had continued their tremendous form, not only in the League but also in the League Cup. Clough's side had not suffered defeat in the League since losing at Leeds in mid-November. Such had been Liverpool's form we were still in touch with Forest, but our win against Manchester United was sandwiched between four defeats which essentially cost Liverpool the Championship. Two points from five matches put daylight between us and Forest, and though we remained unbeaten in our final twelve matches, registering nine victories, Forest never faltered. As Bob Paisley said later, when asked to reflect on his time as manager of the club, 'Of course we knew bad times at Liverpool: we once finished second.'

I had continued at centre-back, more than happy that there had been no recurrence of the calf or knee problems. If anything, I felt better in myself than I had done for some time. I did the job I had been asked to do to the best of my ability and went forward when-ever an opportunity presented itself, no more so than when we entertained Leicester City at Anfield in early April and my forag-ing forward resulted in me scoring twice in a 3–1 victory.

Bob's changes to the team had proved seamless. Kenny Dalglish ended the season with twenty League goals, and thirty in all competitions. Not for nothing had the Kop crowned him 'King Kenny'. Graeme Souness provided steel and guile in midfield, and when called upon, Alan Hansen had proved himself to be Bob's type of cerebral central defender, eminently comfortable on the ball when bringing it out of defence before playing a telling pass. Naturally we were very disappointed not to have retained the title, but credit must go to Forest. Following that defeat at Leeds in November they remained unbeaten in the League for the remainder of the season.

Historically Liverpool had never done well in the League Cup, but this season we went all the way to the final. To get there we defeated Chelsea, Derby and Coventry City (all 2–0) and Wrexham (3–1), before being drawn against Arsenal in the semi-finals. The first leg took place at Anfield, and though goals from Kenny and Ray Kennedy gave us a 2–1 victory, for once Liverpool were not favourites to progress. A crowd of some 50,000 attended Highbury for the return, which proved a taut affair. With minutes remaining and the tie goalless a chance fell to Graham Rix some six yards from goal. He pulled the trigger but I managed to slide across and block his goal-bound shot; I even managed to spring to my feet to block Frank Stapleton's follow-up effort. Joe Fagan later remarked, 'Tremendous, Smithy. It was as if they'd turned back the clock.'

'Thank the stars they didn't,' I quipped. 'The pace of that game, I don't think I could have lasted another ten minutes.'

The 0–0 draw was enough to take us to Wembley to face Forest.

Having at one stage thought my career at Anfield was all but over I was delighted to take my place in the team for yet another Wembley final. I had overcome the initial problem with my knees, worked hard at regaining fitness and, having been given a chance in the first team, had played sufficiently well to retain my place. This pleased me no end as competition for places was arguably hotter than ever. Having been given good reason to ponder my future some months earlier, I couldn't believe how things had turned about.

To be honest, I felt I was now playing some of the best football of my career. My experience in the game was reaping dividends. I never had a great deal of pace and I was aware that at thirty-three I was slowing up. Football is mainly about speed over the first four to five yards, but as Bob told me, 'You're producing the goods because with your experience those first two yards are in your head.' I knew what he meant. I had a reputation as a hard man, a player with a sledge-hammer tackle. I could still tackle, but my reading of a game resulted in me winning possession of the ball more through interception than tackles. With my experience I also knew how to get through a game – what to do in certain situations, how to keep possession and take the heat out of attacks from opponents, when to go forward, when to drop back – and I passed this knowledge on to younger team-mates. But I knew I couldn't defy time. A professional footballer never loses skill, it's the legs that go. I was acutely aware that it would be only a matter of time before that happened, but in the meantime I was determined to enjoy the warming glow of my Indian summer.

Nottingham Forest could score goals, but underpinning their successful return to the First Division was a resolute and well-organized defence. Along with Clem, Peter Shilton was one of the best goalkeepers in the world, but he had taken no part in Forest's League Cup run as he was cup-tied; his place in the side had been taken by Chris Woods. The Forest back-line of Viv Anderson, Larry Lloyd, Kenny Burns and the veteran Frank Clark seemed average on the face of it, but, Viv apart, it was a defence that contained a lot of football experience, and Clough had them playing with real guts and determination. Clough and his assistant Peter Taylor had instilled in their players the value of keeping a clean sheet rather than taking to the field hell bent on winning a game. They went out with the objective of not losing. Forest didn't possess a twenty-goal-a-season forward, far from it. John Robertson was their joint leading goalscorer in the League with twelve goals, and seven of those had come from the penalty spot.

Just about every player in the Forest team, however, was capable of scoring. The fact that they shared their goals was one of their great strengths, and having taken the lead in a match they knew how to preserve it.

I was only too aware of Forest's defensive strengths, but nothing prepared me for how the League Cup Final panned out. In all my years of playing football I had never come across a team happy to fight a two-hour rearguard action, which, due to the game going into extra time, is what Forest did. In the break between normal time and extra time Clough and Taylor remained seated on the bench, never at any time offering advice or encouragement to their players assembled near the centre circle. The press later made much of this, but what could Clough and Taylor have said? Forest's sole plan was to defend, and that wasn't going to change. We probed and prodded but never made the breakthrough. Terry Mac had a goal disallowed, but that was the nearest we came to breaking the deadlock. I had never played in such a one-sided game and not ended up on the winning side.

The replay took place at Old Trafford and it was as if we were facing a different Forest. They attacked from the start and created more chances in the first ten minutes than they had done in two hours at Wembley – not that that was hard to do. Having weathered the early storm we seized the initiative, and it was Kenny, of all people, who squandered two gilt-edged chances. Forest began the second half as they had started the first, coming forward in numbers. John O'Hare latched on to a through-ball from Tony Woodcock, Phil Thompson caught him, and the referee pointed to the spot. I wasn't having that, and neither were the other Liverpool players. In my opinion – and I had a good view of the incident – Phil made contact with O'Hare outside the box. Television pictures seemed to indicate that our protestations were justified. No matter. The penalty was given, and John Robertson drove the ball wide of Clem's outstretched arms.

Undaunted, we poured forward, and a matter of minutes later

Terry controlled a pass from Kenny, sprinted forward and swept the ball past Woods and into the net. Aware of how difficult it was to score against Forest, relief swept through my body. That relief suddenly turned to anguish when a linesman flagged and the referee adjudged Terry to have handled the ball while in the process of controlling the pass. Peter Withe turned to me and said, 'Looks like it's going to be our day, Tommy.' I was determined to prove him wrong, but deep down the voice of experience was telling me he was right.

We pounded Forest but found no way through. Having totally dominated the first game at Wembley and having had the upper hand in the replay, we were gutted not to have won. Especially as we'd had two goals disallowed, the second of which the press described as a 'controversial decision', and also conceded what television pictures proved to be a very dubious penalty. Our dressing room was like a condemned cell as we struggled to come to terms with the result. Our disappointment did not prevent us from going into the Forest dressing room and complimenting them on their success, though. Credit to them, they had put up a tremendous fight and managed to score the only goal of the two games. Having shaken hands with all the Forest players we were filing out of their dressing room when I thought it only right and proper to offer my congratulations to Brian Clough too.

'Thank you, Tommy,' Clough replied, shaking my hand warmly. 'I know how difficult this has been to do for you and your team-mates, but I want you to know it is much appreciated. In football, greatness is not just about winning trophies, it's also to do with how you react to defeat and disappointment. Remember that, because you lads still have much to play for this season.'

The dashed hopes in the League Cup were more than compensated for by our defence of the European Cup. For the first leg of our quarter-final we travelled to Portugal. Benfica were not the force they had been in the days of Eusebio, Torres and Simões, but they were still a highly rated side. It was what the press called a 'tricky' tie. Backed by 70,000 home supporters, Benfica proved how 'tricky' they could be when they took the lead through Nene, but we were soon back in the game with an equalizer from Jimmy Case. I always felt we had the measure of Benfica, and when Emlyn scored in the second half it appeared their players believed it too. Thereafter they never really threatened and we returned to Merseyside confident of capitalizing on our 2–1 away success. We had a little scare in the first half when Nene once again proved he was no mean taker of chances in front of goal, but strikes from Cally and Kenny gave us a half-time lead. We totally outplayed them in the second period, and although further goals from Terry Mac and Phil Neal sealed victory, in truth the final scoreline of 4–1 flattered Benfica as we had overrun them.

The semi-final pitched Liverpool against old adversaries in Borussia Mönchengladbach. Borussia had home advantage in the first leg, and they had a score to settle. Both sides featured a number of changes in personnel from Rome, and if anything they appeared to be a better side. They surged into a 2–0 lead, but in Europe even such a deficit is no cause for panic. We didn't, and as the game progressed we began to dictate matters. One of our strengths was that we kept going to the very end. Our physical and mental fitness was such that we were as strong in the final minutes of a game as we were in the opening minutes. We continued to take the game to Borussia and two minutes from time our perseverance paid off when David Johnson scored a morale-boosting goal.

In the home leg the early resistance applied by Borussia was simply swept away. Ray Kennedy and Kenny gave us a 2–0 lead at half-time, and when Jimmy Case added a third midway through the second period I knew we were home and dry.

A season that had at one stage seen me wondering if I had a future at Anfield was now sweet. I was about to play in my second European Cup Final in successive seasons. The venue was Wembley, our opponents Bruges. I was looking forward to the night immensely, confident that we could maintain our dominance in Europe, but fate was to play me a cruel hand – or should that be foot?

Sue and I were in the process of developing our home in Blundell Sands. I'm quite a practical guy and had set about working on an extension and developing our back garden. In the days leading up to the European Cup Final I was working at the back of the house when a large sledge-hammer fell from a wall and landed on my foot. It was only on my foot for a second, but it did its worst. I was taken to hospital and was horrified when X-rays revealed I had broken a toe.

If you have been unfortunate enough to have been involved in an accident, you will know that your mind flashes back to the moment the incident took place and you tell yourself, 'If only I had done this, or that, I could have avoided all this.' When the doctor told me there was no way I would be fit to play in the European Cup Final, my stomach turned over. Initially I was filled with anger at the injustice of it all. I had battled to regain fitness and worked hard to get back into the side only now to miss out on the biggest game of the season because of a silly domestic accident. I felt really badly done to. I then began to reappraise my situation. Rather than view the incident in isolation, I attempted to see the big picture. I had been with Liverpool for eighteen years and in all that time I had not sustained a career-threatening injury. I thought about all the players I had known, or heard of, whose careers had ended in their twenties due to serious injury. I reflected on all the success I had enjoyed with Liverpool. From the time I first established myself in the team, Liverpool had been in the hunt for honours every season. On occasions we had fallen a little short, but my trophy cabinet contained more than enough major medals to demonstrate that I had enjoyed a very successful career in football. I had been so very fortunate in this respect. Above all, I had a happy and loving family. No perceived disappointment in football could ever detract from the happiness and contentment I gained from my family. I thought about players whose marriages had, for whatever reason, broken up, and the effect this had had on their children, their wives, and them as men. I thanked my lucky stars that I had never been through such a thing. All these thoughts enabled me to get my broken toe and the fact that I would miss out at Wembley into proper perspective. Sure I was devastated, but in the greater scheme of things I knew I had much to be thankful for.

Phil Thompson had returned to fitness, and he partnered Alan Hansen in defence against Bruges, Phil Neal and Emlyn occupying the full-back positions. Bruges could have been forgiven for thinking they were at Anfield as the vast majority of the 100,000 crowd inside Wembley were Liverpool supporters. The atmosphere was electrifying, but the game was anything but a classic. In truth, it was dull, a sharp contrast to Liverpool's success in Rome the previous year. Bruges were content to defend, and the only goal of the game was scored by Kenny Dalglish who, after being played in by Graeme Souness, coolly chipped the ball over goalkeeper Jensen from an acute angle. The goal, in the 66th minute, sparked Bruges into action, but at this stage Liverpool had the game by the scruff of the neck and wouldn't let it go.

To retain the European Cup was a tremendous achievement, and it cemented Liverpool's reputation as the undisputed top club in Europe. Liverpool had risen from being a mid-table Second Division outfit to arguably the best club in the world, and I was proud to have been a part of it all. I didn't miss out at Wembley either. Though the broken toe resulted in my being sidelined for the final, I had played the required number of matches in the preceding rounds to qualify for a winner's medal. I can't say I received it with quite the same *joie de vivre* I'd felt in Rome, but I was nevertheless proud and happy to have played a role in yet another great Liverpool success. I made a point of relishing this fantastic occasion for the club, for I knew that for me there was not going to be another.

14

SWAN SONG

DURING THE SUMMER OF 1978 BOB AND I SAT DOWN TO TALK. I still had a year of my contract remaining and Bob was happy for me to stay on at the club, but he made it clear that I did not feature in his plans for the first team. I told him I didn't think there was much point in staying at the club, that it would be better for me to move on. He thanked me for all the years of loyal service I had given him and Liverpool. We laughed about the early days when I was a groundstaff lad and he had me sawing the 'girder of girth', and reminisced about the players we had known and the experiences we'd shared. He said some very complimentary things about me, warmly shook my hand, and I left his office and Liverpool Football Club.

Of course a part of me was sad, but I can't say I felt any disappointment. I had known great days at Liverpool and enjoyed a career that had exceeded my wildest dreams. I had been associated with the club as a player for eighteen years and had given my all. Liverpool Football Club had been good for me. In many respects it had shaped me, made me the man I was. I felt I owed the club, and football, a lot.

I had some statistics to contemplate: 632 first-team appearances, forty-eight goals, four First Division Championship medals, two FA Cup medals, two European Cup medals, two UEFA Cup medals, one European Super Cup medal (courtesy of a 7–1 aggregate thrashing of Hamburg at the end of 1977) and five Charity Shield medals, a World Youth Cup medal and several runners-up medals of various descriptions. I would be keeping Duraglit in business for years. I had also been awarded the MBE and had represented my country at schoolboy, youth, under-23 and full international level. I was far from rich, but my family had a comfortable lifestyle. I had enjoyed my career at Liverpool immensely and relished the friendships I had made, not only with team-mates and staff but also opponents. How could I possibly have any regrets?

The same message had been delivered to my great friend Ian Callaghan. Between us we had played close on 1,500 first-class games. That's a lot of football. Cally and I still felt we had a couple of years of football left in us, however, so we began to put out the feelers.

Some players who have enjoyed a fruitful career at the top don't wish to step down and play for a club in a lower division; having known nothing but top-class football, they would rather go out at the top than ply their trade in a lower league. My mindset was different. I loved football so much I wanted to continue in the game. With my experience and the fact that I was a dedicated pro whose enthusiasm for playing had not waned, I felt I could 'do a job' for a club in a lower division, perhaps help younger players develop their game by teaching them good habits and offering practical advice. I was seeking a new challenge, and I knew enough about the game in this country to realize that every day is a challenge for most clubs in the lower divisions. If I could in some way contribute, help a club enjoy better days, I would be putting something back into a game that had given me so much.

I was contacted by Walsall, Bournemouth and Wigan. Hereford

were interested in me as a player-manager. I met with their board and was informed that the chairman did all the buying and selling of players. Sorry, but I thought the job of a manager was to run the show. Shanks had asserted his authority very early on at Liverpool to ensure there was no interference at board level. I had learned from him that it was the only way to run a football club. The chairman told me they did things differently at Hereford. I said, 'Perhaps that is why Hereford are in the Third Division and Liverpool are again European champions.'

I was still waiting for a response from Bournemouth, Walsall and Wigan (I still am) when I received a telephone call from Tosh, who was player-manager of Swansea City. Tosh and I had had our occasional differences, but neither of us had allowed that to result in a falling-out. I had always been of the mind that Tosh had some great ideas on the game; what's more, he possessed the ability to put those ideas across to players. It came as no surprise to me when he entered management. Tosh had done very well at Swansea too, guiding them to promotion from Division Four the previous season. Now he was looking for Swansea to make an impact in Division Three, and I thought I could help.

'I'm offering you an opportunity to give it one more go,' Tosh told me. 'I've had a word with Cally and he's up for it if you are.'

I had no hesitation in saying yes, but certain matters had to be sorted out first, and I don't mean money. Swansea were in the Third Division – I wasn't going there for the money. It was the challenge and the opportunity to carry on playing for a while that appealed. I told Tosh that I didn't want to uproot my family and move to Swansea, and Cally was of similar mind. Sue and I were settled in Liverpool, the city in which we had both been born and bred. Darren and Janette were doing well at their respective schools and had reached an important stage in their education. I fancied giving it a go at Swansea but not at the expense of up-setting family life. Tosh understood all this. It was arranged that Cally and I would continue to train at Liverpool and we would travel down to Swansea for home games and stay in a club house. Should the family ever come down, we would be accommodated in a hotel on the Gower Peninsula. Many of Swansea's away games were in the north at places such as Bury, Tranmere, Chester and Blackpool. It was agreed that on those occasions Cally and I could meet the team at the venue, or else I would park my car and we'd be picked up at a motorway junction.

The last thing we talked about was money. Tosh didn't deal with it. The Swansea board did, so I met with them. The chairman told me that as a Third Division club Swansea were not in a position to pay First Division wages. I informed the board that I completely understood. 'The most we can pay you is £150 a week,' the chairman said. I was flabbergasted. It was the same basic wage I had been on at Liverpool, the highest basic wage I had ever been paid while at Anfield. It made me think, 'Have I been selling myself short all these years?'

In many respects joining Swansea softened the blow of leaving my beloved Anfield because there was a strong Liverpool connection at the club. In addition to Tosh and Cally, my old team-mates Phil Boersma and Alan Waddle were also on the books. It was like a little bit of Liverpool once removed. I joined Swansea prior to the start of the 1978–79 season and was impressed by the squad Tosh had assembled. Tosh himself was still playing, and there was Cally, Phil, Alan and me. Geoff Crudgington was a very experienced goalkeeper who had seen service with Aston Villa and Crewe. Right-back Wyndham Evans and midfield player Chris Marustick were also very experienced, having respectively played some 300- and 600-plus games for the club. Les Chappell had seen service with several clubs including Rotherham, Reading and Blackburn Rovers. And then there were the Welsh internationals Leighton Phillips, Robbie James and Alan Curtis, and some promising youngsters such as Nigel Stevenson and Jeremy Charles – at least they appeared young to me.

I made my Swansea debut at home to Lincoln City on 22

August. Swansea had previously drawn at Colchester on the opening day, and a crowd of 16,704 turned up at the Vetch to see us enjoy a comfortable 3–0 win. The attendance was as heartening as the performance. Victory over Lincoln was followed by three successive wins and a somewhat bizarre 4–4 draw with Rotherham which took Swansea to the top of Division Three. It appeared that my days of winning medals might not be over after all.

As the season developed Swansea continued to post good results and were never out of the top three automatic promotion places. Tosh, Alan Waddle, Robbie James, Jeremy Charles and Alan Curtis proved a real handful for opposing defences. A consummate pro, Cally was directing operations from midfield, and I had formed a good partnership at the back with Nigel Stevenson. The travel arrangements were working well too. Cally and I met up with the team for away games, sometimes at the venue, sometimes we were picked up along the way. If we were playing in London, Cally and I would catch a train from Lime Street on Friday around noon and link up with Swansea at their London hotel.

Playing in the Third Division was somewhat of a culture shock, though. I remember one game at Brentford when we entered the away dressing room to discover it had not been cleaned after the previous game. Even the bath and showers were full of mud and silt. The Swansea lads simply swept everything aside and proceeded to change. It brought back to my mind Liverpool's visit to Romania when Shanks ordered us back on the bus and threatened to take us home unless the dressing room, showers and toilets were cleaned. There was no such protest from the Swansea camp, so I just went along with it.

Having beaten Newport in the first round of the League Cup, everyone was delighted when Swansea were drawn against Spurs in round two. At the time Spurs were the subject of much discussion and many headlines as their manager, Keith Burkinshaw, had signed the Argentine World Cup stars Ossie Ardiles and

Ricardo Villa. They were among the first overseas players to arrive in England, certainly the only big-name players to have done so. Such was the interest in the tie that a capacity crowd of 24,500 crammed into the Vetch. The game was only minutes old when Steve Perryman played a through-ball and Ardiles made to get on the end of it. I came across, took the ball cleanly, and my momentum carried me forward. Ardiles went up in the air like a Guy Fawkes rocket and came down just as ignominiously. The Vetch roared its approval. Ossie lay on the ground as if he had been hit by a bag of hammers. I went over to check he was OK and, satisfied that he was, said, 'Welcome to English football.'

We drew 2–2 with Spurs, and I was of the mind that they were more than happy to escape with the draw. In the second half only some desperate defending on their part had kept them in the cup, and for sure they hadn't relished the devilish aggression we all displayed. The following day I had cause to speak to Bob on the phone because Liverpool were due to play Spurs at Anfield that Saturday. 'We softened them up for you,' I told him. That Saturday Liverpool hammered Spurs 7–0. On the Sunday I received a call at home from Bob, 'We've softened them up a bit more for you lads,' he said.

Though we had been the better team at the Vetch, few outside Swansea gave us much hope of achieving a favourable result at White Hart Lane. We, however, were confident that our attacking style would cause Spurs all manner of problems at the back. Come half-time we were two goals to the good, courtesy of Tosh and Jeremy Charles. Spurs made more of a game of it in the second half and pulled a goal back through Villa, but when Alan Curtis made it 3–1 the reporters in the press box were penning 'Cup Shock'.

The consensus of opinion then was that the foreign players arriving in our country would simply adapt to our style of play and be absorbed into our football culture, or else sink. In the early days this proved to be the case, but over the years as the influx of overseas players, and managers, gradually developed from a trickle into a flood, it has been English football culture that has changed. As television became more involved with football and money poured into the game, English football became the Holy Grail not only for top overseas players but anybody who was half decent at kicking a football. Just as schoolboys will try to replicate what they see top players doing, many clubs in the lower leagues aped the policies of the big clubs. We now have overseas players playing even in non-League football in this country. In December 2005 a pal of mine told me that Chesterfield reserves fielded six overseas players in a game. With all due respect, if these players are not good enough to get into the Chesterfield first team, what the hell are they doing here? The presence of these players in such a team surely prevents homegrown youngsters from developing their game. A player normally reaches his peak around the age of twenty-seven, but in order to do that he has to have been playing for six to seven years. A lad will not develop if he's sitting in the stand or playing at a level of football that will not enhance his game.

English football appears to be suffering from myopia. I have told you how Shanks, Bob and other members of the Anfield boot room spent countless hours working with Kevin Keegan to develop his game and help him achieve his full potential. I'm not sure there are many managers and coaches who want to invest so much time these days in working with a player of potential. It seems to me that most would rather sign an experienced player from overseas and get a 'quick fix' as opposed to investing time and expertise in the development of homegrown youngsters. I'm not against overseas players or managers plying their trade in this country – without doubt the game has benefited from the presence of many of them – but there are now too many in British football, to the detriment of indigenous talent.

Following Swansea's headline-making victory at White Hart Lane, we exited the League Cup in the following round at the hands of QPR, but the good form in the League continued. By this stage I had assumed the role of assistant manager to Tosh. Results were going well and everyone was happy, including me, but several months of incessant workload seemed to be getting to Tosh and he decided to take a short break in mid-season. We had been tracking Neil Robinson, a full-back in the Everton reserve team who we felt could do us a job. After watching him play for Everton reserves against Sheffield United I rang the Everton reserve-team coach, my old pal and adversary Colin Harvey. Colin was upfront about Robinson: he told me the lad had a problem with a knee injury. We decided to go ahead with the transfer anyway, but as a precaution we agreed to pay Everton the fee in instalments.

Tosh's mini-break coincided with the arrival of Neil Robinson at Swansea. We had a reserve-team match scheduled against Bristol City and Neil asked me if he could play. I asked him if he felt fit enough and he assured me he was fine. He was keen to prove himself as he had not played for our first team at this stage, so I included him in the team to face Bristol City.

I was staying at a local hotel at the time, and on the night of the reserve-team match, unbeknown to me, the telephone in my room was out of order. Late at night I received a knock on my door. A member of the hotel staff asked if he could check my telephone as I had received a number of calls and not responded. The check revealed that the telephone was not ringing, which explained why reception did not receive a response from me when trying to put through the incoming calls. The porter told me it was the club that had been calling. As it was now late at night I informed him I would return the call the following morning.

The next day it became apparent that there was a bit of a panic on. 'You must get down here quickly,' I was told. I didn't think too much about it, but I showered and changed and headed into the club. When I arrived at the Vetch, the club doctor was there. 'Neil Robinson's cartilage has popped out,' he informed me, crestfallen. 'We were trying to contact you last night to ask what we should do.'

I was quite philosophical about the matter. 'Get him into hospital and operated on. If we leave it until Tosh gets back, it'll only get worse. Better we act straight away. The sooner the problem is resolved, the sooner he will be fit.'

Neil was admitted to hospital and subsequently had his problematic cartilage removed. I felt that that was the right thing to do. I was thinking about the implications for the player, not the money we had paid to Everton.

When Tosh returned from his mini-break and was told what had happened he was not best pleased.

'Why did you sanction the operation?' he asked.

'Because it had to be done, and sooner rather than later. He hasn't played for our first team as yet, so just put the payments to Everton on hold until such time as we are happy he is match-fit.'

I was trying to adopt a logical approach to the matter, but Tosh was angry. He just kept shaking his head at the thought of our new signing having a cartilage operation before he had kicked a ball in earnest. It was a warm day for the time of year, but a sharp frost had descended on his office.

(Incidentally, there was a touch of irony to Tosh's absence from the club. Swansea remained unbeaten that month. I had been in charge for two of our four games, and Tosh received the 'Manager of the Month' award. I couldn't help but smile.)

The matter died down, and we got back to trying to guide Swansea to promotion, but the Neil Robinson incident made me realize that management, in whatever form, was not for me. I just didn't want the hassle that went with the job. I was happy in life, and I reasoned, 'Why should I undertake a job that in all probability will result in problems for me?'

Swansea continued to feature among the promotion hopefuls and I continued to play my part in the renaissance of the club, both off the field and on it. The old legs still occasionally propelled me forward, no more so than during a game against Hull City when I scored twice in a 5–3 win. I was aware, however, of the recurrence of the problem with my knees. As the season progressed, so did the knee problem. It wasn't at this stage debilitating, but I sensed it would be only a matter of time before the pain returned and I would have to give up playing altogether.

As the campaign moved towards its climax, Swansea yo-yoed between top and second. A second successive promotion was on the cards and I was determined to see the job done. We enjoyed an unbeaten run of twelve matches at the end of the season, but it was so tight at the top that even this good form did not result in us winning the Third Division Championship. That honour went to Shrewsbury Town, who finished a single point ahead of both us and Graham Taylor's Watford. Any disappointment we felt at not winning the title was more than compensated for by the fact that Swansea had gained promotion to Division Two. The club had been on the brink of folding a few years earlier, but Tosh had triggered a remarkable renaissance; he would later guide Swansea into Division One.

I played my last senior game for Swansea in a 3–1 win at Blackpool on 21 April 1979. A crowd of around 7,000 were present at Bloomfield Road, and when the final whistle sounded I walked off a pitch for the very last time. I threw my boots in my bag and joined the rest of the Swansea players for a quick drink before they headed for Wales. Cally and I drove back to Liverpool, knowing that my career as a player was over. For the remaining games I sat on the bench, fulfilling my role as assistant manager. Promotion was sealed and duly celebrated when Swansea triumphed 2–1 over Chesterfield before a full house of 25,000; Tosh scored the winning goal, which seemed entirely fitting. It took his tally for the season to fifteen, just one of five Swansea players to reach double figures. To the best of my knowledge, that's the last time that happened in English football. I was happy to have played my part in the club's success that season. By and large it had been fun and I had enjoyed the experience. Cally too had enjoyed his football, and he decided to stay at Swansea for at least another season.

The 1979–80 season went well for Swansea in Division Two. We remained unbeaten in our opening four matches, and though there was a long way to go I knew the team were not going to struggle with their newfound lofty status. I, however, was struggling. My knees were deteriorating. I was experiencing soreness rather than pain, but it was enough to prevent me from playing so I concentrated on my role as assistant to Tosh. I continued to train with Cally at Liverpool, but found things increasingly problematic. After one such training session in the autumn, Bob took me to one side. He asked how things were going for me and I put him in the picture.

'Why don't you come back here and look after the youth team?' he suggested.

This came as a surprise. The idea of returning to Liverpool was greatly appealing. I had come to terms with the fact that I had played my last game of football and the thought of working with the youngsters at Anfield was enticing because I felt it was an opportunity for me to give something back to the club that had given me so much. I talked the matter over with Sue and with Tosh, then I rang Bob and said, 'You're on.' Initially I was as keen as mustard. Just being involved again at Liverpool gave me a tremendous lift. The boys in my charge proved eager to learn and for the first few months everything went extremely well.

Once again Liverpool had won the First Division Championship in 1978–79, but Bob had continued with his seamless tinkering with the team. One of the players to fall by the wayside was Emlyn, who during the season had not been able to command a regular place. It seemed he was not happy about this. He wanted away that summer, and he was granted his wish.

One morning I received a message that Bob wanted to see me in his office.

'I've done the bastard,' he said as I took a seat.

'Who?' I asked, not having a clue who he was referring to.

'Emlyn,' Bob informed me. 'I've sold him to Wolves and I've done him.'

Bob went on to tell me that on hearing of Emlyn's desire to leave Anfield and secure regular first-team football elsewhere, Wolves had made an approach. Apparently Emlyn had travelled down to Wolves for talks during which he had said some very uncomplimentary things about Liverpool, the news of which had got back to Bob. Emlyn was leaving Liverpool on a 'free', but apparently he had asked Wolves for a £50,000 signing-on fee. When Bob heard of the things Emlyn was alleged to have said about Liverpool, he spoke to Emlyn to express his displeasure. Knowing that Bob was privy to these remarks, Emlyn realized there was no way he could ever stay at Anfield now, even if the Wolves deal fell through. According to Bob, he rang Wolves and persuaded the board to pay Liverpool the £50,000 and not Emlyn. There was nothing Emlyn could do about the matter. He couldn't come back to Liverpool and had little alternative but to sign for Wolves, in so doing forgoing his request for the signing-on fee.

'What goes around comes around,' said Bob. 'Great player, but the only guy I know who Mother Teresa would have wanted to smack in the mouth.'

The Liverpool junior teams played in the Lancashire League, the league I had played in when I had first joined the groundstaff. A few months down the line I was standing on the sidelines watching the youth team play when it occurred to me that I had come full circle. I was now back to where it had all started for me, and to be honest, as the weeks went by that notion didn't rest easy with me. The knee problem was becoming progressively worse too. There were times when the pain was so bad I found it difficult even to walk around the training ground, let alone run. It affected my enthusiasm for my role as youth-team coach. I became frustrated at the fact that I couldn't run, and that frustration soon turned into disillusionment. I just wasn't enjoying the job. My great football adventure was over.

Liverpool were still the dominant force in English football in 1979–80 and once again finished the season as champions. The side more or less picked itself: Clem, Phil Neal, Alan Kennedy, Phil Thompson, Ray Kennedy, Alan Hansen, Kenny Dalglish, Jimmy Case, David Johnson, Terry McDermott and Graeme Souness. Only six other players featured in the first team that season, but in each case they played only when injury affected any of the preferred eleven. Bob had exceeded all expectations as manager. Shanks was a tough act to follow, but Bob had emerged as not only the most successful manager in the history of the club, but the most successful manager English football had ever seen. No one was more pleased for him than me.

I told Bob that I was calling it a day. I explained my reasons and he thanked me for my honesty. At one point he suggested I might take a break, get the knee problems sorted and return in some capacity as a member of the backroom staff. Again I thanked him, but I felt it better to break from the professional side of the game altogether. So, in April 1980, I cleaned out my locker, took my boots and kit home and stored them in the attic. Then I sat down and thought about what the future might now hold for me.

I had a number of business interests in the city, mainly property development, and for a number of years I devoted my time to this. At one time, as I mentioned earlier, I co-owned the lease on the Cavern club. In the main the businesses went well, but there came a time in the 1980s when I'd had enough of this too and my business partner and I went our separate ways. I continued to hold interests in property and development into the early nineties, but when other work began to consume my time I left property development altogether. And to think I could have been the Sarah Beeny of Liverpool.

I wouldn't have swapped my time in the game for anything. I

enjoyed phenomenal success with Liverpool and more than fulfilled my childhood dreams. There was, however, a price to pay for my twenty years in football. Over the years I underwent so many operations on my knees and elbows and I had so many plastic joints fitted that I was fearful of sitting too close to the fire in case I melted. Throughout the 1980s I think I must have spent more time in hospitals than the cast of *Holby City*. I was fitted with two plastic knee joints, a plastic right elbow and an artificial hip. As I once remarked to Sue, 'There are three ages of man: hip, formerly hip, and artificial hip. I have now reached the final stage.'

At one stage the pain I was enduring in my knees and hip was so chronic that a surgeon severed the nerves to try to give me a certain amount of comfort, but it didn't work. I went to see a specialist. 'I have good news and bad news,' he told me. 'You have the physical body of a twenty-five-year-old but the knees of a seventy-five-year-old.' I was diagnosed as having osteo-arthritis (crumbling of the bones) and also rheumatoid arthritis, a disorder of the blood that weakens the joints. At one stage I was so debilitated I was confined to a wheelchair. I shall be forever grateful to all the doctors and nurses who treated me; they were magnificent. I counted my blessings that I lived in an age when medical knowledge is such that painful joints can be replaced and arthritis treated.

The bulk of the damage was sustained while wearing the red of Liverpool. It is only when your playing days are over that you suddenly realize just how wearing on the body a long career in football can be. I never thought twice about going in for a tackle of any sort, but my body certainly paid the price for some of those bone-crunching moments.

I meet people at sporting dinners today and some are still of the mind that I was a ruthless player. Those who knew me or saw me play on a regular basis know this not to be true. I loved to tackle and put everything behind each one, but I always did it properly. I wasn't sneaky or underhand. I never went in late or over the top.

I played some 650 competitive matches and I was only sent off once, for dissent, and cautioned on only three occasions. There is the real me and there is the other me, the one that exists nowhere else but in the memories of some supporters. Hopefully by this stage of my story you have got to know the former.

There is a curious side-story related to the problems I had with my knees and hips. It began when I, among others, was invited to take part in a penalty shoot-out for charity prior to the 1996 FA Cup Final between Liverpool and Manchester United. I wasn't really up to it, but seeing as it was all for charity I agreed to give it a go. It wasn't long since I'd undergone a major operation on my hips. I was confined to a wheelchair for a time, and someone advised me that I could claim benefit from the DHSS. Apparently there were three levels of benefit for people with my condition and I qualified for the middle grade. At first I declined, but I was told, 'You have paid into the system all your life and never claimed. You're entitled to this benefit, so fill out the form.' I subsequently completed one and was duly awarded payments. Come the day of the FA Cup Final, I hobbled across the Wembley turf and managed to toe-end the ball towards the goal. No one took the penalty competition seriously, it was just a bit of fun to raise money for charities, but an employee of the DHSS watching the build-up on TV saw me take the penalty kick and reported me to his superiors.

To cut a long story short, I was ordered to attend an interview at the DHSS offices in Manchester to explain why I was claiming disability benefit when I was capable of 'playing football at Wembley'. It appeared ludicrous to me but I answered the investigative panel's questions as best I could. My main defence was that hobbling up to take a penalty hardly constituted 'playing football', but if they felt my appearance at Wembley contravened rules and regulations regarding benefit, I would be happy for them to stop payments. The 'interview' took place on the Friday morning; the very next day I received a letter from the DHSS informing me that my disability benefit was to be downgraded to the lowest level.

It can take months for the DHSS to respond to an application for disability benefit, let alone award it, but within twenty-four hours I had received notification that the few pounds I had been encouraged to apply for were to be revoked.

The story made news in the national newspapers. I don't think anyone believed I was out to take advantage of the benefits system, though. I had, after all, been a reluctant claimant. All manner of stories circulated about the incident, the most common being that the DHSS employee who reported me was an Everton supporter. To this day I don't know if that is true or not. Even if it is, I'd suggest that his reporting of me had more to do with him as a person. Fortunately the story did not do any harm to my character or reputation. On the contrary, the consensus of opinion was that the DHSS employee had been petty-minded. Though I must emphasize that at no time did I ever hold any sort of grudge against him, whatever his motivation.

In September 2006, exactly ten years on from the incident, I arrived at Anfield for Liverpool's game against Galatasaray and on approaching the foyer was told by a steward that a supporter would like a word with me. I told the steward that I was just on my way to meet corporate guests and was running a little late.

'He says he has some good news for you, Tommy,' said the steward.

I was directed towards a supporter kitted out in one of the club's replica shirts.

'Tommy, you don't know me, but I work for the DHSS,' he informed me. 'I have come to see you because I have some good news for you.'

I wondered what on earth this news could be. I had not had any dealings with the DHSS for ten years. Surely there weren't some outstanding benefit payments payable to me?

'Good news?' I enquired. 'What is it?'

'Remember the DHSS employee who shopped you at the Cup Final?'

'Yes.'

'He died last week!'

But death, under any circumstances, can never be a fit subject for humour. There are times when football seriously affects your judgement about life, occasions when we lose all sense of perspective and reality and are blinded by our passion for the team we love and support. Shanks took it to the extreme when he made his famous quote about football being more important than life and death. I never believed that to be the case, never more so than in the wake of the Heysel Stadium and Hillsborough disasters of the 1980s.

I was at Heysel on 29 May 1985 when Liverpool faced Juventus in the European Cup Final. I was also at Hillsborough on 15 April 1989 when Liverpool met Nottingham Forest in an FA Cup semi-final. Those days will forever live with me and will forever cast a black shadow across a part of my heart. I do not wish to go into the details of what occurred on those fateful days; the tragedies are well documented elsewhere. I will, however, say that in my opinion both disasters could have been avoided.

In the wake of Heysel, UEFA banned all English clubs from European competition for five years, but did they ever indulge in self-examination? In my opinion Heysel was a tragedy waiting to happen. It was a tired and crumbling stadium totally inappropriate for staging a major football match. It simply did not bear close inspection on the safety front. In saying this I am not ignoring the unacceptable behaviour of those fans involved in the ugly scenes I witnessed. To me it is an undeniable fact that no one can make excuses for the behaviour of some so-called Liverpool supporters that led to thirty-nine Juventus fans losing their lives. That said, I feel that had the game taken place in a more up-to-date stadium, one that adhered to modern safety requirements, the loss of life could have been averted. UEFA totally ignored Liverpool's official protests regarding crowd segregation. Peter Robinson had been highlighting the club's fears in the weeks leading up to the game, but his concerns and those of the club fell upon deaf ears.

Ninety-six Liverpool supporters, whose number included children, lost their lives in the Hillsborough disaster. Hundreds were also injured, some seriously. It transpired that a senior police officer had ordered a gate to be opened, allowing supporters to surge into an area behind the goal at the Leppings Lane end of the ground, crushing those already at the front of the terracing. I feel I am not alone in thinking that some senior police officers, and one in particular, 'froze', in the words of the official enquiry, when ordering that gate to be opened. In his report, Lord Chief Justice Taylor subsequently vindicated Liverpool supporters and severely criticized the organization on the day and the response of the police. But football's governing bodies must also take some blame for what happened. For years they had allowed the game to decline and supporters to endure below-standard conditions at many grounds. It took a tragedy such as this before the powers-that-be forced football to get its act together and seriously think about the way it treated its paying customers.

When I think about Heysel and Hillsborough, I don't just think about the 135 innocent people who needlessly died, but also the effect these tragedies had on thousands of individuals, particularly the families and friends left behind. Sue and I maintain contact with a lady called Lynn Rimmer and her son Paul and daughter Kate. Lynn lost her husband. The immediate families suffer to this day, denied justice by successive governments and still unable to come to terms with that horrific day. Now I am well aware that some people outside Merseyside may be given to thinking that we dwell on these disasters too much. But we all know someone who died, or are aware of a family who suffered, so we never forget. No one, irrespective of where they live or what team they support, should ever forget Heysel or Hillsborough, or indeed the Bradford fire disaster, for we must continue to learn the lessons.

★

In the 1980s, when I dissolved the property development business partnership I had, I continued my weekly column for the *Liverpool Echo*, which I still pen to this day. I couldn't live on that alone, of course, and because we were not so well off that we could live for the rest of our days on the money I had put away from football, I had to find some sort of alternative employment.

I had always been comfortable talking in public. Quite often when the Liverpool players needed someone to speak to the media, I would be asked to do this. I was also a spokesperson on behalf of players in numerous negotiations with the Liverpool management and board on different matters. The fact that I had a few interesting stories and anecdotes about my time in football prompted me to ring a few agents who handled after-dinner speakers. At first I was a little unsure about how I would go down, but within a week of having spoken at a couple of dinners I began to receive invitations from all over the country. Since that time, after-dinner speaking has formed the bulk of my work. I have spoken not only at sporting dinners but conferences, product promotions, you name it. I have even visited oil rigs to entertain the workers. I tell my audiences about what it was like to play for Liverpool, and I relate a few funny tales and the odd joke at the expense of football and the footballers of yesteryear and today. If my diary is anything to go by, these speeches seem to go down very well.

In addition to the speaking and my column for the *Echo*, I appear on radio and television as and when invited. Of late the television appearances have dwindled, though. It seems to me that television, being what it is, requires even contributors of football to be what producers term 'sexy'; that is, they must have visual appeal as opposed to being able to fulfil an objective or, heaven forbid, have a highly controversial opinion on football. I listen to some former players on TV today – players who won next to nothing of note in their careers – pontificating on the game and I shake my head in wonder. Football is, as Shanks always maintained, a simple game, but listen to some of these former players and you'd think it was marginally less complicated than quantum theory and relativity.

But Sky Television came to the rescue when English football had reached its nadir, and for that one must be grateful. At least in one sense it did, for it is not true to say that at the time football in this country was at its most unpopular. The image of the game may have been at an all-time low, but not attendances. Having registered record low attendances in 1985–86, League matches enjoyed a year-on-year rise in the six seasons leading up to the inception of the Premiership. In 1991–92, the last season of the Football League in its old format, aggregate attendances rose to 20,487,273 – an increase of four million from 1985–86. More significantly, attendances for the first season of the Premiership were down 200,000 on the previous season, the last of the old-style First Division. So while the involvement of Sky and the formation of the Premiership have indeed greatly benefited the game in this country, it is not true to say that they breathed life into an ailing game. If attendances at matches are anything to go by – and how else can one measure the game's popularity? – Sky and the Premiership simply took advantage of a growth trend. Somehow along the line, however, the myth has been perpetuated that they 'saved English football'.

Now English football and television enjoy such an incestuous relationship, and the money is so great, that TV is very wary about allowing any former player or football writer to criticize the game on air. Former players (visually appealing ones) who now work as TV pundits are reluctant to go out on a limb for fear of upsetting someone and losing their job, or else they are incapable of commenting objectively on the game. So we now have cosy discussions between presenters (increasingly former players) and pundits on TV. To me it comes across as trite and polite – the way TV, I believe, wants football discussion to be. You even see interviews in which a presenter will phrase a question in such a way that he or she provides part of the answer they require. Hence the pundit beginning his reply with the cliché, 'Very much so . . .'

You never find such restrained and cautious football discussion among supporters. One of the few places former players and supporters can get together to really speak their minds on matters football is the after-dinner circuit, which is another reason I like doing them. In Q and As, which often form part of a dinner, former players such as me and supporters have an opportunity to put forward no-holds-barred opinions on the game. Say what you like about sporting dinners, but increasingly over the years, in addition to providing entertainment, they have become a rare platform for honest, unfront talk about the modern game.

Talking of which . . .

15

A DIFFERENT BALL GAME

IT IS STILL 'THE BEAUTIFUL GAME', BUT IN MANY RESPECTS FOOT-
ball today has changed almost unrecognizably from the game I
knew as a player. In saying that, I'm not making the case that football in my day was better, only that it was very different.

In these pages I have already visited several topics that exercise
me, including that of overseas players in this country. A proportion
of them have brought wonderful skills to our game and generally
speaking made a significant and positive contribution to football in
this country, but in my opinion the greater proportion have had a
negative effect. It's a case of the old Steve Miller song 'Take The
Money And Run'.

Take goalkeepers. In the 1970s England boasted two world-
class keepers in Clem and Peter Shilton; at one point there was
also Gordon Banks. In addition to these worthy custodians of
the England jersey, the seventies also boasted goalkeepers of
the calibre of Phil Parkes (QPR and West Ham), Joe Corrigan
(Manchester City), Jimmy Rimmer (Arsenal, Aston Villa, etc.),
Jim Montgomery (Sunderland), John Burridge (Villa, among
many others), Paul Cooper (Ipswich Town), Alex Stepney

(Manchester United), Graham Moseley (Derby and Brighton), John Osborne (West Bromwich Albion) and Mervyn Day (West Ham). Then there were the international keepers from the other home countries: Pat Jennings (Arsenal and Spurs), David Harvey and Gary Sprake (Leeds), Iam McFaul (Newcastle) and Jim Platt (Middlesbrough). That's some roll-call of top-class goalkeepers, even if you only consider those of English birth. One of the gripes today is that England does not produce top-class goalkeepers in the numbers it once did, that the current contenders for the England jersey are 'so-so', the best of a poor lot. There is every case for saying, on the basis of his age and talent displayed thus far, that Ben Foster promises to be an excellent goalkeeper; but it is little wonder that England has struggled to produce a crop of con-sistently good world-class goalkeepers when there are so many overseas players. Throughout February 2007 I made a point of noting how many goalkeepers in the Premiership qualified to play for England. There were only five: Paul Robinson (Spurs), Scott Carson (Charlton), Ben Foster (Watford loanee from Manchester United), David James (Portsmouth) and Robert Green (West Ham). Really, is it any wonder?

The wider picture is also a cause for concern. In 2007 only around 40 per cent of starting line-ups in the Premiership were homegrown players, as opposed to 70 per cent in Italy, 65 per cent in France and 63 per cent in Spain; and people wonder why England fail to do well in major international tournaments. There are a number of reasons, of course, but one is that you can't pro-duce a strong, successful England team when only just over a third of players starting Premiership games on any given weekend are qualified to play for the national team. When I hear the media trumpeting the superiority of our football in Europe courtesy of Arsenal, Chelsea, Liverpool and Manchester United, I am reminded of what Bob Hope said when asked to comment on the fact that Russia had beaten America in the space race by becom-ing the first nation to put a man into orbit. 'All it proves is their

German scientists are better than our German scientists,' he said.

There are many things about football today that are far superior to the game I knew. No one in their right mind, for instance, would want to go back to the days that begat Hillsborough, Heysel and Bradford. We now have wonderful stadiums, as opposed to grounds, and without doubt the facilities afforded to supporters are much better. English football is once again the family game I knew it to be when I started out as a player, and no one is happier about that than me. But money dictates more than it has ever done. One of the saddest aspects to the regeneration of the game in this country has been the alienation of the traditional working-class support at the expense of those with disposable income. The elderly and those on low incomes could once afford to watch top-division football. Not any more.

In January 2007 the Premier League negotiated a three-year deal worth £600 million for overseas TV rights to games, in addition to which there is a £1.7 billion deal with Sky and Setanta to screen matches in Great Britain and Ireland, and a £400 million deal struck with internet and mobile phone companies. Premiership clubs currently share some £900 million a season from broadcasting rights, a deal that will run until 2010. Yet admission prices for Premiership matches are the highest of any domestic league in the world. Given the colossal amounts of money swilling about in the game, to say nothing of the revenue generated by commercial ventures, such prices simply cannot be justified. To their credit, Blackburn Rovers suggested that the vast amounts of money from the broadcasting companies should be used, in part, to slash ticket prices. Then again, Blackburn are one of the few Premiership clubs that don't sell out their home games, unless one of the 'big four' pays a visit. Those clubs that do enjoy bumper attendances will, I feel, pay little more than lip service to Blackburn's plea, and this is where the problem lies. The power in the game rests not with the Premiership as a whole, but with half a dozen rich clubs. Some might even say four clubs.

I have just cause to be familiar with most parts of the report published in 1990 by Lord Chief Justice Taylor in the aftermath of the Hillsborough disaster. Taylor advocated the need for all-seater stadiums and said that this could be achieved at a price to each supporter of £6. I'm no Gordon Brown, but allowing for inflation I estimate that in 2008 that would mean fans paying around £10 for a seat at a Premiership match. The average price is now around £37, and if that's the average price it stands to reason that some clubs are charging more. Since the inception of the Premiership, admission prices have risen in excess of 500 per cent, way in excess of inflation. Again, how can such a rise be justified?

The hype generated by television, radio, the press and other media has ensured that attendances at Premiership matches remain healthy. But the average attendance in the Premiership depends on which teams are contesting it in any given season. There was a little hullabaloo during 2007 when it was reported that the average attendance figures were down; at the time, however, the league contained Watford and Charlton as well as Wigan, Fulham and Blackburn, none of whom attract truly big attendances to home games. Sunderland were at the time in the process of winning the Championship; when the Wearsiders are in the Premiership they contribute greatly to attendance totals. For example, in April 2007 more spectators watched Sunderland at home to Barnsley than Chelsea at home to Liverpool in the Champions League the following week. The best-supported league in Europe is the Bundesliga in Germany. In 2006–07 the average attendance for Bundesliga games was in excess of 40,000, some 25 per cent above the Premiership. Yet German supporters can buy tickets for as little as fifteen euros (around £10) and literally thousands of tickets are available for all games, including those of champions Stuttgart, for twenty-three euros (around £15). What is just as appealing, to my mind, is the fact the Bundesliga is truly competitive. Several clubs are in contention for the title every season.

Our beautiful game has been the victim of carpet-bagging. As more money has poured into the game, it has increasingly become a magnet for the rich and powerful, which is why so many top clubs are now owned by foreigners. And the richer the game becomes, the more it distances itself from its traditional working-class bedrock support. You only had to look at the swathes of empty seats in the corporate areas of the new Wembley during the second half of the 2007 FA Cup Final for an indication of how the genuine supporter has been driven away from the game. Mind you, given the quality of the game in the first half I don't blame the 'prawn sandwich' brigade for staying within the confines of their catering areas for the second period.

I spoke earlier of myopia in the game, and nowhere is this more pronounced than in the coverage of the game by broadcasters and the press. After the Bundesliga, the best-supported league in Europe is the Premiership; third is La Liga in Spain and fourth is the Championship, as it is now called. Yet scan the pages of some of our national newspapers on a Saturday morning and you would be forgiven for thinking the Championship didn't exist. Quite often on a Saturday the only coverage given to the fourth best-supported league in the world is the fixtures for that day. The *Daily Telegraph* and the *Guardian* pride themselves on their coverage of the game, yet on a Saturday they are obsessed with the Premiership, particularly Manchester United, Chelsea and Arsenal. There are more clubs in the Football League than in the Premiership, and more people attend Football League matches, yet the coverage, other than brief match reports, is minimal in comparison. I have just cause to love Liverpool Football Club and I enjoy the Premiership, but I will always ignore a sycophantic club PR- or agent-generated piece about a Chelsea or Manchester United player in favour of what is increasingly now a rare article on a lower league club, manager or player, and I don't think I am in the minority.

Another disconcerting aspect to the game is the prices

some clubs charge visiting supporters of certain clubs. Increasingly, clubs, those in the Football League included, are categorizing home matches, hiking admission prices for what they perceive to be 'A' grade games. In essence this is clubs cashing in at the expense of other clubs that enjoy good support. Away support in England is unique. You don't get five thousand Stuttgart supporters travelling to Werder Bremen or a similar number of AC Milan fans travelling to Palermo. And I am not simply talking about fans of Liverpool, Manchester United or Arsenal. In 2007 Stoke City significantly increased admission prices for visiting Sunderland supporters. It begs the question, why? Stoke would have enjoyed an increase in revenue anyway as Sunderland's travelling support is considerable. Seemingly that was not enough for them. Likewise, Manchester United supporters were subjected to a price hike when they visited Fulham in 2007: the cheapest seat at Craven Cottage that day cost £45. Why should away supporters be exploited like this? All-seater stadiums were the appropriate and required response to the Hillsborough tragedy, but it seems to me that many clubs have taken advantage of this – justifying their high ticket prices by providing services and facilities that fans may not want or need. And anyway, as Manchester United fans discovered when visiting Lens and Milan for Champions League matches in 2007, seating is not the all-encompassing panacea to the ills that once beset the game.

When I was a player I often heard the call that football should be run more like a business. Well, it is run like a business now, and not just any business: it is run like a global company. If anything, there is now justification for saying that in order for English football to be returned to the genuine fan it has to be run less like a business. Fat chance of that happening, though: the money-makers and those with financial wherewithal who are out to make their crock of gold have seized power. The people who run the game and clubs today seek only to attract those whose income is such that they can afford grossly inflated admission prices, corporate hospitality and the myriad commercial peripherals sold off the back of club loyalty. When I began my career in the game, football was essentially a working-class pursuit, accessible to most. Sadly, this is no longer the case. Before the letters come flooding in, let me say that I acknowledge some clubs have been at pains to offer admission incentives to low-income supporters, particularly those clubs in the Football League. There is no denying the fact, however, that by and large the game has become increasingly elitist.

The actual football apart, it is the way the game is portrayed, or rather 'sold', to supporters these days that I find disconcerting. The actual football produced more often than not will not live up to the weighty hype that precedes the match. Every fixture between Manchester United, Chelsea, Arsenal and Liverpool is now portrayed as being a potential 'classic', but invariably meetings between two such sides are damp squibs because they tend to cancel each other out. Take the first FA Cup Final at the new Wembley between Chelsea and Manchester United. On the whole it was a dour game; the first half in particular was dire. This is because when today's top teams meet, often they are content to wait until the opposing team makes a mistake that will result in them scoring a goal, rather than adopt a positive, attacking approach and seize the initiative. But the higher the standard of football, the fewer mistakes there are. Sure I played in games that failed to live up to expectation, but this has never been more the case than in top-class football today, and that is largely due to media hype.

There are some great players in the game today – John Terry, Micah Richards, Steven Gerrard and, dare I say it, Fernando Torres – but a truly great player will have a great game in the great games. George Best and Bobby Charlton in the 1968 European Cup Final; Kevin Keegan in the 1977 European Cup Final; Bobby Moore in the World Cup Final, and against Brazil in 1970; I could go on. The first FA Cup Final at the new Wembley was a great occasion for today's great players, but none displayed his talent. Cristiano Ronaldo, for example, was virtually anonymous. He had any number of super games for United in the course of that season, but he also turned in several performances that were so uninfluential that you forgot he was on the field. Such was the talent and consistency of Kevin Keegan, Kenny Dalglish, Bobby Charlton, Billy Bremner and Bestie, to name but five players from yesteryear, you never forgot they were on the field.

I love music, but it seems to me that no preview of a game is now complete without a backdrop of rock music. It's totally unnecessary and irritating. It has reached the extent on TV where we are treated to short, sharp cuts of images of games at a speed greater than reality accompanied by frenetic music which gives the impression of football being even more exciting than it is, which invariably results in anticlimax and disappointment. Radio, too, is guilty. It can be a great way of following football, but who wants to hear frantic snippets of past commentary to a backdrop of loud music in an attempt to persuade us to tune in to the commentary of a game? The beauty of radio commentary is its immediacy; snatches of commentary on past games are inappropriate to the medium, particularly when they verge on the hysterical, such as those from the self-opinionated Alan Green of whom Jimmy Greaves once said, 'When commentating on a near miss on goal he sounds like a man whose pants are on fire.' Radio, like young people's television, makes the mistake of thinking it has to shout in order to keep its audience.

In the sixties and seventies, at around half-five on a Saturday, BBC radio's *Sports Report* used to afford five to seven minutes of air-time to a well-known football writer such as Ken Jones, Bryon Butler, Geoffrey Green, Hugh McIlvanney or Brian Glanville during which the scribe would offer an insightful and objective personal view on some aspect of the game. Superbly written, these vignettes were a joy to listen to, football journalism and radio comment at its very best. There are no such opportunities on radio now. Following commentary on two matches, after five p.m. on FiveLive a much-shortened results and reports service gives way to yet more match commentary. 'Over to our third match commentary of the day,' the anchor proudly boasts. Overkill, more like.

As for 606, FiveLive's radio phone-in, it is simply a case of a missed opportunity. Rather than encouraging heated debate on issues that really affect supporters, the bulk of the programme appears to consist of fans ringing in to say how brilliant their team have been of late or how well they did that day, or cries for a manager to be dismissed. I suppose FiveLive would say the content of these calls is purely down to listeners and what they wish to talk about. To a certain degree that's true. But does the presenter not have a duty to use these calls as footbridges to more fertile pastures? In the early years the programme was presented by Danny Baker and the content was rich, insightful and often humorous. Helped by Baker, football fans across the nation were introduced to one another, and in the days of segregation that in itself was revealing. Fans related their experiences at games, of travelling to matches and meeting their heroes; they talked of their superstitions and foibles, and the things they did to entertain themselves at matches, such as relating the squad numbers from the programme to the menu of the local Chinese takeaway. 606 was hugely entertaining as a result, and it acted as a social glue for fans of whatever hue. Sadly there appears to be no place for such humour or irreverence on radio and TV today as far as football is concerned. There are some exceptions – Alan Brazil on talkSPORT and possibly *Fighting Talk* on FiveLive – but even these do not engage with serious issues and take the game's authorities to task.

Supporters' response to the constant bombardment of matches has been to have their appetite for televised football blunted. Genuine supporters, as opposed to consumers, will go and watch their own club, tune in for the odd Champions League match and settle down to watch England. I love football, I'm an ex-pro, but

I would feel ashamed of myself if I tuned in on a daily basis to watch every televised game going. Like many others, I like to think I have a life.

In addition to speaking on the after-dinner circuit, I also appear in a theatre show alongside other former Liverpool players. The line-up can vary – just as it was at Anfield, no one has a regular place – but in the main Cally, Jimmy Case and Joey Jones accompany me at these shows, and they have proved very popular. The second half consists of a Q and A with members of the audience. One of the most frequent questions I am asked is, 'Would players such as you, Cally, Jimmy and Kevin Keegan be able to play in the modern game?' Leaving myself out, players such as Keegan, Dalglish and Callaghan, to name but three, were of such quality and skill, they could play football in any era. Invariably I also say, 'Another question is, could modern players play in the game we knew in the sixties and seventies?'

I ask this simply because things were so very different then. Players today enjoy pristine pitches whereas my generation played on Christmas-pudding surfaces for much of the season. The ball today is overly light; the footballs we used were of regulation weight, exactly sixteen ounces (one pound, or a little under half a kilo). Try crossing the old regulation ball with accuracy on a pitch resembling stewed prunes with Ron Harris or Nobby Stiles snapping at your heels; yet this was consistently done by the likes of Steve Heighway, Cally, Mike Summerbee, Alan Hinton, Cliff Jones and Dennis Tueart, to name but a few. Then there was the physical side of the game. Match officials had a much more lenient attitude to physical play, basically because physicality was seen to be an intrinsic part of football.

I remember once playing against Burnley, who had a flying young winger in Steve Kindon. He really did possess a turn of speed, I didn't, and early in the game he took me on the outside and left me for dead. Remembering the words of Stan Lynn, when

Steve took up his position on the wing again I moved alongside him and snarled, 'If you go on the outside of me again, I'll break your leg, son.' Steve turned as colourless as ice. Once he'd got over the initial shock he ran over to the referee, who, if my memory serves me well, was Mr Baker from Rugby.

'I've just been threatened,' blurted Steve. 'Tommy Smith said if I go on the outside of him again he's going to break my leg!'

'Well,' said Mr Baker, 'if I were you I wouldn't go on the outside of him again. It's a man's game, son. If you can't look after yourself, go do something else in life.'

Steve got on with the game, as did Mr Baker, who'd obviously assumed that I had simply indulged in some verbal psychology with Steve and saw nothing wrong with it. Somehow I can't imagine a referee responding in such a way today. Nor can I imagine a player resigning himself to 'getting on' with the game as uncomplainingly as Steve did that day.

There were also a lot of very skilled players who could display their technique and talent whether they were playing on a mud-heap or a frozen pitch. 'In your day, was there a player who displayed the level of skill of Cristiano Ronaldo?' I was once asked at a theatre show. I replied, 'George Best, Alan Hudson, Rodney Marsh and Jim Baxter, to name but four, all possessed an abundance of skill, though different skills to Ronaldo. Ronaldo can do things with a ball they couldn't, but then I saw those players display skills I have never seen Ronaldo perform. I suppose it's all relative, but yes, the game did possess very skilful players. What's more, you can go back – Matthews, Finney, Shackleton, Mannion. Every generation has its skilful entertainers. What you've got to ask yourself is: could Ronaldo display his skills on the pitches of the past?'

One aspect of the game that has stayed remarkably consistent over the decades is its administration. I have never been too enamoured of the people who govern the game in this country, and never less so than now. I can never watch or listen to FA chief executive Brian Barwick without thinking he would do well as a foil for Patricia Routledge in *Keeping Up Appearances*. In my opinion Barwick showed himself to be a bungler of the first order when overseeing the hunt for a successor to Sven Goran Eriksson and attempting to lure Phil Scolari. Barwick is a former TV executive. I rest my case.

The key officials in the Premier League also showed themselves to be lacking when dealing with West Ham in 2007 over the Carlos Tevez affair. I am sure West Ham were more than happy to receive a £5.5 million fine and no points deduction. In essence the club was able to 'buy' continued membership of the Premiership. Surely a precedent has now been set? In future, clubs must expect a fine and not a points deduction for fielding ineligible players. I am sure the Premier League hoped that the imposition of a record fine would generally be seen as an acceptable and appropriate punishment, but many people simply saw the Premier League as having 'bottled it'. Bury were removed from the FA Cup for fielding an ineligible player, so why were West Ham punished with a fine for a similar offence? The game's administrators fine and suspend players on a regular basis for not having played the game fairly; seemingly the Premier League's administrators feel they do not need to adhere to similar rules of fair play.

For over a hundred years football has enthralled and captivated millions of people. Throughout the Victorian age and the first half of the twentieth century the game evolved as its rules were fine-tuned until they were as good as they could be and we had a game most understood. Football administrators, however, simply can't stop tinkering with the rules, and not always to the betterment of the game. As a former defender I always understood the offside law; not any more. I have spoken to several current referees, players and managers, none of whom was able to explain the current ruling because it is based on a subjective decision on whether a player is 'active' or not – a totally arbitrary judgment that can change from game to game. It begs the question, if referees, players and managers don't fully understand what offside now is, why have we not reverted back to the original ruling? Surely that's the answer to the current confusion? You knew where you stood, as a defender quite literally, with the old offside law; now it would appear most do not. The current law is open to interpretation, which often leads to trouble.

In my opinion, then, reverting back to the old offside law would eliminate confusion and improve the game. The following are just some more personal suggestions for how the current game could be further improved.

Scrap the transfer window. The fact that this now applies to non-League clubs is preposterous. In theory the transfer window is supposed to help smaller clubs; in fact the opposite is the case. A small club facing financial difficulty is unable to sell a player when necessary to ease its financial problems, as it was once able to do. I am no lawyer, but the window would appear to me to be a restriction of trade. The fact that we now have 'emergency loans' suggests to me that it does not work.

More games to return to a Saturday kick-off at three p.m. The time and day of kick-off was originally settled upon because it was considered to be most convenient to supporters. I am of the mind that it still is. Television has run rough-shod over the needs and conveniences of the genuine supporter. We now have a situation where not one FA Cup quarter-final tie takes place at the traditional time of three p.m. on a Saturday. It's monstrous that genuine fans are being ignored and the history, tradition and culture of our game is being eroded. On 6 October 2007 only one Premiership game kicked off at three p.m.: eight games took place on Sunday the seventh. The National Supporters Club voiced their protest to the Premier League but it fell on deaf ears.

Impose a minimum number of homegrown players to be fielded in teams. UEFA are trying to introduce a regulation that allows for this, but are meeting resistance. English county cricket does it, why not football? We need to give indigenous talent better opportunities to develop, which will give more options to the England team.

Reduce the number of televised games. Some hope of this, given the recent deal struck by Sky and Setanta. The average attendance of matches in Serie A in 2006–07 was 16,700. There are several reasons for the decline in crowd numbers in Italy, one being saturation coverage of games by television. I don't know about your home, but Sue and I were on the point of sandbagging in an attempt to prevent more matches being beamed into our house, until she reminded me the TV set does have an on/off button. The pudding has been over-egged to the extent that one televised game blurs into another. Football is very popular at the moment but, just like gardening make-over TV programmes and boy bands, eminently susceptible to the evanescence of trends.

Stop TV and radio commentators indulging in insipid superlatives. 'Genius', 'brilliant', 'truly magnificent' – these are often the responses of commentators to a run-of-the-mill goal scored by a big name in the Premiership. I do hope current top players watching videoed matches don't believe such nonsense. 'Heighway, Toshack, Keegan, one-nil' was all that needed to be said in the seventies; such commentary was indicative of how a defence had been clinically breached. It wasn't genius and it wasn't brilliant, it was simply a football team playing to their optimum. Genius is the preserve of the likes of Einstein, Lennon and McCartney and Picasso in their respective fields and only a handful of highly gifted men in football.

Reduce admission prices and make football accessible to all. See earlier musings on this. On the subject of buying tickets for games, I am once again a supporter. Have you tried to buy tickets for a game on behalf of a group of mates so you can all sit together? At best it is time-consuming, more often than not it is impossible to do. Every effort should be made to allow groups of fans to sit together, to reintroduce the social glue that once existed on the terraces.

As an experiment, no TV cameras at a Premiership game, for example Liverpool v. Everton. Every incident and each moment of a game is now captured on camera, which leaves nothing to the imagination. In the days before saturation coverage of the game, supporters would debate and discuss incidents at work or around a pub table for a week. The fact that fans only had their own eyes to depend on when witnessing 'the moment' fuelled debate and enriched conversation about the game. Supporters were energized, their particular view of an incident mattered. Now they are spoon-fed everything.

A greater and fairer distribution of wealth throughout the game. The new deal struck with TV means it will take a Championship club such as Burnley or Stoke City some thirty years to earn from TV revenue what the club that finishes bottom of the Premiership earns in a single season. This imbalance is detrimental to the long-term future of the game. The rich are becoming richer, the poor becoming poorer. When I was a player at Liverpool, even though we were all-conquering, I believed we were a part of the great family of football, that clubs such as Mansfield and Doncaster contributed as much to the game of football as we did. All these years on, my view hasn't changed. Relegated clubs from the Premiership enjoy a marked financial advantage over other clubs in the Championship. In 2006–07 Sunderland and Birmingham immediately returned to the Premier League, and West Brom featured in the play-off final. A fairer and more democratic distribution of wealth throughout the divisions would promote competitiveness.

Offer former players key roles within the game. Not one former player holds a position of authority within the FA (Trevor Brooking does not have a say in matters of policy), the Premier League or the Football League. What other industry is run by people who have no practical experience of their business?

Clamp down on cheats, diving and the like. I am not saying this didn't happen when I was a player. It was wrong then, it is wrong now. But to me there appears to be more of this sort of unacceptable behaviour on the field than ever before. Every instance undermines what the game should be about – the pursuit of sporting excellence.

Stop TV dictating to the extent that it is now instrumental in the design of strips. Clubs whose strips feature stripes or hoops, such as Reading and Sheffield United, have had to change their strips at the behest of television. While the fronts of shirts are still of a traditional design, the backs are a block of colour so that TV viewers not familiar with players can read their names. We now have a situation where some teams appear to be wearing two distinct and separate styles of shirt. It is ludicrous, and again it is an erosion of the traditions of the game purely to accommodate the needs of television.

Greater distribution of tickets to supporters of teams competing in World Cup matches and major cup finals. The allocation of 17,000 tickets to Liverpool and AC Milan for the 2007 Champions League Final was a disgrace. Half of the tickets for the final in Athens went to – well, you tell me. On the night there were five thousand empty seats because advertising hoardings encroached on to seated areas. The ticket organization for the 2007 Champions League Final was a shambles. Fans with forged tickets gained admission to the game, and a number of fans with bona fide tickets were refused admission on the grounds the stadium was full. I am not defending fans who bought forgeries, but many touts also sold genuine tickets. As 50 per cent of tickets for the game did not go to the respective clubs, UEFA must take its share of the blame for the chaos on the night. Instead, they blamed Liverpool supporters. Of course I am going to stand by Liverpool fans as they stood by me throughout my career, but I do not do so blindly. If I genuinely thought Liverpool fans were in the wrong I would say so; but when 50 per cent of tickets for the final are distributed to heaven knows who and only 17,000 to each club, you can't blame genuine supporters for travelling in the hope of buying a ticket on the day. There were, as I say, plenty of touts selling genuine tickets, which begs the question, where did they get them from? Not from the two respective clubs, that's for sure. UEFA, and our own FA in the case of the FA Cup, should get their priorities right and increase the allocation of tickets to supporters of the competing teams.

When I watch football today and see certain players going through the motions on the pitch seemingly with one eye on the ball and the other on their wage slip, I often think back to those days when Shanks, Bob and Joe Fagan were in our dug-out demanding we sweat blood for Liverpool while entertaining the supporters in the process. One particular end-of-season trip, to Benidorm in 1973, sums up for me the importance of commitment and passion – and how much football has changed since then.

We had agreed to play a local team in lieu of the cost of the trip. The domestic season was over and the lads were winding down after a long, hard year, keen to get some sun on their backs. We had been sunning ourselves and getting into the swing of the holiday for a couple of days when one evening all the players hired a bus to take us into a nearby town where we were going to enjoy a meal and a few beers in a taverna. As we boarded the bus I turned to Shanks.

'Are you sure you won't join us, boss?' I enquired.

'No, not me,' replied Shanks. 'It would kill me to see you lot enjoying yourselves.'

The following morning Joe Fagan entered my room.

'Tommy, get them all up and changed into kit. We've got a game this morning,' he said.

'A game?' I asked, bleary-eyed. 'I didn't think we were playing for a couple of days.'

'The boss only arranged it last night,' Joe said. 'We want everyone in kit and downstairs in twenty.'

I went up and down the hall knocking on doors and issuing the order. Within twenty minutes the players had assembled in the hotel foyer wearing their strips and boots. We boarded a coach and were driven to a small ground that would have been pushed to be accepted for the Mid-Cheshire League. The pitch was baked earth rather than grass, but given the time element in arranging the match a healthy crowd of some 3,000 stood four and five deep around it. Whatever the game it was always important to our pride and prestige that we won, and won well, particularly before such a crowd of locals.

In what passed for a dressing room I asked Joe Fagan who we were playing.

'A local team,' he replied.

'Are they professionals?'

'Yes, they're all professionals.'

Of course, our opponents were as keen as mustard and wound up for the occasion; we had spent the previous night gorging ourselves and drinking copious amounts of lager. The match started and it soon became clear the game was going nowhere. The opposition ran about like mad but were nowhere near good enough to stretch us. We just went through the motions, playing the ball around among ourselves, occasionally allowing our opponents to have possession only to win the ball back at our leisure. After half an hour or so of this pantomime I looked across to the touchline and could see Bob and Joe were fed up with the whole affair. Joe saw me looking at him and beckoned me over. Thinking he was about to issue an instruction, perhaps to score some goals, I went across to him.

'Start a fight, Smithy,' he said, as calmly as if asking me to push on a few yards.

'What was that, Joe?' I said, believing I had misheard him.

'Start a fight,' he repeated earnestly. 'Let's give the crowd something to get worked up about. They're falling asleep, and so are we.'

I took up my position in defence and the next time the ball came near their centre-forward I was straight into him. The opposition were suddenly screaming and shouting; the crowd woke up and so did we. The next ten minutes saw players launching into tackles, elbows flying, you name it. We reacted by scoring three goals before half-time. It was mission accomplished as far as Joe was concerned. He hadn't asked me to do anything sinister, it was just the old Shanks trick of jerking players out of complacency. We won at a canter, but the crowd were happy, and so, curiously, were our opposition, who thought they had been involved in a real ding-dong with a top European side.

After the game both teams enjoyed a drink together and a bite to eat. As I chatted to these lads I asked what they did for a living. Invariably the reply was 'waiter' in a bar or restaurant. I asked how much they were paid for playing football. 'We are not paid. We are – what you say? – amateur.'

As we journeyed back to our hotel to enjoy the remainder of our holiday I confronted Joe.

'You conned us,' I said. 'You told me the team we were playing were professionals.'

'They are,' replied Joe defensively.

'They're all waiters,' I informed him.

'Yeah, but professional ones. They don't do it for nothing.'

One of the greatest aspects to my career as a player was that I had so much fun and so many laughs. It saddens me when I see today's players on the park, or conducting interviews. For all the trappings of wealth they enjoy, they appear solemn and devoid of humour. I'm sure they do enjoy a laugh as much as the next person, but only away from the game. When my good pals Ian St John and Jimmy Greaves were informed by ITV executives that their very popular TV series *Saint and Greavsie* was to end, they were told, 'There is no place for an irreverent programme in what is now the very serious business of football.' That says everything to me about the attitude that currently prevails in the game.

Writing this book brought memories flooding back to me, and many of them centred on players having a good laugh. I've already had a few giggles at Bob Paisley's expense over the trouble he had remembering the names of opposing players. What I haven't mentioned is that he would invariably refer to any opponent as 'Duggie Do-ins'.

Prior to a Liverpool game against Barcelona, Bob was, as usual, talking us through the Barca team using the tiddlywinks and the green baize cloth to illustrate his points. He got to the Barcelona outside-right and, as ever, could not recall a name.

'Their outside-right, Joey [Jones], he's a decent player. Has a turn of speed, but doesn't like being forced inside. So, Joey, I want you to force . . . to force . . . er . . . What's the name of this Spanish lad?'

'Señor Duggie Do-ins?' enquired Joey, and we all convulsed with laughter.

Bob was not devoid of wit himself. When I was a member of the Liverpool coaching staff I remember being in the dressing room at half-time when Liverpool were trailing 1–0 to Southampton. Bob was very unhappy with the first-half performance and gave full vent to his anger by laying into every player.

'Clem, you're one of the best keepers in the world and you let a powder-puff shot beat you at the near post! Bloody Nora, Clem, what the hell were you doing?' he roared, his face as red as the shirts the team were wearing. Turning his attention to Phil Neal, Bob let him know what he thought of his performance in the first half, and it was far from complimentary. Then it was the turn of Alan Hansen and Phil Thompson. That done, he turned to Alan and Ray Kennedy. 'And as for you two,' said Bob, pointing an accusing finger at the pair of them, 'they shot the wrong Kennedys!'

As I said, the memories have come flooding back. They don't tend to focus on medals won or the success enjoyed with Liverpool on the pitch so much as on the sheer joy I derived from playing football. I loved every minute of it. I also loved the camaraderie I shared with my team-mates (all but one, anyway) and opposing players. I remember many things, some seemingly inconsequential images, many of which have been lost to football for ever.

I remember, I remember . . .

During the severe winter of 1962–63, when many matches were postponed, on what was a bitterly cold and snowy day, playing for Liverpool reserves against Sheffield United reserves at Anfield before a crowd of nigh on 25,000.

The majority of supporters on the Kop in the sixties wearing a collar and tie to the match.

Again in the 1960s, not knowing the results of other mid-week games because they weren't broadcast on TV or radio, and having to ring the sports office of the *Liverpool Echo* to find out, or else wait until the following day when the morning newspaper was delivered.

Watching the build-up to the FA Cup Final on television and paying particular attention to the footage of games in the feature 'How They Got There', because prior to this we hadn't seen 'how they had got there'.

The long walk up Wembley tunnel, for much of which, because of the gradient, you could only see sky. You emerged into the stadium to have your ears assailed by a deafening noise before commencing the gladiatorial walk to the halfway line. Sadly, this experience has now gone for players. At the new Wembley players emerge from doors near the halfway line and simply step out on to the pitch, which affords no sense of occasion, excitement, reverence or fevered anticipation.

I remember, I remember . . .

Playing on snow-covered pitches, the only parts to have been cleared being the lines, which had been sprinkled with sawdust. The backdrop to certain grounds on such days was snow-covered roof tops.

Playing at White Hart Lane on a pitch totally covered with sand. Players used to call it 'the beach'.

Steve Heighway leaving the pitch after the 1974 FA Cup Final and being collared for an interview by the BBC's David Coleman.

'How do you feel?' asked Coleman.

'Adjectives fail me,' replied Steve.

You don't get post-match soundbites from players like that any more.

Photographs of cheery, smiling supporters in the immediate aftermath of a goal having been scored. When a camera hones in on supporters today when a goal has been scored we are treated to snarling faces and clenched fists.

Advertisements for Austin cars, Lucas headlamps and Mitchell and Butler's beer adorning a stand at Villa Park, reminders of areas' industrial heritage in which the vast majority of supporters worked. These companies were people's lives. How many companies whose logos you see emblazoned across the front of shirts today are you so intimate with?

The atmosphere of a match often being interrupted by an appeal on the public address system on behalf of the police for a supporter to remove his car which was causing 'an obstruction'.

The flagpole that sported the club flag, which was visible above the turnstiles at the entry to the Kop. It had once been part of the topmast of Brunel's *Great Eastern*, one of the world's first iron ships.

Archibald Leitch's gable in the centre of the main stand at Anfield, on which a large board proudly proclaimed 'Liverpool Football Club'.

Twelve steps down, touch the 'This Is Anfield' board above my head, five paces along the concrete floor before ascending five more steps, then out into Anfield.

Slipping a folded sheet of paper into the hand of my pal Jimmy Greaves as Liverpool and Spurs players prepared to take to the field at Anfield. The look on Jimmy's face when he opened it and saw it was the menu from Liverpool Infirmary.

Having had a shower following a game on a very hot day, and being unable to towel myself dry due to constant perspiration.

The pride and honour I felt when holding aloft the Football League Championship trophy and the FA Cup. They are beautiful trophies. The aesthetics of their design suggest glory and style. The current Premiership trophy is vulgar to look at. It looks like the sort of cup one sees presented to a pub darts team. Then again, perhaps its design is in keeping with the Premiership and the money-driven game of today.

The dedication and sportsmanship of my great friend Ian Callaghan, who in playing nigh on 850 games for Liverpool was booked just once, and that was unjustified.

The joy of playing alongside Kevin Keegan and Kenny Dalglish. Kenny was the most natural player I have ever seen in a Liverpool shirt – and that is saying something.

The way Shanks and Bob became father figures to me following the death of my own father.

I remember, I remember . . .

Joe Fagan, a wonderful guy and a very funny man. 'One Russian is a poet, two Russians a chess game, three Russians a collective, and four Russians the entire Moscow Dynamo defence. Their goalkeeper's hopeless.'

Following the 1974 Charity Shield match in which Kevin Keegan and Bremner had been sent off (it was actually Johnny Giles who perpetrated the foul on Kevin, who turned and mistakenly confronted Billy), me also being called to the subsequent FA disciplinary hearing. On presenting myself before the committee one FA official began by saying, 'You started all this.'

'I beg your pardon?' I said, aware of the fact that the FA official in question had been on holiday at the time of the match. I was furious. This was supposedly a hearing to establish what had happened in order to bring those responsible to book. This man was the first to speak, and he'd already passed judgement.

'You started all the trouble with your very first tackle of the game,' said the official.

'You weren't even at the game, how would you know?' I replied.

'This is a democratic hearing of the evidence, you're not allowed to ask questions,' said the official.

I burst out laughing at the absurd contradiction in his reply.

Thankfully, Matt Busby was on the committee and at this point he stepped in.

'I saw what happened. That'll be all, Tommy, thanks for coming,' he said.

That was it; all that way just for that. I left the room wondering how it was possible that a person such as that committee member could have a key role in the running of football in this country.

I remember, I remember . . .

Arriving at Milan airport prior to playing Inter, and a group of about fifteen Italian journalists surrounding Shanks, all talking excitedly and simultaneously. Shanks turned to our interpreter and said, 'Tell them I totally disagree with everything they're saying.'

Sitting with Peter Cormack and Cally, signing autographs at a garden fête to help raise money for a local hospice. A lady approached and said, 'Do you remember my husband? You visited him in hospital three years ago. You sat and chatted with him for quite some time. It meant so much to him and really helped him.'

I had visited countless hospitals over the years and, to be truthful, I couldn't place her husband, particularly as she gave no further details.

'Of course I remember him,' I said, not wanting to appear insensitive. 'I'm glad he enjoyed our chat.'

'Oh, yes,' said the lady, 'it really perked him up.'

There was an awkward silence as no one knew what should be said next.

'How is he?' I asked eventually.

'He's dead. But never mind him. Here, sign this.'

I remember, I remember . . .

A representative of the US Soccer League visiting Liverpool prior to our tour of the USA. Shanks took him on a guided tour of the city. He pointed out famous landmarks only for the Yank to ask, 'How long did it take you Brits to build that?' Whatever reply

Shanks gave – five years, six years, whatever – this guy replied, 'Gawd, Bill, in America that would have been constructed in less than six months, tops.' This constant boast began to irritate Shanks. Eventually he and his guest arrived at the Liver building.

'How long did it take you Brits to build this one?' asked the Yank.

'I don't know,' replied Shanks. 'It wasn't here this morning when I passed on my way to the ground.'

Surging forward against Stoke City at the Victoria Ground, playing a one-two with Peter Cormack and rifling the return past John Farmer from twenty-five yards. As I returned to our half of the field, Geoff Hurst said to me, 'Bloody hell, Smithy, next thing you know they'll be telling me you can tackle as well.'

The pride I felt when making my full international debut for England against Wales in 1971, playing alongside Larry Lloyd, Chris Lawler and Emlyn at the back, the only non-Liverpool player being Terry Cooper (Leeds). The game ended goalless. As defenders we felt we had done our job, but only Terry retained his place from that back four.

'Run it off!' being the advice shouted from the dug-out to a player carrying an injury, whether it be a strain or a broken leg.

Rattles and rosettes, the latter worn by supporters only for FA Cup ties, made of tissue paper in the club colours, the centrepiece of which was a cheap tin cup whose only resemblance to the FA Cup was that it had handles.

The magic sponge, the precursor to sprays and ultrasonic treatment, at its most effective on a winter's day when taken from a bucket in which the top of the water had turned to ice. Applied to any part of the body, any pain felt would immediately be replaced by shock.

Half-time scoreboards with letters of the alphabet that denoted specific games, the key to which could be found in the matchday programme. These boards were the only way supporters knew what was happening elsewhere in the country, and they would emit a collective gasp whenever they saw a sensational scoreline posted.

The idiosyncratic features of the grounds I played at. The hooped railings of the perimeter fencing at White Hart Lane. The bulbous frontage of the main stand at Villa Park. The 'chicken run' at Upton Park. The Archibald Leitch-designed crisscross wrought-iron design of the frontage of the main stand at both Goodison and Roker Park. The wide open spaces behind either goal at Stamford Bridge with the greyhound lights ringing the pitch. The rows of small windows in the rear of the main stand at Craven Cottage which made supporters seated on the back row appear in silhouette. The rows of poplar trees behind the east terrace at St James's Park. The multi-span roof stepped in triangular sections on the east side of Molineux.

Shanks turning on a reporter who had had the temerity to suggest that Liverpool's form had dipped of late. 'Aye, you're right, son. We're struggling at the top of the League!'

The thrill of playing alongside my boyhood hero Billy Liddell for Liverpool reserves.

Bob Paisley – six League Championships, three European Cups, three League Cups, one UEFA Cup, two European Super Cups – on being asked the secret of his success as manager of Liverpool saying, 'There's no secret really. I just carried on the good work. Why change something that isn't broken?'

Playing for Tampa Bay and having the unenviable job of trying to mark my hero Pele. The memory of playing against him will live with me for ever.

When I began this book, I made mention of there being two Tommy Smiths, the one my family and close friends know, the other the player who lives in the memories of many supporters. I hope you, my friend, now know the real me.

To those of you who cheered me and inspired me throughout my football career, may I take this opportunity to offer you my sincere thanks. To those of you who booed and cat-called me, I thank you too: you inspired me to even greater effort! Take a bow Bill Shankley, Bob Paisley and Joe Fagan – the three people who influenced me the most in my life. And a big thank you to all those footballers I played alongside and against. Back then I thought we were simply trying to entertain people and win a game. I didn't realize you were all helping me create my memories.

The sixth of June 2007 will be forever imprinted on my mind. That day I was happily busying myself in our garden when I suddenly felt a little queasy. I had a slight pain in my chest which I took to be indigestion, and I made a mental note to take some indigestion tablets when I finished the gardening. Having weeded the beds, I then mowed the lawn. I had just about finished with the mower when a sharp sensation slammed my body. It was as if I had been hit by someone.

I felt very tired, and I sat down on the garden seat. From where I was I could see the clock in the dining room, which told me it was three p.m. I just sat and rested for what I thought was a minute, then I glanced at the clock again. I was taken aback because it said a quarter past three. I couldn't understand where the time had gone. I wondered if I had blacked out, though I had no sense of this happening.

I went into the house. Sue was on the phone speaking to Darren. I told her I felt tired and hot and was going upstairs to lie down. I took my shirt off and lay on the bed, but rather than feeling cooler I felt even hotter and was aware I was sweating profusely. I couldn't rest so I got up, put my shirt on and went downstairs. Darren had now arrived, and when he saw me a look of concern swept across his face. He asked how I was feeling.

'Not too good,' I told him.

I told Darren and Sue what had happened and Darren immediately picked up the phone and rang an ambulance. I muttered something about this not being necessary but was then so overcome with tiredness that I sat down in a chair.

Minutes later the paramedics arrived. One asked me what had happened.

'You've had a heart attack,' he told me. 'We have to get you to hospital straight away.'

His words shocked me. A heart attack? How could this be possible? I've always kept myself reasonably fit, I'm not over-weight, I eat the right food. I began to shake, with fear I suppose. Funny thing is, I thought to myself, 'If I'd known I'd had a heart attack out there in the garden, it would have come as such a shock to me I would have had a heart attack.'

I was taken to Fazackerly Hospital where a doctor confirmed the paramedic's diagnosis. I spent two days in bed resting. I don't like being in hospital – what with the operations on my knees, hips and elbows I had seen enough of them – but I consoled myself that I was now in the right place in the right hands. After a few days in hospital the doctor told me he was sending me home. Though not keen on hospitals, I told him I wasn't too happy about that. Later in the day I was informed I was being transferred to Broadgreen Hospital under the care of a heart specialist by the name of Dr Pullen.

Dr Pullen informed me that he was going to perform a bypass operation within forty-eight hours. 'Three-way,' he said. In the event he conducted a six-way operation on my heart. When I recovered he told me he had found more blockages which necessitated a 'bigger operation'.

Even though I was told the operation had gone well, I didn't sleep for two days. I was afraid to go to sleep in case I never woke up again. The days passed and I simply lay in bed recuperating and dwelling on events. I have been at pains to tell you in this book that I have always appreciated what has come my way in life. As I lay in bed I thought again about just how wonderful life is. How important your loved ones are to you. That no matter what problems arise, they're nothing if you have your health. I was far from being in the best of health, but so very, very grateful still to be alive. Still alive to see and be with Sue, Darren and Janette, to cuddle my grandchildren and see them grow up. OK, I thought, you've had a heart attack, but you're a very, very lucky man, Tommy.

I was stunned by the number of people who visited me in hospital or sent cards and messages conveying their best wishes for a speedy recovery. Old team-mates Ronnie Moran, Ron Yeats, Roger Hunt, David Johnson, Cally, Joey Jones and Chris Lawler visited, as did Nobby Stiles, Kevin Ratcliffe, Gerry Marsden and numerous other friends. I received get-well wishes from hundreds of pals including Jimmy Case, Tommy Docherty, Kevin Keegan, Peter Cormack, Norman Hunter, Tommy Lawrence, Alan Ogley, Gerry Byrne, Gordon Milne, Peter Thompson, Jimmy Greaves, Lou Macari, Michel Platini, just about everyone at the PFA, Elton Welsby, the publishers of this book, my agent Julian Alexander, my pal and collaborator Les Scott, and Joe Fagan's widow Lil. Brian Hall and Wally Bennett at Liverpool FC were tremendous to me, as was John Thompson and all the staff at the *Liverpool Echo*. I received countless cards and letters from Liverpool supporters, including one from Brian Phillips, who's known me since my days as a groundstaff boy at Anfield. Space does not allow me to list everyone who visited or sent their good wishes, so for those whose names I have not mentioned, may I take this opportunity to say a very big thank you to you all. You know who you are, and I will be forever grateful to you. Your good wishes helped me in no small way to overcome the biggest problem I have encountered in life.

After four weeks in hospital I was allowed home and told to take it easy. Relatives and friends continued to visit. One day Jamie Carragher called and asked how things were. I told him I was making a good recovery, but I was a little frustrated that I couldn't do what I used to do, like keep on top of the garden. Jamie told me he would sort that out for me, and, ignoring my protests, he did.

I shall never forget the expertise and care of the staff of

Fazackerly and Broadgreen hospitals, particularly that of Dr Pullen. Above all, I shall never forget and always appreciate the love and support I received from Sue, Darren, Janette and the other members of our family. Through it all, Sue was absolutely amazing. All these years on, I love her more with every day that we are blessed to be with each other.

As the days passed I grew stronger. I still get tired easily, especially at night, but my recovery was such that in a matter of six weeks from being discharged from hospital, Dr Pullen said he was so pleased with my progress I could drive again, which came as a very welcome relief.

At the end of August I was invited to attend Liverpool's game against Chelsea at Anfield. It was great to be back, and I thanked Brian Hall, Wally Bennett and their respective staff for all their good wishes and support. I was asked to go out on to the pitch during the half-time interval. I wished to do this as I wanted an opportunity to say 'thank you' to all the Liverpool supporters. I was stunned when I walked out on to the pitch, because I did so to a standing ovation and loud cheers. I walked, albeit slowly, over to each section of the stadium to applaud the fans. At one point I found myself looking up at the section containing the Chelsea supporters. I wondered what sort of reception they would give me. They too took to their feet and gave me generous applause. I was so full I was fighting to hold back the tears.

Slowly but surely my life is getting back on track. I returned to work on this book and resumed my column for the *Liverpool Echo*. I have also started to accept after-dinner engagements again, though obviously I'm careful not to take on too much. My life and that of my family have settled down. We are all together still, and for that I shall always be so very grateful.

I have lived a lot of life and, God willing, there is much to come. I have known great days and enjoyed success beyond my wildest dreams. I have also known troubled times, having spent a lot of time in hospitals and endured the pain of debilitating injuries and conditions such as crippling arthritis. At times such things get you down. But in conclusion may I say this: I wish you happiness, but in those moments when life gives you a bad time and you may feel everything and everyone is against you, be mindful that that's not the case, and have faith, because you'll never walk alone.

Picture acknowledgements

Unless otherwise stated, pictures are courtesy of the author. Every effort has been made to obtain the necessary permissions with reference to copyright material, both illustrative and quoted. We apologize for any omissions in this respect and will be pleased to make the appropriate acknowledgements in any future edition.

Illustrations, Section One

TS at childhood home: © Liverpool Daily Post and Echo; TS with Chris Lawler and their wives: © Stan McLeod; TS with Sue and Janette Smith: © Mercury Press Ltd; TS with Jack Charlton Touring XI: © Edward Sanderson; TS at home with family: © Liverpool Daily Post and Echo; TS boxing: © Harry Ormesher.

Illustrations, Section Two

TS with Chelsea players: © Herbert Sündhofer; Celebration of winning Championship, 1964: © Mirrorpix; Referee at FA Cup Final, 1965: © Mirrorpix; Celebration bus: © Mirrorpix; TS with car: © D&C Thomson Ltd; TS at Nottingham Forest ground: © Mercury Press Ltd.

Illustrations, Section Three

TS with Liverpool line-up: © Gary Talbot; Shanks presents TS with trophy: © Central Press Photos Ltd; TS runs with Liverpool team: © Harry Ormesher; TS with Colin Bell: © Colorsport; TS hit by bottle: © Mirrorpix/Harry Ormesher; TS scores goal: © Liverpool Daily Post and Echo; Liverpool team on balcony: © D. Rice; TS with Bobby Charlton: © Liverpool Daily Post and Echo; TS with Bob Paisley and backroom staff: © Express Newspapers.

Index

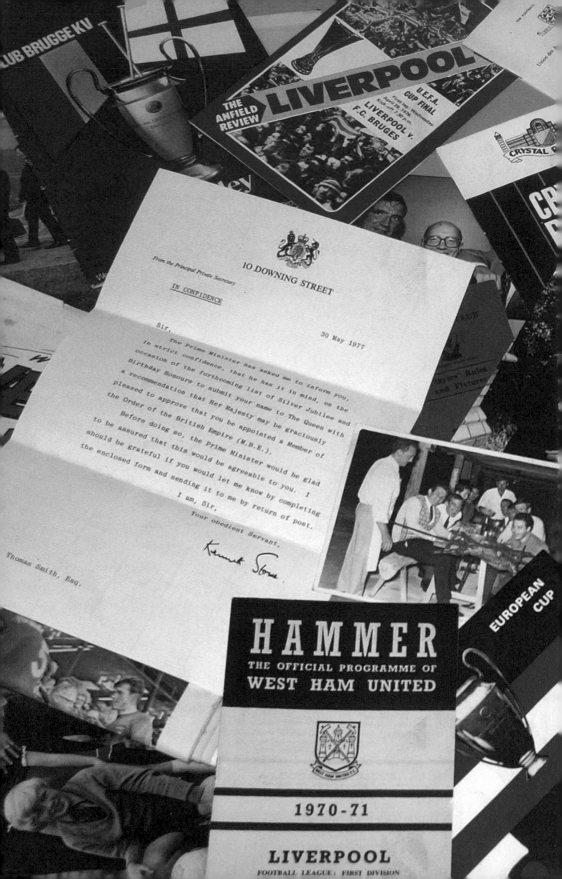